I Say Me
FOR A
Parable

Photo by Bill Records, 1971

I Say Me
FOR A
Parable:

THE ORAL AUTOBIOGRAPHY
OF MANCE LIPSCOMB,
TEXAS BLUESMAN

AS TOLD TO AND COMPILED BY
Glen Alyn

W. W. NORTON & COMPANY
NEW YORK · LONDON

Permission to reproduce the lyrics to the following songs by Mance Lipscomb is gratefully acknowledged: "Baby, Let Me Lay It on You," "Big Bossman," "Captain, Captain," "Ella Speed," "Freddie," "God Moves on the Water," "Jack o' Diamonds," "Johnny Take a One on Me," "Key to the Highway," "Going to Louisiana," "Motherless Children Have a Hard Time," "Night Time Is the Right Time," "Out and Down," "Rock Me Mama," "Rocks and Gravel," "Ain't It Hard," "Sugar Babe," "Tom Moore's Farm," "Willie Poor Boy," "You Be Kind to Me," "You Got to Reap What You Sow." All songs © by Tradition Music Co. (BMI), administered by Bug Music Co. Mance Lipscomb's recordings are available on ARHOOLIE RECORDS—for a catalog write: 10341 San Pablo Ave., El Cerrito, CA 94530.

The text of this book is composed in Century Schoolbook with the display set in Caslon. Composition and Manufacturing by The Haddon Craftsmen, Inc.

Book design by Charlotte Staub

Library of Congress Cataloging-in-Publication Data

Lipscomb, Mance, 1895–1976.
    I say me for a parable : the oral autobiography of Mance Lipscomb, Texas bluesman / compiled and edited by Glen Alyn.
        p.   cm.
        1. Lipscomb, Mance, 1895–1976.   2. Blues musicians—Texas—Biography.   I. Alyn, Glen.   II. Title.
    ML420.L67A3   1993
    782.42'1643'092—dc20
    [B]   92-46560

ISBN 978-0-3933-3327-5

W. W. Norton & Company, Inc.,
500 Fifth Avenue, New York, N.Y. 10110
W. W. Norton & Company Ltd., 10 Coptic Street, London WC1A 1PU

1 2 3 4 5 6 7 8 9 0

To "Ma,"
who sat me on her lap
and told me her "adventures"
in the Texas Hill Country with
a hearty chuckle and fondness
for detail and accuracy.

Grandma Ida Archer-Holmes
brought to life scenes erased
by the hands of time and migrations
that had turned a rural population into
an urban one by the 1960s.
My ears got bigger as her words got better.

And to another master storyteller and his wife,
Mance and Elnora Lipscomb.

All three were children of the 1890s.

Contents

CONTENTS

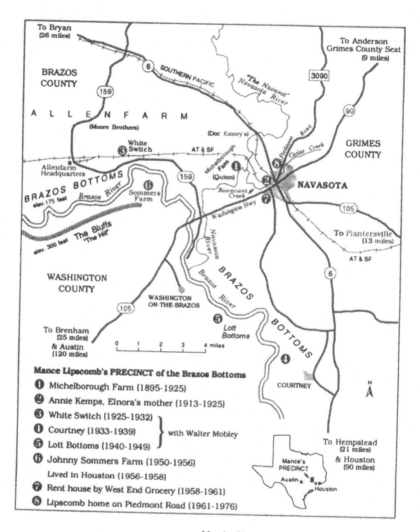

To Bryan
(26 miles)

To Anderson
Grimes County Seat
(9 miles)

BRAZOS
COUNTY

SOUTHERN PACIFIC

6

159

"The Navasot"
Navasota River

3090

90

A L L E N F A R M
(Moore Brothers)

(Doc Emory's)

GRIMES
COUNTY

❸ White
Switch

AT & SF

Cedar Creek

❺

Allenfarm
Headquarters

BRAZOS BOTTOMS
elev.175 feet

Brazos River

159

(Quinn)

❶

❷

NAVASOTA

❻ Sommers
Farm

Boonmont
Creek

❼

105

Washington Hwy

To Plantersville
(13 miles)

The Bluffs
"The Hill"
elev. 300 feet

Navasota River

Brazos River

AT & SF

6

WASHINGTON
COUNTY

WASHINGTON
ON-THE-BRAZOS

105

B R A Z O S

To Brenham
(25 miles)
& Austin
(120 miles)

0 1 2 3 4 miles

❺ Lott
Bottoms

B O T T O M S

❹

Mance Lipscomb's PRECINCT of the Brazos Bottoms

COURTNEY

N

❶ Michelborough Farm (1895-1925)

❷ Annie Kemps, Elnora's mother (1913-1925)

❸ White Switch (1925-1932)

❹ Courtney (1933-1939) ⎫
⎬ with Walter Mobley
❺ Lott Bottoms (1940-1949) ⎭

❻ Johnny Sommers Farm (1950-1956)

Lived in Houston (1956-1958)

❼ Rent house by West End Grocery (1958-1961)

❽ Lipscomb home on Piedmont Road (1961-1976)

To Hempstead
(21 miles)
& Houston
(90 miles)

Mance's
PRECINCT

Austin ★

Houston

Map by Glen Alyn and Dr. Dennis Fitzsimons

Acknowledgments

At first, I thought I was putting this book together by myself. Time passed, and so did the thought. I am grateful to the named and unnamed for helping to make this "parable" possible.

The Lipscomb family made me feel welcome, and treated me like one of their own. I especially thank Coon and Pie (Willie Lipscomb and Lillie Davis), Mance, Jr., Jude, Helen Jones, Blue Gal (Annie Hall), Punkin (Ruby), Richard, Jimmy, Charlie Brown, Cricket, Francis, and their families.

In Navasota, Mark Bouliane kept me out of jail and gainfully employed when necessary, while his wife, Nancy,

11

provided my first in-depth account of Mance; her parents—Mr. and Mrs. Bingham—extended to me the same graciousness they had once offered to Mance and Elnora Lipscomb.

I am grateful to others in Mance's "precinct," for their friendship, support, cooperation, and insights into Navasota: Mary Kathryn Crawford, Eddie Pratt, Earl Valentine, Fred Baldwin, Wendy Watriss, and Anders Saustrup. In Waller, Edna Webster and Sonny and Nanny V Lewis drew out Mance's tales of Frank Hamer and other times gone by. In Cameron, Dr. George Bowman (and family) showed off other sides of Mance through his "teethiz," his parties, and his admiration for Mance. In Washington-on-the-Brazos, Ed and Lilly Lathan and James "Beck" and Georgia Lee Wade were good neighbors and true friends. I'm also grateful to Johnny and Chang Ewing, Boy Scales (for watermelon knowledge), T Roberson, Roosevelt Roberson, Sammy Keys, Carolyn Cochran, Gerry and Sherry Humphreys, Reba Dickschatt, Skeeter Stolz, Lucy Loscocco, Mark and Sara Madera, and Jody Blazek. Skip Gerson produced the sound for the Lipscomb documentary *A Well-Spent Life* in 1970 and stayed on to contribute to my efforts a few years later.

For critical editorial assistance early on, hats off to Don Gardner and Dave Crossley. Their contributions plus early manuscript readings by Bill Wittliff and later by Billy Porterfield helped clarify my intentions and open up possibilities for the book's presentation. And for generous use of their photographs, I thank Bill Records, Burton Wilson, Ed Badeaux, Lucy Loscocco, and Tad Hershorn. Marcus Mallard provided access to his extensive historical photographic collection of the Grimes County area.

Many others made significant contributions to this work. Among them were Joe Lomax, John Jr. and Mimi Lomax, Pete Seeger, Chris Strachwitz, Les Blank, Bruce Willenzik (whose dedication to Mance was unconditional),

Alan Willenzik, Jane Hardey, Kurt Van Sickle, Eddie Wilson, Bobby Hederman, Jane Lott, Lee and Amy Fikes, Pam Murfin, Tary Owens, Nathan Pearson, Tom Whitbread, and the University of Texas at Austin's Folklore Department and Student Government. Mike Tolleson and Nancy Moore laid the legal framework for the Lipscomb/Myers/Alyn Collection at the University of Texas.

Rod Kennedy first introduced me to Mance Lipscomb in 1972. Stephen Oates inspired me by making history alive; his example of discipline and excellence, plus his faith in my talent and his generosity in sharing the mysteries of creating a book, led me to believe I could put one together myself. Roger Abrahams was my mentor; he provided a scope, focus, breadth of knowledge, plan of action, and continuing inspiration for me to complete the work. Tuffly Ellis and the Texas State Historical Association administered a grant on my behalf for over two years.

Don Carleton's comprehensive academic editing and support throughout grounded me and gave the book a richer quality. For their help with the Lipscomb/Myers/Alyn Collection at the University of Texas at Austin's Center for American History, special thanks to Don Carleton, John Wheat, Carol Williams, Ralph Elder, Bill Richter, Kay Ahrendt, Denise Mayorga, Allison Beck, and other staff. All photographs used in this book are housed there.

Director William Ferris at the Center for the Study of Southern Culture in University, Mississippi, Dick Waterman, Mance's East Coast booking agent, Director Russell Cushman at the Horlock History Center in Navasota, and Director Kathleen Hudson at the Texas Heritage Music Foundation in Kerrville all contributed to the latter phase of completion—as did Frankie Westbrook and Tad Hershorn by reading the manuscripts.

Angela Smith and Sally Baker at the Austin Writers' League led me through the maze of locating John Ware, my agent. John believed in the book more than I did my-

ACKNOWLEDGMENTS

self, and steadfastly refused to let it gather any more dust. I couldn't ask for a more honorable and effective partner. Gerry Howard's patience and his sensitive yet unflinching editing have allowed me (and possibly a lot of readers) to see the forest for the trees, the swamp rabbits in the woods, the cotton on the stalks, and Mance himself. Gerry deserves the editorial byline. Taj Mahal has kept the music alive since he was Mance's student in the early sixties. I am deeply grateful for his contribution of a unique global perspective in his foreword to this book. Don Carleton's academic editing has been the icing on the cake of a dozen years of acknowledgment and support of me to bring this work to fruition.

And most important, I acknowledge my children, Shannon and Sequoia, for supporting and tolerating their father in his vision.

I Say Me
FOR A
Parable

The Sage

From the past we are encouraged to take the best and leave the rest. Mance Lipscomb was a sage, a songster, a responsible elder, a self-made man—the best! Every generation seeks to define itself through modes of dress, behavior, music, philosophy, and art; and during the sixties many young people looked to the past with fervor. All forms of traditional music were studied, the blues especially. Everybody had a blues band, it seemed. However, in this youthful quest for authenticity and perhaps masculinity, many would-be blues musicians gravitated towards the big-city-style electric blues, overlooking many fine solo artists, perhaps because of their obvious rural roots and rural themes. This is a shame, because much was lost. As the great Bukka White (I believe) said, the blues came out of a man plowin' behind a mule, with little or no hope for better days. For much of his life that described Mance Lipscomb.

Furthermore, the eventual commercialization of the blues led scores of would-be blues musicians to believe that there was one mythic, monolithic blues style that was played only in the key of E major, or occasionally in the key of A. In contrast the forefathers and foremothers of our present-day tapestry of musical styles and tastes often had played in widely diverse styles, if only to be flexible enough to work the many traveling shows that criss-crossed the South and even the North. Many of the shows played for both black and white clienteles, changing their repertoire as the occasion demanded. This is the diverse tradition that Mance came up under and carried on.

I first became aware of Mance Lipscomb through a college acquaintance who had grown up in Texas near the area where Mance was a local hero. In those days (the early sixties), artists with local reputations might also garner a national following through being recorded by folklorists who traveled great distances, or by themselves traveling to larger cities to cut records. Even though Mance had been recorded by Chris Strachwitz of Arhoolie Records, his records were unavailable in Navasota at that time. My Texas friend was unaware of the existence of any Mance Lipscomb records; so when he found one, he was eager to share his discovery with anyone who would listen. This fellow was a fan big time, and we spent many an afternoon and evening listening to these LPs until the scratches on the records grew louder than the music they contained.

The thing that struck me was that Mance played so many different types of music in his own style with powerful conviction. This is where I take issue with many people's idea that Mance was strictly a bluesman. He was actually a songster, in line with the great tradition of the West African griots from Mali, Senegal, Gambia, Guinea, and southern Mauritania.

In person, he was a handsome, intelligent, sparkling-eyed man of great patience and love for all people of good will. Even in his late sixties, he had the energy of a man forty years his junior. Full of stories, funny jokes, philosophies, and recollections, he was never at a loss for encouragement to young and eager fans. He always carried himself in a dignified manner and received great respect from everyone whom he met or knew. Mance spoke of his triumphs, troubles, and tribulations in the hope that we, the youth who loved him, would lead better and richer lives. Yes, Mance, we certainly have had a better, richer life for knowing you!

Mance Lipscomb spoke the truth about his life. He hid nothing. One particularly telling story was that he was always coming in late for his lunch or dinner, and his wife told him if he kept on letting the hot food she was preparing for him get cold, she would never again eat with him at the dinner table. She kept her word, and so he ate at the dinner table without her for the rest of his life, while she sat in her favorite living room chair with her plate in her lap. He must have told this story many times, for I heard it from quite a few other sources. He always stressed that it was his own hard-headedness that got him in the fix in the first place.

Tilting his head back, closing his eyes, and thumping that Harmony Sovereign and later the Gibson J-200, Mance brought the past to the present and turned the present into story, into song, and into life. I have been lucky enough in my life as a musician to have had personal contact with this great man, to play music, to learn, to listen with my inner ear, to be in his rich company.

Yeah Songster! That was what Mance Lipscomb was.

But most of all, he was a wonderful human being who traveled from a rural farming community to place a great light in the world. You are holding in your hands the life story of one of the best that's been, so enjoy yourself. This book is a labor of love for all who have participated in its realization. Yeah Mance! The Sage.

Taj Mahal
May 3, 1993

P.S. I would also like to offer my personal thanks to Chris Strachwitz for his many years of dedication to the recording and preservation of great traditional music and for making wonderful recordings available for the world at large. Through his Down Home record store and outlet in El Cerrito, California, he has shown the same independence of spirit and the will to share the real thing as the great musicians themselves. Thanks ever so much, Chris.

Introduction

On a hot Texas day in July 1973, I was driving east out of Austin for my first look at Mance Lipscomb's home in Navasota. Locusts rattled in the trees like some distant train through my car windows. To get my mind off the Texas heat, I was imagining what the home of one of America's leading country blues artists would look like. Navasota lay deep in East Texas, 120 miles east of Austin and 90 miles northwest of Houston. Probably some quaint Victorian farmhouse built before the turn of the century, needing some work but possessing plenty of charm and character. It would have to be on the outskirts of town or nestled off some dirt country road, peaceful and secure.

Surely purchased with the money Mance had made over the last twelve years, as he rose from being a nonentity in 1960 to being a star at every major folk and blues festival he had time for, and playing at countless universities and major clubs all over the United States. After all, I daydreamed, he was listed in *Who's Who in America*. Movies had been made about him. He was written up in dozens of magazines. His posters were plastered all over Austin. We're talking rich and famous here.

The cedar-covered hill country of Austin was replaced with a narrow strip of pine trees that ran through Bastrop, thirty miles east of Austin. As the hills flattened out thirty miles farther up the road near Giddings, the stands of oak, hackberry, pecan, elm, and other deciduous trees mirrored the increased rainfall as the land began to roll into the Gulf plains. The trees grew larger as the towns grew smaller, all connected by increasingly thick prairie grasses dotted here and there with cows. Radio stations disappeared off my dial, while the locusts and the hot wind droned on. Secured in the trunk were the tape recorder lent by the University of Texas Folklore Department and the $125 of reel-to-reel tape I'd purchased with a $200 UT Student Government grant. I'd saved the other $75 for motels and food, hoping I could stretch it to two weeks thanks to the $10-a-night motels Lipscomb had assured me still existed in Navasota. My math was poor, but my hopes were high.

A hundred miles east of Austin, I turned northeast off U.S. Highway 290, drove through the Washington County seat of Brenham, and found myself on State Highway 105, a two-laner. By the time I reached Washington-on-the-Brazos, the live oak trees had become huge and thick, and the elms towered above even the telephone poles. In just over a hundred miles, the annual rainfall increased from about thirty to forty-five inches. As I crossed the Brazos River bridge, I looked out onto an expanse of flatness that extended to the horizon. This is the true beginning of the Gulf Plains, an ancient seabed that rejoins the Gulf of Mexico 150 miles farther southeast, at Galveston. The elevation drops from a thousand feet in west Austin to 150 feet where Highway 105 cuts across the southern edge of Allenfarm. I was to discover that this former 20,000-acre cotton plantation stretches for fifteen miles along the Brazos River, while part of its eastern border is defined by the Navasota River just before it flows into the Brazos. In a little over two hours, I had driven out of the Old West and into the southwestern edge of the Deep South. My Volkswagen was rolling between two rivers like a marble across the lush green tabletop called the Brazos Bottoms. This was Mance Lipscomb's homeland, what he referred to as his precinct.

A hundred and twenty miles east and slightly north of Austin, the Navasota City Limit sign announced, "Population 6,000." Four miles back, I'd read a sign sporting a bee and a cow proclaiming, "Welcome to Grimes County, Land of Milk & Honey." Downtown Navasota resembled Vicksburg more than Fort Worth, though it contained flavors of both. Scores of wooden Victorian and pre-Depression brick mansions attested to the town's former prosperity. I effortlessly glided to Navasota's one stoplight and completed my last leg following the simple directions Lipscomb had given me over the phone, after I had revealed, with hesitation and resolve, my intention to write a book about him.

He had said, "Well, you come out an brang yo tape recorder. I'll set an talk over it. I'm good at that. Kin you drive one a them pushbutton caws? Inyhow, I got aplenty caws. I got some friends we kin go see. We kin show have us some fun. An if inythang come outa it, I'll git half an you git half." Mance never asked for a contract. He was a man of his word and expected the same from others.

As I rounded a curve on the Piedmont road, the houses

became more shut in and bleaker, and concrete driveways gave way to dirt ones. Just a stone's throw away from the northern Navasota City Limit sign were two houses set in the middle of five acres of prairie grass with a couple trees and a basketball hoop. Through my windshield I saw a lone Jersey cow staked on the outside of a chain link fence, a 1950 Chevy pickup truck and four cars strewn around the yard, a small white frame house propped up on cement piers, some chickens, a huge pile of old rotting lumber, and a low rambling house with a blue asphalt-shingle roof inside the chain link fence. On the side of the house an antique black cast-iron caldron sat upside down in overgrown grass. On the wood porch beneath the roof, Mance and Elnora Lipscomb sat patiently, greeting me with a hearty welcome as I arose in a pool of sweat from my car.

One side of the house contained a tight living room, a dining room and a kitchen, and a bathroom. The other side held Mance and Elnora's bedroom and two other bedrooms for whatever grandchildren were in need of them at the time. I had been right about Mance Lipscomb's house being old and Victorian, but wrong about what it looked like. As I learned later, it had been reconstructed from two Victorian mansions that had fallen into disarray and then been torn down.

Posters, photos large and small, and other mementos from his music career were tacked up on the walls of every room, along with a calendar portrait of Jesus. The living room walls were painted bright red, and after a half hour or so I noticed that the wallpaper was made of old newspapers. This last detail shocked me. How was it that a famous musician was living in a place like this? I suddenly found myself sitting in Mance Lipscomb's reality, not my own, and I realized that if I was going to write about his life, I would have to do it by leaving my prejudgments back in Austin and living in *his* world for however long it took me to come to know it.

We spent a week talking before the tape ran out, making practically nonstop rounds from friend to relative to party and back again. I was astounded at the energy emanating from this seventy-eight year old man, who slept hardly four hours a night. Little did I know then that these tapes would form the substance for this book or that publication would occur twenty years down the road. By then I'd discovered a lot about Mance and knew there would always be more depth of character and experience to look into.

Mance Lipscomb was born on April 9, 1895, in Brazos County on the banks of the "Navasot" River, at Michelborough Farm, a couple miles north of the town of Navasota. He was the son of a man who had been a slave and a woman who was half Choctaw Indian. He picked his first fifty pounds of cotton at age eight. By the time he was eleven, he was the man of his household, plowing the fields behind a mule whose harness he had to grow into. From 1906 to 1908 Texas Ranger Frank Hamer befriended Mance and gave him a brief respite from sharecropping. He learned the rudiments of music from his father, a professional fiddler who taught his son to bass behind him when Mance was still so small that he had to be placed on a soapbox. That way, the little boy wouldn't get stepped on at the Saturday Night Suppers. Mance later was to amplify those skills as a solo guitarist and songster.

Except for two years in Houston (1956–58) and his weeks on the road during 1961–73, Mance spent his entire life in his three-county precinct of Washington, Grimes, and Brazos counties centered around Navasota. They all met just west of Navasota in a triangle occupied by Allenfarm, the former plantation and prison farm. Mance spent his life there farming with mules for halvers (giving half of every crop to a landlord) and later rent-farming for thirds and fourths (every third bale of cotton and fourth bushel of corn). The 2-song repertoire he started with as a teenager had expanded to a 350-song collection forty years later. It ran the gamut from field shouts to blues, rags, ballads, Broadway tunes, spirituals, and children's songs—all set to the dance rhythms of the Saturday Night Suppers. He became one of the best cultivators and *the* best musician in his three-county precinct. He picked up blues from personal encounters with two of its early giants, Blind Lemon Jefferson and Blind Willie Johnson, while circus carnival musicians Richard Dean and Hamp Walker brought him songs from vaudeville and black minstrel shows. Bessie Smith, Memphis Minnie, Big Bill Broonzy, and scores of others came to him through the horns of the 78-rpm crank-up Victrolas.

The first outsider to discover Mance came through Navasota in the 1920s. Jimmie Rodgers—the father of yodeling country and western music, known by many as the Blue Brakeman for his blues-influenced singing style—asked Mance to go on tour with him, but Mance declined. He was not rediscovered by the outside world until nearly four decades later, when folklorist Mack McCormick and entrepreneur and music enthusiast Chris Strachwitz stumbled on him in 1960. A year later, an audience of 41,000 went wild over him at the Berkeley Folk Festival. On that stage, Mance commenced his thirteen-year career as a concert musician with the likes of Pete Seeger.

Before he died in 1976, Mance Lipscomb had influenced a whole generation of musicians, including Bob Dylan, Janis Joplin, Taj Mahal, and Ry Cooder. As a participant in the folk and blues revival of the sixties and early seventies, he lived to experience the effects of the civil rights movement on the nation, his hometown, and his children. By virtue of his music and his magnanimity, he was an emissary of civil rights.

But the essence of Mance Lipscomb existed only here in Navasota. His aura of authenticity and his astounding musical prowess were always present onstage; these qualities, along with his accessibility and genuine compassion for his fellow human beings, drew people to him like a magnet. But in order to re-create who he was and to uncover the origins of his music, Navasota was the only place to experience him. I would spend five years living and working in the three-county area Mance called his precinct (with the help of a private grant for two of those years) from 1974 to 1979. During that period I transcribed sixteen hundred pages of taped conversations with Mance and corroborated most of the material contained in the following pages through oral history sessions with Mance's relatives, friends, neighbors, and other Navasotans.

Mance grew up in the days of steam locomotives, mule-drawn wagons and plows, and horse-drawn buggies. Airplanes did not exist. By his death he had flown on airliners to gigs all across the United States and had seen a man walk on the moon, via television—a medium of communication that not even Jules Verne had imagined by 1895. He was born in an era when African-Americans were denied the right to vote. He lived to witness the enactment and enforcement of the first civil rights legislation since Reconstruction.

The span of Mance's music was no less breathtaking. Born a slave, his father became a professional fiddler after Emancipation. He taught Mance songs from the Civil War, old-time fiddling reels and breakdowns, and black minstrel songs like "Arkansas Traveler." Mance was cutting his musical teeth when three parallel and innovative musical styles were developing out of the blues: jazz, ragtime, and Dixieland. All these styles crossed and recrossed paths, blurring the boundaries between city and country music and between blues, rag, and jazz styles. While Jelly Roll Morton was perfecting his walking bass jazz piano style in New Orleans, Mance was developing his hard-driving independent-thumb blues guitar style as a one-man band for Navasota Saturday Night Suppers. Mance was playing strong when rockabilly and rock 'n' roll converted jitter-buggers into rockers, and he was achieving national prominence when psychedelic rock exploded onto the pop charts.

Mance will probably be best remembered for the scope and quality of his repertoire and for his ability to convert all of it into an unmistakable dance beat and signature. He neither fully mimicked the artists whose songs he made his own nor so innovated as to stand completely apart from his fellow country blues artists. Yet every song and tune he played can be identified as distinctly Mance Lipscomb's.

Blind Lemon Jefferson and Blind Willie Johnson were two blues innovators who shaped how the blues is played today. Jefferson's melodic runs and free-form delivery challenged blues guitarists to improvise beyond the accepted limits of what a guitar was supposed to produce. Johnson's open tunings and slide guitar style created the possibility of microtonal music by producing a fretless instrument capable of re-creating the African musical traditions where drums imitated the full range of the human voice. Prior to World War I, Mance tuned Blind Willie Johnson's guitar on the streets of Navasota. From 1917 to 1921 he watched Jefferson enthrall crowds down on Deep Ellum Street, a section of Dallas that has achieved fame as a seedbed for blues musicians. In the twenties and thirties Mance listened to Memphis Minnie, Bessie Smith, and other "race record" artists on Victrolas and jukeboxes, while he first heard Lightnin' Hopkins in Galveston in 1938. In the forties jukeboxes brought him Big Bill Broonzy and other blues innovators. As Elvis Presley was imitating Chuck Berry's torso movements and cleaning up Big Mama Thornton's version of "You Ain't Nothin But a Hound Dog" in the fifties and as rockabilly artist Jimmy Reed came into his own, Mance picked up an electric guitar to try to bolster his temporarily waning popularity. But by the time the Beatles and the Rolling Stones were recording Chuck Berry songs and other tunes by African-

Americans, Mance had moved on to such prominence that he was directly influencing folk, blues, and pop artists like Bob Dylan, Taj Mahal, and Janis Joplin and appearing onstage with the Grateful Dead, Pete Seeger, Earl Scruggs, Doc Watson, and scores of others.

In May of 1972 Rod Kennedy founded the Kerrville Folk Festival, 120 miles west of Austin. He had been a music enthusiast, promoter, and entrepreneur in the state capital since the 1950s. His appreciation of good music ranged from classical and flamenco all the way to blues and German beer barrel polkas. He introduced me to Mance Lipscomb at the festival. Prior to that, I hadn't known Mance existed. I had only recently learned "Travis"-style finger picking, which employed an alternating bass thumb, and did not play my first note of finger-style blues until my first semester of music theory that fall, when I discovered the triple-beat rhythms employed in most blues songs.

What first struck me about Mance Lipscomb was his awesome guitar style. Except for Carlos Montoya and Andres Segovia, I had simply never heard one person make that much resonant noise come from a guitar all at once. And I had never heard some of the sounds Mance produced. Although clearly from another world of experience and style, his music managed to cross over into my experience and seemingly everyone else's. Mance was producing something universal, and I had no idea how he was accomplishing it. While Mance was singing about mules, cotton, love, and sex in a thick East Texas black accent I couldn't fully understand, I knew somehow what Mance was communicating. I just couldn't verbalize what it was.

When Mance walked offstage, I spent the afternoon following him around and talking with him. As I watched while he interacted with others, and laughed as his sense of humor and passion for life got the best of me, something much deeper resonated within. Mance was the same person offstage as he was onstage. He was for real. Nothing about him was affected. His authenticity flowed out of him like water from an artesian spring. He was *naturally* authentic because he made no effort to be so. I decided that day to read the book that had no doubt been written about such a fascinating character and influential musical figure.

Six months later I still found only an undergraduate paper written by Nancy Bingham, of Navasota, and a couple of dozen magazine articles. There was no book on Mance Lipscomb. And though I didn't feel qualified to write it, I decided that someone ought to. I'd heard that Dr. Roger Abrahams had a long association with Mance, and rumor had it he was planning to write Mance's life story. Abrahams, formerly head of the Folklore Department at the University of Texas at Austin, was then head of its English Department. I made an appointment with him. The conversation went something like this:

"Are you going to write a book on Mance Lipscomb?" I interrogated.

Abrahams paused, gave me a long, searching look, and then shrugged and said, "Probably not."

"Well then, I am. And I want you to help me do it."

A pixieish smile crept across Dr. Abrahams' face and a twinkle emanated from his eye. He got up, ascertained that I was either glued to my chair or had no intention of getting up, turned his back to me, and walked over to a wall covered with books from floor to ceiling. He began to pull down one book after the other, until he had set a dozen of them on the corner of his desk.

With a fierce grin, he pointed to the books and told me, "Take these. Come back when you've finished reading them, and we'll talk."

This began an association that I found richly rewarding and that Abrahams found possibly amusing. A year later, after I had read books about Jelly Roll Morton and Big Bill Broonzy, Alan Lomax's *The Rainbow Sign*, books written by W. C. Handy, Eldridge Cleaver, James Baldwin, Sam Charters, Paul Oliver, Mason Brewer, and others, we talked again. From then until the first draft was completed, in 1979, we met about twice a year. Roger was brilliant in his ability to keep me focused on the tasks at hand, while his scope and understanding of folklore, black history, and the blues were enormous. He told me to be sure to record Mance's boyhood experiences with Texas Ranger Frank Hamer. Had it not been for Dr. Abrahams' support and expertise, this book would very likely not exist.

Mance at seventy-eight had a clear sense of his place in history and of who he was. His detachment from his successes and failures was matter-of-factly even-tempered and honest, while his ability to laugh at his own foolishness was disarming. My job was primarily to keep the tape going so that I could get it all down, and then piece it all together so that it made sense as a literary piece.

As a musician, I marveled at the rhythmic and dynamic diversity of Mance's rich and poetic delivery of language. He was darn near as masterful an oral storyteller as he was a blues guitarist. This was what had been missing from Mance's recorded repertoire. Although over a third of his complete musical repertoire and probably most of his active songs had been recorded, and the sound of his speaking voice was preserved in documentary films, the impact of Mance's vocal delivery did not effectively transfer to the printed page. When I attempted to translate his speech into standard written English, so much of the humor, poetry, and musical quality of his voice was lost that it appeared barren. I heard dynamic rises and falls in Mance's speech, tones of inflection indicating humor or seriousness, variations of turns of phrase and story renditions like reflections off a fine-cut gem, and rhythmic variations of syncopation and counterpoint. To me these facets of speech were mirrored in the musical delivery of blues and jazz.

Mance's dialect was as distinct and American as the blues. The best way for me to preserve it, I decided, was to preserve as much as I could of the oral quality of Mance's speech. I sought a balance between standard and phonetic spellings and between traditional and nontraditional use of grammar and punctuation that would reflect how Mance actually spoke. I tried to come up with something that readers could *hear* with their eyes. If a word looked to me like it sounded, I used a phonetically oriented spelling. If it didn't, I standardized it and let the language flow on. If a colon could indicate a rise in tone to cue the listener that what followed would relate to what was just said, I used it. If a comma could indicate a short pause while a period indicated a longer pause and a dash indicated a shift in thought, I tried it out. The quality of his speaking was simply too rich to let it go unpreserved.

Mance's storytelling style is a twentieth-century version of an oral tradition reaching back thousands of years. Indigenous peoples used repetition to remember how a story went and what happened. So do a lot of good poets. Repetitive "hook lines" and choruses in today's songs are extensions and acknowledgments of that tradition. It works. And just when this redundance began to get boring, people as distant in time and space as the Australian aborigines, the !Kung of southern Africa, the Montagnards of Asia, the Vikings and the Visigoths of Europe, the Druids of England, and the Cherokees of North America would all offer variations of content and style that could stir the imaginations of the worst television addict. Chronological delivery took a backseat to thematic content.

Coming from a tradition that placed less importance on linear time, Mance at age seventy-eight delivered his stories thematically. To demonstrate a point, teach a lesson, or carry on a metaphor, he could jump in midsentence from an anecdote out of the 1920s to a thematically compatible episode from that day or the previous week—and vice versa. He would refer to life or a story as a "go-along," as the current in a river just "goes along." I have chosen to organize this book chronologically, chapter by chapter. However, each chapter is organized thematically to reflect Mance's storytelling style and delivery, and the chapters acknowledge Mance's poetic license in being called "go-alongs"—because that's precisely what they do. And that was the quality of Mance's conversational tone.

Mance closes his book with a modern variation of a tale straight out of the African Anansi storytelling tradition. When slaves from the African Anansi tribe were settled in Georgia and the Carolinas, along America's southeast coast, they mixed with the indigenous Cherokees. The Anansi's master storyteller was a spider man who wove stories so incredibly that he trapped even the gods into doing his bidding. Giant spiders were plentiful in the Anansi's homeland. Tarantulas did exist much farther west (in Texas, for instance), but the rabbit was plentiful in the land of the Cherokees. As the blood and cultures of Anansis and Cherokees mixed, so did their creation myths. All good storytellers know that their subject matter must be either mighty enticing or relevant to the experience of their audience—especially where children are concerned. It was these creation tales that the storytellers used to teach children what it was to be human and what their identity was as part of a larger tribe.

The spiders of the Anansis gradually blended into the rabbits of the Cherokees, because the symbolic trickster figure of the two cultures was fundamentally the same. The trickster is known to some as the knowledgeable fool, sort of like the clever coyote in Roadrunner cartoons. Through generations of renderings, the Anansi stories were misheard or forgotten enough that they became known as Aunt Nancy stories. "Aunt Nancy" had come to have a familiar English ring to it, useful since it had become dangerous in this new country called America to carry on the tribal traditions of Africa. As centuries passed, the Anansi tribal memory may have changed into the memory of a word sounding like "Aunt Nancy"; finally, even that word became nearly forgotten.

When a white child named Joel Chandler Harris (1848–1908) arrived faithfully night after night at an old black man's cabin in Georgia prior to the Civil War, perhaps he was confused as to why an "uncle" should be telling him Aunt Nancy stories. In honor of the teller of these cherished childhood stories that had such an unforgettable impact, Harris wrote them down years later and renamed them *Uncle Remus, His Songs and His Sayings*.

Why establish a relationship between Native American and African-American peoples? Because it is there. Mance's mother was half Choctaw Indian. His wife, Elnora, was part Indian. Andrew Laster was their distant neighbor when they lived from 1945 to 1956 on the Bluffs in Washington County. Laster was born around 1880; he lived above Camp Springs, where everyone in the area used to bring wagons to get drinking water. As a child, Laster remembered seeing tipis clustered around Camp Springs. It had been a favorite camping spot for Native Americans. For hundreds or thousands of years, it offered good water, good hunting, and open ground for safe campsites. There were three hundred Indian tribes living in Texas prior to the coming of Europeans. It is generally conceded that Mexicans and Mexican-Americans have a mixture of Spanish and Indian blood. What is less widely acknowledged is that many whites and blacks whose ancestors were born in Texas prior to 1880 have some Native American blood. In the Navasota area, most of the African-Americans I interviewed remembered having some Indian ancestry, while substantially fewer European-Americans recalled such an ancestry, whether their features suggested it or not. There is a striking resemblance between Mance Lipscomb's profile and the aquiline features depicted on a child's Big Chief writing tablet.

I Say Me for a Parable is an oral autobiography of Mance Lipscomb. I invite you now to immerse yourself in Mance's world. Imagine you've just driven up to Mance's home. You've gotten mud all over your clean car right after you turned into the driveway past the Navasota City Limit sign and bounced through the first big puddle.

You get out of your car and look up to see Mance Lipscomb sitting on the front porch. He is a thin black man around seventy-eight years old and about five feet nine inches tall. His hair is graying but still mostly black. He is sitting on his sofa, or maybe an old oak chair, alternately talking to several of his old cotton-picking and Saturday Night Supper friends, his wife Elnora, Little Mance and his kids and a bunch of grands and great-grands, and a fair sprinkling of Mance's white fans. He invites you to take your seat somewhere among the group. You might see somebody you know, or you might just wade over and set down with somebody you'd like to get to know. As you do so, you hear the locusts and katydids and other bugs, and maybe a meadowlark. There's no way you can screen out the sounds of Mance's great-grandchildren playing ball or chasing squawking chickens or just plain getting into mischief.

Mance has his guitar in his lap, or maybe he's put it down on the pine floor for a bit. He might even be getting a bite to eat at the kitchen table wedged between the Frigidaire and the glassed-in pie saver turned china cabinet. He's talking and chuckling about his life and his music, what it was like and what he's like and maybe what you're like. Telling more than a few jokes, and sometimes seeing how credulous your face can contort before you realize he's caught you in a hooraw.

The front porch is overcrowded with listeners. Some have spilled out onto the grass in the yard surrounded by the chain link fence and are dodging fire ants. Some of us are backed up beneath the shade of the chinaberry or fig or mimosa tree. You're invited to join the group, and listen to this storyteller songster. Ask him a couple questions if you get a notion, because that's what the rest of us are doing. And then you've become a part of this book.

Mance Lipscomb, July 1973, at the home of Edna Webster and Sonny and Nanny V Lewis. *Photo by Glen Alyn.*

Mama and Papa and the Back Life

Mance called pre-adulthood "the back life." It can be interpreted as "where I came from," "how I was brought up," or "the life I came up under." It is what shapes the adult, from one's family and cultural heritage to the experiences of birth, infancy, childhood, and the bridge of adolescence where one jumps back and forth between childhood and adulthood. In the rural culture of turn-of-the-century Navasota, children began to be assigned adult responsibilities generally by age ten. Black males were expected to shoulder a man's responsibilities and workload by the time they turned sixteen. Mance Lipscomb was born into this Navasota back life in 1895.

The fundamental influences on Mance's back life were Mother, Father, the immediate family, the church, and cotton culture. The first three go-alongs are organized around these themes. The first go-along introduces all of them, the second focuses on his mother, and the third relates to his father and his musical contribution to Mance and the community.

Mance expounds his version of the Christian experience in the first go-along and sprinkles it throughout the rest of the book. He built his life and made his choices standing upon this philosophical "Rock of Ages." The influence of the black Baptist church on Mance's life cannot be overstated. It became a source and funnel for the profound folk wisdom exhibited in black rural culture, the bedrock upon which African-Americans shaped the meaning of their lives, and the paradoxical seat of judgment rubbing backs against the celebration of worldly sensuality known as the Saturday Night Supper. When Mance was turned out of the church at fifteen, he was forced to choose between the two opposites. He drew his own interpretation of Christianity and carried it through his life, adjusting it to explain what he encountered as the proponent of the Saturday Night Supper's "devil music" and as a hardworking farmer.

Two generations after the end of slavery, African-Americans continued to re-create their meaning of family. Drawing on African, Native American, and European traditions, they brought new meanings to some commonly used terms. For example, when Mance refers to his mother being a "widow," he means that her husband was not present for the most part while she raised their family. A father being gone or dead amounted to about the same thing. In order for such a family to have a legitimate place in the sharecropping system, a son or another man had to step into the position of head of household. Mance began filling those shoes at age eleven.

Generally, blacks classified close family members of the same generation as brothers and sisters and those of more-distant blood ties as cousins, similar to how first cousins are differentiated from second and third cousins. Gainesville (Gainsvul) is defined by Mance as his "brother" because Gainesville's father, George, was the brother of Mance's father, Charlie. Mance refers to his mother elsewhere as a "one-man woman," while he calls his father a "twenty-woman man." Though it is possible that Mama Janie gave birth to both Mance and Gainesville, it is unlikely and in this case irrelevant. Gainesville and Mance simply became "brothers."

Mama Janie Pratt, Mance's mother, was half Choctaw Indian. Like Native American families, where children traditionally called anyone bigger than they "Mother" or "Father," black families used different guidelines than white families to establish the definitions of relationship. Until after the Civil War, many slave owners intentionally broke up black families and encouraged loose sexual relationships among their slave populations, while they further separated themselves by insisting on a strict puritan way of life in their own families. Ironically, the mixing of red, black, and white bloodlines was more common than family histories generally concede.

Typical of his culture, Mance's tongue and music were rich with these nuances of meaning and a host of refreshingly well-coined words and idioms. Though most of their meanings become self-evident in context, "brets" and "freznoes" deserve honorable mention here. Up until the introduction of tractors in the 1940s, teams of fifteen to thirty laborers performed most of the kinds of work required to maintain an efficient crop of cotton and corn. This team and the specific portion of land they could work were referred to as "brets." A "frezno" was a farm and road-building implement introduced in Navasota about 1930, and a predecessor to the front-end loader. It required three mules to operate. A bucket or blade would scoop dirt and transfer it to a wagon.

This book represents a critical shift in point of view. Mance Lipscomb presents *his* view of his culture and of the white world from which he was largely excluded for much of his life. He is looking at us, rather than the other way around. With a sense of humor or of gravity as the situation warrants, he makes a contribution to all of us.

THIS IS MANCE LIPSCOMB TALKIN. You know, they oughta have sumpm where thangs done went on in this world, they kin go down in histories. As the years come an go by. Now I dont understand much about writin poetry, or sumpm like that. All I kin hep you out in is: words that you ask me ta explain what they meanin. An inythang you see fit ta ask me, why jest give me time ta thank over what I'm doin. Cause you want it ta go through right, you see. Ya dont ever wanta do sumpm that aint no count.

I dont know how ta operate no tape recorder, cause I never had had em. But I know how ta operate in talkin, an know whats ta be said. One thang: once I git in the mood a talkin, I dont waste no time in talkin no foolishness. I know it dont hep the tape out. Dont hep me out. An if its not right, I'm wastin time.

See, there was a count-up fur it, Sonny. Younger race a people, who hadn never seen me: they would git some re-poat on me, after they come in the world. They'll go up in that. Generation ta generation. They left a lot a thangs undone, when they misst Blind Lemon. Leadbelly. An other players like me, an Mississippi John Hurt. Freddie MacDowell. Let them die. Without them in history.

I kin always hep you out in speakin opinions. An tell you some thangs: inythang about my life story, how I come up in the world. I'm willin ta do that cause you see I'm good at that. Because its not no strain on me ta tell the truth about myself.

An then people might near kin hear my records an my sangin, an picture it out might near as much as I could ta tell you about it. Cause they set an listen. Onto my records.

I bet ya I have done mow regularly recordin, outa my eight albums, than the odd man who was cuttin the albums foedy or fifty years ago. Well say he stawt cuttin the albums when Bessie Smith was out: I wadn nothin but a boy.

They was usin them old cup records. Jest like these flat records, but it was jest made diffunt, you know, when they cut them records befoe. First record ever I seen, it was about that long, like my awm. I call them cup records cause they was round an had a hole in it. Jest like one a them old biscuit rollers what you roll biscuits an pies an thangs, but it had nary shawp ends on it.

An they was the simplest thang you ever saw. It hookt into the machinery what you sung over, makin the record. You slip it over a sleeve, an buckle it down. An then, had a little switch there you turn it on, it go ta sangin. An it turnt over round an round til it git through wit it, it had a cutoff. An take that one off. Boy, you could hear it three or foe miles.

That was way befoe yo time. Thats the way our records come out when they first stawt ta makin records. An Bessie Smith did a lot a recordin on them.

I got two a Bessie's songs: I Plays "Bumble Bee," thats the first song she made in her life. An the other song called "I Wanta Do Sumpm fur You." She got a backup man doin that with her: Kansas City Joe. An then so miny people come out behind her, makin records. They jest whirl in here quick. Here come Leroy Carr, he's Bessie's piana player. An then, there was Clara Smith—foe Smith girls, an none of em wadn no kin.

You know, Edison was a smart man, who stawted lectricity an diffunt thangs. He's the first man ever performed these here Vick Torries, an cut the records. You couldn git a record playin over the air, without Edison's name was on it. An we went on with that Edison Vick Torrey, an Edison records fur years.

Them thangs come round here, somewhere in about 1912, 1913. I wadn playin half a nothin when them thangs come along. First song I played that I could rememorize was, oh, about thirteen an foeteen years of age, I was bumpin on a gittah. Playin two songs: "Sugar Babe" an "Out an Down." "Out an Down" was the first blues come out in state a Texas. Represented what the blues was. Well we playin "Out an Down," but we was playin the blues and didn know what it was.

What was "Out an Down" about? Jest somebody on the road, tryin ta go somewhere an make it ta some place. An

Political rally for W. E. Barry on Railroad Street in Navasota, Texas, circa 1895. Note steam locomotive and preponderance of African-Americans in the crowd. *Photo courtesy the Marcus Mallard Collection.*

you dont have iny money no way ta catch a ride. Jest
nothin but freight trains in them days. You could catch a
freight, when it slowed down or take water at a tank. A
train'd come up to a tank an slow down, it had a big old
pipe where they hold that water. Pull it over that boiler an
they'd fill that up, an it'd last fur miles an miles.

Well now the people who was, we call it hitchhikin now,
they knows when it was time ta take water. Well, we called
it we was goin beat our way an catch a train an ride. An
the brakemans, if they seed us git on there, they'd put us
off. We'd git back up in the cawbox, unbeknownst ta him,
an hide. Til we git ta the next station.

An if he didn see us, he wouldn look fur us. But he saw us
git on that train: we call it a big force arunnin? Why, he'd
wait til you git ta the next station, an he'd walk on top a
that train, an spot ya, an you hafta git off. An then he'd
turn you over to the policeman.

All right, we wanta go somewhere, fur better wages. Better time. Probly somebody that you knowed: say this is
Navasota. An somebody live in as close a place as Hearne.
We wanta try ta git there. We git out on the railroad track,
an we know exackly about where the water tanks was. He
stop there, an we git on an git in a boxcaw, an ride until it
slow down fur the next town. Then we jump off.

A lot a people got kilt tryin ta jump off that train. Jest
found em on the railroad track dead. Didn know how ta
catch a train, didn know how ta git off a train. But a lot of
em *knowed* how ta git on an off an walk em, because if you
once fool around wit a train—they'll know the speed it was
runnin: they could git off them trains jest like you jump
out that doe. Ya know, a train sucks wind to ya when ya git
off it. Its kind of a motion: jump off it, an lean back. Cause
its goin pull you forward, you see. An when you straighten
up, why, you had a balance that you could run down from
the dump an git yoself safe. When you jump off that train,
it got stirrups on them cawboxes. You hit that stirrup ta

git off: you better know how ta git off, or else you is a dead person.

People didn do nothin but jest steal away in them caw-boxes. Go hunnuds an hunnuds a miles! They had been ware where they wanted ta go an git off there an find what they lookin fur. Somebody or either some good job, ya know. They git up there an do well, an if they didn do well then they'd say, "Well, I blieve I'll go back home." Wait til another train come along an git water, an they grab it an come on back home.

I been knowin what that was, oh, when I was about eight years old. People call hitchhike thumbin a ride wit caws now: walkin, an tryin ta git somebody ta give you a ride. But we knowed about hitchhikin wayyy back in years, but we called it hitchhikin on a train: beat a ride.

We didn have iny caws. Didn have but very few hawsses. They was real good saddle hawsses then. An if you didn have one of your own, you couldn hawdly borry one ta go a nearby town, three or foe miles. No, they was crazy about them hawsses, man. Wouldn let you ride em. Unless you did sumpm fur him, you know.

Now if he's a fawma, why, he had a good hawss: you work out in the field. We'd work whole days ta git ta ride somebody's hawss. We uz glad ta work that day! We'd work two days if we couldn git the hawss.

An if they didn loan it to us, we gonna steal em out the lot that night. We had a way gittin to it. Oh yeah, we stole hawsses, boys. An rode hawsses all over this country where I showed you where I was bawn an raised back in them bottoms. On a mile an a half outa Navasota, goin ta Bryan. Used ta be a railroad bridge on this side a the Nava-sot River, on yo left goin outa town. I'd say about a half a mile down that river. Goin west. Eighteen ninety-five, on the ninth of April. Jest about plantin time. Bawn right on the banks a that river, right where that old railroad bridge at today. An I was raised on that fawm. Old fella named

Mista Ed Nickelbuck [Michelborough]. Funny name. That was his fawm. He was crippt up, an rode a old white hawss.

My uncle had the best saddle hawss ta ever come in state a Texas. Bred up from a colt ta be a saddle hawss. Course, you never did see none of em, but you read about these speedy hawsses, could go so fast wit a two-wheel gig. What you call a gig: got two rubber-tired wheels, like a buggy. But jest room fur one man ta sit in there. An no top to it.

An say, "Tell me how they go about racin them thangs?" Well, they give you a certain limit ta go. Maybe it was two miles. An you have a hawss there, an you say, "I bet you five dollas or ten dollas my hawss kin out-saddle or out-run yo's or out-singlefoot."

Then you have a judge. If you goin a mile nawth, that judge'll be up there when you got there, so he know who was in the lead. The man what you stawted off with, he didn give no account a how fast that hawss was goin, cause the judge is settin up yonda where you made it ta that mile or mile an a quota, ta time ya.

An when the first hawss beated there, he win the race. Sometime hawss have about, oh, half a length. Then, if its even: if he jest got im by a nose, well they wouldn give ya that. Now right up in about three quotas of a length from his neck, that was counted no race. That hawss'll be showed up. Hafta try it over again. They wait fur the one that kin beat the othern up ta the point, you know. Half a length, he win.

Man, a lot a people lost a lot a money on them races. Oh, people jest go out there on Sunday, thats the day's work end days. They'll let people run races, an people didn hafta pay ta go see it, you know. Now you got ta pay ta see races. Not in my come-ups. Jest go out in them shade trees, free.

We had a racetrack right down the road here. Bout two miles outa town. An the people'd stawt soon in the mownin befoe day: they git ta the racetrack, be there when the hawsses stawt ta racin. Had the hawsses out there in a big lot, an had men ta care fur them hawsses, an feed em at night.

Them hawsses are anxious, man. They knowed their way around, as good as a man could talk. They know what they're out there fur. An kep em separated. You had yo hawss in a pen, my hawss wouldn git in yo pen. They'd fight! Them hawsses had sense enough ta know that they was gonna race, an they didn like ta be beat.

So, is a lot a fun. A whole lot a diffunce in the time we havin our fun now than it was when we come up.

We walkt foe ta five miles, ta git ta the ball game. Go ta foe or five miles distance ta git to a church. No hawsses. No caws. We'd stawt early enough ta git there, so we'd make it there. Its a church right up this road, about two miles nawth from where I was raised an bawn at: called Saint John. Its been there over a hunnud years, I reckon. Seed aminy babtized, miny people go ta the church, an even join church.

Built it on a hill. Didn put it down there in the Bottoms where it'd git washt away. Well see, they used ta come from that church down here ta Navasot River. In wagons an buggies an walkers.

We had places located, would qualify fur people ta be babtized. We had a deacons ta go out in the water, an wade out there ta git the water straightened out where it'd be up ta the preacha: near about a little above his waist—somewhere along his titties? Then he stop. He had a stick he'd poke down in the water, so he wouldn go too far out in the water.

An he carried the preacha out there first. An then he go git the people who goin be babtized: carry em one an two at a time. An it'd be a hunnud an fifty, two hunnud people up an down that river, an the preacher'd be sangin an the people sangin up an down that river fur miles. People be shoutin, so glad people was gonna be babtized. An a lot a times, they had better church on that river than they did in the church house.

An the deacon'll go up ta the bank, an brang the people who gonna be babtized. The womens an mens all had gowns on, you know. White gowns! An when they stawt ta sangin, they stawted ta sangin befoe you git in that water. Preacha go out there an stood in the water until the deacon brought the patients out there to im.

An the whole gang a people on the bank, they would come there ta see the people babtized. Everbody sangin along together on babtizin day. An that preacher stawt ta sangin, as the deacon brang em out ta the water.

An when he git em out ta the water, the preacha git one of em by the hand. Dont babtize but one at a time. First thang he say, "I babtize my sister in the name a the Father, an the Son, an the Holy Ghost." Down under the water you went. Ever time he was babtizin a person, it was the same word he used over the first, up to a hunnud. Me an everbody would say the same thang, over the person who was gonna be babtized. An when they carry that one out he babtized first, somebody'd throw a dry cloth around her cause she uz wet.

Well, you take in the Bible: that Jesus Christ, he was babtized by Moses. Thats intended fur God Amighty. He had a unknown Son come in this world, experience mown inybody in the world.

You know he was twelve years old: Jesus Christ was goin round healin the sick, an lettin the blind come where they could see. If you had sores on ya: you a poe man, Labbuth [Lazarus], you might a heard about Labbuth. He's full a sores. An he could heal him. Jesus Christ jest put his hand on him, an them sores got well. Blind man: he jest put his hand on him, an he come ta see. People couldn talk, he had em ta talk.

See, he set ta do thangs couldn no man do. God sent him

here as His Son, so he could die fur you an I. Hey, he gives us His lovin Son, so we would all be free. You know thats a wonderful God, aint it?

People dont understand—now dont stawt me in ta preachin, cause I got a whole lot a religion in me. Whenever we go out an say we know thangs, we don know nothin, we jest guessin our way through.

God dont make nobody wise as Him. God say, "You's a saint." If you done done Right, you gonna live long enough ta reap yo right deeds. An somebody gonna treat me right if I keep on doin Right. I say me as a parable: may be two years, but you gonna live ta reap what you sow. A lot a peoples done died, an didn reap all they wrong deeds. Wrong deeds overtuck ya befoe ya die. But yo righteous thang gonna come back to ya.

Aint nothin in the world did without a cause. An takes His time, fur ta reach here. He say it aint gonna come in one day. Cause He works in a mysterious way. Work when you sleep. He's never without us.

Now you take a little two-, three-year-old infant, he's not been here long enough ta do no wrong thang. Yo foeparents takes up yo deeds, until you git a certain age. Do you know how long it take you ta realize Wrong from Right? You done got in the stage of teenage: foeteen years of age. Yo sins is on you then. Now these people say, "I babtize this child, eleven years old." Aint no sich a thang as that. You caint confess ta hope in Christ til you git the age on ya, til He know you able ta understand what you doin.

Now you git yo Bible—it might not be in the Bible but its in my mind an in my hawt. Cause I been converted myself. See, I wadn nated ta gittin a religion when I was going ta church regular. With my parents—my mother, mostly. I was jest goin ta church as a alibi, jest goin there. They told me how ta pray an what ta say ta the Lawd. He wadn payin me no attainsion! Cause He know you too weak ta say, "Lawd have mercy," an mean that. An "Forgive me for my sins." You aint got no sins til you git foeteen years old! See?

But when they stawted ta runnin revivals: at a certain time a the year they babtize ya. Long in September an October, thats cotton-pickin time. A lot a people come up there an pray an say, "I got religion," an git a preacha's hand an say, "I done got a conversion."

Well, they join church. On they word. But lot a people jest pretend they blong ta church. Oh you kin howl an hoop all you wanta. If you jest say, "Lawd have mercy," an dont mean that, why, aint nothin gonna hapm. He dont let thangs hapm. Cause he is a jest God! When you say, "Lawd have mercy," an mean that, you git credit fur it. Its a bright place in yo livin. Right there. You dont see it. He let you feel Him.

Certain prayers cause you ta git converted. No, I didn felt it the first time. I workt at it maybe three or foe weeks. An when I did say the right prayer: told the Lawd if He free my soul from sin, that I would serve Him the balance a my days. I askt him ta convert me.

Convert means free yo soul from sin. An then, you dont see Him. He send you a spirit: that's a feelin. You be happy the minute He touch yo hawt that you is converted, cause you gonna tell everybody, you goin shout so people kin come ta you. Yo hands look new, yo foots look new. The whole world changes, why when you got converted. You see people an they look bettern you ever saw em in yo life. You see thangs bettern you ever saw in yo life. An you, you's Happy.

I was converted one Satiddy night. I never will furgit it. I prayed, prayed, a night an day. I prayed in myself. I prayed in the field. Walkin an plowin, an choppin. Askt the Lawd ta convert me.

But until I got ta pray the right prayer thats the moment He heard me. Fifteen years of age: I was in the church house. Everbody was sangin an shoutin, an I was prayin

49

fur the Lawd ta convert me. Them "Amens" goin on all around me, preacher callin us ta God Amighty.

An after while I commenced ta gittin this feelin, from the inside out. I went up an sat down on the mourner's bench. Me an seven or eight others was settin up there. An man, I was shoutin an happy, an they couldn hold me. I didn know exackly what I was doin. I was so stout, it taken two, three people ta hold me! Well, that was the Holy Ghost, the Spirit had hit me! Man, a person git a religion you caint hawdly do nothin wid im! Hafta turn him loose! Let him go! Until he settle down. One man like me kin handle three or foe mens. You got some power. He give you that Holy Spirit, He give you the Power.

He has got the Power ta send it down ta you, by air. An by feelins. He sent His power down ta you ta make you happy. An know its some change in life done made in you. Conversion means a whole lot.

An from when I confessed ta hope in Christ til I got home that Satiddy night, I couldn tell you exackly what hapmd, cause I dont know what hapmd. But I kin tell you one thang: I went out that doe an went on home, talkin bout religion all the way! Lay down that night. Couldn sleep nohow. Jest tossin around on the pallet, you know. An people hear thangs fur an near, "I heard Mance got religion last night."

I was layin in a pallet in the flow. Mama said, "Yeah, my child got converted last night."

Say, "Well I come ta see im."

An I woke up an I say, "Now listen." Ta myself. I say, "I caint tell the people I got no religion. I jest told em I made a mistake. I dont feel up ta facin people an tellin them what the Lawd did fur me."

An they say, "Well tell him ta git up."

I got up an went ta the doe, an I say I wadn gonna tell it.

An then I heard some people comin down the road, an they was sangin praises ta Jesus. An when I got ta the doe an met those people, I was tellin everbody I met. Jest resht out there an told em I was converted an how I was so glad about it. I'd jest turned somewhere between foeteen and fifteen years of age. Jest Happy, you know. Its a gift from God. That Spirit hit you. An everwhere I went, in the hot sun everwhere I jest walkin the road, hollerin an hoopin an tellin the people I'm so glad.

An I was tendin church, purdy briefly. I had jest learnt how ta play gittah. Three or foe good songs. I wouldn look at that gittah. I wouldn touch it. I went an joined church, an stayed in church.

Wadn there, oh, about half a year, befoe they turnt me outa the church. See, I couldn understand what they were doin. They couldn understand what they were doin ta me. An I couldn see in my mind what they was doin, cause it was a false pretense went out on me.

Jest a few people told it out that I wadn converted, because I was playin my gittah. See, I kin tell a tale on you, an it could stick. I wadn playin the gittah, cause I had done decided ta give it away or sell it. But they told the wrong repoat.

See, I had respect fur them peoples whats in the church. Deacons an pastors, church members. An they tellin me I didn blieve in God Amighty, you know, that went harder in me. It made a looong time—I dont know how long—befoe I revealed a yen fur what they said about it, an then I wanted ta be a church member. Because I had a good open hawt all my life. An I didn thank that I was ware a bein turnt out.

An so finely three or foe of em got together, the deacons an some a the church members. I went ta church an they had foe or five of us up there on a table, bookin us ta turn us out. You got ta give an account a yoself, how you was livin in the church. They say, "Well, we gonna turn him out."

I take it so bad. I said, "Well, I dont know what ta do.

51

Because I had done made up my mind ta be a church member. These people dont know what they talkin about. Cause theys somebody lied on me."

But I didn know. God Amighty knowed how ta git me back in church. I dont care what the people said, God knowed yo hawt. But I was figgerin the people oughta compromise wit me. I wadn thankin I could go ta God Amighty an git forgiveness in prayin ta Him, cause I was a young man.

Finely, I said, "Well, they turnt me outa the church. I jest as well ta go back an play my gittah. Thats all I got."

An, first thang you know, they commenced ta sayin, "Well Mance, play us some good music, inyhow."

That stawted me off playin music. Fact, I never woulda played music no mow. But I had sumpm worthwhile: ta do my music playin cause they turnt me out the church. An they was sorry. Because I was a good songster, an I was a quiet man, an everbody like me, couldn give me no bad recommendation. So I got on, commence ta playin the gittah back, to an fro. Then I never did go back in the church.

I didn quit church: church quit me. Cause they didn want me ta play my music. An they say I was a sinner. I'm not a sinner. I been converted. An I'm got religion.

But I learnt a whole lot about religion. If you got a religion, its in yo hawt. Not in the church house. You kin talk wit God Amighty right now, like me an you talkin. This is not a church house. You kin talk an hear Him right here in this house. You dont hafta talk loud, either. Jest, you kin talk in yo hawt an mean it. You say, "Lawd, take care a me. Forgive me fur what I done."

He want you ta ask Him fur forgiveness when you make a mistake. He want you ta repeal ta Him, that you done did sumpm or other, that you ought not ta do.

So I tote my church right along in my hawt. Ever day. Everwhere I go. When you see me wake up in the mownin, I done thankt God fur ablin me ta live ta see this day. Sayin my prayers at night. Dont miss it. Because I have a conscience. An when I do that, it release my feelins. I say my prayer befoe I git out the bed, say my prayers befoe I git in the bed. Then its well done.

Now, aint nobody dont make a mistake in this world. Folks say, "You too old ta git out here an play music. You oughta be servin God." I'm servin God ever night an day. I aint makin a mistake. You know why I aint? Cause God give me chance ta do this! He could cut off both these hands! If He wanta take this away from me. Or one a my awms. Or put me in a fliction where I couldn move my fangers. But He give this talent ta me, what I got, an He satisfied in what I'm doin, til He wanta make a change in life.

There's nothin in the world between you an God Amighty. If He give you religion once, He dont take it away from you. What He give you, He dont take it back.

Some people say, "Well you a backslider." Its not no sich a thang as a backslider. Cause you dont be in church, an yo name on the church list? Yo name with God! An you kin do thangs through God by prayin an thankin Him. An trustin Him. Dont care where you is an where you go.

No, I didn git no hatred wit em. An no trouble. I kin take thangs easiern iny man you ever met. I never go round makin no big ta do when a person do wrong ta me: why I dont git out ta cryin, an hoopin an talkin about it, an tryin ta make a big thang outa it ta dispute an squabble. I never was a squabblin man. I was a peaceful boy all a my whole life. I didn like ta spute people's word. I jest went along, had my own mind made up ta be sociable an kind ta people.

Remember me tellin y'all, in my go-alongs: if I go places, an people look like I couldn git along wit em, I quit foolin wit ya an go some other way. I dont wanta brang no hatred. Because if you kin have happy feelin, you know thats the best part a yo life: Happiness. You not mizable. You not worried.

Why I dont live ta be confused an ta have people have the bad opinion a me: I wanted ta live Right wit people. Then I'm pleasin God up yonda. You caint please the people here on earth. You try ta please God, an He'll open the Way fur ya podna, as long as you live. You have thangs ta come ta you so miny ways you dont know how it come.

Why? He sees inside a you, you got the right desire. It aint yo flesh! Aint yo blood! God lookin at yo hawt. Now, what is yo hawt? You got a desire ta do Right inside a yo hawt. You wanta live Right wit people, wanta treat people Right, you wanta like people.

I dont care how purdy you is, if you got a bad hawt you a ugly person. I dont care how you are dresst—got all the fine clothes an fine shoes an automobiles, nice home—if you got a bad hawt inside, you aint got nothin. Cause you caint enjoy it.

An you kin take sumpm from me, an say, "I tuck this from old Lipscomb. I own this. I'm enjoyin it." You caint enjoy that cause you tuck it away from me an you oughtn ta tuck it. Its sumpm inside a you. That conscience is worryin you so you dont know whats a madda wit you, but you know its a feelin in there.

You say, "I'm a man." Yeah you a man but what is a man? A man aint nothin but his mind. A mind aint nothin but his hawt. See? I'm talkin right direckly ta God Amighty. He sot the day fur me ta come here an talk wit you all. I didn know it til I got ta talkin. An then He gonna let you feel that religious gift that He sent down here with the Power. He work with Power. Not talk. Thats a mighty man, aint it? He kin set up there in heaven, an kin send that Power down here an do what He want wit it.

Say, "How its gonna reach me, man?" He send the Power down here.

"What sorta power, man?" He send blessin. It come fur the righteous man. You'll reap some good deeds. You'll come aware a doin some good thangs. Maybe inherit some money. Good car. Its so miny ways He kin come at you an reach you, you dont know nothin about. Cause ever time He turns around wit His Power up there, He turn it right down on Right. He's under the earth. He's on top a that earth. He's in the air. Now how you gonna dodge Him? He kin git you iny way He wanta. Now what you gonna do wit a man like that?

You know what religion is? You got ta *live* religion. You got ta *do* religion. You got ta live Right. Then God kin feel that in you, He know when ta come ta you an when not ta come to ya. Wit His Spirit.

Now you watch my appearance: I'm livin religion. Cause I like everbody I meet. You caint hate people, an say you have religion. But you kin hate their ways, an git away from their way. You kin walk away from a wrong thang. You jest stay here, an be in the midst a them people who is doin Wrong: well, first thang you know you'll be in the middle a that same stuff. You wrong fur stayin there wit em, an kneelin to em, an let them push you around.

People dont understand what the world is. They say the world is gittin worser. The world jest like it was when it first was created. The people is gittin worser. People is of the world. They doin so much criticism. An God dont like whats goin on. See God, He's against us goin on what stawted from way back, generation ta generation: tuck from yo parents—if you didn have some rich parents. Tuck from my parents. Tuck from the Mexican over there. An beat im an tuck all their land away from em, an run em outa there. An left it fur they kids.

Looka how miny doggone hurrikins an floods an thang. Earthquickens. How miny thangs hapm here, in some certain part a the world? Now destroyed, aint it? See, He lettin these people know its a God somewhere.

It was already a sayin, "Its gonna be wars an rumors a wars." Thats one war right at anothun. You read that in the Bible? We lived ta see three wars, aint we? God knowed that was gonna hapm befoe it come here. But He's tryin ta show us in the way its gonna hapm wit a Bible He put out here on earth fur em ta read that, wit a Scripture.

An then git the meanins outa the Bible: wars an rumors a wars. An its gonna become a time, as mothers against daughters, daughter is against mother. Fathers against sons. Sons against father, aint it that? Right now? He sent this here in the world, fur these ta come about. He knowed hunnuds a years back this is gonna hapm, cause His Word does not fail! We didn know what that meant, but we done lived up to it ta see what it meant. To experience what it meant. In this time. We understand that now. We jest thought them words was readin words.

An somebodys gonna live ta see sumpm another change. An some of us aint gonna be here ta see it. But its gonna make a change in this world. Because God said, "Now it lookin low." He's dissatisfied in the way people is livin among one another.

Cause he made this world fur you an me. You as much as me, an I'm jest as much as you. Its not none a yo world. Aint none a mine. Its mine an yo'n. But some of us gonna stand on potions a the world dont blong to us. Take it away from you, an I inherit all of it. Thats where these wars started! Fightin people about they land, an we aint got no bizniss over there in Germany. We wadn raised in Germany. We wadn raised in Nam. Thats a diffunt part a the world. Let them people stay over there, an do what they wanta do over there an we try ta take care a our part a the world. No, we gonna go over there an fight them an take their country.

Caused a lot a bloodshed too, aint it? Lot a powder an awtillery an bombs, guns. Wasted in the ocean, out on the land burnt up.

Well, we havin judgment right now. We aint gonna see no Judgment Day, talkin bout the world gonna burn up. Thats jest all a propaganda. We dont know nothin about the world, back in the time they talkin Noah built his Awk. That was the first world, God come in here an first created it. An He turnt around an destroyed ever durn bit of it. He was jest showin people in a pattern, what could hapm. He didn say was gonna hapm. He's powerful enough ta do those thangs, but He didn say He was gonna come here an set the world on fire.

He send earthquickens in some potions a the world. Like it went over ta Mexico, Califownya, Guatemala. We aint had no earthquickens here yet. We aint had no floods here yet ta wash away. We dont know how soon, but maybe its comin.

But we kin prevent those thangs. You know how we kin prevent em? Jest git tagether an try ta live Right. All right. Thats what happenin over there some people in Los Angeles: is so miny people dont blieve its a God. He lettin em know in a way, it *is* a God.

Listen, if we wanta have a good world, me an you all of us here wit me, we'll git tagether an claing together. An like each an one another. Then we got thangs goin the way God is suited at. Do you know we'll have a peaceful world right here? We in a big world right here, communin. We dont need no mow world jest ta git right here an git tagether. This is our world, ta live peaceful an happy wit one another.

God dont kill you. He dont kill me. You do thangs ta kill yoself. You dont know when its gonna hapm or how it hapmd. But you do them thangs, some way another you gonna brang it on ya, brother.

No, I havent played in church very often. See, they criticize me cause I'm a blues songster. You know what I am? Blues is in the church! I kin prove it ta you in one word: What is the blues? Blues is a feelin. If its a feelin out in these nightclubs, its a feelin in church.

Say, "What sort a feelin?" Its a sad feelin, an a worried feelin, an a thang that'll concentrate on yo mind. An thats worrinated. Thats the reason they say its the worried blues. Well, you feelin sorry. Disorderly. It communicates a whole lot a ways, the blues do. But it dont come back unto you wit no happiness.

Aint the people unhappy in the church when they settin up there lookin at somebody in the coffin, dead? Church house caint say a word? They hate ta see im in that shape. Say, "Thats the last a him." Then when you sang an pray over im, fixin ta put im in the ground, some a his relatives or close friends has got ta shed tears. Aint they got a feelin?

Blues aint nothin disorderly. Its sumpm what you done lived with all yo life. But you jest comin aware a what it is: its nothin but a feelin.

Listen, I played songs last night with that knife, "Mother Had a Sick Child, She Thought It Would Die." That feelin went through everbody. Cause God give me the power ta carry it. An present it. I didn come! God sent me here. Ta talk ta you young people. An play my music.

Music is talent. What kinda talent? He give me the power ta learn this music, an ta play this music, an play it wit a feelin. Ta spread it from town ta town, places ta places. Cause I could not a been here today, talkin, if God didn intend fur me ta be here, mista. I coulda been dead or somewhere else! But I'm here, doin his commandment.

An if you wanta know sumpm: it aint nothin in the world got a feelin to it, if you dont sang these old back songs. An play this back music. Because thats the generation a music. An we brang that to y'all, in the light, who dont know nothin about it, in yo age. See, we know about it; well, we brangin it to ya.

Now you take Blind Gary Davis: plenty a time I met him. He's a nice fella, an he plays some rail good gospel song. He knowed the Bible, an knowed all about these old back songs.

Well, he wadn sposed ta sang blues. He sot out ta be a

preacha. Now listen, dont say he couldn sang it. He thought in his mind cause he was a preacha: blues is a criticize. Cause people jest go up against the words say "blues," they dont wanta put it in the church an say, "Thats a blaspheme on the church."

But he sangin the blues all the time. Cause he had that feelin, ta sang his spiritual song. He was happy over what he sangin an he made people happy.

"Lookin for My Jesus"? I'm glad you mentioned that. That was the first stawtin, when Christ was in this world, an Mary was Jesus' mother. Mary was virtuous. She was bawn a chile. He didn have no daddy. She revealed Him in her womb. God had the Power ta convert a son in her womb, that He called Jesus Christ as the Son of God.

He didn come down here an mated wit Mary. he revealed her, that she gonna inherit a chile: say, "This chile was bawn, is gonna be the Son of Me: Livin God Amighty. An He's gonna be virtuous. He's gonna come here wit no sins hangin to im. He's gonna come here wise an do thangs couldn nobody else do."

He aint dead! He wadn dead when they kilt im. They thought they had im kilt. Buried Him in a grave, they call it a tomb then. Tuck them there nails outa His hands. An outa His feet. An He was tuck down ta be buried in the grave.

Them fellas put im in the ground. An went on about their bizniss, say, "Well, we got him."

Next mownin, his mother Mary went ta the grave. She knowed they buried im, but she didn know where He was: was he in the grave, or where he done got away. They had a bump a dirt layin there.

Know where Jesus Christ was? Flyin in the air! You heard that song say, "Shine like the mownin star?" He's shinin you got a glimpse of Him. He so bright that they couldn look at Him. They seed a sky: nothin but diamonds. Jesus imitated, as a mownin star when he was flyin off back ta heaven. They never did find im in the grave.

But now Mary went ta the grave. An she fell down on her knees on the ground, an you kin see that robe. Say, "I'm huntin fur my Jesus." Mary was weepin.

Marthy was His auntie, that was Mary's sister. An Sister Marthy come amoanin. She say, "Kin you tell me where kin I find Him?" Them verses printed in the Bible.

Thats the song I'm sangin. Mary come right back an say, "They crucified my Jesus." They hand the verse, from one to the othun. Jest like you heppin me sang: you use a verse an I use one. Its a hand over. An put it ta some good rhythm ta where people kin understand it. It aint hawd ta understand, cause if you got a hawt in yo body that feelin gonna come to ya.

See, they carried the blues ta the church. An they carried it away from the church. Cause its livin tween you an everbody else that feelin is here. I dont know what sorta feelin you got on you. You dont know what I got on me. An if you dont tell me how you feel I dont know. An if I dont tell you how I feel you dont know. But ya know sometime I got a diffunt feelin.

But all them feelins come ta you in one way an come ta me in anothun. Thats why the blues travels so miny diffunt directions. Goes from you ta me.

Now dont git me wrong. Its plenty of us do's wrong thangs. I've put myself as a parable: I'm a man, too. Well now, what I'm talkin about, I been wrong fur thankin. But some people go ahead in performance a that wrong thang til sumpm hapm to em. Or they cause a lot a violence ta be.

When I found out I was thankin wrong, then I turnt right round, said "I'm sorry I had that in my mind." Pushin you around, an doin thangs ta you I oughtn ta do, why thats what you call a bad doin. My wrongness was bad feelins, cause I didn know where I was wrong or right til I fresht up my own mind.

They come ta me an say, "You treatin him wrong" or "You goin the wrong way. You sayin the wrong words." Then I kin halt right there. It dont take me long ta consider.

You know, thats that same thang I'm tellin you: all that *is* goes in conscience. An I know I done so much bad thangs. I dont have that conscience on me. I'm jest as clear inside a me as I was when I was bawn. Cause I always wanta do the right thang. It dudn take me long foe I know I'm goin the wrong direction, an doin the wrong thang. I check up on myself. You dont hafta tell me. I kin tell you quick, wit my own feelin.

Thats why I stay out a lot a trouble. I been in this world seventy-eight years, an I aint paid a nickel fine in my life. Thats a good record, idn it? Dont be worried about askin people about me! I dont have inythang ta hide behind.

They goin tell you, say "Well, if you wanta know his reputation, he's a good fella." White or black: they know I've got kind of a, what you call principle.

I kin git help, quickern iny colored man from white folks here than it is in the state a Texas. But I never was a man ta beg. An borry. I try ta earn what I got, work fur it. An lot a times I be broke as a hank when I was comin up. Befoe I stawt that music career. I be so hongry. Wanted ta git sumpm an couldn git it. I stand around an go ta town, places. An I want sumpm so bad, it hurt me inside. You never hear me sayin, "Let me have so-an-so." If I didn have it, I jest toughed it out.

An these people here got all this money: they not satisfied. They worried ta death! They scared somebody gonna take it from em. Thats one thang they worried about.

An they want mown they got. If they had a million dollas, they want two million. When you find out about rich fellas goin ta heaven: dont you never blieve that. Rich person aint goin ta no heaven.

Thats right. The people that He have mercy on are people who suffered. Like you an others. Work hawd. Earn yo's.

These rich people, they was bawn wit a silver spoon in their mouth. Papa inherited his, befoe the child was bawn. An he left it here fur his child. He dont know how he come by it. He kin spend a million dollas a day; it dont hurt him, cause his papa give it ta him. Or either he stole it from somebody. But once he got out there an works fur it, he know what ta do wit it. You know I'd appreciate you an me an everbody else. The rich people dont know how ta—they dont appreciate me an you.

Sang one about like that? I dont know if I kin sang, but I kin show talk it.

[Mance sings, "When Yo Lamps Go Out":]

When my eyes git so I caint see no mow,
What you gonna do wit yo 'ligion
When yo lamps gone out.

When my feet git so, Lawd, I caint walk no mow,
What you goin do wit yo religion
When yo lamps gone out.

When yo lamps gone out, when yo lamps gone out,
What you gonna do wit yo 'ligion
When yo lamps gone down.

When my hawt git so, it caint beat no mow,
What you gonna do wit yo religion
When yo lamps gone out.

Nose git so, Lawd, it caint smell no mow,
What you gonna do wit yo 'ligion
When yo lamps gone out.

What you gonna do? I heard that song when I was a little bitty kid. Six or seven years old. Everbody caint understand that unless they been burnin them coal oil lamps. An aint got no mow coal oil, an that lamp goes out.

Well, thats yo life. But we been sayin fur a parable, say, "When yo eyes git so you caint see no mow, when yo nose git so you caint smell no mow." All yo whole body. And when yo lamps gone out, yo hawt stop beatin. See, everthang gone out. Thats one a the grandest songs I've sotten ta hear, Mama an them sung when I was a little kid. An all them thangs is come back ta my remembrance.

Well, you see my voice? My voice taken right after Mama. Oh Lawd, man, Mama had a good strong voice. No, she never would sang wit Papa. They had a bad life ta live. Papa didn do nothin but run around. Had diffunt womens an kep Mama confused. An go off an leave Mama, weeks in an out. An come back, an Mama didn know where he was until he come back. Played that fiddle, an he woe his good clothes. Mama was a nice-lookin woman. Hawdworkin woman.

Now she couldn talk plain, til she got behind bein mad wit ya. She git mad, all you could hear is jest bawl. Indian talk, you know. She could cull up all them turkeys from out in the woods. An they'd hear, an they'd come runnin an sailin cross the prairie. An she could call a chicken out in the prairie some kinda way, an them chickens flied plumb ta the house! She had that instain, outa her bein half Choctaw Indian.

Nooo, she didn sang wit my daddy. Papa an her lived disagreeable. Listen, Mama had eleven kids ta my daddy. He quit her mow times than I could count. He'd go off an stay a while, til a new baby was bawn. An when she'd git shed a one baby, he'd come back, an she'd bust anothun fur im.

An he'd go off an leave her again. Papa stayed in the gutter with them old bad womens an half-crazy womens. Iny woman'd do him jest soon as he'd git away from Mama.

So, I knowed Mama an Papa wadn gonna make it when I got ta be about ten or eleven years old. Cause they'd fight an fuss so much. One day I thought he'd kilt Mama. Knockt her plumb down ta the flow. But she got right back up. An they went on a little further after that come about.

So finely, Mama was settin in the doe worried about Papa one night. An he brought a woman right front a her doe! Come right by!

Mama say, "Who is that? Looks like that Mista Lipscomb comin yonda."

He say, "Yeah, thats me. If you hadn been settin in the doe you wouldn seed me. You watchin me."

She say, "I aint watchin you. I jest saw you. I was settin here in my doe. I wadn botherin you." An the woman was on the other side. She said, "Who is that you got wit ya?" She had heard the repoat bout he was goin with that woman.

An he say, "None a yo bizniss."

An Mama walkt out ta see who it was. An she hit that woman like a dog. All us chilluns jumpt on Papa an the woman an run em away from there. An she bloodied that woman.

Brung that woman right by the house! Oh, man, my daddy was onry. So you caint count them times, cause they separated an lived so bad until she jest finely quit im. We got big enough so ta hep her work, then she didn notice im no mow.

Yeah I hadn pickt cotton, miny years when that come about. I could throw a boll a cotton so hawd: man I wade away an then, Va-dddddddr! hit a fella right in the head! Man, that man show did git hurt.

He said, "Somebody done hit me wit a rock."

Tuckt my head down. Commenced ta pickin cotton like I hadn done nothin.

Mama said, "Who is that chunkin up here?"

I said, "Wadn none a me, Mama."

Man says, "Well, somebody chunkt cause I got a knot in my foehead. I catch who done it, I'm gonna knot him."

Field hands at Allenfarm, near Navasota, circa 1900s. *Photo courtesy the Marcus Mallard Collection.*

My sista she's oldern me, she say, "You gonna chunk im again?"

I said, "No. Mama might find out who chunkt."

Well you take the landowners, what me an Mama, Papa, an all of us workt under: they would qualify you could do a whole lot mow in the field than you could do. They'd push you, an git yo limits ta how much you could do. Had people pickin cotton, say "Well, I want you ta pick so much today. You aint doin nothin." Well I git out there an try ta do it, cause I fraid of em. Didn wanta git whuppt an knockt.

First time I was about ten or eleven years old. I never will furgit it: Mama had me in the field. Said, "Boy, you got certain amount a cotton ta pick today."

I said, "Mama, how much I got ta pick?" I couldn do nothin but count one, two, three, to a hunnud, you know.

She said, "You pick fifty pounds, you kin go home."

That was the hawdest day ever I saw in my life, ta pick

fifty pounds. But I workt, I workt. Sun was hot an I was sweatin. Kids had little old croakasack they drug. Now them old long sacks what the grown-ups toted: sometimes you could put a hunnud pounds in one bag. Thats bout the furtherest as it should git, cause you got a whole lot a cotton when you put a hunnud pounds a cotton in one sack. Oh, man. One of em was too much fur me, when I was young.

Whats a croakasack? Tow sack, you call it. See, thangs done changed in words now. When I was comin up we called em croakasack. I dont furgit that word yet.

So I pickt that fifty pounds a cotton, an man, I was so tired. I tried ta eat suppa. An lookt like I'd eat a little, lay the piece a bread down. Pick it up again an my awms was hurtin, my legs was hurtin, my back was hurtin.

Mama said, "Well you better eat yo suppa befoe you go ta bed."

I said, "Well, I woke tired." I didn do nothin but sot there at the table. Half went ta sleep an woke up, right there at the bread again. Went ta bed hongry. Cause I was hurtin all over.

Next day I was a little supple cause, when you once do a thang, why you kin be a little strained up to it. But you be ware of it the next day. So, next day I got my fifty pounds a cotton early. I was out in the fields playin with other boys.

An from then ta that whole year round, all I was taxt fur: fifty pounds. Then I go'd up the next year, I had ta pick a hunnud. He'll shove the limit up, as years come around. That landowner dont let you slack off with nothin, man.

An first thang you know, the next year I was pickin a hunnud an fifty. Went up from one-fifty ta five hunnud pounds a cotton one day in my life. That like ta kilt me, it hurt me so bad, man all over I was achin. I told him, I said, "I went ta the limit. Caint pull a boll mow."

He said, "Well, I blieve you is. You hold that ta foe hunnud, you kin git by wit me."

An from that back down ta foe-ten, an three-fifty. I found out I jest strained up myself cause I couldn go it. An I had regular average: I cut down ta three hunnud pounds a cotton, an I figgered I could hold up at that.

Then I had a brother could pick six hunnud, six-fifty, an then turn around an pick five hunnud pound another day. See, he wadn no average picka. Charlie was two years older'n me. An I didn know but what he was doin but he was pickin it. Nor how he got it. He was liddlern I was. He was a swift cotton picka. Swift at inythang he tuck. He run that big steam engine down there at the Shoemocka [Schumacher] Oil Works, fur years and years.

An I try ta pick along wit im, he pick so fast, I leave half my cotton on the row, tryin ta keep up wit im.

He look around an say, "Boy, you better go back an pick that cotton. Leavin the cotton! You caint keep up wit me. You jest pick like you pick."

Cause he pickin it clean. See, what they call a clear picka, a clean picka, well he kin pick his cotton an fill his sack, an wont be nothin but cotton in there. Thats how we done it most all the time in Navasota. An in these bottoms around here.

Now what you call pullin cotton, thats a diffunt thang. Jest go ta grabbin inythang you kin. Git old leaves an sticks in that sack. You kin git six, seven hunnud, sometime a thousand pounds a day pullin. But wont be half the cotton in that croakasack as pickin it clear.

Well finely, I give up tryin ta follow im. Say, "If I dont git off ta myself, I caint keep up wit im an too do the job right. Cause first thang you know, I'm gonna git a scoldin about leavin my cotton on the row." An I gaited myself away from there. See, aint no use tryin ta be like nobody else, tryin ta do what the other fella do. You come ta find out what you kin do best. An do that, an be satisfied wit it. Caint nobody fault you fur that.

But that brother a mine pickin five hunnud, iny day he

67

git a notion fur it. He wadn average picka. Average picka, like what you call my mama, had pickt the same amount ever day. See, she was a workin woman, she could pick three hunnud pounds a cotton ever day she go ta the field.

Boy, you talkin bout a man who had it tough. We wadn gittin but foedy cents a hunnud, an fifty cents a hunnud. When I was raised up, I had that brother Charlie. An I had a sista; her name's Annie. She was two years oldern me. An I was the third child, third boy. There was one mow in there, befoe me. But it died a little bitty baby. I never did see that one.

An so, my brother Charlie, he purdy thrifty. He caught on quick. An he loved ta drive mules an thangs out on the levee camps. Is roads here now was built by mules. He slipt off, blieve about foeteen years of age. An left my mama— but he'd come home ever Satiddy night an brang her his pay. Then he go back Sunday evenin. Cause he was a good driver, an he knowed his way round on them roads.

People would have tents, all round them roads. An mule lots built! An they commence ta likin him. Because he could show drive mules. An he could use those slips. They had two little handles, one on each side, an had a point like a shovel, but it'd hold a lot a dirt. An you scoop em down under that soft dirt an bear down on them handles an fill it up, an then the mules'd pull it up an dump it in a wagon. An thats what lowed em over ta build them roads.

Next thang come frezno over there. Big frezno got three mules ta them. Do the same job, but it'd haul mow dirt. Thangs commenced ta immigratin: bout two or three years at a time, diffunt equipments would come up. Freznoes come in here somewhere in about nineteen-thirty.

Now a levee camp is where people are out there buildin roads, highways. Yeah, work camp, loggin camp. You kin call em what you wanta. But they didn give but one name. But we say we goin over there an be where a log camp:

thats a levee camp. All of em is levee camps. But we was doin diffunt thangs there.

Certain time a the year, we was required ta work on the roads fur the county, you know. You had a road ta run along side a yo house, or nearby, why you would work sich-an-sich a length a time on that road, in place a payin tax on it. You an everbody else. An the big landowners'd hire somebody ta work in their place.

Now you take in the fields we was doin diffunt thangs, an doin the same thang. Cause we go ta the fields we might near plowin or choppin or pickin. But whatever it was, we was always workin.

Oh. When we git in the field, its daylight. An we go out the fields somewhere long about, little befoe sundown. But now in the fieldwork, we didn have no limit. If I go ta the field only what limit we had, we had ta be out in the field when daylight come ta see how ta hitch up our mules. An workt until night.

So, we would go an talk about "Caint ta Caint." People heard us say "cane ta caint"; they didn know what it was fur a long time. But we understood what we was talkin about.

Like you come into a strange place. We say, "Well, boys, here's old Caint ta Caint."

They look around an say, "What're you talkin bout? Cain da Kaynt?"

"Caint *tuh* Caint: you caint see when you go ta the fields, an you caint see when you come out."

He say, "Man, I'm gonna quit this caint ta caint. I'm goin hunt me somewhere else ta go."

Yeah, I pickt that first hunnud, eleven years old. When I was eighteen, I'd pickt three-fifty an three hunnud. An doin a man's job, befoe I got eighteen. When I was eleven years old, I was plowin mules out in the fields like a grown man. I wadn tall enough ta reach up ta the plow handle.

Well, I be tryin ta git between a pair a plow handles, an I had ta reach up to em. I would plumb give out, holdin em from the ground up ta the top a them handles. So I grow up ta gittin a little taller enough ta git up even with those plow handles where I wouldn be in no strain, havin ta reach up. I could kinda reach down front a me. Then I was flyin, man!

Then Mother, she was a widow, an she had ta vouch fur eleven head a kids. See, Mama didn have no papa ta stay wit her wit all them kids. She jest had ta be stranded. He'd go off an leave her an come back, maybe a week or ten days an go off an leave her again.

An my brother he left home after he got grown an married, an he was about eighteen. I was with Mother, ta help her tote that load a kids at the house. So I stayed with Mother until I married. I was eighteen years an some months old.

I got one boy. An twenty-three grands. I raised foeteen, an three of em what I raised is adopted. Off a one son. Thats right. An all them were his kids. He has foe wives, two dead an one divorced.

I been married jest the one time. You know, I got a record a lot a people aint got: fifty-eight years wit one woman. This comin December the thirteenth, we'll be married fifty-nine years. Married nineteen-thirteen. An I been vouchin fur that one woman, she got mow a my earnins than— now aint nobody perfect. I done some thangs in my young days, cause the womens jest tore out after me. Musicianin. A music man, he does right smart by the women.

What you talkin bout? I coulda quit my wife, if I'd a listened at women. They dwell round me, talk that sweet talk. Nice lookin. I went fur em til a certain distance. When git ready we go home, I go where that wife was. An I didn never lose no time—enough so my wife ta miss it.

But I knowed: I had one wife that I really loved. I jest liked the others. Cause I'm in the midst of em, an playin that music an they dancin. All them big legs, you know, showin an man I tuck a fickle. Fur a while. I go with that other woman. She say, "You know, you jest dont love nobody but yo wife."

I say, "I dont sposed ta love nobody but my wife."

Say, "Oh, you could have a good go wit me."

I say, "I thank I'm doin enough wit you fur a while." An when night come, or day come, I'm goin home ta see my wife.

LEMME SEE NOW. That five hunnud come long about the same time a bein a teenage boy. About sixteen years of age. An it hurt me so bad, I said, "I dont wanta thank about it no mow." An I remembered it all right, cause that lookt like the last day I was gonna live. Hot sun was on me. Man I was achin, an I was thumpin like somebody had the jerks. I was hid way up in the night befoe I could git myself realized.

An went ta sleep that mownin. I woke up. Mama was tellin us, "Well, git up. Git up, boys, git up!"

I said, "Ooh, Mama, I'm stiff."

She said, "Well, dont you go out an pick that much cotton today. You kinda slow down. Dont care what the Man say about what you doin. I'll tell him you my chile, an I keep him from botherin you."

I was scared a that white man. But Mama, she'd whip em. If you wanted ta have a fight outa her, you say sumpm ta one a her kids you oughtn ta say it. White or black! An she'd pull off her sack, put her hoe down. She kep her dress tuckt up about middle way up her leg. An when she git through workin the fields, she'd drop it down. She come an said, "Looka here, man! You got iny black chillun?" She talkin ta the Boss Man, the man who shoot you down, knock you down.

Say, "Oh, he aint doin so-an-so."

Say, "He doin what I told him, an I know he caint do no

71

Will and Mary Cotton, with two grandchildren and tow sacks in hand, at Allenfarm, with the Bluffs in the background, circa 1900s. *Photo courtesy the Marcus Mallard Collection.*

mow. Let me tell you: dont you do no wrong ta my child if you dont wanta kill me. Cause, man, I'll fight you long as I live bout these chillun."

An they knowed it! Say Mama didn have good sense. Cause she'd talk up fur her chillun, fur herself. An she has that old Indian blood in her. Man, them white people could say those thangs ta *her*. But you git ta messin wit her chillun, man, she like a hen wit a bunch a chickens, she'll fly into ya.

Oh, man, listen! I dont know whichun she loved the hawdest, but she would git around ta me: I was a quiet child. I didn do miny wrong thangs. The rest of em would do thangs; she'd whup all of us when she found sumpm was goin on wrong. An then it hurt me so bad fur her ta whup me, an I didn do it, you know.

After a while, she'd turn around: "Boy, what you cryin about?"

I wouldn say nothin.

She'd say, "Dont you hear me talkin ta you?"

I'd say, "Yes'm."

"What you cryin about? I thought I jest whuppt you."

I say, "You did, Mama. But you whuppt me, an I didn do nothin. Them other boys an girls did it."

Some of em oldern me, some of em wadn oldern me. But I dont blieve I got ten whuppins in my whole life. The rest of em got foedy or fifty a day. An I stayed good, an stayed in my place. I dont care how much fuss an how much saind them kids'd git in, I never would git out an do thangs behind our parents' back. No. I always had a certain mind made up. I'm one fella wouldn let up on that. Cause I was always ware a what a whuppin meant. I knowed whuppins wadn good ta eat. An the rest of em take a chance, but I dont take no chances.

But now they bloodied them kids. They were so bad I felt sorry fur em, but they, soon as they got that whuppin today or tonight, tamarra they doin sumpm little worser.

Say, "Come on, lets do so-an-so. Aint nobody gonna tell Mama. She wont know it."

I say, "You kin do what you wanta, but I aint gonna be in it. Somebody's gonna tell it, or Mama gonna find out."

"Aw, you crazy!"

I say, "I dont care what you say. But you do it, well as long as you kin git by, I aint goin tell on you. The only way I'll tell on you, she'll ask me who done it. Then I show aint gonna lie fur ya."

An they would git at me an say, "Dont let old Mance see you do nothin, cause he gonna show tell. He's a old pimp."

Now I tell em, I say, "You gonna git a whuppin."

"I dont git nothin if you dont tell it."

I say, "I dont hafta tell it. Y'all better quit that."

An they standin on their head, tear down cotton patches. Kill chickens! Inythang they could git in they'd do it, an I'm settin there, wishin they wouldn do it.

But night come, call the roll: "What you did, an what you did?" She had everbody settin down, askin em questions. "Come on in here, Annie. Come in here, Charlie. Come in here, Ralph." An got em in a line. An podna, when she got through with them, tamarra they had ta do sumpm or other else cause they show gonna git a whuppin fur today's pass.

The first thang you know, she commence catchin up an watchin her kids, who was wrong an who was right. Mama said, "Well, I'm gonna whup ever one a y'all but Mance."

"Why you dont whup him? He was in it too!"

"Thats yo lie. I got one chile that I blieve wont tell me a lie. I know Mance didn do what y'all was doin. An if he did, y'all caused him ta do it. I been whuppin im when I ought not ta been whuppin im."

An them kids would git at me, scoldin me, fightin me around. "You dont do nothin but tell everthang we do."

An they jump on me, ya know. I said, "I dont care what you do! I aint gonna do what y'all tell me ta do. Cause I aint gonna git no whuppin fur y'all."

Now Gainsvul, he was a rowdy guy. That was my brother by my father's side. His daddy, George, was my daddy's brother. He would fight white, black, inybody blue or brown. Dont care how big you was. An shot a lot a people.

Yeah, he died about three, goin on foe years ago now. He was crazy about me. He was about thirteen years oldern I was. You could tell im I told a lie, he say, "Wait a minute, what you say?"

"Mance damn show told me a damn lie."

Say, "Well wait, dont cuss im. I'll go see im if he told a lie on ya, but dont cuss im."

74

So when he come, he'd walk ten miles ta git ta me. See how it was arranged. An I'd be done furgot about it. An say, "Did you told a lie on Soanso?"

I say, "I dont know nothin about no lie."

He said, "Well, Soanso called you a damn liar. An I'm goin back an see about it."

I say, "Oh, dont you go back an stawt nothin. Talk dont hurt me. That fella jest had sumpm another he wanted ta say about me."

He said, "Well, he couldn cuss ya."

I said, "Well, he done cusst me. That aint gonna hep me."

He say, "Yes, it will. Cause when I see im, he gonna eat that up." An he had ta eat it up or either kill Gainsvul. I had a *BAD* brother, man! You had ta shoot it out or cut it out.

Man, that wadn nothin but ta see a fella git kilt. But you know what? I been here all a my life. Never was raisin no stirryment. An I had few fights. Listen at me good: in my teenage, boys'd git off an make up fights. See who was the best man an all like that. I been at places where they carried me off in the woods, hunt puckawns an simmons an diffunt thangs. We go out in brets: fifteen or twenty of us go out there, an we go ta knockin wit our fists, see who could out-knock.

An I was a smart guy. I could beat the average man knockin. I could beat the average man rasslin. When I didn have no brother an no kinry wit me, then they pickt at me, ya know. I was purdy stout, purdy active. An so, they jumpt on me one day. Three of em jumpt on me. Cause one couldn handle me.

An so, they bloodied me. So I told em, "Thats all right. When you know a pay back one a these days."

So I went on home. My brother was oldern me, an he was off workin. When Satiddy night come, he'd come home an brang Mama his pay. An he was crazy about me. Charlie say, "How is thangs goin along wit ya?"

I said, "Willy an Sam an Garfield, all three of em double-teamed on me an whupt me this week."

He was big as they was, an he would fight too! He said, "Well wait til tamarra. I wanta see about it." That was on Satiddy night.

So, we went back. I was scared cause I thought they was gonna whup me again.

My brother say, "You come on. I want you ta tell them jest what you told me."

So, he went down there where they was playin, shootin mobbles an playin ball. Say, "I heard three a y'all jumpt on my brother."

They say, "He told you a lie."

An I say, "I aint tellin no lie! You did! Three a you. Two brothers an one cousin jumpt on me."

My brother say, "Well all right, they gonna pay fur it today." So when I told him that, he jest true as a rifle: he carried a round rock in his pocket an iron tap. An he thowed an hit one, an knockt im down. An hit one right here in the mouth, an split his lips. An then the othun an him hung up. An when his last rocks an thangs was gone, my brother downed im an beat im til he hollered "Mercy."

Charlie say, "Come on. Lets go home. They wont bother you no mow."

An show nuff, they didn bother me no mow. He whuppt all three of em.

So I grew up that way. You kin raise chillun up in the time I raised my grandkids, my son's kids over there: they'll mind ya. All of em come here, all of em grown what I raised? When they come in this house, they goin respect me. I dont hafta hit em. Dont hafta say no hawd word to em. Cause they lookin fur me ta object when they do wrong. Cause thats the way I raised em.

But these kids comin up now, yo chile an my chile, they sayin, "I'm people."

You say, "Why you say that, Lipscomb?" Cause it takes time fur everthang. God didn make this earth in one day. Took him seven. Little baby dont make a man in one day. Not in one year. He got ta first talk, an then walk, commence ta gittin round. Come ta know how thangs is, an how ta do em. An grow up into a man's place.

So, thats why the world is so critical. Cause they comin up in a fast way a livin. Fast doin. They dont take time ta realize what they gittin into, until its too late. Well its the way the world is tangled up now. Generation behind generation. They got diffunt reaction in their mind, an doin diffunt thangs. An they wadn raised ta that. Dont know no better.

Mama Janie and the Third Reader Scholar

Mance's mother, his family of origin, and his limited formal schooling are the centerpieces in this go-along. Mama Janie Pratt gave him his birthname, correctly spelled "Bodyglin," even though it was pronounced like "Beaux D. Glen." Some of Navasota's earliest European settlers were French, and the community's black and white bloodlines contain a fair share of French stock. Disliking the name, Mance took up a series of nicknames or second names, among them Crackshot and Pots. During his coming of age, Crackshot chose the name Mance—the name of a friend of his oldest brother, Charlie. Bodyglin became "Mance Lipscomb" from then til his death.

Names and language construction distinguished the Brazos Bottoms black culture from the white. African-Americans developed an innovative economy of language free from grammatical regulations. They were predisposed to drop letters out of words, and words out of sentences. For example, the correct spelling of Mance's wife's maiden name is Elnora Kemps. Had she been white, it would likely have been spelled "Elenora." Coined by her grandchildren, her second name was Myno, short for My Elnora.

Neither Mance nor Myno recalled their relatives further back than their grandparents. Delving deeper into their roots required a broader approach. Black family trees were hard to come by. There were few written records for blacks, while the tradition of naming them after their owners further masked these origins. Also, as noted earlier, many black, white, and Chicano native Texans born prior to 1890 had varying amounts of "Indian" blood, whether their records revealed it or not. Indian blood was no asset in those days, as Indians were considered practically "wild game." Prior to Hispano-European exploration and colonization, there were over three hundred Indian tribes in the Texas territory. Only the Tiguas and Kickapoos now remain within its borders as distinct tribes, along with the displaced Alabama-Coushattas, relocated to East Texas. Although Choctaws are not listed as a Texas tribe, historian and naturalist Gideon Lincecum interviewed several Choctaw chiefs while in Mississippi, before he came to Texas in the 1830s to become one of its first botanists. According to their oral history, which differs from most anthropological accounts, the Choctaws migrated from their origins in Mexico and moved northward through Texas, including the Navasota area, then northeast until they settled in the Mississippi region.

Mama Janie was essentially an Indian healer, possessing vast knowledge of native herbal lore. She would have been considered a *curandera* had she been part of the Mex-

ican-American culture of the Southwest. One of her reme-
dies came from the yellow flowers of "Camile weed," or
"cam-eye weed," which is short for "chamomile weed."
Though it looks a bit like a shaggy relative, it is botani-
cally unrelated to the mild, sweet-tasting herb used to
make a relaxing tea. Camile weed is bitter as gall. It contains enough natural quinine that a half dozen of its flowers placed in bathwater reduces a high fever. I bathed in it
and drank it, and still can't decide whether the cure or the
acrid taste was more miraculous.

On the subject of Mance's formal schooling, he referred
to himself as a "third reader scholar" because his elemen-
tary school education ended somewhere in the middle of
the blue-backed Webster's third-grade reading book. My
grandmother learned to read from the same edition during
her childhood in the Texas Hill Country over two hundred
miles west of Navasota. A contemporary of Mance's, she
was born in 1890.

As with certain other dates in this book, what may seem
to be a five-year discrepancy in Mance's choosing of his
name is explained simply by his having actually been born
in 1895, five years before the turn of the century. He remembered dates on the basis of either his birthdate or the
turn of the century.

One of this book's underlying themes is the nature of
language itself. The ingenuity of the language of African-
Americans arose in part out of the limited choices pre-
sented to them, between formal education and innovation.
Through their use of English, they developed their identity. Mance and others in his culture were very inventive
in developing a language coding system, or a set of "by-
words," as Mance called them. They economized the language. They used formal names, secondary or nicknames,
and then intimate names to identify the levels of familiar-
ity and confidence between speaker and person spoken to.
They combined words to produce new ones, such as

"nated," derived from "related," "mated," and "originated." They produced phonetic variations to create an additional nuance of meaning, such as "instain" to mean "predilection" or "blood-given instinct and imprint." They transformed antonyms to synonyms, such as when Mance used "segregation" to mean "integration" and "bad man" to mean "admirable or good man." To make the English language their own, they changed the syncopation, dynamics, and inflections of the sentence structures to suit their African speech rhythms. All these language elements mark and enrich the distinct musical form known as the blues.

IT WAS A BIG WAR. Everbody was fightin there! That first big war, lemme see, nineteen-seventeen when it first broke out. An ended it in nineteen-eighteen. October twenty-fifth, I blieve.

Let me tell you the truth: these awmies wasted a lot a mens an a lot a money an a lot a materials. Boats an bombs! Talkin bout we short on fuel. Hm-mm. No. Thats what they doin wit it: puttin it into the awmy.

I know durn well its a fraud in this awmy. Its a way in an a way out if people git ta the right people. See, you hafta git in that racket. I'm down there wit my head hung down, dont know whats goin on, cause I'm not in the racket.

All right, you work here like I did, fifty-nine years! Out a the racket. Doin yo job, ta git paid. Everthang I got, I got it the hawd way. But if you git in the racket, you kin git some thangs easy.

Say if nothin but y'all two settin here talkin ta me, an say, "Mance. I'm drivin a truck. I haul meat, lard, or sugar. You meet me on the road sich an sich a time, an when I load my truck, I put in enough stuff in there fur ya, an you kin jest give me a little sumpm another outa it."

See? Like you was in Houston or here in Navasota: while you're loadin that truck, yo boss man be doin sumpm another else, an you slip a dab a meat in there fur me, an they'll be five or six dollas worth a meat. An I give you a dolla fur it. An if inybody's in the way where you couldn give it ta me goin, say, "I'll see you when I come back." Come back, throw me that hunk a meat off or whatever I buy.

Thats a racketeer. Everthang. Clothes, shoes. An them there high-powered rifles, they wrappt em up an stole them. Come home on the furlough an broke em down where they could git it in a suitcase. Them thangs cost you a hunnud an fifty or two hunnud dollas. They brought em here an sold em fur ten or fifteen. Go back on their furlough.

[From Mance's version of "Rocks and Gravel," circa 1918:

> Got a man in the awmy, wants a furlough home,
> Say, "Git back, rookie! You aint been here long."]

Generals were in on it. They put you out workin under him; he said, "Well now, hush yo mouth, an I'll let you sell this stuff. An you give me half, an you take half."

If they found out, you the man went ta jail. Not no generals, man! They got rich in them awmies.

See, they rationed us. We could git what we wanted. No flour, but once a month. An no meat—wadn no once a month in it, didn git none at all. We was on the fawm. We got stuff from the commissary. Thats all they would put out there, an thats all we got. But then later on, why, they have stamps. Like there's three in the family, they had three stamps. When them three stamps run out, we couldn git nothin else. Til next month.

But you know, I'm glad that I was a wise man: when the first world war one stawted out, I was registered. But I didn go. I went over ta register wit the boys who went over there, an a lot of em got kilt.

So, I was fixin ta go ta the awmy I reckoned, cause I had

a class 1-A cawd come to me. But when my mail come, I didn git it in time. Cause I had done moved to another place about five miles from where they sposed ta send me my mail.

Then I was a good worker, fawma, had all that suppoat on me ta keep me out the awmy. See, I had my wife, an one chile, an my twin sister an brother, call em Coon an Pie, Willie an Lillie fur a real name. An my mother.

So, I got myself satisfied, after the landlawd went ta Bryan an talkt ta these people up there in that office where you go up an give an account a yoself. See, I didn hafta do nothin but go up there. He done all the talkin. An got me way back in the foeth class. Exempted. My mama went. An showed herself up, an they sided I had a real mother, you know. My kids, they didn require ta take them up there.

An so, he got me out of it. Old man John Quinn, he been dead now. Had a big fawm, what he tuck over there where I was bawn an raised at. An I was workin fur him, fur my mother.

Well, we stawted ta plantin in April. We git our last freeze an thangs down, so we come up wit a regular right time. Them seeds wadn gonna lay there in the ground when its warm, over three days.

Oh yeah! Show, we planted by the moon. My mother was a seance on when ta plant. Never misst it in her life. People come ta be schooled by her, on the fawms where she workin on. She was known aware. See, she had sense enough ta not plant, an sense when *to* do it.

Jest like people say they go to a two-headed man or a two-headed woman. Like that woman in New Waverly. They kin read yo mind. Well, that what you call a seance. Yeah. They know yo intellect, an know what ta do without you tellin me. Have sense enough fur thangs other folks couldn do.

Mama was a Indian woman. About half or little bettern half. She didn know nothin bout the way a life a colored people. What we called ourselves, my daddy called hisself a African. They do thangs a whole lot funny than other nations a people. Irishman do thangs whole lot funny than other nation. Everbody nated ta his nation. His instain, thats seance too, see. Got it inside.

An she had me fur ta be the plowhand. Cause I was the biggest boy she had. If she didn have somebody ta break her land, cultivate her land, she couldn git no openin on a fawm, see.

Said, "Jane, you got ta have a man in there wit ya, do yo plowin. We caint furnish you no hand. Hafta do yo own plowin an yo own choppin. I aint worried about you not choppin, cause you kin chop mow cotton than ten hands."

My mama never did give out. Man, you have a hawss ridin behind her, an then she jest choppt that cotton, sangin. That hawss'd walk, jest walk along slowly. When she got ta the turnrow, she got there ta the end, choppin. Went to an fro.

You never seed a turnrow, is you? The street is about like a turnrow: That road what you brang them wagons an mules an thangs down ta the field. Here the lower end an the high end. The turnrow is where you turn an go down, or either up the next row ta plow, cultivate, chop cotton, pick cotton, whatever you was doin. An then the field whats separated from the next field over, why we call that a cut. Cause see, them turnrows cut the fields up into diffunt sections, in them big plantations down there in the Bottoms.

She didn ever stop movin in her legs an foots. An never stop sangin when she wanta. "Ohhh, Lawd," all kinda songs like that. She was a religious woman. She talk plain as I'm talkin until she got happy, either mad. Then you couldn understand nothin she said. Go ta wailin or cryin or shoutin. No, I never did learn none a that Indian talk. Cause ever time I go ta askin her what it is she sayin, she likely ta whup me or pop me wit sumpm. Yeah, she broke me a that right quick. Dont care what she was, either way I was a disturbment ta her. When she in that kinda ether, you know.

See, sometime I see Mama'd be cryin in the field, an I didn know what she cryin about. She had the spirit ta her. Gospel could hit her iny time. When she git her hawt full, everthang was under pressure in her, an it could jest boil over. That give her some way ta git it off her. An she'd git happy, either upset. She had ta stop an consider what she's doin, an set an be relaxed. Cause man, that hawt'll bust wit ya when ya git that hawt full.

An she would git worried about Papa, diffunt thangs happenin ta me an her, or my sisters an brothers raised up. She'd git ta worryin over us an bust out in a big cry.

I was a mama's chile. I clung ta Mama, mow than iny chile she had. I would always dwell wit her, an agreed wit her in inythang she said. Right or wrong, I went along wit her, an kep her compny. An that caused her ta have release from me. I didn cause her no worrynation, see.

Look like I could tell when sumpm was goin on wrong wit Mama. But I didn know exackly what all a her worry-nation was. Sometimes she'd be in her way a talkin an sangin. She sang them old church songs, sometime she sang them field songs. An I couldn keep up wit her. A mule wit a singletree go along behind her, an she'd keep up wit im. I jest come on behind her. When she got ta the turnrow, she turnt round an hept me back ta the end.

Not only me. Some mow that was there—she had eleven kids. I was the third kid she had. An the kids was jealous a me an Mama, because she do some thangs that she would hide from the others.

She said I was bawn fur good luck. But now, long time befoe she would tell me what that luck meant.

I said, "Why you say that, Mama?"

She say, "Because, you been nice ta me ever since you been big enough. You was obedience ta me." They say a disobedient chile—she tot me that—wont come ta no good end. An she say, "You dwell wit me, an I never askt you fur a favor what you didn turn me one."

An you know what? Thats why I'm got my reward: precious gift come ta me. You rewarded fur what you do, an what you dont do. I'm tellin you why I'm gittin my reward right now—seventy-eight years of age, an I'm not have no worrynation on me, only jest a little old worrynation in this skin. An its gonna git woe away one a these days. Cause the mow rest I take, aint no pains, aint nothin that I kin lay down an dont sleep. An when I feel like goin somewhere, I kin always git up an go.

But you know I have a faith in God Amighty. One a these days, He gonna move it offa me. Thats my docta. I done spent over foe or five hunnud dollas with the other doctas. I did that what my wife say: "Go ta the docta." She didn know I was goin ta Docta Jesus ever night. Wit my hawt.

In these days comin up, you git sick now, you go see a docta. Go ta the hospital. Now, in my come-ups—when did I first see a real docta, besides my mama? Oh, nineteen hunnud an eleven. Come down with the pneumonia. Typhoid. Lemme see, I caught that, oh, in the early stage of life. Somewhere long about fifteen years old. Well I used ta love sweet milk until I got sick, an they fed me on sweet milk an raw eggs. Lost my taste then. An ta this day, when its cool, I kin drank buttermilk once a day. But dont brang me no sweet milk, an eggs either.

Fifteen years old an never seed nary a docta but Mama. I didn know what a docta was, man. They used ta come to ya in buggies, an ride hawsses in there. Wadn no car. I'd see em ridin by an ask Mama, say, "What is that person goin down the road yonda?"

She'd look up an say, "Oh, they call him a docta."

Say, "What *is* a docta? They dig graves or go ta preachin, or what?" I didn know nothin about no docta, man.

Iny kinda cold, sores an achin in our back in our limbs,

fevers! Bleedin or done got swole up! Mama'd go out in them woods—in there she never woe a coat—an down next ta that water, in what you call them branches. Give her a minute, she'd come right back outa there wit some old weed, piece a bark, or some old sumpm. An first thang you know, whatever it was we had, well we didn have it no mow.

I know several thangs that she would see growin. She'd hunt mullein, an brang it out ta the house. Big old stalks. An hang it up. You have a fever, sumpm like back or crow? We called em mullein. Green leaf when it come out in the spring? Wide open big old leaf, wit kinda little old gray hairs growin on it. You ever see tabacca? Well, mullein look jest like tabacca leaves. But you kin tell its bacca if you git a whiff of it. You kin tell its mullein if you break a little leaf off it an taste it. Tabacca got a strong taste, when its a young plant.

Jest like, we swimmin in our limbs, or pains crimpt up in me. They'd boil that mullein an let it cool, an put it on our leg or foots. Whatever the swellin was, it'd go down. Go down! It didn do it the first time, you jest keep adoin it. First thang you know you back ta back, reacted again. Mullein.

All right. When we was young kids, Mother an a lota old folks'd go out an git those old broomweeds. You been out on the prairies an see whole lot a green weeds buncht up growin, an they'll have little straws in em? Used ta make brooms out of em, when I was comin up. Do you know, when we didn have money ta buy brooms, my mother an them would take bunches a those thangs, an put em together, an tie a string above the roots of em, an that end of em you could sweep flows wit em. They grow out an they'd git where they git some tops on em, they shade the ground. They got stickers, an they got yella flowers on em when its green. We call em camile weeds.

When its dried up, why the flowers waste away off it.

You kin take that un befoe it git too dry, an boil it fur a fever. Camiles. Take a cup a that old stuff. It was bitter as it could be! Miny a time Mama'd give me a dose a that stuff, an man, I'd throw up. She'd say, "Take another, take another."

Camiles. Broomweeds the same thang. We give inythang two names, you know. I hunted rabbits all my life out on these prairies, right round in here. An rabbits jest settin up under them there weeds. See, everthang in this world, its useful but you dont know what use it is if you dont know the nature of it. Or until somebody teach you what it is. Ever tree, ever plant grows, its sumpm another in there thats worthwhile!

I called mullein an camile weed. Well now, thats only weeds that I know as valuable—on the prairies. But now you take a red oak tree, you know the diffunt trees? We called em red oaks or pin oaks. Grow straight an tall. They got small leaves on em. Bunch of em. You kin go ta the nawth side a that tree, when its in the sap in the spring. That sap dont never die out of it, but you'll git it briefly if you'll wait til April, May, an June. Then go an gitcha a ax or a hatchet, an chop some a that bark off that tree, an carry it ta the house an boil it so it'll git strong enough fur ta turn the color: it gonna turn red or brown. Leave the chunks in there. Then you strain it through a rag or sumpm like that, an put that in a jar an keep it. An if yo kids have a runnin off, like diarrhea? You kin give em two doses a that, an man, its gone!

Now, all I kin brang in remembrance: that red oak, camile weeds, an mullein. Mama knowed mown I did. She knowed ever plant in the world growed! You say, "How come she knowed all that?" Was nated ta her. Did you know Indians got sense enough ta know ever weed in the world whats value? They take a big old pot, an hang it on a rack like a pole. Tie a wire in each end, let it swang up, an let the blaze come under the pot. An boil it.

Them old chief Indians: somebody git sick, he go ta that person an cure im. Cure his own people. They dont know about no docta. He's a Indian docta. You know there's a Indian docta amongst all tribes? You have no read that? An they know what each one says, dont care if its a Choctaw or a red Indian or what.

Now some a Mama's people, her mother was might near full, Mama told me. I didn know my grandmother. She said her mother couldn talk atall. She'd eat all her food half done. An she told me bout her mama's tribe, what she come outa. I didn know one side from anothun til I grew up into knowin what the Indians was. An read about diffunt tribes. I jest thought all of em's the same.

No, Mama Janie wadn aware a her people, cause her mother wadn really full. I dont know how she come ta be nated ta Indian where her father wadn no Indian. You know people git scattered an git caught up with thangs unworthy. Her mother coulda been out in the woods an contacted a Indian an got that chile—my mother—out in the woods, dont know how she come here.

So, I give it ta Mama she was half. Sisters an brothers ta her was a other mother's chillun, ya see. Fur as I could thank back—I'm jest considerin myself ta how these thangs come about. But ta know her mother, I never did see her mother. I seed her grandmother, an she was dawk as I am. Thats why when Mama come in there, musta been sumpm or other offbred from some other Indian somewhere.

She had, oh, foe or five half sisters an half brothers. They didn have that kinda nation ta them. They all Pratts, jest like their father. They jest straight out colored people. Brown-skin folks, but they didn have no reaction a bein no Indian. But my auntie what nursed me—she lived til I was a grown man an had chillun—her ways was diffunt from mine. An my uncle—Mama's brother—I remembered him. Them two come up purdy close ta Mama. They would come visit her. An they had diffunt reaction. Yeah, they had diffunt ways.

So we had a bunch a little kids settin down on the flow, you know Mama'd go an work fur the white people an cook an wash an iron all day. An they'd give her a big pan a food ta feed us on. We sot down on the flow, an starved all day til she come back wit a big pan on her head.

Some of us were lookin fur her, an somebody would see her. An she wouldn give none of us the mowest. Jest give me jest as much as she did the next one. An boy, we was happy.

Then we wouldn see her no mow til the next night. Then she'd git up an go ta her work again. In them times, they didn give ya too much money: fifty cents, a dolla, an thats a whole lot a money. They'd feed her. Oh, I was too little ta know what was happenin but that food. I wadn no school age then.

My oldest brother an sister, they was school age. They didn have nothin ta go ta school in, didn have no clothes, no shoes. Til she pick cotton in the fall a the year. Then she'd put em in the field an make em pick cotton, so ta git a dress, an old pair a duckins, or sumpm like that, ta try ta keep em in school til work time come.

You know, when I first stawted ta school I was livin about two miles nawth a where I'm livin now. Goin towards Bryan an Millican. That was Doc Emory's place. You wadn allowed ta no school, when I was goin, until you got eight years old. I stayed in school about three years, off an on, an I was eleven years old when I quit. That give me three years, didn it?

Well, we didn go ta school mown five months, in them days. Wadn no school in the fall. Why? Cause we out pickin. Had ta git them crops out the field. An, come springtime, long about April, we'd take off again. Cause then we was plantin. Or breakin the ground, gittin ready ta plant.

That class a kids thins out in the fall, an in the spring yet, round in them fawmin communities.

But what broke me a goin ta school was my oldest brother Charlie. He run off an left me there, the oldest boy in the famly. Cause see, Papa had done run off, an I had ta answer fur a man's place. Thats why Mother put me out in the field. How I'm gonna go ta school, when I be out there plowin an choppin cotton, pickin cotton, hoein weeds an thangs? Man, I was doin a man's job when I was eleven years old. Doin much as I could do now, nearly.

See, people talkin bout havin that Pression an hawd times—they didn have no hawd times, man. You all had it easy all yo life. They oughta come along when I was comin up. I been so cold until I had ta put my hand under my awm, try ta git my hand unnumb. Barefooted, didn have no shoes. I've got mawks on my legs there now, where I went through the briars an thangs, try ta git food fur Mama an hep her out.

First pair a shoes I woe: the old brogan. The red leather what they made em outa old cow leather. They jest hawd as that rock nearly. When you first git em out the box, you might could wear em, but some water or either rain come on em, you never would git em on no mow. Big old thick sole. Had a brass buckle cross yo instep here. You carried it over an buckled it down. Wadn no tongue in em, no laces. They cost about a dolla an a half or a dolla, cordin ta what size you woe.

I didn know what a sock was, man. Talkin bout a sock— sock you or sock you up aside yo head.

First pair a shoes I put on, I was somewhere long about sixteen or seventeen years old. Courtin! Man, an the first pair a long pants I put on, I was about, oh, fifteen or sixteen years old. An the first duckins I woe, Papa or Mama one give em ta me Christmastime. They called it Santy Claw brought us. An she handed em me. Man, I slept in them

91

duckins. I went ta bed in them duckins. Show, man! Somebody might steal em.

I wish that I had a could gotten my learnin. Then I dont regret it, because all the learnin I got is about a third reader scholar. An then I didn go there but jest about one week, after I was promoted ta the third. You know what grade I was in? The first grade, that was the first book you read at. See, I read in the second grade a while, but that didn give me no way ta understand how ta write my name in the second reader.

I had a old blue-back Webster? Them is the hawdest books in the world ta fool wit. Well the back was blue, an the words was hawd ta spell. Sometimes it be ten an twelve alphabets in one word! We had ta git em aaall correck. Didn, that teacha would take that strop an brang it back there an see what was the matter witcha. Thats right.

Thats where I got my neglect goin from gittin my learnin. See, I was scared a the schoolteacha. An I would go ta the schoolhouse wit a bunch a kids. We'd walk foe or five miles a day ta go ta school. Twice a day! Goin an comin. Didn have no hawsses ta ride, no trucks or buses. We walkt.

An on my way ta school, I would talk ta myself. Say, "Lawd, let me git my lesson. I dont wanta git whupt today."

Man, when I got there, that teacha would call me out some words. An lookt like I was apt ta say them words, an some people had been goin ta school, ta the seventh an eighth grade: I could beat them spellin an beat them readin.

But I was scared. In other words, I wanted ta git through wit it. You know inythang you do is worthwhile, its a mind made-up thang. Inside of ya. Say, "I'm gonna do that. An I aint gonna stop until I do do it." But when you stop, you unfinish. See, I had it in my mind ta keep them whippins off me, an explain myself ta people.

[From Mance's version of "Johnny Take a One on Me":

One a these days, I'm gonna act like a fool,
Gonna take up my books, go back ta school.
Oh, Johnny, Johnny, take a one on me.]

An so I told Mama, "Well, I'm goin ta school." I had buncha dogs'd follow me.

One a the kids say, "What you doin wit all these durn dogs?"

I say, "You let em alone. They my dogs."

When I git halfway ta the school, I've learned ta swerve it ta the right an go over in the woods, an catch me a bunch a rabbits. I know at foe o'clock when they gone turn out, I come on home right with the school kids. They all knowed me. Didn know what I was up ta.

Say, "Man, that teacha say she goin whup you!"

I said, "She got ta first find me." Oh man, I was about twelve years old.

So, Mama thought I was goin ta school. An somebody sniffled off on me. Mama said, "Boy, is you goin ta school?"

She said, "Well why you quit school?"

I said, "Mama, I'm scared a that teacha. That teacha liable ta whup me."

She said, "She aint gonna whup you unless you give her a cause. Boy, you better go on ta school! I'm fixin you a bucket up here fur you ta go ta school. You go on an eat up yo food, an hunt rabbits all day."

I said, "Well Mama, I caint face that teacha. I done quit school, an them kids told me that she gonna whup me. I know I aint goin there."

An so the teacha, she tuck a likin ta me. An one evenin, the kids was comin from school. Playin, talkin. Here come the woman wit that little old sorrel hawss, she drove a two-wheel gig ta school. Call em a sulky. She stayed right down the road.

So, she lookt an saw me over there. Come on down the road, an she called me by my real name, "Bohdyglin!" Spell that B-O-D-Y-G-L-I-N. I didn like that name, an I wouldn never answer by it. From this size on up I wouldn have it. We didn call people out by their real name. We called em a nickname, a second name. I called myself Mance out among my playboys an thangs. An so they commenced ta callin me Crackshot. They tried ta git me ta take up wit that name.

Now Crackshot, that was meanin a fella was true about shootin a gun or true about throwin a rock. Or stick. He was a crack shot, didn miss nothin. Thats true right on, ya see. So you would jest say, he's a fella that kin be true ta do sumpm.

We had a word a whole lot diffunt from y'all havin em now. They laugh at me sometime I say a byword, an they look at me an say, "What you mean by that?" Well, y'all know what explaynation what y'all done read up on, an what you oughta learnt in yo young days. An I done learnt sumpm diffunt in my old days. Way back yonda up until now: you wouldn know what I'm talkin about if I didn tell ya.

An first thang ya knowed, it was a fella used ta come see my oldest brother, ever Sunday. An the people saw that boy comin ta see my brother, they say, "Yonda come Mance." An we got in the habit a callin his name comin up ta our house.

An I caught on ta that name. Spelled it M-A-N-C-E. So I swore off from that Bodyglin an switcht over on ta his name. I been callin myself Mance ever since I was about nine or ten years old. Everbody called me Mance after I commenced ta likin that name, an got ta playin music around.

Nobody never knowed nothin about no Bodyglin. But see, my teacha come up there in that two-wheel gig, an caught me lopin longside the road there, an say, "Bohdyglin, how come I dont see you in school no mow? You been feelin kinda offly?" Wadn nothin hawd in her voice.

Couldn lie ta her. I say, "No, ma'am. I jest, hadn felt like comin."

"Well, how come you aint made it ta the schoolhouse? You aint fraid a me, is you? You know I aint give you nary whuppins."

Now that was the truth. But you know, I seed her whup other kids. She whuppin kids today—tamarra I wouldn be there. So I told her, "Yes'm, I know you aint. But you whuppt them other kids so, I didn want you ta go an whup me thataway." I didn tell her where I was goin, when I wadn in school. See, if you kin cut it off from sayin thangs they dont ask you, then you dont hafta lie.

An she say, "Well, you do like I tell ya, an do yo work, I wont whup ya. I whup them other girls an boys cause they dont do what they oughta be doin. Now you come on back ta school, an git yo learnin. You dont hafta be fraid a me."

So, I went on back ta school, fur a little while after that. An I couldn even write my name when I left school. I had a hawd time in the learnin. So, I'd say I was robbed outa my schoolin.

But I went a long ways since then. I kin figger. Spell inythang I wanta an write inythang I wanta. My mama said I was the aptest chile she ever was bawn in her life. I taken up thangs, consideration jest soon as somebody say it—if it was worthwhile—I didn furgit nothin. I learnt it by ear. Jest like I come ta where you workin, doin whatever you doin, standin round you maybe a hour or two: I be done learnt sumpm what you doin.

No, man, I learnt how ta read an write good as you wanta see a man. Cause I was busy fur a night school. Colored fella'd come ta my house, around seven nights a week. Monday up until Sunday night. An a bunch a us kids would be home, like at my house tonight, five or ten of us, or fifteen, twenty people there. An he would teach us. An the next night he'd move somewhere else, an I'd go over ta their house. An the next night he'd move somewhere else, and I'd go over ta their house. But when we were around here, he done teacht us seven nights. An thats the way I got my learnin from him, how ta read an write.

He was a educated old fella. He's a half Indian. His name George Jones. I was, oh, I'd say foeteen years of age when he come around there. An he learnt us mown iny school-teacha ever learnt me. An a lot a others, they didn git ta go ta school. But he would learn us out ta our home. I'd say he was a backbone to us.

An I pickt up mow, after I got up in the teenage, after he quit lettin us go ta school from him. Pick up little old scraps a paper, tow up piece off the flow. Turn it this way an that. Try ta reckonize whats on that piece a paper, see.

Why, I wadn long catchin on. I couldn write my name a bit mown a durn spider. Maybe about the second year, he stawted me out. He give me some kinda information how ta stawt it with the pencil. I didn know how ta hold the pencil, didn know how ta write. An when I stawted up ta the top line, when I'd end up I'd always be down on the bottom line. Jest like a snake crawlin!

He call me Pots. An he be talkin right at Mance when he say, "Pots, thats yo name, but you carry it straight across." An man, I ruint aminy piece a paper tryin ta write my name.

So he showed me how ta write it, an say, "Now you stay on the line. That be bit mow purdier. You got a purdy handwrite." Brag on me, you know. Encouragement. Hell, I wadn doin nothin but jest twistin from the top ta the bottom. But that was my name.

See. If you wanta git a young player ta play a gittah, brag on im. Dont cull im down, say, "You aint doin nothin." That throw him off. Maybe he quit. You got ta say, "Well ya know, you doin good." Then that'll give him encouragement ta do better. Thats why I got so miny friends with the young players.

So finely, after I commence ta coatin, I commence ta fig-gerin this out: that girl in there's my wife. Talkin bout Elnora. I said, "Now I got ta learn how ta swap letters wit my girlfriend."

Man, I went an bought me a whole big old thick tablet. Woe it out! When I got through writin, wadn nothin right in that whole thang. I couldn read it. Didn write nowhere but ta her. That was about the second girl—third girl—I coated. So, I wouldn send it ta her, cause I know she couldn read it. That was a waste a paper.

Finely, I got you ta write fur me. Or him. An I'd tell you what ta put on it, an the boy who could write, he write it like I told him.

I'd look at it: I didn know what he put on there. Cause he wrote it, he coulda said, "Come up here an kill the hell outa him." I wouldn know.

He say, "Thats all you wanta put in here?"

I say, "Yeah. Two sheets is enough."

An so finely, I was right—in the wrong position: my girl—same one these kids call Myno [My Elnora]—she say, "When you comin over?"

I say, "I thought I wrote you a letter day befoe yestiddy, an told you I'd be over there Sunday." See, we couldn git nowhere on the weekadays, til on Sunday, or Satiddy eve-nin, cause we workt ever day. Well we was like a old mare in the woods an prairies, you know. We didn have no trans-portation, no mown our feet.

She say, "You aint wrote me no letter."

I say, "Oh yeah! I wrote you a letter."

Say, "No! You didn write me no letter."

I say, "Well, I'll tell you the truth. I couldn write. Willy wrote a letter fur me."

You know what she told me? Say, "Willy give me the letter fur hisself."

Oh, I was show nuff outdone! I come on home that night, got out on the flow. I commenced ta scratchin, scratchin.

Mama said, "What you doin there, boy?"

I said, "I'm writin."

Said, "Caint nobody read that."

I said, "Well, one thang: they gonna read what I wrote. They wont read nary other letter the boy give her fur hisself."

She said, "What?"

I said, "I been gittin Willy ta write fur me, an that rascal's writin ta my own girl. Now I got ta learn how ta write, cause I caint trust Willy no mow."

She said, "Well, you show right. You better learn fur yoself cause, if they doin you thataway, they take all yo girls."

Finely, I got ta foolin around, spellin thangs backuds, an I said, "Well, I'm gonna try ta do sumpm another fur myself, cause these boys aint gonna git me pooged up an fool around wit me."

About two weeks, I wrote a purdy good letter. Aw, it was all crooked, on the top a the first line an down ta the bottom an half used.

Finely, she got that letter. She read it. She wadn too much of a good writer herself. She wrote a little bettern me. But she said, "That was a nice letter you wrote me."

I say, "Yeah? Well, could you understand it?"

She say, "Yeah. I finely understood it."

Man, that give me a gift ta thought I was writin! An first thang you know, I was writin well enough where we could pass a note back an foeth in Sunday school. I coated her two years, befoe we married.

Whats hapmd, you try ta tell the kids right. An here come their parents, say, "I dont want you ta be scoldin my chile." You not scoldin em. You were tryin ta keep em from gittin in trouble an tryin ta teach em how ta read an write. Thats what a teacha is fur: ta keep the kids outa missstress an bad thangs.

Well, I know one teacha, call im Hawd Hat Henry. He

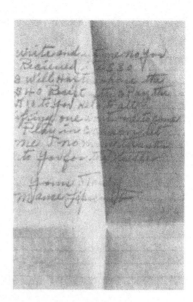

The handwriting of the "Third Reader Scholar" in a letter to Dr. George Bowman dated November 7, 1967. *Lipscomb/Alyn Collection, Center for American History, University of Texas at Austin.*

was a man preacha, I mean teacha. He would belt those kids. He's a heavysot brown-skin fella weighs about, close ta three hunnud pounds. Used ta be a football coach.

Well see, there's two of em go round. Mista Henry an Mista Jackson: that old fella was purdy tough too. He's the one got in that mess wit the police. Tuck the police's pistol, an the police shot hisself an kinda claimed *he* shot im. But Mista Mow an them got im out of it.

[From Mance's version of "Tom Moore's Farm":

Tom Mow tell you, without a smile or grin,
Stay out the cemetery, I'll keep you out the pen.]

He used ta teach out ta the Allen Fawm. Then they turnt im in ta be a principal in that old school, called it G. W. Carver when it was nothin but colored kids goin there.

See, they done built two or three schools here recently now. Since that segregation [Mance means "integration"] done come in here. Now, he digs up these kids who dont go ta school like they oughta. He big enough ta dig em up.

Now he's a nice fella, but he's got so much ta go through

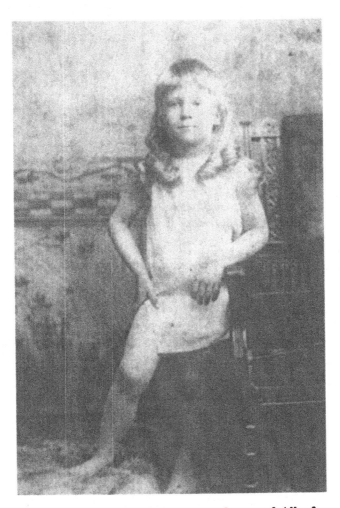

John D. Rogers, born July 2, 1886. Owner of Allenfarm shortly after Mance's birth. *Photo courtesy the Marcus Mallard Collection.*

wit. Wit these young kids. No, they dont go. An ya know, I blame the parents fur that. Well you take a kid, when he out in that school age, I thank they oughta keep em in school. Because nary em without a learnin like it is now, you caint hawdly git by wit a *learnin*. Thangs are so changeable.

A chile say, "I'm gonna stay outa school about til the foeth reader." An he turnt im loose an he git grown, why he's a star Nigra fool! Because everthang done went on so much, he caint catch on.

You got to be in this forward life now. You take me: I couldn git a job. All the good jobs in the world passt by me. Cause I never did go no further than this third reader, ya see. But you cheated out yo degree, you cheated out yo life nearly.

If you wanta know sumpm, my wife, she stawted ta cookin fur the white people out in the kitchen, long about twelve years of age. Her mother was a chef cook. An my mama? I wadn nothin but a kid when I'd watch her carry a water bucket on top a her head, an had one in each hand: she's dancin around fur the white people an didn spill nary a drop. They'd give her a nickel jest ta see her do that.

Now, you're measured out ta cook. If you caint read it out a book, you caint be no cook. Everbody want ta make a fool outa ya if they find you a fool.

An cheap wages. They liable ta tell ya, say, "I'll pay ya five or ten dollas a day." Aint no mow five or ten dollas. You aint gonna hawdly live out the twenty dollas now, the way thangs goin up.

But you know, I'm lucky. Boy, after I got grown an workt, fifty-nine years on the fawm: I did some a everthang but kilt a man ta make a livin. Two thangs I didn do—steal an kill nobody. If I had ta steal an rob, I speck I'd a been jest dead or sumpm. I'd rather be dead than come up here an take sumpm dont blong ta me.

If you got sumpm, I want you ta let me have it wit ya own

free goodwill. Then I kin go home an rest. Cause befoe I git home, you gonna come up here an say, "What you— Mance, where is so-an-so you tuck?" Thats what I'm fraid of.

Crime's up an paid ya, hear? Say what you call crime: unjest. Dont stand long, befoe they find you out. They break in these stows here. Mista Love had his stow broke in an all around in here. An Mista Hall. But I didn hate about Mista Hall. Cause his old lady was so ungodly mean up there. I didn care what hapm, cause she's tuck some money from me an everbody. Try ta shortchange ya, iny-thang she could git by wit. She had it comin! When they done sumpm in that stow, like her stow, they jest gittin even wit her.

[From Mance's version of "You Got ta Reap Jest What You Sow":

> After all I did fur you,
> You say you love me, now we're through.
> You got ta reap jest what you sow.]

Like I say, the best thang in the world you got ta have now is yo education. If you dont, the people look over you as nothin. But when you git that degree, you jest got ta the stoppin point. But whatcha gonna do wit it if somebody dont lead you in the right direction?

There's two thangs you should thank about. Principle an Pride. You got ta love first: love yoself. Then the rest is in yo*self*. You aint got nothin but a old piece of, pair a shoes: love that. You may be the ugliest person ta the peo-ple in the world, ta love yoself.

Then after while, you kin spread it out wit Principle. You say, "Well, I aint goin rob Lipscomb. I aint goin kill him, do sumpm ta him set his house afire, cause I dont want him ta do me that way." Its a hibitation between there.

Thats the fine point right there, that thang called Princi-ple an Pride. Is a little thang ta thank about. Is a great thang when you understand it, though. See, the teachas is got a whooole lot ta say in these books. But they dont have nothin about no Principle an Pride in them books. An I havent had no school. Its hawd ta git the understandin. Understandin beats inythang in the world. You got ta like yoself first. An when you love yoself, you kin kinda venture out an like me a little, an have a feelin toward me.

But you tell me you done got a education when you git there an aint got no Principle an Pride? Learn jest how ta rob banks. Learn how ta go in an write diffunt handwrites. Make everthang easy. Say, "I got enough sense ta do what I want. I got a education." But what you gonna do with that education?

Listen, my daddy told me sumpm when I was eight years old, an I remember it today. He caught me doin sumpm in a untidy way. I was out on the turnrow, choppin cotton, me an them other kids. An I had my mind made up on sumpm else, wadn thankin about no cotton.

I was lookin round, leanin on that hoe. Listen at the birds or some little sumpm another. Sometime I'd hit at a old weed, might jest as easy chop out a piece a cotton.

An Papa come up there. Say, "Is that a hoe you got in yo hands, or a willa stick?"

I say, "Aw, Papa. It be so hot out here. I'm tired a cuttin at these weeds." I wadn tired. Wanted ta go play wit my playboys.

He said, "Boy, listen at me good. Whatever you do, dont care what it is, you give it the best lick you got. Then you dont hafta be hung down an sorry fur what you done. You'll have a good feelin towards what you done. An towards yoself. Now, you go on an take that hoe, an chop it like it oughta be choppt." See, he was teachin me ta take pride in what I was doin. In my work, an in myself.

An so I went on, an choppt a little. Choppt a little further. Direckly, I got ta not feelin so bad about bein there, an all my friendboys hollerin an runnin out cross the fields. Cause I was payin attainsion ta what I was doin.

An direckly, Papa come back an say, "Well, that look a little better. I reckon you done a good amount today, son. You kin go on an play now." An I'd done forgot I was dissatisfied wit what I was doin, an wanta be some other place.

Somebody gonna take teasey ta what I'm sayin, say, "You know, old man Lipscomb told us sumpm we hadn never thought about." An then you tell others. Word spreads.

Now you go ta stand in one place. Good reputation in front of ya, that bad reputation in front of ya. Yo reputation is there waitin on ya. Best thang in the world fur you ta have is a good reputation. The folks say, "Money's all I need." No. That reputation is a whole lot further than money.

Awkinsaw Travla, Come from Alabama with a Banja

Just prior to the Civil War, a black family of unknown origin and name was shipped from Alabama to Texas. It was composed of a father, whose first name was George, and his two daughters and three sons. Their mother had either died or been sold to another family. Since Galveston was the main port of entry for the Texas slave trade, they were likely inspected and purchased there by a Mr. Lipscomb, who may have been from Dallas. As was customary, the owner renamed his newly acquired property after himself, effectively branding them under his ownership. The family soon found its way to Navasota, in East Texas, where Mance's grandfather became George

Lipscomb and Mance's father became Charles Lipscomb.

Around the time that Mance's grandfather would have been shipped from Africa to Alabama, the 1840s and 1850s, slaves arriving there and in Haiti were being shipped mostly from the Voodoo tribes of equatorial Africa. Odds are good that George was among them. In any case, many expatriated Voodoo tribal members came from Alabama, probably with their beliefs in their pockets, in the form of rabbit's foot charms and other "mojos." Many would label those beliefs "superstitions." In the Voodoo religion, "mojos" were potent talismans used to gain power over others. Mance retained a vestige of these beliefs throughout his life, and resorted to them when modern science and Christian faith failed to meet his needs.

This sense of mystery was evident in Mance's frequent use of the word "ether." His definition fits its more archaic sense, from the era when alchemists theorized there were five elements: earth, water, fire, air, and ether. Ether was the unseen atmosphere that encompassed the mysterious, the psychic, the worlds within the mind, the inexplicable and magic, the unknown. Whatever didn't fit into the other four generally wound up in the "ether" category. Ether surrounded and bound the other four with its invisible film and magnetism. Mance had profound respect for such spiritual unknowns.

Voodoo or not, Mance's father, Charlie, personified the character portrayed in the song and skit "Arkansas Traveler." This pre-vaudeville song sprang from the black minstrel tradition of the nineteenth century, when blacks would travel the country by train, entertain black and white audiences, and be forbidden to sleep or eat in many of the places where they entertained. Minstrelsy's upbeat performance style became so popular that whites blackened their faces and took over the minstrel shows. The melody of "Arkansas Traveler" was created by a black fiddler and was later converted by a white musician into

"Turkey in the Straw." Itinerant musician, jokester, and rogue rolled into one, Charles Lipscomb could have his children and everyone else rolling on the floor laughing one day, and knock his wife to the ground the next. He was humanly paradoxical.

In the absence of psychologists in those days, such behavior was commonly attributed to possession by the devil. And what an effective phenomenon to relieve one of responsibility for one's actions! "Dan" was the name most often ascribed to Satan. Sam Collins was the neighbor of little Crackshot Lipscomb who first introduced him to guitar-based "devil music," and Mance's father was the expert fiddler of that genre who thoroughly initiated him into it. The concept of "The devil made me do it" surfaces twice in this go-along. In the first, Sam Collins takes on the devil's identity in a passing reference. In the second, "Dan" is clearly identified. Rather than Mance, it might well be "the devil" who speaks and sings parts of this go-along. The old folk song "Old Dan Tucker" might even shed some light on this devilment. Or the word "hooraw."

In the arena of otherworldly behavior, Mance and his father developed a peculiar ability that even a Buddhist monk would envy. Playing twelve to eighteen hours straight for Saturday Night Suppers was no mean feat. While acquiring this stamina, they each learned to play music or talk and sleep at the same time. I didn't believe this was possible until one morning around three when I witnessed Mance's eyes roll back in midsentence after everyone but myself had fallen asleep, and he finished the sentence with a snore. During several later occasions, I sat by while Mance told certain stories on automatic pilot into the wee hours. During one twenty-four-hour period in 1972, fellow friend and musician Kurt Van Sickle and I spelled each other while Mance went from one performance to another, pretty much all that day and night. Afterwards we calculated that one or the other of us had witnessed him playing his guitar for seventeen of those hours. Mance was seventy-seven at the time.

This go-along closes with an outstanding instance of black economy of language. The Navasota River forms the border between Grimes and Brazos counties and drains into the Brazos River at about the center of the eastern edge of Washington County. Within this three-county area, blacks distinguished between the town of Navasota and the Navasota River with the omission of a single letter. "Navasota" always referred to the town and "Navasot" always to the river. "Navasota" was also the name of a now extinct tribe of Texas Native Americans who once inhabited the banks of the river. Most of today's occupants of Navasota are unaware of those former inhabitants.

WELL MY FATHER WAS SOLD in slavery time. His daddy brought him from Alabama here. He would set down an talk like me an you talkin, an explain ta me what he went

The Brazos River, just above where the "Navasot" flows into it. The left bank is Allenfarm. Washington-on-the-Brazos is about six miles down on the right bank. *Photo by Glen Alyn.*

through with. His mother wadn livin when he come from Alabama, but his daddy brought him an two sisters an two brothers here when he got off the boat. Papa didn know about no mother. They crosst the water an unloaded in Texas, an his daddy was sold with the five chillun, ta slavery. Under jurisdiction of his daddy. My grandfather.

You see, people would go git people—jest like you got a bunch a cows. Well, you would transfer yo cows from place ta place ta try ta git what you could fur em. Well them people in Alabama, they was brought here in a boat. Then the people, you know, pickt the people off the boat what they wanta buy.

If you go an buy a hog, you'd want a fat hog, wouldn ya? Well, thats the way people graded people off them boats. If you was healthy, stout and able-bodied, they'd rush ta buy ya. But if you was slender an haggly lookin, why you'd be the last one they'd pick. You was culled back. Then they'd itemize down ta the size an what you lookt like you was able ta do. Cordin ta how big you was an how thrifty you was, they'd go buy you quick. An they unloaded you here in Texas.

Well no, he didn talk much about—he didn know nothin about slavery, because he wadn grown when they fit that war an the peace was declared. I dont know what year, but he was under his papa's thumbs, what you call it: his daddy was a sayso over his famly a people. He had ta do what his daddy say. His daddy tuck care a him, an he got im outa miny places that he didn hafta go in, because he was too young. Eight years old. He didn do no hawd work, until slavery had done come out as freedom. As my daddy was growin up ta be a young man, he didn know much about white people, cause his daddy kep him at home all the time.

But he went under his slavery name. When he come from Alabama, I dont know what he was named then. But when he landed in Texas, the Lipscomb people bought him an he had ta be goin in the Lipscomb name. White Lipscombs.

They bought the whole bunch tagether. Didn buy one at a time.

My granddaddy was named George Lipscomb. Aw, he died way back when I was a little bitty kid. I was bawn in 1895, an he shoulda died when I was about seven or eight years old.

See, I didn know too much about im, but I knowed im by bein close to im. An I was fraid of im, because he was a gray-facedid man. Other kids oldern me, they takened up wit im, but I never would let im git me ta sit on his knee. Cause I didn like that hair on his mouth. An I'd cry when he'd call me. He loved us all, ya know. Chin whiskers all over his face! An gray mustache. We all called im Granddaddy George.

When slavery times ended up, my daddy was eight years old. He didn know nothin bout a pair a pants, an didn know nothin bout a hat. He woe a shirttail, old low shirttail til he was foeteen years old. He told me a lot a times.

An he didn know nothin bout but three letters in food: Meat, Meal, an Molasses. Three Ms! No flour. No sugar. No coffee. An always got some milk when you go out ta the cowpen. From where he carried the milk into the landlady's house, boss man's house. He was a good milker. Uh-huh, I was raised on them three Ms.

Them days, dont madda if you's fifty years old, you had ta go ta bed this time a night. Along about nine o'clock. If you wadn sleepy, you still had ta go ta bed! An you wouldn go in town less you had a permission ta go ta town. Stayed right out in the woods an on fawms.

Yeah, my daddy told me that. Thats over a hunnud years ago. Jest a few white people was over here. All the colored folks come from Alabama an over ta Africa. But now, after they commenced cumulation, colored an white, Mexican an all that come inta the same town.

Walter Davis, that was my ex brother-in-law. He's maybe foe or five years youngern I am. An he was bawn an raised

John D. Rogers (1828–1908), in Confederate uniform (circa 1862), owner of Allenfarm when Mance was born, and grandfather of John D. Rogers, pictured on page 100. *Photo courtesy the Marcus Mallard Collection.*

an stayed at Waxahachie. But see, he hadn got out a the fear a bein mistreated in Waxahachie, cause it retcht from Dallas on back here ta Navasota.

Other words, its so miny people here done done so bad ta me, an done kilt my people an robbed me. An I was scared ta go down the street, without gittin off the street. If I meet a white fella, he's down the street an he had his nice clothes on, I had ta give im the street. An dont touch up against a white lady. Do, you gonna git kilt, Nigra. Thats way e'er befoe yo time. This town here is rotten with that! An I lived through that.

We was raised under that ether, what my daddy an mama said. Jest like the white kids, we was tot those thangs. We'd set down on the flow, we didn have no chairs an good places ta set. An we look up at their face, an they would estimate thangs went on. An teacht us those thangs.

See, we went by our bylaws, by Papa and Mama sayin it. Everthang they say, we thought it was true. Everthang they done, we thought it was right. You know, when you young, you dont know no better. You got ta be tot those thangs.

Thats why I dont fault the white boys an girls fur what they doin now, because *they* didn *do* it. Their foeparents done it. Well now, what a man done a hunnud an ten years ago, I couldn hate you fur it when you aint but twenty-three or twenty-five.

But you take this young white race a people now: been so nice ta me, because they wanted ta mix up wit us an be people as people. But I'm scared ta go around a lot a white people. I hate ta say that befoe y'all cause you white people. But we all white now. See, I gives consideration, an look into it in a diffunt view. An so in the go-along, I was takin thangs sincerely in my mind. Puttin em ta good use.

An when I got ta be eight years old, I could remember what went on. First thang I could remember I got a rail good whuppin about was stealin sugar. It aint but two thangs I stole. I stole watermelon, stole sugar.

They used ta have them little old thangs called saves, what people put up in the house, where you safekeep yo plates an yo knives an fawks. Had a little winda to em in the front. An I was stealin sugar. An Mama, she was by the side a the house washin. She was a good songster. An she's sangin, sangin. I knowed I had her. Cause I could hear her sangin on the outside. So I got in the house. An the chair nearby it was high. An I had ta kinda clam up in the chair ta reach up there ta open the safe.

An the doggone chair fell over wit me: "BLAM!"

Mama, she quit ta sangin. Wanted ta know, "What was that?"

Well I didn have but one doe ta come out. An Mama was in that un, cause she right next ta that doe rubbin wit a old washbode, when she heard that noise: I done turnt the chair over, turnt the bowl over, waste all the sugar, an there I was hemmed up in the house.

Mama jest peept in an say, "Uh-huh! I see whats the madda." An so, she got in the house ta whup me.

Well then, I broke ta run. Then Mama caught me goin out the doe, an put my head in between her legs, she say, "Uhh, its too late ta holla now!" Cause she had the doe blockaded. Man, you talkin bout hollerin! That woman was tearin this end up back there. God Amighty!

An I couldn git aloose from her, she's a stout. An she whupt me so, I say, "Now I aint gonna do it no mow, Mama!"

Say, "I know you wont."

An she'd hit me so hot til I bit her. Bit her in tween where you know I had my head—I bit her on the thigh. Down here *some*where. An she opened her leg, then she said, "Go, you bitch, you!"

I say, "I'm gone!" An I scottered out from tween her legs an run off.

I stayed off aaalll that day. Went over down ta White Switch Bottom. My daddy was livin down there, oh, about three or foe miles from where Mama an Papa was separated. So, I went down there ta stay all night wit Papa.

Papa knowed what was the madda, cause he saw me comin. Say, "Yo mama done got holt to ya over there, huh?"

I say, "Yeah, she whupt me an I run off."

He say, "Well, I'm gonna go an carry ya home tamarra, an tell her dont whup ya. I'll talk fur ya."

So, Mama hunted me, all that evenin an all that night until she went ta bed. Put the dogs on my track an couldn find me. An finely I come in home from bein quartered over ta Papa. I never will furgit it, he had a old blue duckin suit: jumper, you know, them old overhauls. I caught holt a Papa's hand.

Mama said, "You need it? An dont thank I aint gonna whup ya."

An I commenced ta cryin. Papa says, "Oh, dont whup that boy."

He was kind of a mean man, an Mama was sorta mad wit im cause he had done quit her. An they got ta fightin. Papa knockt Mama down. I come back an got Papa offa Mama.

She was bleedin. Finely she got up an got the blood off her, she say, "I'm gonna have you arrested."

He say, "I told you not ta hit that boy."

An so Mama got the whuppin offered me, but she got one too.

An I remember after I went back home, I wadn quite nine years old. People would plant a row a watermelons in the field, or a row a potatuz. Bunch a us kids would git tagether, an we would find out where that tatuh patch or watermelon row was in the field: five or six a us boys would go, in the nighttime when our foeparents asleep, an slip off an steal watermelon an sweet potatuz. Dig em up wit a fawk.

I was standin in the road watchin fur the man, an they was about seven or eight boys in the patch. They had me fur they alibi. Least I didn let the man slip up on us. Ya know what hapmd? The man was in the patch. Settin down on a stump. Sleep!

One boy say, "Wooo! Here's a great big un."

An I was lookin down the road. I said, "Well come on out the patch. You got one."

He said, "No, I'm gonna bust it over this stump." An he rared back ta hit the stump: hit the man over the head, an watermelon went everwhere an the man jumpt up an run. He runnin from us an we was runnin from him.

All us boys got in the road, an walkt on down the road ta my house. An we thought we was home free. Had done made our gitaway.

We wadn thankin bout no durn tracks or nothin. Daylight come, this man what the boy busted the watermelons over, he come on back ta his patch, an got ta scratchin round there: spied all us boys' footprints. In the dirt all around that tree stump. An the tracks would verify us. Jest like he was trackin a old coon or sumpm. Except we left a trail, about like a strang a mules windin up the road. An he jest follad em on up that road—it was a dirt road, ya know—till he come by my house an one footprints turnt right in ta the gate. An I got whuppins about that.

No, white folks didn raise nothin like that. They didn raise nothin but cotton an cone. If you was workin on halvers, or thirds an foeths or sumpm another, well, you could slip an plant you a row a watermelons in the field. An raise potatuz on one row, an plow it with yo plow.

Sandy land wouldn grow nothin but watermelons an peanuts, an sweet potatuz. That nature a land wadn strong enough ta grow no cotton an cone. A little old patch a saind maybe fur as from here ta that road: they'd give it to ya, an you could plant you a watermelon patch in there. An go an plant tatuh patches right next to em.

My nerves is strong as they was when I was, oh, I'd say foeteen or fifteen years old. I a little shy when I was that age cause I wouldn go an see people. Oh, I'd go an play fur a little party here an there, maybe fur some friends or some little sumpm like that. Well see, I was mongst my people who seed me ever day and ever night. I used ta those people. Nated to em. Wadn no face shy there.

An then long about fifteen years of age, turnin into sixteen years old, my daddy quit ta fiddlin fur the Satiddy Night Dances. Turnt it over ta me with the gittah. An the people commenced ta gittin crazy about that gittah style I had. Always could memorize my songs, an play loud gittah, clair gittah. So they jest run races ta git me ta play fur em on Satiddy night.

An the songs I was playin, thats what I figgered out wit my own ears. My music come ta me by hearin, or what you call ear music. I caint read music. But I learnt a lot a songs from people, jest hearin em: sang em an whistle em an play em in their way a playin em. That I dont like, I dont pay no attainsion to it. But if I like it, that music jest go right in my ears, an it gonna be drillin in my ears till I play it. An I tuck it an turnt it around an made my music diffunt from them. I stole a lot a songs from people. An when they hear em again, made em sound diffunt.

Thats the best music in the world, ear music. Cause you dont hafta git the book fur it, you dont hafta do nothin but jest listen, it come to ya.

Jest like I go ta sleep sometime. Wake up. I git ta thankin. Some a them songs come across my mind, what I havent finisht. An I lay down a while, cause I say, "Oh well, I know what I'm gonna do tamarra. I'm gonna complete that song." You caint complete a song when you first stawt that song. You got ta stay wit it. An when it come ta yo ears perfect—have a sound exackly how you like it—well then you leave off a that one an go on ta the next one.

I tot myself by my own ways an actions from my ears. An my fangers al*ways* had a quick movement under em. I kin move my fangers whole lot quickern a whole lot a you young people kin.

Where I pick up my tunins? Ear. Kinda tune it the way I feel. You kin figger em out, how they oughta be. Dont nobody show you, you jest study on em til it sound right, in yo ears. All up an down this gittah, so miny codes you kin make, too.

But Papa, he was a fiddla, an he had that music goin to an fro. A gittah an a fiddle got the same sound on it. But the reaction's diffunt. An I could hear it—I'm a ear man. An Papa was a ear man.

I wanted ta play fiddle when I first stawted out. An I give *out* drawin that bow across. I said, "Papa, I caint do that."

He said, "Boy, you'll make a good fiddla."

I said, "Nawsuh, my awm's give out."

Fooled around with that fiddle, til my mama bought me a old piece a gittah. With three strangs an all busted up, an I jest went crazy about that old gittah.

Eleven kids in the famly, an ever one of em could play some kinda music. So I been playin gittah mown ary un in the famly. I left my older brothers behind outa sight a me when I got about foeteen years of age. They played ahead a me. One was two years oldern me an the other one was about four years oldern me. They was real good gittah players. See, I didn have no gittah—I was too little. But when I did git one, I passt them like a pay car passin a tramp. Into my fangers.

Where I learnt ta call the notes? Well I didn read up on em. My daddy was a fiddla. He was knowin those codes, an he learnt em to me, he say, "G, C. . . . Now play it so it sound like what I'm playin, boy." An show me how ta put my fangers on that neck, as fur as he knowed, about five or six codes. There's a G, C, an A, an F. I was raised up under them foe codes.

No ma'am, I'm self-tot. Cause I cumulated from my ears

an goin about, an figgered out there's mow codes than that. Til I taken my gittah an felt fur em. An then I found its a diffunt code here. I tuck my own time, an seed somewhere else ta put that, up an down this neck.

My daddy made his first fiddle out of a cigar box. You know you had diffunt brands a cigars. One was what you call a old cheroot cigar, the old strong cigars. Liddle old box about that long: wrist ta my elbow, I reckon. Got some tacks, an nailed a plank neck on to it. About that long. Fiddle is a liddle thang. It would jest sound off some way, you know. He didn know what it was doin, even though it was soundin off.

He found that box in the road somewhere, I thank. Nothin but a boy, he pieced im up old piece a fiddle out of a cigar box. I tell you what he told me. See, he bound ta be my daddy an knowed sumpm I didn know. All right, he sayed when he's comin up, he tuck thread. Numba eight thread. Wadn but foe strangs on that fiddle. An twisted it round an got it doggone stawted, an he done purdy good. Playin with that fur chillun. Didn play fur grown-ups. No, hmm-m.

An stretch that thread cross wit a liddle old piece a plank went under there, thats his bridge. If you didn raise up on that, you couldn hear nothin. Its flat. Thread was jest layin there. But when you pull up on that thread, why it stretches them thangs fur as you could git it tight. Then you could hear it.

See, he didn know whether it uz tuned up or untuned, he jest went on the way he wanted. He's out there doin sumpm ta satisfy him. An everbody's jumpin around that dance wit im, an he there "Twadadrrtwa-Twadadrrtwa!" An man, they danced behind that old cigar box fur years!

Until he become aware of a fiddle. He never did play no gittah. He jest find his fiddle. He could make that thang talk, man. Say inythang you wanta. He could make it say, "Our Father Who Art in Heaven." I aint heard nobody that could pass im on that fiddle, man. From then up until now.

That was his young days. My father was about ten or twelve years old. No, I never did see that thang. When I first seen Pop, he had a old piece a fiddle somebody sold im or he—I dont know where he got it.

Wadn miny instruments in the world when Papa come up. Wadn but a very few when I come up. One gittah was spread all over the whole country. Its sumpm *strange* when you hear a gittah come through the country in fifteen or twenty miles.

The first thang I heard was an old cordion. That thang, jest pull it open an "Yahhh-Wahhhyy-Yahhhhhu"—he jest pumpin around an havin fun. Call that a airjammer. I didn know what them thangs was, but know they made music.

Next thang come up was a banja. Old five-strang banja, people play it now. An then we thought we was gittin somewhere.

Next thang come up was a little old piece a gittah. An that gittah lasted around there five or ten years. One man ownin it. You want him ta play it, why then you could hear him play it, but you better not touch that gittah. Cause that was his hawt, man.

No, he wadn from around here in Navasota. He lived over there where I was raised at, on the Navasot. Yeah, the river. Oh, its a old fella. They called im Sam Collins. When I was eight years old, I could remember Sam Collins' name, an tell you how he lookt: he was jest as light as inbody in here. He lookt like he was white, but he was jest a red colored fella. Had a red mustache.

An I was scared a him because a that old red mustache. Come out there an he git ta "Rhaa rhaan rhaa!" an hear me, an we'd jest fly. We didn know that kinda natured fella, but he was a colored man.

An he played his old gittah, oh I reckon, around us fur years. I always hear it. Slip down by his house an eaves-droppt im, git on a cotton stalk or cone stalk. See, that cotton used ta git high, an thick. Sometime be tall as the boss man's shoulder, ridin his hawss through that turn-row: jest could see over it. An I'd clam up there, an sneak up there an hear im. An we thought that was the best thang in the world, "Weawuwe. Blum-didablum blum-dida-blum blum-didabl." All night. Until you went ta sleep.

An he put the old gittah down an next night, some kids would run out there, "Reckon Sam Collins gonna play that old gittah tonight?"

I say, "I dont know. But if you wanta hear it, we better sneak down there befoe it git too late."

Well sometime it would, sometime it wouldnt. It was all accordin ta how he felt that night. Cause he was workin hawd, befoe day in the mownin an it was night when he come out. But ever Satiddy night he got out an played that old gittah. Thats his alibi on Satiddy night. But sometime he's too durn tired ta play that gittah.

But we jest went out there an snifft around an hear what he was doin. An if we stayed too late, we were headed over a *head* Sam Collins [a head-on collision], cause we were gonna git a whuppin. Nine o'clock we better be in the bed, podna. If we wadn asleep, but *be* there, whisperin. Thats the hour limit. An if Mama caught us out after nine o'-clock? If it was nine of us, nine of us got a whuppin.

An I got a good whuppin, one time I never will furgit it. Mama come in there an caught me doin sumpm I ought not ta do. Wadn long after she bought me that gittah. We come out the fields long about noontime, fur ta eat dinna, you know. An I got done eatin, an went over there pickt up my gittah. Commence thrailin at it. An I git stawted with that thang, didn know when ta quit it. Cause the hours jest resh by ya when you doin sumpm you nated to.

An so, direckly Mama say, "Mance, put that gittah down an git ready ta go out ta the fields. You know you aint got time fur that foolishness."

I say, "All right, Mama." An I put it up against the wall, an come on ta the field. We all out there workin. An direckly, I say, "Man, I show wanta play that little tune. Blieve I go play it jest fur a minute. I'll have it down an I come right back out here an go ta workin. Wont nobody miss me jest fur a minute or so."

I go on back ta the house. Pick up that gittah. Go ta matchin them strangs with that little tune goin round inside a my head.

Mama, she out in the field with them other kids. An she heard sumpm, say, "Uhht! That dont sound like no mockinbird ta my ears."

She come on back ta the house, see who was makin that sound. An I'd done furgot all what I was doin an where I was, settin in there with that gittah in my hands. I in there, real quiet, you know: "Blum. Blum."

"What you doin in here, boy? I told you ta git in the field!" Man, she went ta beatin on me, one side up an down the other side. She was hot, man. An I thought I never would git away from her! Followin me out jest runnin, all the way out the fields, whuppin me an knockin me wit a old piece a willa branch.

So we knowed our rules, wit our parents. Now you talk about whuppin, we'd a got Mama ta pick up this—whatever she git in her hand first thang, our papa or her would whip us wit a big old rope or switch or quirt, a bullwhip, inythang.

Papa had a old belt. Called it a gin belt. Ginnin house used ta have belts around them wheels. An they had holes in em, so the cloth would go over an catch holt. Then Papa got a old broke piece a gin belt, an he woe it. An thats what he whuppt us with. That thang had holes in it, platted from end ta stawt. It suck ya meat in it ever time he hit ya, an them thangs put a dent in yo meat.

Papa put a whelp on me when I was twenty-one years old, could be under there now. Cut me right round under

121

here, under the bend a my leg. Well I abused that whuppin cause I was fightin. An they caught me fightin.

They said, "Well come in here. I'm gonna stop you from fightin."

Well I done done my devilment, an I knew that. I didn know he was gonna whup me as hawd as he did. He cut me with that old buggy whip he had, ta drive hawsses wit a buggy. Call it a quirt. The thang was limber at the end, it'd fold up an it catch you round yo fleshes an some blood was comin. An that thang would whistle foe it hit ya: "Fwwwitoo fwwitoo," an then when it'd hit ya it'd bend double on ya clutch.

An he hit me right in the calf a my leg, an I hoppt around there two weeks. Two weeks, I was jest on my toes! He felt sorry, but he was mad an I was due that whuppin, but not the way he give it ta me. He coulda whuppt me a little diffunt from that.

Now, Mama didn break out a limb, didn put our eyes out. But we had them whelps on our skin. . . . Mama lookt like the pictures of health. Lookt like she was well, an hawdy. But she still was down wit strokes she had stroked—oh, I blieve it was nineteen foedy-one. An then she got ta that place where she couldn stand up good, an she couldn walk atall. An they put her in a wheelchair. She was good an stout by then. An I would lay her on a big wood bode, over the tub an poe water over her ta bathe her.

But now she was a real good hawd worker, befoe she had those strokes, you see. Yeah, I seed her befoe she died. When I went ta the hospital. John Sealy. In Galveston? That where my twin brother and sister Coon an Pie live at. An she talkt jest like me an you talkin. Didn frown a bit. Didn have a pain, she said. She passt in nineteen fifty-two.

I dont take it good now. Oh, I'd taken dreams a her, you know. Even since she passt. Plenty time. Up til recently time, maybe last month, or last week. Cause see, I loved my mother an I always thought of her.

Mama Janie Pratt with her children, Coon and Pie (Willie and Lillie Lipscomb), 1950. Photographer unknown. *Photograph owned by Lillie Lipscomb-Davis.*

When aaalll this music you hear me playin: some a them words are wrote across my mind about my mother. My sister caint take the songs that I play about "Motherless Chillun." She caint take the song that I play about "See ta My Grave Kep Clean." If she's laughin when I play either one a those songs, she git outdoors an cry. Hafta catch her.

Well, cordin ta the Scripture in the Bible—we've got ta go on an survive by what the Bible say—if you die a Christian, you'll go ta heaven an meet the people who died an went ta heaven. But me knowin or you knowin? Nobody dont know whats gonna hapm. But we appreciated her, the way she carried herself. Mama was a Christian woman.

She mighta lived a few years longer, if she'd a stayed at home. Out here in the country, where me an Elnora was at. But she couldn git around hawdly, fur years befoe she finally died. An I dont blieve we coulda pulled her out a that house, when it burnt up on us up there on the Bluffs. Jest did git Ruby outa there, she's my granddaughter. An lost everthang we had, but the clothes on our back. That place burnt up, I blieve fifty or fifty-one. So, I reckon she'd a been dead, one way or the other.

So Papa left her, an he could call Mama from his house where he stayed at sometime. He left her fur another woman, which wadn none a his wife. My mother was his lawfully wife. But he wanta go wit another woman, which he did stay wit her until he died. He died with the woman what he quit Mama fur.

An the way they found out he was dead: he had a way a gittin up, foe or five o'clock in the mownin. An he's stayin wit a colored man called Ben Cawvud. He had about two hunnud acres a land, an a bunch a kids a his own. An my papa was stayin there workin by the day fur im. Ben Cawvud, they called him the well-ta-do man, he had the purdiest mules an hawsses ever been in Brazos County. Had tossels on em on the bridle. Jest like you tie a strang on yo bridle? An it hung down, the mules would keep it floppin. Its about that long. An he had a red tossel on ary one of em. An them mules walkt fastern iny mules inybody ever brought in that country.

So my papa was stayin out ta Ben Cawvud's place. An one mownin he didn come outa the house. An everbody stayed around there knowed he was a early riser. So, long about dinnertime, they went in his house ta see about im. An there he was, stretcht out on the bed dead. Died in his sleep. Oh, my daddy died in nineteen twenty-two.

My mother, she was a one-way woman. Papa, he was a twenty-way man. He had about twenty-two chillun, an see eleven of em was some outside kids. That made them be half, from Daddy's side. My mother, all eleven a her kids were the same mother an the same daddy.

But we didn count half brothers much. We look at them

as sumpm comin down the road. But Mama taught us, "Thats yo brother." An we didn feel like that was our brother, because we wadn bawn an raised in the same house, same famly.

An we criticized them, say, "They aint no brother a mine." Until we got grown. An then we commenced ta realizin what was happenin, an done hapmd. I got one brother, he go fur wit me as my whole brothers—Gainsvul.

[From Mance's version of "Careless Love," by Bessie Smith:

Can't you see what careless love have done?
Can't you see what careless love have done?
It'll rob you outa yo silver, rob you outa yo gold,
Then turn around it'll rob you outa yo soul.

Dont never drive a stranger from yo doe,
Dont you never drive a stranger from yo doe,
Mustn't never drive a stranger from yo doe.
Could be yo brother, yo may never know.]

Now I was here when my daddy first stawted out ta playin. First song he ever let us know what he was doin: "Whoa Mule, Let Me Git the Saddle on Ya." I got that gittah banja tunin:

Hit that mule, he wouldn gee,
Cross his head wit a singletree.
Whoa, mule, let me git the saddle on ya. Whoa, mule.

Foedy-dolla mule an a foedy-dolla saddle
Goin out west ta herd them cattle.
Whoa, mule, let me git the saddle round ya. Whoa, mule.

That mule gonna kick, that mule gonna pitch,
Hold that mule til I git im hitcht.
Whoa, mule, let me git the saddle on ya. Whoa, mule.

You take Sally, an I'll take Sue,
Taint no diffunce between the two.
Whoa, mule, let me git the saddle round ya. Whoa, mule.

[Mance then sings, without pause, "Willy Poe Boy":]

Willy. Willy. Willy, poe boy. Do Lawd, remember me.

I went down ta dinner to my true lover's house.
Hadn never been down there befoe.
She said, "There you are love." A hawss trough!
Aint goin back no mow.
That old mule. Aw oh. Do Lawd, remember me.

Raccoon up that old simmon tree,
Possum down on the ground.
Raccoon says to the possum,
"Go on, shake me some simmons down."
That old mule. Aw oh. Do Lawd, remember me.

Well, I went down to the old cone patch,
Git me a load a cone.
Well, the raccoon sickt his dogs on me,
An the possum blowed his hone.
Oh mule. Oh my. Do Lawd, remember me.

I would not marry a nappy-headed gal.
Tell you the reason why.
Evy time she go ta comb her head,
Naps begin ta fly.
Oh mule. Oh my. Do Lawd, remember me.

Thats seventy-five years old. My other brothers done fur-got that. Eight years old I could remember sumpm, right now.

I kin remember some thangs he said, an verses. Naw, I couldn remember all the songs, cause, see, I couldn sang inythang back then. I was jest listenin. Eight years old, I was wishin I *could* sang. But I hear what he say bout his "Masta Promised Me":

My old masta promised me
When she died she'd set me free.
Oh Lawdy, oh Lawdy. Lawdy, oh Lawdy.

She lived so long, her head got bald,
She give out a notion a dyin atall.
Lawdy, Lawdy. Lawdy, oh Lawdy.

Well, thats all we want a that. Didn try ta add no mow verses to it. Oh, that jest tickled us ta death. It wadn nothin but, oh, two or three verses ta put to it. That was a whole song.

An when Daddy turnt around, tell a little joke, say, "You know what, boys!" An we settin right down on the flow, listenin ta them jokes. He played the "Awkinsaw Travla." I remember the verses he would say in that. You dont hear that much now. He played it wit his fiddle, an I couldn play it with the gittah. [Mance sings the melody to "Arkansas Traveler."] It sound ta you sumpm like "Turkey in the Straw"? M-hm.

So he play it one piece, say, "I'm goin down the road . . ." His fiddle dont say inythang. "Purdy briefly, I pass by a fawma's house.

"An he say, 'Hello!' Fawma come out, spoke ta me.

"An I'm travelin. What you call a Awkinsaw Travla." Thats my daddy talkin, say, "Mista, how fur this road go?"

"Fawma turnt around an say, 'Well I tell ya the right answer: I been here foedy-two years an I aint seed it go nowhere yet.' "

Then he resin up the bow purdy briefly. Then, Daddy stood up another word ta say.

"Awkinsaw Travla say ta the fawma what come out his house ta greet im, 'Mista, kin I take this road down ta the next town?'

"Fawma turnt around an sayed, 'Mista, they dont *need* no road down there, its already one down there.' "

Man, we jest laugh an cry over them little old verses. He was doin sumpm, but what it was, we couldn catch up whether it was true or untrue. Hoorawin, you know.

My daddy was a real good fiddla. He would stay drunk

five or six days in the week. But he knew how ta drank, so he could always play good as you wanta hear. He'd be up there playin, an his eyes be half closed—I learnt that from him—an he could sleep while he was playin. He could play all night that way.

Now you say, "Aw, Lipscomb, dont gimme that. You hoorawin me." No, I'm tellin you he could stand right up there an play them songs an old reels good as, no, bettern inybody in the precinct. An he'd be right there sleep! Jest as restin as him layin cross the bed. Yeah! Thats the truth.

Show you what I'm talkin about, he'd tell me, "Now I know you'll git tired an give out. So you jest tap me on the foot when you gits tired." I was tryin ta play gittah behind im. Bassin im. When I was little. An they had me up on a box, some kinda crate or sumpm another. Had me back behind im out the way, cause I wadn big enough in my young age ta see. Well, some a them dancers an people drankin, reelin to an fro, they liable ta step on me, or knock my gittah outa my lap. An sometime I had ta git out the way.

An, two three hours pass by. I begin ta git a little tired. Say, "Reckon I'll pull Papa's coattail, an git down off here." See, I wadn nated ta playin them Suppas all night long, in my young days. Papa was used ta that. Never would stop.

So, I git down off that box. Rest my gittah someplace back out the way. An reach down, tap his shoes like he told me. An he keep on crossin that bow against them strangs. Reach down, go ta tappin his feets again. He wadn knowin I was even there! Shuh, man! I might near woe his shoes out tryin ta raise him. Cause I was done give out!

Oh, Papa played about five times as miny songs as I play. I caint remember what he played, all the while, because he played the fiddle an I played the gittah. I called myself backin him up. What you call bassin im, wit a old gittah didn have but the biggest foe strangs on it. I was strommin along, "Blam Blam," behind im fur certain length a time, an I got ta the place where I wanted ta do my own thang. I knowed I couldn play a fiddle. An I couldn git a chance ta play much gittah behind his fiddle, because I had ta stay behind his fiddle an hit along, thrail along. When I wanted ta always pick. An thats what I'm doin now.

So, I backt him up in waltzes an two-steps. [Mance plays "Missouri Waltz," also called "Til We Meet Again," a World War I song, and "Over the Waves."]

You call that "Over the Waves"? Thats it. The purdiest waltz in the world. Thats what I used ta set behind im an bass im, an he's playin the tune clair, on the fiddle.

Now, he played those "Saint Louis Blues." Thats the only blues that Papa could play. I learnt it after he turnt me loose. I was jest bassin im behind there. But I plays it clair, now. That song's fifty, sixty years back.

An people used ta call "Saint Louis Blues" one a the best blues come out. Back when that come out, people was playin blues an didn know it was *blues,* what they was playin. See. They was playin blues fur years befoe inbody give it a name. Say, "What kinda song is that you playin? Too slow ta two-step wit it."

Say, "Oh, I'm jest playin my feelins, what stirrin me inside." When the blues first come round here, I'd say long about nineteen hunnud, nineteen an ten, had a slow way a playin it. Set yo mind ta thankin, maybe you'd motion, sway to an fro in yo chair, git out on the dance flow an shuffle yo feet. It wadn no dance piece. But this "Saint Louis Blues," well you could dance ta it.

"Soap an Water Keep Yo Boody Clean"? Ohh Lawd, thats a dirty song. I caint play that! WHOO! Doc? You say they's jest nice people here? Well they aint no nice words I'm fixin ta use. Maybe after most everbody's done gone an went home. But you know I caint play that in front a these womens an young chilluns an thangs.

I dont git a chance ta sang them low-down songs, unless

I'm sangin out amongst us men. Like that song "The Dirty Dozen," an all like that? I learnt that when I was about eighteen years old. You know, people would git mad witcha when you put em in the dozen. You know what the dozen is?

Say, "I'm gonna heave you in the dozens."

Say, "You might try it, but I'll kill you if you do."

Dirty Dozen is talkin bout yo mama an yo sister. What kinda shape they in, an who they are. They dont put no man in the dozen, when I was comin up, if you didn wanta fight. An so they call that song, "The Dirty Dozen." Well, we tuck it fur an insult when we was comin up. Boy you'd git hit in the mouth, or kilt or staubed, shot down! Cause inybody got iny sense, they loves their mama. Dont want you ta talk about his mama. You kin talk about *him.*

An so, we had a way a gittin up a big disturbment amongst a bunch a boys. Git ta hoorawin, we call it. Gaggin one another. Say thangs that you caint match. An git you mad or git you upset. We got out in a bunch an git ta talkin bout the Dirty Dozen an diffunt thangs:

"Boy, yo mama walk like she's done had so miny men she caint stand up," an all like that.

"Yo sister, she's done woe herself out wit all kinda race a people."

Well, you dont like that about yo sister an yo mama. They knowed that when they stawted. Thats a prank they doin, sumpm ta git sumpm another outa you so you kin fight over it. Git kilt.

So, one little old quick word I kin say is this ta y'all: "My woman got something, it works like a C C pill." You know what a C C pill is? Yeah, its a pill that you take fur a kidney. Say, "An when she stawts ta workin it, I caint keep my backbone still."

People say, "Where'd you git that?" Thats over fifty years ago. But I never used them words, you know.

An there's another song say, "Mama around the corner, an she pickin up sticks, an yo sister's in the backyawd, suckin off dicks. You be kind ta me, I'll be good ta you. Take soap an water, keep yo boody clean." Yo boody's yo asshole. Thats stinkest part you got. I dont care how much you wash it. See, that hole there it never do be clean.

All right, go an say, "Ever time I go ta pee . . ." You know, people talkin bout clap, gonorrhea the same thang. Thats when yo dick runnin, yeah with puss. An when you git it a hawd-up, it hurts ya. You got ta cool it off, cause man, that thang hurt ya so bad. It sore inside. An so, say, "Ever time I go ta pee, I thank about the woman that give this ta me."

See, woman give it to a man. In other words, she kin have it, an she dont have it. She got a filth inside a her. An yo dick's already hurtin when you have the clap. Say, "Ever time I go ta pee, I shet both eyes an grab a tree." Cause it hurts.

An when you play it, git it all ranged, this is how you match them verses:

[Mance plays his version of "You Be Kind to Me":]

>   (Soap an Water Keep Yo Boody Clean)
> Keep on talkin, you made me think
> Mama wouldn look at you, Daddy wouldn blink.
> You be kind ta me, you be kind ta me,
> I'll be good ta you,
> Because soap an water keep yo boody clean.
>
> Mama told Papa, Papa told me
> You got ta learn how ta do the Shivalee.
> You be kind ta me, you be kind ta me
> I'll be good ta you.
> Soap an water keep yo boody clean.
>
> You play at a man, say be a man in the full.
> Let your nuts hang down, like a Jersey bull

You be kind ta me,
I'll be good ta you, I'll be good ta you.
Soap an water keep yo boody clean.

Mama, Mama, look at Sis,
In the backyawd she's doin that twist.
You be kind ta me, you be kind ta me,
I'll be good ta you.
Take soap an water, keep yo boody clean.

Mama, Mama, look at Bud,
In the backyawd tryin ta act like a stud.
You be kind ta me, you be kind ta me,
I'll be good ta you, I'll be good ta you.
Soap an water keep yo boody clean.

Pull his britches below his knees
An shakin his dick at who he please.
You be kind ta me,
I'll be good ta you,
Because soap an water keep yo boody clean.

Mama in the backyawd, pickin up sticks,
Sister's in the cone crib, suckin off dicks.
You be kind ta me, you be kind ta me,
I'll be good ta you, I'll be good ta you.
Soap an water keep yo boody clean.

Ever time I go ta pee
Thank about the woman that give this ta me.
You be kind ta me,
I'll be good ta you.
Soap an water keep yo boody clean.

You aint got that on, too! Oh, man! I didn say that, you
hear me? Cut that off when you git down there, huh? That
was *Dan* slippt in there on Mance. Mance wadn there
talkin.

Well now, you got some part thats bad on there, finish
this bad part out. Then we'll talk about sumpm good after.

Frank Hamer, Alias Charlie Hayman

The level of racial violence and subjugation endemic to Navasota from 1900 to about World War II had a lifelong impact on its African and Native Americans. Those conditions were encouraged by the imposition of the Jim Crow system of racial segregation around 1900, and the loss of black voting rights before that time. Telling the whole truth in any circumstance during that forty-five-year period could have cost Mance his life. He survived by developing a sense of humor, a dry wit, and a high degree of compassion. We can see evidence of Mance's inbred caution in his insistence on using the name Charlie Hayman as an alias for Texas Ranger Frank Hamer during his entire account in this go-along. By using an alias for a Texas legend and juxtaposing potentially life-threatening facts with yarns, Mance may have conceived that he was putting some distance between himself and some former enemies who were still walking the same streets with him.

Brandishing his skills as a master storyteller from the African tradition, Mance and his lawman friend "Charlie Hayman" go on a romp, kicking up enough metaphorical dust to blur the fence line between fact and fantasy. Mance carries this off all the while protecting his backside with thinly veiled anonymity and varying degrees of exaggeration—a bit like his ancestors the Anansi storytellers who were spiderpersons. These artists caught their listeners in a gossamer web of illusion. They knew how to blur and overlap truth and fiction. By making the boundary indistinct, they challenged their listeners to inquire beyond their preconceptions into the nature of reality.

As Mance tells it, "Hayman" nearly stretches himself into Pecos Bill. "Charlie Hayman" was in fact the Texas Ranger Frank Hamer—the lawman who tracked down and killed Bonnie and Clyde. He was in fifty-one other gunfights, wounded by shotgun blasts countless times, injured by bullets twenty-three times, ambushed four times, and shot down and left for dead twice. Among many other stories, he told Mance of his rescue by a black man during one of those last occasions. This explained to Mance why Hamer was so committed to giving blacks a fair shake.

Many of Mance's recollections of Hamer's escapades are corroborated in the biography *"I'm Frank Hamer": The Life of a Texas Peace Officer,* by John H. Jenkins and H. Gordon Frost. Born on March 17, 1884, Hamer had almost grown larger than life by the time he enlisted on April 21, 1906, as a left-handed private in the Texas Rangers. He was six feet three inches tall and weighed 193 pounds. As a child, he made up his mind "to be as much like an Indian" as he could. His extraordinary sensory powers were legendary. Like Ted Williams, who claimed he could read the label and count stitching on a fastball headed his way, Hamer said bullets looked to him "like a bee enveloped in a tiny cloud of heat waves produced by friction between lead and air" and a shotgun blast looked "like a swarm of gnats." He could call shots before they hit their target. In one pistol-shooting match, Hamer hit a small glittering stone over a hundred yards away. On another occasion, he shot more than one hundred consecutive butter dishes thrown into the air. His fancy footwork was likened to *savate*, the French science of foot fighting.

In the two years prior to Hamer's arrival in Navasota, its population was diminishing itself through dozens of shoot-outs and at least a hundred violent deaths. He became the city marshal of Navasota on December 3, 1908. That very day, the patriarch of one of the twelve aristocratic "old guard" families stood across the street and let fly a rebel yell. Hamer calmly threaded his way across the board path through the muddy street and said, "I'm Frank Hamer, the new City Marshal. You know there's an ordinance against disturbing the peace." When the old man yelled again, Hamer recalled, "I just reached up with my left hand and grabbed a handful of white beard, put one foot up on the sidewalk, stepped back, and threw him like you would throw a cow, right out in the middle of that mud," and put him in jail.

A week later, he was informed by a leading citizen that the local Ku Kluxers "don't allow our kind to be arrested." That night he arrested one of them. No one in the crowd responded to his challenge. By the end of 1910, Hamer had made Navasota a safe place to live for blacks and whites alike. On April 20, 1911, he resigned and went to Houston to work for Mayor Baldwin Rice. Hamer was an expert poker player—though he never gambled for money, of course. In later years, his poker club met weekly. Their fancy poker chips bore a wealthy Texan's initials. After

Saturday street scene in downtown Navasota, circa 1895–1900, with children on the footbridge by the fire bell. *Photo courtesy the Marcus Mallard Collection.*

raiding and closing the man's gambling house outside of Houston, Hamer had kept a souvenir set of chips.

The serendipity of this crossing of destinies of two legendary Texans is remarkable. Two extraordinarily talented men in unrelated fields meet on the wooden slat sidewalks of Navasota. One is a man moving into the prime of his law-enforcement career. The other is a boy just learning his first song, unaware of what he is to become. Yet Hamer asks the boy to be his guide while the man goes on to tame Navasota and get to know some of the boy's family. The fourth go-along closes with Hamer and his sidekick deputy Bailey's encounter with Mance's brother "Gainsvul." An ex-convict, he bore the name of one of the three state prisons where so many blacks spent time: Gainesville, north of Dallas; Sugarland, just southwest of Houston (where the consummate country bluesman and twelve-string guitarist Leadbelly resided before being pardoned by the governor); and nearby Huntsville, forty-five miles northeast of Navasota.

This leg of the journey requires a final set of directions. Mance places a couple of subtle road signs on the border between facts and stretching them into yarns. When lots of detail and facts accompany an incident, it is a true story. Boasting and exaggeration indicate a hooraw coming on, as does a continual attribution of the story to someone else.

Now, YOU TAKE WALTER DAVIS. He's born in Waxahachie. But he reacht on down here an married a sister a mine at Courtney. From Courtney he went ta Houston, I dont know how miny places he done been. He been a fawma around his hometown, between Ennis an Dallas. Thats where my sister found im, up there in Waxahachie.

Yeah, we used ta run around together, in our young days. Go ta gamblin. Drankin. Carryin on. An I was tellin you about how the people always bothered him when he was gamblin an they thought he was a coward, you know. They got im stirred up one night, an I hapmd ta not be down there where they was gamblin, in Courtney.

"God damn y'all! Kill all you son of a bitches! I'm tired a y'all takin my money!" An Walter broke up the gamblin game. He done had this pole, tryin ta catch up wit em. Man, they goin ever whichaway. The boy called Queen a Hawt, he done run clear til he jumpt over in the well! I had ta go there an stop it. That Walter. He aint got good sense when you stawted. Woo-oo! An he run that whole bunch away from down there. An I'd go out ta the well—I couldn keep up wit im.

He got African an Indian blood in im. Grandmother was a fullblood an her mama too. An Sonny Lewis' daddy was a half Indian, an his mama part Indian too. Jest like my mama: She's right at about half Indian. Iny a them people git mad, you couldn understand what they say. I never did try ta learn none a that Indian talk, cause the only time

137

she spoke it was when she'd git mad. I didn wanta be around her then, cause see thats when she was likely ta whup us kids.

Oh my daddy, he had hair jest lookt like the way mine is. I have my daddy's futures, an color. Ya know my mother's a brown-skin woman. She come from out in Grimes County. An her mother is right at three-quota. See, they run the Indian people outa this territory. They moved em up towards Oklahoma, back in there. They got em outa here. An kilt em out.

An way back in a hunnud years ago when freedom was declared—you know when *we* come up, we was slaves. What you call slaves? We wadn lowed ta do no mown what the white man told us. Til we got orders.

An whatever we got, he issued out to us. We didn have no money comin to us. We stayed right in one settlement, under my boss man. Now, he might have a hunnud Nigras workin fur him. Go right cross the fence, there's a hunnud Nigras workin fur *him*. An you know what? Ever one of em has a diffunt name. But they was all Nigras.

Say, how come they make em change their names? If you's white, yo people's name in yo daddy's name. But you—jest like you branded some cows? Inythang—mules, cows, sheep. An they woe yo brand, an yo name. An right cross the fence, there's somebody else had *their* brand. An their people who workin fur them went in their name. The white folks' name. Didn madda what their real name was, what you brung from Africa or Indian or inywhere. U-uh. Jest went in the boss's name.

An you know who's doin that? The Merican man. I'm talkin bout white folks. Everbody that white folk aint got the same nation. German, an they got a Italian, Australian, Irish, English. White people what was bawn an riginated got together here in Texas. But they got diffunt color—got dawk color, red color, an white color. But they all white, cause they got white color. An so, if he speak pure-blood English—everthang he talk is plain—an he got white color? That's what you call a Merican man.

He wanta be mown inybody in the world, the Merican man. Cause all he got in this world, that Merican man he tuck it from sombody. Tuck it. He didn work fur it. Cause once you work fur it, you know how you come by it.

Thats a lot a thangs hid behind people's jurisdiction, that oughta been opened up foedy years ago. Fur a better world. We didn have no schoolin, an we didn know nothin but what the Man told us. An we couldn go ta town, unless we had a what you say permission ta go. We couldn go ta the white church. We couldn go ta the white school. Thats hid from you, cause you wadn here, maybe wadn bawn. It dont look like its true fur me ta tell you what we went through in life. You say, "Well, I dont blieve that. I wouldn a done it." Cause you know why you dont blieve it? Cause it didn hapm ta you.

You say, did we mess around in our come-ups? No, man! We was workin. Choppin, plowin, hitchin up our mules. Pickin. We was all the time workin. Yeah, you go messin round if you didn suit that boss man, cause he would mess around wit a stick over yo head if you dont do what he told you ta do. Either a ax handle or hoe or shotgun or sumpm.

Well, they come in the field an said horrorish words, an tell me what I had ta do. I'd stand the cussin. Cussin dont bother me. Its hurtin you, it aint hurtin me. See, I understand that.

[From Mance's version of "Big Boss Man":

> Standin in the turnrow, wit his pistol in his hand.
> He done shot that woman, gonna kill that man.
> Cause he a Big Boss Man, caint you hear me call,
> "Well you aint so big, you jest tall, thats all."]

But a lick would bother me. Jest dont hit me, you kin cuss all you want. Cause I aint gonna hit you, an if you hit me, I'm gonna hit you back or die. Try ta fight you back.

They wanted ta whup me. But, the way I come up in the world, my parents was scared of em. An we had ta be scared of em cause we was raised under that ether. An they tot us ta be scared a the white folk. Cause when we were bawn, we were bawn scared of em.

Now you take my grands, an the age they at now? See, I had ta be scared cause I was tot that. I didn teach my kids ta be scared. An my son dont teach his kids ta be scared.

But you know, I call myself the hawt a the famly. All of em blieves in me, an they thank I'm tellin em the truth when I'm hoorawin em. Sometime I say a little funny joke, they look at me—an I turn my head off. I say, "What you lookin at?"

"Do you mean that?"

I say, "Yeah, I mean that."

Said, "Well, if you say so, you mean it. It must be so."

Cause if I say no, he say, "Oh, dont hooraw me like that. Had me blievin everthang you'll say."

I say, "I aint said ta blieve *everthang* I say, cause I'm gonna straighten you out befoe I git ya wrong."

But I love ta have fun out a lot a young people. Cause I raised so miny kids, I'm aware of em. An then, back in my young days, I tell ya what I was doin: obeyin Mama's orders. I wadn scared. I was scared ta not mind Mama. Because she knowed thangs that she was goin through with, she would hibit me an tell me ta turn around, an not do thangs that I wanted ta do. Such as bracin up to em.

An when they said sumpm they meant that, an meant fur you ta do what they told you. Else you couldn stay there, an if you run off, they gonna git you an brang you back.

Now you might say, "Well, I blieve I'll move over here across the fence, with this Mista Soanso. I dont like the way he treatin me." What you gonna move? The same durn thang over there where you movin as it was where you left.

He wouldn treat you no bettern the other fella what you gittin around.

So, I come up under that ether. Didn know no better. An come a Satiddy night, we'd be at the Suppas. Aw, man, you couldn never tell what them people was up to at them Satiddy Night Suppas. Sometime they go ta fightin an shootin, I'd go ta gittin up under the bed. Sometime break a gittah over somebody's head. Break gittah strangs, tryin ta play so loud where all them people kin dance behind my music. When the crowds git so noisy, you know, that culls ya down. But I've played places where you kin hear a pin drop. I kin play purdy briefly fur the people at those places.

You know where we passt today goin into Houston? Jest passt that T, used ta be a planation up there. Right back in that little patch a woods, off the highway about five miles thisaway, towards Waller. Call it the old Giddins Fawm. Buster Brewer an Jewel, an A C Kiels an all them boys follad me up ta dance behind my music. An they knowed I was playin there at Hoe Station.

I was livin in Courtney then. That was somewhere back in the backwoods, back up in Hempstead. Lemme see now, I was talkin in the way back. Maybe twenty-eight or thirty somewhere. But its no need a sayin when it hapmd, cause it done hapm. Some white guys had some colored women goin wit em, an they knowed I was playin music. An them colored girls bantyshaw with the white men, come out there ta hear me play so they could dance. They was nicelookin colored girls. All of em had big hats on, them colored women an the white men both. An the white men carried em on out there in them buggies, an some of em had caws.

An come right over cross the prairie since about past that T, on past Holiday's place, an comin right up the road ta the right, befoe that pastor. Them old white people set there in the caw, til they seed A C, Buster, Jewel an all

141

them colored folks dancin with them white men's colored women. An come in there an got them womens outa there an whuppt them colored women an made em leave there. An they tuck em out the hands a Buster an Jewel an all a those, an thats their own color. Yeah. Old man Tommy Holiday used ta call hisself a hoodoo, say he was two-headed.

See, the whites had their go, but the coloreds couldn mix with the white women. But the white men could mix with the colored women. An couldn do nothin about it, cause they was Klu Kluck. You bump up against one a them, you know you gonna hafta take em all on.

You ever heard a talk about Klu Kluck? That mean a buncha men'd git together an do what they want. Nobody could stop that Klu Kluck, cause its too miny people there, an one had the other one's same mind.

So them white boys, white men, took them girls an put em in the caws an buggies where they got outa whatever they was in, an carried them away from there.

They used ta call Hempstead Six Shooter Junction. Bad town. So miny people shot their pistol off an got kilt an kilt one another: so much colored folk got paid up in there wit pistols an fightin an drankin an killin. Few whites went down in that.

The next un was Navasota: a dog call that a dirty hole, thats what I call it. Thats the dirtiest place there in the world, Navasota. Mow niggas kilt there'n iny place in the world. Yeah, man! They kilt niggas fur the fun of it. Specially if a man try ta hold up fur his rights, they gonna kill him. Git rid a him. An that'll steer the other colored folks out the way. Say, "Well, that nigga got kilt, an I'm gonna try ta stay here. I'm gonna do like old boss told me if I wanta live."

Listen good, show you what I'm talkin about. Now whether it hapm or not, thats too fur back ta know what everthang hapmd. But what they was doin, an who all was in the caper, they kin figger that out. But I kin figger this out, why they went ta git im:

A colored man was throwin up his hands. "I didn mean no hawm! Aw, dont mess wit me, boss!"

An this other guy, he had went ta the penitentiary. He was a nervy guy. His name John Cameron. An they knowed he was nervy. But they didn know how nervy he was, until he lookt ta see this colored guy throwin up his hands. Right in Navasota.

An he say, "Looka here"—he was a nigga too—say, "Nigga, why dont ya hep yoself? You jest throwin up yo hands an hollerin, 'Oh this!' Why dont you hep yo damn self?"

An a white fella turnt around an said, "I'll give *you* some of it."

John Cameron say, "You might, but it wont be easy as you thank."

An he drawed back ta hit im with the ax handle, an John jest grabbed the ax handle. He was left-handed, an he cut the white fella right cross the neck. An the blood come outa his neck an he thought he was dead an he fell an he fainted. White fella fainted. Jest scratcht im enough fur the skin ta break.

An then the whole town would git down on one Negro when a colored person done hit a white man. Everbody in town git ax handles, shotguns, Winchesters, bullwhips, an circle around that Negro. Dont I have no show.

An so the law put im in jail, that day. That fella what cut this fella on the neck. Gonna lynch im that night. Maybe fifty or a hunnud mens got together, ta decide they was gonna git im out an lynch im.

So, bout this time on a Satiddy night, these bad white folks a Navasota told the jaila, "Pitch me that damn key!"

Jaila say, "Fur what?"

Say, "We're goin down there an git John Cameron out."

He said, "Well, I wont hand it to ya, but I'll throw it to

ya. You aint got no bizniss killin John Cameron. That white man aint dead. John was jest speakin right. But you aint gonna git me ta give you the key. Cause I'm violatin the law ta let y'all take that man out the jailhouse an lynch im, cause I know thats what you gonna do. But I'll throw it to ya. Cause I know I caint whup the whole damn Navasota."

So he pitcht em the key, an they wint down there on hawsses, an walkt down ta the jail, an called John Cameron, lockt up in the jail: "John! Come out!"

An he was a colored *man,* you know wadn scared. John say, "No, make me come out."

Say, "Yeah! We gonna make you come out."

Say, "Well if I had what y'all had, I'd make *y'all* come out. I aint comin out no way. Cause I know damn well you gonna kill me. But, I'm gonna die in this jail. An I aint gonna come out there an give you a chance ta kill me out in the light. I'm already lockt up. Y'all come an git me."

So they broke the jail open with the key. Wadn but one doe to it. An commenced ta shootin at im in the jail. Oh, they jest had a great big time, guns goin like firecrackers. They shot im in mincemeat pie: "Blam-zum blam-zum blam-zum blam-zum!" All over the jail. I dont know how miny times they shot im, but they shot im enough times ta have sister holes in im all over.

An befoe they would go in there an git im, one fella says, "You reckon he's dead?"

Anothun said, "Well, I know: Shine yo flashlight." Wadn no lectric lights back then. Jest a few city lights. Gas lamps, you know. Shine the flashlights in there, that jailhouse was lit up wit flashlights. An he was layin there on the flow.

"Be show he's dead cause this damn nigga's dangerous!" Shot im again! Already dead!

An one fella says, "Well, he dont move!"

Drug him out the jail an say, "Well, throw that rope around his neck."

All of em had hawsses—wadn but two or three caws in Navasota. Throwed a rope around im, an wrappt it around the hone a his saddle. An struck a lope. Headed south towards Hempstead. Draggin im round the neck.

An when he got ta the corner, downtown turn ta the right, went two blocks down, an rode behind one another draggin im down the road.

Say, "What you gonna do wit im?"

One fella say, "Well, jest gimme a hand, an I'll git up on this post." Carried im to a nearby telephone post. Fella steppt on those irons til he got up high enough ta tie a rope around his neck. Then they put a loop around his neck, an throwed the rope up ta him.

An he wrappt it around that piece a iron what you walk up on—call em stirrups—an he say, "Well, now I got the end of it. I'm gonna throw it down ta y'all, an you put it back round the hone a that saddle."

Pull it up there an say, "Is he clear?"

Say, "Yeah, he cut clear!"

"Well tie it round that post." An come off an leavin him. An hoopt at im an shot back at im again. Man didn have a face! Body near about like mush. Shot im ta pieces in the jail!

He hung there all night, but he was dead befoe they strung im up there! You know a man draggin by his neck: the hawss was lopin, draggin im, he's dead if he didn have a bullet in im. An he had boots on, an he had bled so til blood was runnin out his boots.

I wadn nothin but a boy. That wadn nothin but ta see a fella git kilt. An this blind boy, Deps? His famly was standin there watchin the whole thang. All right then, the white folks, they left im there.

An so, they was all waitin fur their daddy ta come home,

out there on the prairie where John Cameron stayed wit his famly. Waitin ta see a loaded old black mule from Navasota comin back over the top a the hill. Didn come home that night. He was a *bad* man, he would gamble an fight. He didn bother nobody, but if they bothered him, you had ta kill im or whup im. So they didn know where they daddy was.

He hangin there from about eight o'clock that night until twelve or one the next day.

By nine o'clock, white lady got in a buggy ta git herself a cool buggy ride. She had a fiiine hawss. So she had her hawss hookt up an went downtown, drivin. Hawss was trottin along. He was gentle, never had been known ta run away. She settin there in her buggy. An got near about ta where that man was hangin up.

First thang you know, the hawss whirlin an turnt the buggy over on the old lady. An she fell out the buggy an the hawss was headed back nawth toward Anderson. Too much blood there made im scared. An she hollered, "HEY, HEY! Catch my hawss!"

An she got up, didn kill her, didn hurt her. An she said, "What in the world was a madda wit my hawss? He aint never tried ta run off wit me."

An a fella overrun im in a buggy, led im back ta her. She told im, "Whats hapm ta my hawss? *My* hawss dont be scared a nothin. This a trained *pace* hawss."

An he say, "I dont know, lady. I caught im, an he was runnin. If he aint scared, maybe you kin manage im."

An she said, "My hawss aint never act this way befoe." Still hadn lookt up.

An the man say, "Oh! Lady. I tell you whats a madda wit that hawss: look up there hangin on that post."

That man hangin up there. All that blood drippin on the ground. That hawss smell blood, he gonna turn around. An she say, "Oh, have mercy!" She lookt up as he told her an she fainted. Right on the ground.

So she went home, after they done tuck her ta the docta. Scared her so she got sick. When she got reconciled, she set down an wrote the govamint a letter. Say, "Y'all got ta come in ta man this town. If you dont, this town's gonna go ta destruction—I'm a white lady—with these white people killin an marmakin up these niggas."

An the governor answered her letter. Said, "We'll take care a the situation." An that stawted these Rangers acomin here. In one week's time: the baddest man ever been here was Mista Hayman. Texas Ranger. An his deputy, Mista Bailiff.

An you ask me what was he like, this Mista Hayman? He was a bad man. Talkin bout *bad* man. He was a Ranger! You know what they is? Texas Ranger, what he is?

No purdy bad in im. He's as bad as they *git*. An he got authorities ta be bad. Cause the governor got im out ta do what they *want* him ta do. An the govamint when they hire a Ranger, he's got ta be strict an right. If he do inythang under kiver, the governor will know it.

They dont hire no man ta be a Ranger, unless he got the nerve ta go an git inybody thats required ta be got. Dont care *how* bad he is.

First thang a Ranger do: see they say, "Brang em dead or alive."

Dont hafta go back an git no repoat from a local district. Say, "Well, I thought he would come, but I couldn git im. He too tough, unless we kill im."

Then they come back an give em authorities ta do that, say, "Well, kill im."

Ranger gonna kill you, when you dont go. You go by what *they* say. See? Cause he got authority ta do that. When they send a Ranger at ya, well you got ta come on or be dead when you git back.

Regardless a who you are: iny way he kin brang ya, he gonna brang ya. Why? Cause he's a Ranger. You be in jail when a Ranger come at you, or be dead. Two ways: he'll

Frank Hamer and R. M. Hudson (later sheriff of Navasota), taken at Del Rio circa 1906, shortly after they had killed several Mexicans. *Photo courtesy the Marcus Mallard Collection.*

brang you live, if you be peaceful. An if you be bad, an say you aint goin, he'll brang you dead.

An this Ranger I'm talkin bout—an let you know I aint leavin off nothin—when Mista Hayman come at ya, you comin ta the jail. Had you done a jail crime, iny kinda crime that he had ta arrest you, he'd rest ya. An you had ta come or die.

Now he wadn fraid a black or white. He wadn no *piece* a man, he was a *whole* man. These civil officers around here, they jest *piece* officers. Cause they hafta go somewhere, maybe Foat Worth, an register another authority ta git you.

But that Ranger, he sent *out* ta git you dead or alive. Thats the reason he call hisself Ranger. I mean rangin all over the whooole state. When that Ranger come at ya, podna, you kin go outa the state a Texas: thats the only way you'll be safe. Cause they comin at ya.

An this man Hayman, I rode away with him jest like I'm ridin wit you. I was stayin on the Nickelbuck Fawm when he come here. But I was about nine or ten years old. I dont know how he pickt me up ta be his buddy. Reason he was *my* buddy cause I was *scared* of im.

Next thang he would kill me birds. Takin practice shoot. On all kinds a bird ever fly up: out of a buggy, an a hawss, either flatfooted, ever time he shot, a bird had ta die or his wing was broke. Fix em so I go pick em up. I had a croaka-sack a birds ever day.

Carry em home. Jaybirds, redbirds, mockinbirds, all kinda birds. I didn know one from the othun. Cause they were all birds, an I carry em home Mama says, "Boy, what you gonna do with this here jaybird?"

I said, "What is a J bird?"

She said, "He aint fit ta eat." Well, I throw him away.

An looky here an say, "Here's a redbird." I eat him.

I say, "Here's a mockinbird."

"Throw that thang away, boy!"

Yeah, stack a birds there wadn no count. But when he turnt me home, he give me all them birds. An I'd carry em ta Mama an have bird stew tamarra.

An he carry me all through the fields. An some a them bad landowners: one of em had nerve ta ask Mista Hayman if I'd open the gate fur im. An I'd stick up tawgits, bones an bottles, so he could shoot at em, see could he hit em. He'll shoot em from Brazos County, plum out ta White Switch. Five miles! An all them landowners comin out an watch him poppin all them tawgits down say, "Well I blieve he's a purdy straight shoota. Better not mess with him."

He's goin all through the fawms, checkin up what was goin on. That was when they had them there county fawms. Where he heard tell of a colored man got beat up on this fawm, he knowed all about that. He go through the fawms, an see how they was treatin ya.

An boss man say—knowed im—"Long come Mista Hayman." An they wouldn be cussin. Wouldn be beatin ya while Mista Hayman's there.

So, Mista Hayman an me settin up there, under a shade tree. "Hi, Mista Hayman!"

"Ayuh!" He didn laugh an carry up wit nobody. Whatever he say he meant that.

Man said, "Mista Hayman, what you doin lettin Mance ride here wit ya? That boy's about eight or nine years old. He oughta be in the field."

Mista Hayman turnt right round an say, "What did you say?"

Say, "That boy there's big enough ta plow." Talkin bout me.

Say, "His damn hands dont fit no plow long as I'm wit im. Who told you his hand fit the plow?"

"Well I didn mean no hawm!"

Say, "Well I dont mean no hawm tellin ya. He doin what I want im ta do, an he aint gonna plow til he quit drivin round an openin these gates fur me. So, what you thank?"

"Nothin, Mista Hayman!" They scared of im!

I set there listenin at two or three of em talkin bout I was big enough ta plow. An so Mista Hayman come back, said, "Mance, lets go over on ta sich an sich a fawm."

We go round the back way, you know. From where I was raised at, plum back on the Baker Fawm, leadin in ta White Switch. An from White Switch ta Allen Fawm. He had a hawss an buggy he drove.

There some cotton choppas or cotton pickas or whatever was goin on. Hollerin an sangin old conefield songs. He stop. Thank a minute.

There's a fella name Peckerwood. That fella could holla five miles! Peckerwood was a convict once. Had a double head like. He wadn scared a nobody. An they were sorta fraid a Peckerwood. An he be out in the field, put his hand up ta his mouth, thisaway. An holla jest as loud as he could.

Mista Hayman say, "How?! Mance, that boy show is got a good voice, aint he? Do you know him?"

I say, "Yassuh, I know im."

Say, "What is his name?"

"Peckerwood." He'd write it down. Well thats all he wanted ta know was his name.

He drive up there say, "Oh, Peckerwood?"

"Yassuh boss!"

"Kin you blow yo hone like you did when I was comin up here?" Talkin bout his voice.

"Yassuh, boss."

Say, "All right, holla!"

He sang, "Work on the road somewhere!" An boy, he could sang that. An Papa used ta play that.

Sat there an listened at im. All the people come out the fields, gatherin round im. Landowner come out his house wonderin what went on.

He say, "Landowner, how you treatin these fellas? Are you givin em the right share?"

"Yassuh, we good ta our hands."

Say, "An you know all this lynchin. An all this colored beatins. Knockin em in the head. You know, I come here ta stop all that. I know people's got ta work fur their livin. Except they oughta be treated like people."

"Thats right, Mista Hayman!" Soon as his back turnt they gonna cut those niggas again.

151

An so, bout two years I rode wit im. An when he left here, I shoulda left too. Cause they hated me, after I was turnin in ta nine years of age.

An eleven years old, I was a man, plowin wit them older folk. Mista Hayman was gone. If he stayed here, I'd a been a lazy man. Eleven years old they had me in from behind the biggest mule! An the handle was so high I couldn do nothin but reach up at it!

M-hm. I know I would a been ruint if he'd a stayed round there. But still, Mama'd a been ruint too, cause she didn have nobody ta break her land, an she couldn git no way out.

Do I thank Mista Hayman done iny good comin down here? Hm-m. I know it! I dont hafta thank nothin. I saw it. An a lot a colored folks know it. Listen: he settled that town, podna. They placed im there ta corral Navasota, keep the white folks from beatin up niggas. An hangin em.

He knowed me everwhere I seed im. I was on the streets one day, right in the middle a town. Lady an Lemon, Jimmy Lee too, they had a saloon. An they had a showcase wit owls an parrots, an all kinda funny birds in the case. An Mista Hayman would come by, an stop. An puck some peanuts or whatever the owl would like in the showcase ta play wit im.

"Hey Mance!" He lookin round. Tryin ta catch somebody doin a dishonorable thang. An he say, "You doin all right?"

I say, "Yassuh!" Had ta say yassuh cause he's a white man, an I jest figgered all white men was—white, you know. Had ta honor em.

An he say, "What you got, Mance?"

I said, "I aint got nothin, Mista Hayman!"

"What you want?" Ten cents was plenty a money. He pitcht me a quota. An I got the quota, an it last me two Sundays! If I dont see im next week, I got fifteen or ten cents left. Cause you gittin loaf a bread fur a nickel. I git a whole lawny sausage fur a dime. Git a whole peppermint

J. H. (Jimmy) Lee's Saloon, where lived the parrot Hamer fed peanuts to. Johnny was a distant relative of General Robert E. Lee. *Photo courtesy the Marcus Mallard Collection.*

stick a candy this long fur a nickel! An so man, I was rich wit a quota.

Go down the street, first thang you know, some white man kick me. Mista Hayman brang him back ta jail.

He say, "Git on ta the jail! I dont hafta folla ya. But you be at that jail when I git there!"

See, the people runnin this place—the white folks—had said, "Well, I'm gonna run this place."

Mista Hayman say, "I thank you got that pitcht over some ways. I'm runnin this place. When you do wrong you got ta go ta jail. An lay there, until the term's come. Dont care how much money you got."

So he said, "Yassuh! Yassuh!"

If he'd slow down, he'd kick im from here yonda ta yo caw. He's a big a man enough ta do it. Strong enough ta do it. Man, he was the purdiest white man I ever laid eyes on.

All I kin tell you is, he was nice lookin. Got black hair. Tall.

An he had a eyes of a eagle. That man had the quickest eyes of iny man ever I saw in my life. He could turn his head this way an see whats goin on that quick. Woe a big white hat, or either a big black hat.

Did he do iny exhibitions? I was givin him exhibition when I ridin wit im in the buggy. I set up sumpm right here, an git back, an let him shoot that off. Stick or bottle. Inythang.

Most times, he done that jest fur hisself. Takin practice shoot. An sometime he git a crowd a white folk: I'd git

Frank Hamer while in Navasota, circa 1909. *Photo courtesy the Marcus Mallard Collection.*

them tawgits set up, an ever time his gun poppt, one of em bust open.

One of em say, "Well, I aint seed nobody take a dead aim like this man done done." Cause he could shoot a gun bettern inybody ever been in this county. An they figgered that he's the best mawksman they ever saw in their life.

When he shot at you, podna, he hit you. Dawk or day. An the other part a the exhibition, when they broke in a stow or did sumpm badly, he said, "HALT!" An you stawted ta run, he said, "Well, you will stop."

When he shot "BOW!" . . . he hit ya in the leg. He didn try ta kill ya. Where he shot at, he knowed its goin where it hit you at.

No, I never did see im shoot nobody. See, he done what he done in the night. Cause he was a night watchman an a day watchman. But I could hear em an find it out, from the next day. Night come, I'm at home in the bed.

Fella broke in the telephone office one night. Went upstairs ta steal sumpm. An they got a repoat ta Mista Hayman, say, "Somebody's up here. Telephone office!" An they was scared ta death up there.

An he wadn ten minutes gittin there. He was lookin all upstairs fur im. An this fella slippt down the stairs some way or other, an slippt out.

An Mista Hayman heard im. An he come down from the stairs, an when he stawted ta go up the railroad track, he said "Wup!" an turnt his ear: this fella jest hittin them gravels up there, goin nawth. Goin right through town. Down there where the bank used ta be, an the Smith Hotel. It used ta be a little lighthouse up there, wit a trainman throwed a switch up there.

Mista Hayman didn know who it was. But he told im "Stop!" An he got way up the road, from here ta the next railway cross there.

An he poppt an . . . He hollered like a calf, "Ohhh Lawd,

Mista Hayman!" He knowed he had im.

Mista Hayman walkt up there an throwed his light on im: he was layin there, with that leg broke right down where he shot im at. You know who it was? A half-crazy boy called Doach. He used ta sang on the street fur a nickel. An then had one teeth up here like me. Chew tabacca. They'd git him ta dancin fur a nickel, an they'd give im a dime ta stop. Cause he didn know how ta stop. That nickel'd make him dance all day.

But Mista Hayman knowed he wadn dead, cause he could hear im hollerin all the way up there: "Oh Lawdy! Oh Lawdy! Oh Lawdy!"

He was laughin at im, says, "Doach. If I'd a knowed that was you, I wouldn a hurt ya. But I had ta give an account a who you were. I had ta shoot you cause you would outrun me. I didn meant ta kill ya. You aint dead.

"Well I tell ya what you do. You caint walk. I'll git a ambulance ta come down here an git ya, an git that bullet thats down in yo leg. Well now, if you had a done halted when I told ya, you wouldn had yo leg hurtin. I'll call, you always stop."

"Yassuh! Yassuh! Yassuh! Oh Lawdy! Oh Lawdy! I'm dead!"

So they wrappt his leg all up, an he come hoppin round there next mownin. Hayman said, "Doach, dont try ta hop. You got a crutch. Now you go home. Stay off these streets, an stealin an tryin ta break in. Because you liable ta git hurt show nuff next time."

He had a automatic in each side. First automatic I ever seed in my life. One a them guns go like a firecracker strang. An he told them folks—befoe I quit ridin around wit im—he said, "Now look. A colored man was the best friend I ever had in my life. Listen, I dont want y'all ta be mistreatin these colored folk. Cause I been a Ranger. A colored man pickt me up, while the Carr boys shot me down. Shot my guts out, an left me layin there. An a colored man come long, an my guts was hangin out. An toted me, an rested, an carried me to a hospital. An let em wash that sand off a my guts, an sewed me up, an I'm livin today."

An said, "I want y'all ta be surer than hell respect em. Thats been done over fifteen years ago. That colored man cause me ta be livin today. No white folks didn git me here. They left me layin there.

"Now I'm strictly fur Right. An if y'all handle me that way we can git along. But when I tell you sumpm, I mean that. An if you dont do what I say, I'm gonna put you in jail, white or black."

An they find that out in about two years after he got there. He told them bad fawmas, an stow muchants. Said, "I'm the only man—me an my deputy—sposed ta wear a pistol in the broad open day or night. We gittin paid fur it. Now if I catch y'all wit a pistol on, I'm gonna put you in jail."

You know what he did? When he caught two or three of em with they pistols on, ahidin it, thought he couldn see the shape of it? He walkt up to a place where he's lookin round on the staves. Had eyes jest like that: he could see them in one minute, man! Sumpm round yo leg, in front a ya, inywhere he retcht fur it, he knowed it was on ya an where it was ta go git it off ya. See, he could size you up from yo thigh wit a pistol here.

You know what he wouldn do? He wouldn say nothin til he git ready ta say it. Then he come ta you, he lookin right in yo eye. Says, "You take that pistol an carry it home. Now if you dont, I'm gonna take it off ya."

"Mista Hayman, I aint got no pistol." Couldn look him in his eye, he had ta drop his head.

"What you goin chasin me that lie?" He done told you: take it off an carry it home. An he meant fur you ta take it off! Dont give him no head about what you aint got. He done knowed you had it. "You aint got nary un?"

157

"Nawsuh."

He grabbed it right there: "What is that?"

"That's a uh uh—"

"Nooo. Gimme that pistol." He'd pull it off an he'd kick you all the way ta the jail.

When you git tired a him kickin you, why, you done got ta the jailhouse. He'll let you rest a while from here ta that caw. Turn around an he was a *man,* he could kick you down. But if he hit ya, he knock you down. He didn have no branch or nothin, jest fistiz: One lick, you goin down. An when he didn wanta hit you wit his fist, he'd kick you.

An go ta the jailhouse, say, "Well, git in." Open that jail "I said, 'Git in!' I done kickt you all the way up here. I dont wanta kick you in the jail. I want you ta walk in there free."

Then he go down the street, whistlin. Lookin fur somebody else. Here come anothun up the street. He say, "I thought I told you ta put that pistol up, next time you come round here."

"Well, I'm is, Mista Hayman but, I jest dont have nary un."

Befoe he got the word out, he'd go ta kickin him. Say, "I want that pistol."

"Yassuh!"

"Well give it here! I mean hand it to me careful. Dont make no funny moves. Do, I'll blow yo brains out. Jest hand it to me like I want it. Jest drop it over there."

He'd take it, an he'd say, "Now git in front a me. Now I aint gonna run! You might run cause I'm gonna whirl you around wit my foots."

An here come his wife down there: "Mista Hayman. How much money would you take ta let my husband out so he kin go home, an git in his nice bed? That jail is too nasty fur my husband."

He say, "Well Miss, he's *my* prisoner tonight. That

money dont talk til tamarra. He got ta stay all night with *me* tonight. He's my prisoner."

She cried an, "Oh, Mista Hayman. I kin tell yo about mean. Thats a white man."

Say, "Yeah, thats whats a madda with this town: white. I'm a white man, but I'm doin my job. He kin come out in the mownin. But he caint git out with no amount a money that you offer me. Cause money dont buy me. I'm already bought, ta take this here position. Now you come down in the mownin bout nine o'clock, I might let im out fur nothin. But he gonna be in there til tamarra."

He such a man that they couldn fool im. If you done sumpm, he could look you in the eye an he could see it. Jest like he say, "You know what? Its bad about so-an-so hapmd." An he lookin right in yo eye.

You had ta drop yo head, he know exackly you done went an done it. But if you could look him in his eye, he'd pass you up. Hunt another fella who hafta drop his head. An he found people jest by lookin em in the eyes, an expressin his mind on what had hapmd.

Boy, he cooled that town down. Poe colored folks was scared ta meet white folks on the street: bout bearin around em, cause they was white an they was niggas, they dont wanta touch up against no white folks. But them white folks commenced ta lettin the colored folks git by. Give some room fur them. But wadn no room fur nobody but whites until *he* come there.

Man, not nary another colored man was lyncht after he tuck the job bein a Ranger there. Until he left there. They put im way from there because he's too strict fur Navasota.

Around nineteen-eighteen, I was livin at White Switch. Thats over there in Allen Fawm, but it had a diffunt landowner. It set over yonda by the railroad tracks. They hung a Negro that year, up in Anderson. But I didn know im.

See, Mista Hayman was gone by then. Left an went ta Houston.

Now I had a good friendboy, call him Jim Thomas, since I was about foeteen years of age. We was so close, we shared the same girlfriend. One night he'd go off an see her, next night I'd be over ta her house, an he'd stay at home. If I run up on him over there, or either he run on me, he'd say, "Hi Mance. You doin all right?"

Say, "Yeah, man. I'm doin all right. How you gittin along?" We never would go ta fightin one another. Fight *fur* one another, but we wouldn never go against us.

So he was seein a white girl, an they was dwellin together on the sly. Right there in Navasota. She wadn no Merican person, way the white folks tell it. Was a Jew: but white skinned.

See, he got careless, went ta see her one night right up ta where she stayed, wit her famly. You know that stow, down there on Washington Street? Well, them what run the stow used ta have a place up on top a there, where they lived. An jest befoe daylight, he come down the stairs, slippt up an knockt over a garbage can. Woke up everbody in the house. An they lit up the lights, an saw him runnin off from there an come after im. But he beat em down the stairs an slippt off, cause see it was night an it was dawk soon as he got outa them house lights.

An they got her ta tell them what they was doin—had been doin all along. An told her, "Dont you tell nobody about what done hapm. If you do, we'll—we'll do sumpm ta you too."

All right, they rounded up thirty or foedy white mens: on his trail with guns an hawsses, dogs howlin an yelpin, pickin up his scent. An he come by my house ta git my shotgun. But I was in the fields an didn see im. I woulda let him have it if I'd a knowed of it, long as he wouldn let on where he got it from. But its a good thang he didn git it, cause he'd a kilt a lot a white folks. He wadn fraid of em. An when they found out it was my gun, they woulda framed me up. Put me in the same fix as him.

So, they knowed he was headed out fur Allen Fawm, cause see, his grandaddy lived out there. So Jim couldn find no gun, cause they was followin im up too close. An they caught up wit im down on the Brazos River, down in them willa thickets. An let them dogs go at im foe they pitcht im up on a hawss an tuck im ta the Anderson jail.

So, they lockt him up in the jailhouse. An they give him a trial. Her famly give the judge a thousand dollas ta hush up her disgrace. Say, "He was up there lookin ta steal sumpm, an he saw her layin in bed there an raped her." Thats the tale they told in the coatroom. Wouldn let him say nothin. An she didn open her mouth neither.

They hung im right there at the jailhouse. They wouldn let nobody in ta see im except those that fed im, from when they drug im in til they hung im. Wouldn even let his mama see im. I rode up there ta see im, tried ta catch a glimpse of im through one a them barred-up windas. But I never could see im. That was long about—I'd say nineteen twenty-six. He was the last man hung up there in Anderson. Tuck em away from here after that.

I cried when they hung im. I'd a done inythang fur him. He was my best friend. But back then, there wadn a thang I could do fur him. Ever time I go through Anderson, I thank a him.

I'll tell you some mow about him some other time. We talkin bout Mista Hayman now. Cause he told people in Navasota, "I dont need that little job. I wanta git sumpm fur my pay. I'm jest foolin round here walkin. Aint nothin in Navasota ta fit me. One man kin do what he wanta in Navasota. I wanta go to a bigger town."

An he said, "Well, I know y'all glad I'm gone. It commence ta gittin hot here, I'll come back, though. Long as it stay cool, I dont need ta come back. But I'm goin out here ta Houston, where there's a lot a people. Aint nobody up here in Navasota."

There he was in Houston: an they wouldn stop them people from gamblin at the Rice Hotel an them big high places there. An he say, "Now, I heard that the whites is gamblin like they wanta. An arrestin all the coloreds. Now the coloreds an whites all gonna git arrested, if I catch em gamblin down there."

So, he wadn worried about the coloreds, cause they was scared a him. But the whites figgered they could buy im out. Talk good talk, an tell im what they would pay im ta let im have a shakedown.

He said, "How come you ask me that?"

Say, "Well, we want ta have our pleasure. We know you the law out here. Kin we pay you so much money so we kin have our own way gamblin? We *white* folks."

He say, "No, you caint pay me nothin. Long as I dont catch y'all, you aint got me. Now I'm gonna tell you one thang if I catch y'all gamblin, I'm gonna 'rest ever durn one a you around the table!"

So he was locatin where they was gamblin at. But he couldn git up there: three or foe nights he sneak up there, an they had a doe watcher. Watch when he come up there an they had some way, like a secret strang ta pull when he got up there, they quick hit on that strang. Then they quit gamblin in there. Taken him a whole year ta catch em.

You know what that rascal done? He come downstairs, an walkt the streets. Clumb a fire escape. Went up on the outside. You know that a fire escape go way up there. An crawled up ta the winda, an peept in there.

An somebody discovered him, but they didn know who he was, cause he wadn dresst up: had a overhaul duckin suit, an old flop-down hat. An one fella said, "What you doin up here?"

He said, "Well, I was tryin knockin on the doe, an y'all

wouldn let me in." He aint knockt on no doe.

Said, "What you want in here?"

Said, "I wants ta gamble. My money's hot! Y'all wouldn let me in the front."

Fella said, "Here's a guy here wants ta come in here ta play poker. Old tramp. Talkin bout he got plenty a money. Y'all wanta let im in?"

Finely, some of em lookt im over here an said, "That damn tramp aint got no money."

He said, "I aint got a whole lot, but I got me enough ta gamble. What is the rate a gittin in here? What you hafta pay ta git in here?"

In a certain class, you hafta pay a hunnud dollas, or a hunnud an fifty, ta git in there. Fella say, "It take two hunnud dollas befoe you git in here."

He says, "That aint no trick." Told the doekeeper, "Let me in! Here's yo two hunnud dollas."

An he eased in there. Went ta gamblin jest like inybody. He could gamble, too. Had that old flop-down hat down on his head—an had that badge inside his duckins.

An he had em a little skit: might near done broke everthang up in there. Say, "What y'all boys gonna do? Gonna give me some IOUs?" Thats a check. Say, "I blieve I got enough a them."

An he caught their names, ya know? As he was talkin to em. Had a pile a money settin there. Said, "Well boys, y'all done let me broke up yo game. An I got enough IOUs ta fold up an burn em up. I dont need all these damn IOUs." Hoorawed em, until they got sorta sore wit im.

One guy say, "Hell. You done broke us, whyn't you give us a stake?"

He say, "You oughta ask it. Maybe I done give you a stake, you coulda went ta gamblin at one another. But I aint gonna stake you ta gamble at me, now."

They say, "What is yo name, inyhow?" Got his name.

So he give em all a little stake, let em go ta gamblin at

one another. Fooled around an got all of em's names, Sonny! Sat round there like he was sleepin, while somebody was callin their names. They thought he was asleep, settin there, like he was noddin.

An when he got *aaalll* their names: woke up, an throwed them two pistols down. Said, "Well, y'all march downstairs, boys."

They look around say, "Who you talkin to?"

Said, "I'm talkin ta all a y'all. Them names you called while ago? An the names I aint got. Everbody march downstairs!" With them pistols, one here an one here, he got behind em. An it was thirty-eight people went downstairs!

An he called a ambulance. Them wagons what you put em in jail with: hoodlum wagons. He stood there until they load up three loads of em! An put em in jail. Rich guys!

An went down ta the cafay, an commenced ta whistlin an talkin. Told em, say, "That was easy done, wadn it? Jest take me a little time ta do it." Man, that man was smawt, Sonny.

Now that repoat come back ta Navasota. That was done after I quit afollerin im. Lots a thangs I find out about im, when he carryin me wit im. He didn have nothin ta hide from me. He told me all about what went on with him, when he was Ranger—you know, out an about.

The next thang, great thang he done: Was a lot a cowboys would steal people's cows, an brand em in their bossman's name. Lot a crooked work was goin on in these cow ranches. They had some guys could ride inythang had hair on their back. But they didn have no womens out there. They workin fur a salary of a month. An if you go git out there, you hafta be rough.

So, them people had went ta stealin from diffunt ranches. You couldn catch em. When they drive a bunch a cows off this ranch, on another ranch or whichaway they wanta carry em: them boys was in the lot, waitin in front with the fire heated up ta brand em jest as fast as they brang em in there.

So they couldn give an account a where them people was goin an who was doin it. So finely, they put him out there.

He told me, said, "Mance. Thats the hawdest job ever I had in my life." I'm a colored man. He called me by my name. He said, "It taken me about two weeks ta catch them people. I had em dead ta the right. But I couldn git em up an prove that I had em, until I got a chance ta git the location of em, where I could make em come under my command. I couldn bust in on em, an tell em I got em. I had ta git aaalll the bad people. Quick shootas, befoe I got ta the lead man.

"I stayed there two weeks. I et to the ranch. They had some best cooks out there on the ranches. Slept an et wit em. An they paid me off."

But now the first thang Mista Hayman told me, he said what was the hawdest thang was him gittin up ta that place. He say he was about a mile from the place: befoe they ever seed him, he was crawlin on his back, in them high hills an mountains. Say, he crawled over a mountain, an be so tired he'll stop an rest.

He say he seed a bunch a cows comin towards him, an they gonna kill im if he didn know how ta git out their reach. He say he got under the wire, an look over in the pastor: the cows was tryin ta git over wire ta git im. So he stoppt. Until they ceasedid down, commenced ta easin away from the fence.

They lookt away from the fence, where a stack a hay was already baled up. Them cows got ta eatin round there, an he slippt up in there an got im a bale a hay. An put his awm through this side, an a awm through this side, an put it on top a his back where he could crawl wit it: his hand is on the ground, where the hole went down, an the hay is on his back.

He say he crawled on that ground, somewhere along a mile an a quota. He said the damn cows was eatin off his back!

An he said about the last dot a the hay give out befoe he got ta the ranch. He said, "I dont know what the hell ta do now cause all the hay is gone. An they probly gonna kill me."

You know what he say he done? When that hay was all about gone, he got on his knees an resht, an got under the fence. An said the cows commence ta hookin at his belly then. Found out he wadn no hay.

That made the people at the house see them cows follerin up sumpm, an them cows commenced ta lowin, "Beeuh! Buh!"

They come ta the poach an said, "What in the hell is the madda?" An there he was standin out there on the other side a the fence: duckin suit. Had his pistols on, old white hat.

First un said, "What in the hell you doin out here?"

He say, "Who is the ramrod here?"

"What you wanta know that fur?"

He said, "Well, I heard y'all was short a hands. I wanta git a job."

Man said, "You hear what that guy say? Out there in the yawd?"

Said, "I hear im." They go ta laughin at im.

"Kin you give me a job?"

Say, "Hell that damn fella, wit his damn duckin suit an hat on. What in the hell you know bout workin on a ranch? You dont know about no ranch!"

Stood there til they talkt an talkt it over.

Say, "What kin you do out here?"

He say, "Oh, I dont know. Most iny little thang. Dig post holes. Stretch wire."

"Ah, we dont need none a that. All our pastors fixt. What else kin you do?"

Said, "Ohhh. . . . I kin—riiide a little."

Said, "Kin you rope?"

He said, "A little bit."

"See how good he is about ropin."

They put him in a pen. Let the calfs come around him an: he misst two or three. Said they stawted ta say, "Hell, you aint no good at ropin. You caint whup no damn cow."

Say, "Wait a minute! I might a been tired. I been walkin so fur. Gimme a little chance in the mownin."

Say, "Hell, you'll hafta do bettern that. If you dont, you have no job here."

Next mownin he'd had breakfast, drunk his coffee an went back ta the lot. An got his rope. Fixt it. An they said, "Man! That aint gonna work! You look dumbly! You aint fixin no damn cow rope ta rope no cows! Hell, all the cows been gone when you git the rope foiled around!"

He said, "Well, brang em by. Lemme see." Had the rope like it wadn right.

After a while, the calfs come out. An he said "Bloonk!" Throwed that cow. Cot im.

Say, "You cot im round his neck! Iny cow catcher kin catch a calf around his neck."

Said, "Let anothun come. Where you want me ta rope this time?"

"Rope him around his damn foefoots!"

He threwed the rope out there an caught the foefoot. Trippt im.

"Purdy good. Now lemme tell you one thang: rope him round his hind foot!" Tried im all kinds a ways!

The reason he got the job: they were smawt. They knowed that sumpm another was goin on. But they didn know he had his badge hid in his pocket. An they said, "Boy, what you come out here fur?"

He said, "I come up here ta git a job."

Said, "Hell, you caint git no job here. You got ta git a job under this jurisdiction a bein a—a roughrider! A good shot!"

So the first thang they done was sight im, see how could he shoot. An say the first shot he made, he coulda hit it, except he misst.

They say, "Aww, got damn, gotta do bettern that."

He said, "Well, gimme a chance. I jest misst one time."

An he told me, next time he didn miss. He knew how ta fire.

An they said, "Well, thats purdy good shootin. Reckon you kin do it again?"

He said, "I dont know. Try me." He shot again, an he hit the jackpot ever time he fired.

Said, "Ooh! Got damn! You about as good as we got! We need you on that shootin bizniss." An they'd drop along with that.

The next time, they wanted ta know could he do iny music?

He said, "Oh, I play a liddle fiddle."

Best fiddla ever come out the world. He playin the fiddle, Sonny, good as inybody! Could he play as good as my dad? Show! He could play all them cowboy songs. Papa couldn touch im in his ooold style. When he git in there in the cowboy arrangements, he knowed all them cowboy songs Papa didn know. The one called "Out on the Foedy Thousand Acres." An could play it so clear.

See, they had im in a dance. Gonna laugh at im, catch im in a lie in front a all those people out there. An they got him playin fiddle one night. An he drug me along like he couldn play good, until the second night. He say, "I could play purdy good if I had a good fiddle." He could play good then, but he made like he caint fiddle.

They brought im a brand new fiddle there the second night. Man, he had em settin, lookin at his hands, when he stawted playin that fiddle. All them cowhands—maybe five hunnud people was workin at that ranch. An they cookt suppa, an they'd gamble, shoot dice, an do all kinda capers up there. They say that rascal had that whole camp lit up. Didn want im ta quit.

He said he got that job two weeks, workin ta git them people located who was doin that doggone cattle rushes an stealin thangs.

Next thang they wanted him ta do: said, "Will you tell me, could you ride—with certain bunches?"

"What you call a certain bunches?"

"Foe of us go in a bunch, thisaway: you take yo bunch—foe of em—go ta the range."

He say, "Oh, I blieve I understand what you talkin bout."

They says, "I want you ta ride east, with foe. I want you ta ride west, tamarra with foe." Change bunches on im. Diffunt ones askin im questions, tryin ta git all they could outa him ta see what he was up to.

So, he rode with them foe one day, an he said, "Well. This job pays off purdy good? When they pay off?"

Say, "That job pays the next time we have another bunch a cows ta go an steal."

"When that gonna be?"

Told im say, "Well—I'll tell you everthang: The land man tell us. We go by orders. Next two, three days, we gonna herd up somebody else's cows."

An he holp em mark an brand em. Said, "Well now, when is next payday comin off?"

Foe of em was ridin wit im. Say, "I dont know. It'll be next month, I reckon."

They done tried ta cross him up, ridin him in diffunt bunches all kinda ways. An here he crossin them up, Sonny! Befoe they knowed it, they tellin him what he wanta know til he done got everthang he want out a them. Now you tell me Mista Hayman wadn sly?

An so he say, "Whichaway I'm gonna ride tamarra?"

Told im: east or nawth or west or south. Ever time he

rode out, they gonna see did he tell all of em the same thangs.

An he said he come out one mownin, an got his foe boys ta ridin near. They said, "You know a den a rattlesnakes up here?"

Said, "Yeah, I heard there was."

Say, "You better watch it, cause when a hawss rare up an turn around on ya, you may be ready, got damn, cause he'll throw you off im. Cause they aint gonna go over no rattlesnake."

An say, they rode up near a bunch a rattlesnakes: "Wwrrrrrrr." He say the hawsses rared up wit im, an throwed him near about off.

Say, "Man, I told ya the damn hawss aint gonna ride over no rattlesnake!"

Another say, "You wouldn a been rodin Old Soanso! Cause he'd a throwed ya!"

Mista Hayman said, "Who's over Soanso?"

Said, "Man, you caint ride Old Soanso an git off im that easy. He's a *bad* hawss. Aint nobody over Old Soanso."

He said, "I want Old Soanso tamarra."

So they told im where Old Soanso was, said, "Well now look. Now if you caint ride, dont you git on there. Cause that hawss gonna kill you."

Said, "Well, I wouldn git up there if I didn mean ta stay live."

Old Soanso you know, he put that saddle an bridle on im, an they put im in the pen. Say, "You ready?"

Say, "Yeah."

An he come out an that hawss was yelpin an jumpin an hoppin, buckin an carryin on. Direckly he fell off Old Soanso. Make it look like he throwed im off, out in the middle a the lot so he wont git hurt.

Say, "Man, we told you dont ride Old Soanso. That hawss gonna kill inythang jump on his back."

An they hoot an holla, hoorawin im cause see, wadn none a them could ride Old Soanso. He's a big old pal-meada: seventeen hands high. He got light brown hair, an long old white mane an tail throwed back behind im: When he gits ta runnin, that wind go ta pullin back that hair straight back behind im.

Mista Hayman git up off the lot, brush the dust an thangs off im. Them cattle rushers bout fell off the fence post laughin at im. Standin round behind the corral an back a the fence an all like that.

He say, "I reckon he's a little shy. Aint been rode in so long."

Say, "Yeah, an aint gonna been rode in longer yet."

"Well, I been ridin all day. I'm kinda tired. Let Old Soanso cool down a while. I'll be rested by tamarra. Lets try him again in the mownin."

So, they go on back ta the ranch house, git em a little sumpm ta eat, an go ta the bunkhouse an go ta bed. An next mownin, here they go back ta the lot. Old Soanso still got his bridle on. Wadn nobody could catch im ta take it off im. All night!

An they git him in the pen, put the saddle on im, an Mista Hayman say, "Open up the gate. Let him go."

An you know what they done, Sonny? Went round an round that lot, buckin an kickin up fence post. Couldn hawdly tell where they at, was so much dust in the air. An everthang he do, Mista Hayman is right wit im. Man, they went round that lot fur about a—musta been a hour an a half!

An so finely, Old Soanso commenced ta coolin down, stawted pacin to an fro. Direckly he was walkin round that lot. Mista Hayman reach up an pat im behind the ear, say, "You had enough, Old Soanso?" An got off im, an led him over ta the gate, an tied im ta the gate. An said, "Well, I blieve he's a purdy good hawss. Jest need a little trainin."

An from that day on, wadn nobody but Mista Hayman ta ride Old Soanso. Wadn nobody else could ride im. Biggest hawss on the ranch!

Next mownin, Mista Hayman said he come out ta the lot ta saddle up Old Soanso: there foe riders in foe diffunt bunches, waitin on him.

One of em say, "Well, we got sumpm new ta do today. You take yo foe riders, an head east. Them foe gonna head west, out on the hills an mountains. We wanta see kin you keep yo riders hid, cause we show as hell gonna keep a lookout fur ya. You reckon you up to it?"

Said, "Oh, I blieve I understand what you doin. How long we hafta stay hid out there?"

The fella ridin over them foe bunches, he say, "Two days pass: first day, we gonna ride fur as we kin ride. Next day, you come alookin, cause third day we ridin back ta the ranch. An, iny one a us bunches git back here without you catchin us, you better not ride back here fella."

Mista Hayman said, "Well, gimme a chance ta saddle up Old Soanso, an you kin go ahead on."

So here they rode out: foe east, foe west an south an nawth. You know what they done, Sonny? He said they kep them foe was wit im, so he couldn run off from there. Tell the high sheriff what they was doin. An had that Ranger badge tuckt under his shirt!

He said he taken his bunch, an rode east til sundown. Others went south an nawth an west. Night come, his boys went ta sleepin. Thought he was sleepin. An that rascal crept up outa his bedroll an went over where the hawsses tied at, an snuck off from there an didn wake a one, Sonny!

An rode all night. Ridin nawth. Day come, he settin there lookin down on them foe. Snuck up on em befoe they woke. An got em ta drop they guns, an ride with him, goin west.

An he done caught up ta *them* foe. Know how he say he done it? They was makin dust in the air, from the hawsses feets kickin up dust off the ground. An he went down in a big old branch, an got out in front a them. An when they rode by he got them foe ta drop they pistols.

An he say he done that wit ever durn one of em, Sonny! An come back ta where he had done run off from them foe ridin wit im who sposed ta keep up wit im. They huntin all round in there fur im, scratchin their heads. Come up on em befoe they knowed it was him. Made em drop they pistols!

One of em said, "How the hell you git away from us, man? An then come back here an we couldn see ya, couldn hear ya comin?"

Three days pass, they lookin fur some a them riders ta come back ta the ranch. Say, "Ah-oh, sumpm goin on wrong now. Hadn none a them foe riders come back. Nawth an south or east or west."

Little befoe dinnatime, long come Mista Hayman an Old Soanso: an lopin long behind em here that whole buncha foe bunches, lowed down behind em. An come up ta the ranch house, an throwed them guns down on the ground—they was a whole crowd a them cattle rushes come out on the poach ta see what was goin on—an said, "Here's y'all's pistols, boys. I reckon y'all kin have em back now."

An lookt at em standin on the poach an said, "Y'all got some dinna cookt up fur us? I'm show is hongry." They thought he was gonna carry em ta the jailhouse, an he turnt right round an tuck em back ta the ranch house.

Say why he done that? Cause he was a smawt man, thats why. He come there ta git all a them cattle rushes, Sonny. He didn come there ta go back an say, "Well, I brung ya this bunch, but I couldn come ta find out who they workin fur." See. He after the top man, the ramrod. An so, them fellas give over ta Mista Hayman. Didn trial im no mow after that. An turnt around an made him the boss a his bunch.

So finely, he come ta find out the landowner's name, all

who they was workin under. An he say, "You reckon Mista Soanso be down this time, when we go ta puttin his brand on them cows we stole?"

Say, "Yeah man. We made a big haul this go around. He'll be down there. Make show everthang done right."

An next day come, he take his foe riders what taken orders under him, an meet up with the whole gang of em. Out there on the prairie, way back in the woods under one a them mountains, so nobody could see how ta find em. An they had a big old corral out there, an bob wire fence made up so they could round all them cows up, what them cattle rushes stole from some other man's place. Big old fire standin round it, an they brandin em jest as fast as they carry em in the lot. Smell that hair singe an meat cookin, brandin so miny of em that quick! Smell like a hog slaughterin.

Direckly, landowner come ridin up: big white hawss, straw hat got a big wide brim. Got his pistol on. He say, "Well boys, look like we made a good haul this month. Reckon y'all could use a little extra pay?"

Mista Hayman, he backt off from that fire. Tuck that badge from out his pocket, an clippt it on top a that duckin suit. Wadn nobody seed what he was doin. They all too busy brandin up cows an changin em up, an thankin bout all the money they gonna git outa it.

An he drawed them two pistols out, level at that whole crowd a cattle rushes. Landowner too. Says, "Y'all all under arrest. Now, you do like I'm tellin ya. Everbody git down off yo hawsses. An dont pull no quick moves."

They stop brandin, pushin cows in the lot, whatever they was doin. Look around. "Who you talkin to? Who say so?"

"Goin by my say-so. You see this badge? An that star in the middle of it? Ranger badge. Texas Ranger." An they knowed its the truth. By that star in it. "Now I want all a y'all ta pull them pistols off, an set them guns in a pile by that fire." Them brandin irons.

"Now I caught y'all red-handed. These cows aint none a yo cows. Got somebody else's brand on em. An you done got yo's, crossin over that brand. You broke the law, an you all goin ta jail. If you dont do like I say, you got ta come or die right here."

An they knowed he meant that. An say, "Landowner? You in this too. Yo hands dirtiern inybody's. Git down off yo hawss, an drop them guns in the stack with the others what you paid ta work fur ya. An do it easy. Dont, I'll shoot you deadern hell." An he do like he say, cause they already knowed he was the best shot a the bunch, from them exhibitions he's puttin on.

An brung all them cattle rushes ta jail, Sonny! Landowner too! An that was done befoe he come here. Them two thangs he told me about, while I was ridin wit im: that colored man savin his life, an that I jest got through tellin ya. He was a Ranger, I'm tellin ya. Couldn nobody mess with him. An he's the one shot Bonnie an Clyde. Frank Hamer. M-hm. Same one.

He done that after he left away from here. See, aminy a thang he done come back ta Navasota, by way a people tellin what he done, from them bein round where he's at when he done it.

But now, he come back a time after he left an went on ta Houston. An that was when Gainsvul got staubed an done all that shootin: see, he was givin a party, call em Satiddy Night Suppas. Make a little extry money an see could he have a good go of it, an everbody else have their fun too. A buncha people was there at his house. He didn reckon on nobody gittin riled up an breakin the place up. But thats near about the way it come about. You caint never tell whats gonna hapm, brang people together an let em go ta drankin an dancin, gamblin. Maybe one see some boy guyin wit his girlfriend. Might be some gambla git sore cause he lose all his money. Or somebody be jest drunkly an caint hep hisself. Cause when one gits ta fightin in a place, all of em stawts ta fightin.

I shoulda let him have his Winchester. But I let im go in there wit his knife: he went in there cuttin. He cut two, three people in there. They in there tearin his house up, man. Stove in the beds. Tearin bodes off the poach. An Gainsvul, all he was doin: tryin ta stop them people where he still had a house he could live at.

[From Mance's version of "Baby Let Me Lay It on You":

Baby dont you tear my clothes,
Baby dont you tear my clothes.
Well you kin cut me an staub me, try ta take my life,
But baby dont you tear my clothes.]

An so, this fella had it in fur Gainsvul. An he was hidin behind the doe: when Gainsvul passt by, he staubed him in the head wit a knife. An when he did that—my brother was young an purdy stout—Gainsvul staubed this fella in the thigh, an he jumpt. That give my brother a chance ta grab im an put his leg around im. An throwed im, an while he throwed im, why, Robert Howard was comin in the doe: tried ta pick my brother up off his brother-in-law.

My brother seed he was resht, an he got up wit his knife, an I met im. I seed they was bout ta double-team on im, an I grabbed Gainsvul an say, "Here yo gun. You got ta shoot yo way through." I knowed he wadn gonna hit nobody hawdly, cause blood was all in his eyes an he couldn see good. But I knowed that Winchester'd scare the others off.

An he commence ta shootin that Winchester. An I was standin right beside a him. He shot three people: Robert Howard, he shot him right in the hip. An he shot Cercy Walker, through a Prince Albert can a tabacca. Thats all that kep him from shootin him show nuff clean through.

But when it hit the can, that bullet slided down, an went out the side a him: flesh wound.

An then, he was shootin as he went, with that thirty-thirty Winchester, an I was walkin longside of im. "They went thisaway," I said. "There! Shoot ta kill!" I told im when that blood runnin all down his eyes.

Well, I snatcht the gun outa his hand, an pusht im outa the way an he fell. An then I'm commenced ta shootin his gun. But I dont shoot nobody, cause I jest shot his gun in the air, git them people ta run off. An then, I shot the gun empty. Kep im from killin somebody.

An when I got Gainsvul in the bed, an washt the blood off im: the next bed, in another room, where lay that fella he shot through the hip. An the boy that got shot, the one with tabacca can. An they was groanin an hollerin.

The law had been made by then: Mista Hayman an Mista Bailiff, his deputy. Same badman I was tellin ya about. They come up there, an I was goin home. I stayed in town. An we went through the pastor, an they come up the railroad track.

So, there was Robert: his people carried im home, put im in the bed, wit a hole in his thigh.

Cercy's little brother, they walkt near about ta town wit me an my sister. He say, "You know I got shot?"

I said, "Aw! Dont you guy me."

He said, "Yeah. But I did. I got a flesh wound. I'm walkin along here shot. But I aint shot bad."

I said, "Listen, yonda go Mista Hayman an them goin up the track. We better be quiet. We go home, they wont know us out here."

So they went an arrested my brother. Hayman said, "Now, Gainsvul, we got to arrest you cause you shot a couple a people. An git some kind a identification, an hold it up in coat tamarra. Now, you come on an go in the jail."

He said, "Yassuh, Mista Hayman. I aint gonna lie. I did some shootin."

Said, "Well. I want you ta tell me the truth. But you got ta pay fur it, one way or the other."

Mista Bailiff knockt im in the damn head, say, "Dont let him talk ta you!"

An Mista Hayman said, "Dont you touch that man. Let him talk! We got him arrested. We need ten mow Gainsvul's like him. Thats whats the madda with this damn Navasota: aint nobody here nervy as Gainsvul."

An his deputy drawed up his leg ta kick im. Gainsvul say, "I'll make you kill me."

Mista Hayman say, "Bailiff, you better not touch that nigga! Let im talk til he give out! He aint hurtin nobody." Mista Bailiff didn like that, but Mista Hayman was the boss.

So Gainsvul carried on, "I mean he better not kick me! Do, he got ta kill me." He gonna talk til he die. He'd talk ta inybody.

So he talkt hisself down, an head was bleedin all wrappt up. Said, "Now, look: I didn shoot fur nothin. Look at my head! I was jest tryin ta command my house."

Hayman said, "You aint done nothin bad. You gonna git out easiern you thank. But jest want the truth about it." An show nuff, he let im out that next day.

So, my uncle—who claims ta be Gainsvul's daddy, an sposed ta be *my* daddy—he was one a them nervy guys too. He was out early that mownin. Walkin along near about the station, when he got the news about his boy. Oh, that made him so mad! He went down there ta the jailhouse say, "Gainsvul! What'd you do?"

"Well Papa, I shot a bout with Howard. But I didn know who I was shootin. I was gonna shoot everbody cause they was tryin ta tear my house up. Thats whats the truth about it. I had nothin against Robert, no mown nobody else. But did they tell ya that I got cut?"

Said, "Yeah, I know that. Who cut ya?"

He said, "I dont know, Papa. But somebody got behind the doe an staubed me."

Uncle George say, "Well, I would hate ta find out who it was. Mista Bailiff? Thats ten years when I find out who snuck up on my boy an staubed im. I'm gonna tell you right ta yo face—all the reason I dont kill im, I dont know who done it.

"If he had a let my boy had a show, he could break. But he slippt up an staubed him behind im. It better not reach ta none a these Lipscombs. Not only me. All his brothers. Somebody goin ta hell. I'm tellin ya, Mista Bailiff: You better keep that hid."

So, I'm the only one ta find out who cut im. At the time that hapmd I didn know, until it leakt out. But I wouldn say nothin ta my brother about it. Because that wadn gonna hep im. An when he died: he didn know who cut im. I kep it hid from im.

Early Musical Influences

The primary emotional elements of the blues are its earthiness and forthright acknowledgment of sex. This gave off a refreshing appeal to many from a white culture that had been too long starved for candor in these areas of life. If there is a cultural or political overtone in the blues, it may be in its allusions that sex is a healthier human activity than is the acquisition of material possessions or the obsession to acquire, control, and manipulate power. Through the blues, many have found a different window to look at sex. If that window gives them freedom, and if giving people freedom from the dominant ethos of any particular era is subversive, then I reckon blues would have to be branded as subversive.

The blues form matured just prior to World War I, long before radio and television came into being. In this go-along Mance portrays how music was disseminated among blacks from the turn of the century up until the 1940s and 1950s. Around 1917, Mance first heard Blind Lemon Jefferson on Deep Ellum Street, in Dallas. Jefferson was one of the first innovators of the blues, and he strongly influenced its current shape. A few years earlier, Mance had tuned Blind Willie Johnson's guitar on the streets of Navasota. With his soulful renditions of gospel-oriented songs filled with "blue" notes, Johnson became a proponent of blues-style slide guitar. Jefferson and Johnson are considered giants in the formation of Blues guitar styles. In the teens and twenties, two traveling carnival and black minstrel musicians named Richard Dean and Hamp Walker brought back songs from across the South when they returned home to Navasota during the off-season. And in 1922, while already afflicted with tuberculosis, Yodeling Jimmie Rodgers played Navasota and asked Mance to tour with him. Seeing himself as a family man and provider rather than an itinerant musician, Mance declined. Rodgers, who became known as the legendary "Blue Brakeman" and the father of country music, was the first outsider who acknowledged Mance's talent before it would be "discovered" four decades later.

Mance intersperses his personal history of how the blues took shape in Navasota with his own music philosophy and how it related to his life, and to life in general. He sums up this relationship by calling his songs "Life Story Songs" and "True Story Songs." From his viewpoint, the following concepts were connected enough to be metaphorical equivalents: Time, Life, Go-along, Rhythm, Beat, Motion, Gait, and Dance.

In addition, Mance defines the term "songster" by giving examples of songsters he knew and by playing or referring to the broad scope of songs that made up his repertoire. "Songster" has a twofold meaning. First, songsters had "big loud" voices; their singing was superior to their instrumental skills. Mance placed Blind Lemon Jefferson, Blind Willie Johnson, and Lightnin' Hopkins in this category. Second, songsters could play in virtually any style; their repertoire was not limited to one or two styles of music. Mance was a songster by this second definition, not by the first.

In the midst of delivering his music philosophy and referring to songsters, Mance brings up several personalities who figure in his life later on. Chris Strachwitz helped to discover Mance in 1960 and went on to found the Arhoolie record label when he issued Mance's first album, in 1961. Woody Guthrie, who grew in fame from the 1930s to the 1950s, is considered the father of modern and especially politically oriented folk music. John Lomax, Jr., was the son of John Lomax, who is heralded as the cofounder of modern American folklore as a disciplined study. Elizabeth Cotton, Mississippi John Hurt, and Leadbelly (Huddie Ledbetter) were country blues guitarists who, along with Mance and others, represent the finest examples of that genre. B. B. King's urban electric blues guitar and vocals have entertained racially mixed audiences for decades; he achieved world prominence in the 1980s. A former student of Mance's who has played the world over, Taj Mahal's piano, guitar and, vocal styles are a mixture of roots blues, jazz, and Caribbean styles. Bill Neely, who also learned songs from Mance, was a country and western songster from Austin, Texas, where Armadillo World Headquarters incubated the emerging "Austin sound" from 1970 to 1981.

The blues is generously seasoned with esoteric and occult references. The spiritual practices of the mysterious

Blind Lady of New Waverly figure into some intriguing aspects of blues terminology. This hoodoo lady lived in the "ether world." She was a "two-headed" woman who could see things with a second head or second sight that most others didn't possess. In talking about her, Mance reveals some voodoo-influenced terminology and practices. For example, the object referred to in Lightnin' Hopkins' song "Mojo Hand" is a lucky charm like a rabbit's foot, or a voodoo doll to cast bad fortune against someone. "Goofer dust"—a sand or powder spread around someone's home or in his hat, clothes, or food—can cause "ruination" in that person's life. Stories of traveling medicine men and gypsy fortune-tellers add to the aura of mystery that pervaded Mance's thoughts and worldview.

Mance goes on to relate his first meeting with Lightnin' Hopkins in Galveston, in 1938. Their reputations had preceded them, but this was Mance's first time to hear Hopkins, who today is often thought of as a link between earlier country blues and the modern-day blues it spawned. Though Mance never played outside of his precinct until he was discovered by the white world in 1960—except for his two-year sojourn in Houston, from 1956 to 1958, when Hopkins first heard Mance—his reputation was carried far and wide in the black community, as Navasota-area blacks migrated all over the United States. Hailing from Louisiana and then Texas, Shirley Dimmick was one of the first white female blues singers. She performed in the 1940s and 1950s. (Dimmick gave Janis Joplin voice lessons.) While in New York in the early 1950s, a member of Count Basie's Orchestra heard that Shirley was from Texas. He urged her to go and see Mance in Navasota because he was one of the best guitar players anywhere. Sure enough, she went there and saw him perform with a piano player—before Mance departed for Houston in 1956. Up to that year, all this sharing of music had occurred without the aid of television and with little or no help from radio in Navasota.

From the twenties to forties there were 78-rpm "race records" played on old windup Victrolas, but it still was almost all literally a word-of-mouth musical culture, or what Mance called ear music.

PART ONE:

BLIND LEMON AND THE BARNUM PLAYERS

I was about foeteen when I stawted playin music. Yeah, first gittah I owned: a gambla come through the fields carryin a beat-up old gittah. He had taken it in pawn. Won it playin cawds somewhere. An I reckon a fella sold him the gittah cause he got broke behind im.

An then he come walkin on down the road, whistlin, an had that gittah throwed over his shoulder like it was old piece a hoe. I was workin with Mama in the fields, choppin cotton. An kids, ya know, could git away from the watch a Mama. She was workin, she couldn pay no tainsion ta us kids.

An so, I lookt back an seed im befoe Mama seen im. I said, "Mama, yonda come a man totin a gittah."

She lookt around an said, "I see im, but I dont know that fella."

An the closer he got ta her, she said, "Oh yeah, I knowed im. But he dont play no gittah."

"Mama, I show wish you'd buy it fur me."

She say, "Well how I'm goin buy that gittah? That man might not sell it ta me."

He'd just pawned it, ya see, had some money tied up in it. He couldn hit a lick on that gittah. He mighta give the fella a dolla on it. He just wanted ta git a return on it.

Direckly, he walk up alongside the turnrow, he says, "How are you, Jane?"

She say, "All right. What you doin around here wit a gittah on yo shoulder?"

"Ah well, I tuck it in suit. Some fella sold it ta me."
Standin there talkin ta Mama in the field, an direckly he
say, "Aunt Jane, you want me ta hep you out? Gimme that
boy's hoe, an I'll hep you ta the end."

So I said, "Let me tote the gittah."

An so, he say, "Kin you play that gittah, boy?"

"Nawsuh, I caint play it."

He say, "You want it?"

I say, "I show do!"

"Well, you git yo Mama ta buy it fur ya."

Boy, you talk about feelin glad when he said that. I said,
"Mama, why dont ya git the gittah fur me?"

An she said, "Hush yo mouth boy! I aint got no money."
Boy, it hurt my feelin then.

Then he said, "Jane, I'll sell this gittah ta the boy."

She said, "You wont sell it then."

"I sell it to ya cheap. I win all the money, an got this
gittah fur a stake."

She say, "What ya call cheap?"

He say, "I'll sell ya the gittah fur a dolla an a half."

"Dolla an a half! Where I'm gonna git a dolla an a half?
We makin fifty cents a day an livin hawd."

Said, "You got *sumpm*. I aint gonna worry bout you not
payin this here. If ya want it fur the boy, let im have it an
you kin pay me when you got it."

Finely, Mama said, "Well, put it under the bush there.
Over against the turnrow. It'll git hot in this sun. Then I'll
pay ya someday. You look like ya wantin me ta have it."

Say, "Yeah, I dont need the thang. I caint play, an look
like that boy gonna die right now, lessin he take that gittah home wit im."

She say, "Yeah, he crazy bout that gittah. He'll be beatin
on that thang all night."

So he said, "Well, its yo gittah." Man, you couldn
hawdly hold me in that field til sundown!

So he put it under those bushes there, an went ta holpin

Mama chop grass an weeds, til dinnatime come an my sisters took im down ta dinna wit us. An he said, "Well boy, I hope you learn how ta play that gittah."

I said, "I'm gonna try."

I come on home with that gittah, "blum, blummed" on them three strangs. Thats all it had on it. Whole buncha kids gathered round, listen at me thumpin. See, you didn hawdly hear a gittah in them days.

One a my sisters say, "Where'd ya git that gittah?"

I say, "He sold it ta Mama."

They were glad about that! Laughin about how old an busted up it was. Daylight comin through that gittah, man!

I didn care how old it lookt, I was lookin at a gittah! Man, I couldn eat no dinna! I had the gittah, an was plunkin it out. We couldn eat with the old people: they would eat first, an the chillun would eat last.

Finely, Mama got up from the table, done eatin.

I said, "Mama, you hear this gittah?"

"Hush yo mouth, boy! You goin crazy with that gittah."

I say, "Yeah Mama, I likes it."

An the kids say, "Well Mama, he wanted one. Ya didn do nothin bad by it."

Man, no one could git no sleep fur my plunkin on the gittah.

I went ta the field at noon an it look like the sun never was gonna go down, cause that gittah was at home waitin fur me ta git there. In the evenin, we toted wood on down that way, with the team. Ever evenin we'd git an awmful, take enough wood ta last all night. So I went on an got my wood quick an got on down ta the house.

An boy, you talk about bad? I didn know nothin ta play on it. I just like the sound.

I put up with it an finely, I come aware a the gittah an

bought strangs on it an tied em up an twisted em up. See, plowman works five days an a half an then, thats what I would go against fur the clothes an such. But on the Satiddy, boss man would give us what we made. I was rich with twenty-five cents, call that *skin* change. Didn git but foe bits a day an workt til Satiddy noon, an that what them dues would buy us.

An ever night Mama an the rest would be up ta me playin the gittah. Say, "Go ta bed so we kin git up in the mownin." They call it a *git*fiddle, "Git that gitfiddle out yo hands an go ta bed!"

An I'd go ta bed an dream about it, hangin up side the wall. "No, dont touch that gittah."

What you thank I'd do in the mownin? Oh man, I'd git up first. I kep that old gittah about two or three years. Then the holes got to it, you know, cracks in it. See, they wouldn make em good as they are now. They'd make em outa old thin planks. Lot a gittahs would warp. They git wet, they swell up, material wouldn hold. Course I didn want nothin but ta learn how ta play em then.

Three- or five-dolla gittah was a tip-top gittah. Now its five hunnud! So thats where I got my first gittah. Fur a dolla an a half. I wadn but maybe twelve years of age.

An when I was foeteen, I could git out an depend on my work, playin. I commence ta learn the sound, an words, how they would go. People were makin up their own songs back then, see.

An so, some fella near by me, he played a liddle gittah, named Robert Tim. An at night I'd slip out in the cotton rows then. I could stand on a cotton limb when I come up. Great big stalks. We'd git under them cotton stalks an hear im play at night.

He the one played "Sugar Babe." First song I learnt in my life. I said, "That show sound good ta me. I'm goin try ta learn that on my gittah."

So I tuck over "Sugar Babe." Same one I got on my records. I played that fur about three years, that one song.

[Mance's version of "Sugar Babe":

        Goin ta town, gonna git me a rope,
        Whup my baby til she buzzard lope.
        Sugar Babe, its all over now.

        Sugar Babe, whats a madda wit you?
        You dont treat me like you used ta do.
        Sugar Babe, aw Sugar Babe, its all over now.

        All I want my baby ta do,
        Make five dollas an gimme two.
        Its all over now.

        Goin ta town, gonna git me a line,
        Whup my gal until she change her mind.
        Its all over now.

        Sugar Babe, I'm tired a you,
        Aint yo honey but the way you do.
        Sugar Babe, its all over now.]

Then I jumpt off a that, an next piece I learnt how ta play was "Out an Down." An when I played them two songs, I could jest play em over an over an then quit. All the people was satisfied at them two songs.

Jest like me an you settin here talkin? Well, they was talkin it, an first thang you know somebody come along an made a song out of it. I say me fur a parable, jest like I say, "Well, I'm all out an down."

You say, "What you mean?"

I say, "I aint got a friend, an I aint got no money. Got no shoes, no clothes, an I aint got nowhere ta go." Now thats what you call old "Out an Down."

[Mance plays his version of "Out an Down," also called "East St. Louis Blues" and "One Thin Dime":]

Mance Lipscomb at Toad Hall, Austin, Texas, October 8, 1969.
Photo by Burton Wilson.

On my way to East Saint Louis
Didn have but the one thin dime,
Didn have but the one thin dime,
Didn have but the one thin dime.

Befoe I would spend it, fur my own use,
Save it fur the lady friend a mine,
Save it fur the lady friend a mine,
Save it fur the lady friend a mine.

All I want, in this wide world,
Is a brand new duckin suit,
Is a brand new duckin suit.
My baby says she'd take me back.

Standin on the Karo [Cairo, Illinois] street one day
When a freight train, come passin by,
Freight train come apassin by,
Freight train come apassin by,

Waved my hand at the girl I love,
Hung down my head an I cried,
Hung down my head an I cried,
Hung down my head an I cried.

Cried, "All I got is done gone"
All I got is done gone,
All I got is done gone.
Sumpm keep atellin me, I wont be round here long.

Aint nothin I brought in this wide world,
Aint nothin I'm goin carry away,
Aint nothin I'm goin carry away,
Nothin I'm gonna carry way.

Follad my woman to the buryin ground,
Down to the buryin ground,
Down to the buryin ground,
Watcht the pallbarriers slow let her down.

Now I'm lookin down in my baby's face,
I'm lookin at my baby's face,
Now I'm lookin down at my baby's face.
"I love you baby, I caint take yo place."

Mmmm, have mercy,
Lawd, have mercy on me,
Aw Lawd, have mercy on me,
Oh, oh, have mercy, on me.

Thats befoe the blues predicted. I was playin right then what we call the old style a blues in *my* time comin up. We didn know nothin bout "The Blues," but we *had* the blues right *on*. Then, after while people commenced ta namin a song like that "The Blues."

You say, "Why you say that, Lipscomb?" All right: Blind Lemon pickt up that song. He was doin that when I tuck the interurban up there ta Dallas, ta hear him sang an play. Nineteen-seventeen: he's standin there on the ground, on the railroad tracks playin that song. He imitated the blues behind that. First man that ever knowed what "The Blues" was made outa. Well then here come "The Blues," stept in behind that song.

An then they invented it from that: "The Blues" style. Now its a thousand million blues they playin. This here's the original blues: that old "Out an Down."

But the same thang what I'm playin right now, that was the blues cause yo all out an down, broke an aint got a dime. An those verses fits in somebody's mind, said, "I follad my girl jest as fur as I could go. That was down ta the jailhouse doe." See, its another way you kin close that song out. Add two three mow verses in there.

Everthang I says in there, why, its compairin with whats happenin in people's minds an in what they were feelin an what they were doin an tryin ta do in them times. It'll make you feel sorry an sad. About yo past life an all like that. Thats the blues: nothin but a feelin.

So, thats where you hafta figger out people's minds when you playin music: brang sumpm cross they mind. People stay woke behind what I'm doin, because some a them thangs done hapmd ta them or somebody they knowed.

191

See, all these songs come up ta me when I was settin down thankin bout somebody's mind, the future a their life.

Now I stole this "Spanish Flang Dang" from a buncha Mexicans come ta my hometown. Pickin cotton. I didn know no Mexicans til I got ta be about, oh, turnin in the teenage. Sometime around first big war come in there. An I was scared ta go out there an talk to em cause I couldn understand what they was sayin. But they had a gittah, while the old mamasita was cookin tawteeyas at night? I slipt out an laid down in between them old conestalks, an heard them playin. You play it in a banja tunin, thats a G tunin.

[Mance plays the instrumental "Spanish Flang Dang."]

You heard that in Mexico? Thats right. Well thats what music is fit fur: if you caint bring remembrance back in music, why, you just hearin noise. What I'm doin, I'm brangin back remembers. Sich as these songs as what ya call True Story Songs.

Now lemme see. I learnt "Alabama Bound" in nineteen-fifteen. I stand around stows, by them bawn dance—same thang that turnt inta them Satiddy Night Dances, thats right. I wadn out there fur nothin: I was catchin them songs. Yeah, then I'd come home an play em. I dont furgit inythang. You tell me sumpm today, an I'll remember it.

[Mance plays his version of "Alabama Bound":]

Alabama bound, Alabama bound.
If the boat dont sink an neither turn around, I'm Alabama
bound.

Well the preacha's in the pulpit, jest awavin his hands,
An the sisters way back in the amen corner's hollerin, "Go on,
man!"

What did the preacha say to the little red hen?
"Wont ya meet me down to the old bawnyawd, bout half past
ten?"

192

Well the roosta crow. Hen flew over on the fence:
"I kin see in yo deep blue eyes, you got ta be confessed."

Well the roosta crow, an the hen reply,
Said, "I kin see, in yo deep blue eyes, ya got ta rise an fly."

Well the roosta crow, an the hen flew down:
"You want ta be a man a mine, you got ta run me down."

Well I'm goin up nawth. Aint goin ta stay,
Got a long tall cheatin brown, gonna pay my way.

Well the preacha preach, all the sisters moan,
Say, "You want this collection I got, you got ta folla me
    home."

When he got through preachin, laid his Bible down,
Says, "Sister, if I miss Navasota church, I'm Alabama bound."

Dont you leave me here, dont you leave me here.
If you leave me here, oh darlin dear, leave a dime fur beer.

Yeah, he make im some money offa that plate, "You got ta folla me home, ta git that money." Thats what the preacha told the sisters in the church. Yeah, thats a good un. That old church was reelin an rockin. Everbody was sangin the words ta that song.

I'm seventy-eight years of age. Reachin back way from there: when the songs I'm playin now come out, I was in my boyhood days. All right, I couldn even play the gittah. Then, my daddy handed that down ta me. He was a fiddla, an my older brother was playin gittah. It jest come up in me as I had ta do these same thangs what they was doin, because I was raised up in that music famly.

All of us played that ear music. Ralph was two years oldern me, an Charlie was three years oldern me. Ralph was a real good songster too. An then the othun couldn sang so good, but he could play like the devil. They played their gittahs *years* befoe I learnt how. Cause I didn have no gittah ta learn on, an I was too little ta pick it up.

193

Then after Ralph quit playin gittah, he could play piana. He was a rail good piana player. Well, I coulda played a little piana, but I was so crazy about that gittah I give up everthang ta learn it. An I'll tell ya why: if you play a gittah, you got ta be of yoself. Inythang that you nated to, you got ta go on wit it. If you play all kinda instruments, you caint do all of em good. See, you got ta throw off yoself in some of em.

Yeah Ralph, he died in Los Angeles, about several years ago. We stayed around one another until somewhere long about nineteen foedy-one. He was in Foat Worth when he left. That big World War Two come up. An people went out ta Califownya in a big booms a work out there, loadin them boats an got a lot a money. An might near everbody here in Texas went ta Califownya—them what could git out there. So he drifted out there an I never did see im no mow.

My sister, she could play awgan. Thats the first something like a piana I saw in my life. Yeah, them old pedal uns: you had ta keep time wit yo feet an yo hand. You doin two thangs. Cause you didn pump it all the time, it wadn no sound to it.

Yeah, we'd stawt ta runnin, walkin til we made it up there ta where that awgan was carryin on that noise: "Flang-flay flang-flay." Boy, thats the purdiest music ever I heard in my life!

The whole family of us could play some kinda music. We could a had us a Lipscomb's band if we'd a knowed what bands meant in them days. Yeah, I heard all kinda music in my come-ups, but I never did take up with nothin but what I was jest raised up under. So it wadn hawd ta git it outa me, because it was already pronged in me, but my fangers jest wadn long enough ta reach over the strangs. An didn know how ta place my hands. An them old songs jest stayed inside a me til I got big enough ta play em.

Wadn but a few songs come out when I come up. Thats when the music first stawted ta comin out: "Sugarbabe,"

"Out an Down." An "Take Me Back," which my daddy played on the fiddle. I carried them three pieces along, from foeteen years of age, on up ta twenty years. An it lookt like I was playin all the songs that I needed ta play.

I couldn reach out an figger out no mow, cause wadn nobody there could sang em ahead a me. Til somebody come in from my hometown an sung a few little songs around. Jest like that song "You Gonna Quit Me Baby— good as I been ta you, doggone." I done wrote that way back in nineteen-eighteen. That song jest come in ta Navasota in a cawnival. I got three or foe words outa it. See, people didn have but foe or five verses to a song, in them days. A lot a these verses I added to it myself, ta make the song go alonger. All my songs got addition to em. I thank about somebody's troubles, somebody's life story, an then I add the verses to em so it'll fit they mind.

Now Richard Dean played a song, called it "Shorty George." Didn play so I could complain. Until I learnt it, it sound so much better when he was playin it, cause it lookt ta me like I wadn never goin ta learn it. I blieve he done "Shorty George" a little diffunt than Leadbelly.

Dean an a fella named Hamp Walker, they would go off an play in them cawnivals? Call em Barnum and Bailey. They had elephants an thangs, an big old tents. An had people playin sideshows, sometime somebody be dancin on the stage wit em. Like that "Buck Dance" I heard played in nineteen-eleven. Ever seed two roostas flappin up along- side one another? Sumpm like that: two men git out on the stage, dancin an buckin against one another, see who could beat. Call it "Stop Time." Try ta git people ta pay two bits or foe bits ta come inside the tent. Cause that first part was free, an thats what Hamp Walker an Richard Dean would do. Oh, they'd stay gone six months, then here they come back ta Navasota an be in town six months. An then, off they'd go again.

Hamp Walker made up that song "She Flagged a Mule

Barnum and Bailey Circus elephant outside Johnny Lee's saloon. Johnny is on left. *Photo courtesy the Marcus Mallard Collection.*

ta Ride." He was a boy was tot. Cause he was country raised, part town raised. An that was his favoright song. Oh man, you kin play that from now until night if you thank a the verses. Boy, he could show sang. I dont blieve nobody on earth I heard could sang bettern that boy. Now, he was a big dawk fella. Big mouth, an shiny eyes. He'd shine his eyes up when he'd play. Man he show could play that song. He done all his pickin right here on this song: "If I Miss the Train, Got a Big Black Mule ta Ride." I didn wanta learn nothin but that un.

When I was a boy eight or ten years old, thats when I was around Hamp, wishin I *could* play an sang like him. See, I could go out sometime, sometime I couldnt. Cause there were places Mama didn allow me ta go out.

Aint no music in the world you kin jest concentrate on

one time an learn it. You got ta hear it mown once. Like what hurt me was, I'd hear it in spots. I'd hear it in the night, next time I hear im it maybe extended fur three foe weeks, or two three months. So that kep me kinda off a pickin up on what he said this time. I'd wanta git around ta hear his gittah so bad. Lot a people jest wanta hear it fur the sound, but I wanta hear it ta learn it.

I done tried my best ta learn that piece an pick it, but my hand was too small ta git across the neck a the gittah. But I had already remembered the song in my ear, what you call ear music. An so, when I growed up ta where I could reach around that neck, I pieced it together. Jest like he played it. Outa remembrance.

After I got up in the teenage, I git amongst a bunch a boys, you know, where there aint no girls around: I could sang as nasty a song as you'd wanta hear. Git you ta laughin. What you call the Dirty Dozen. You heard talk about Iggie an the Dozen? "Yo Mama, yo sister, yo Papa, he done this thang. . . ."

An was some songs people would sang when they was workin. It wadn no music to em, jest sung conefield songs. You take a colored gang a people where I was: there may be foedy or fifty people in one settlement right there in a cut a cotton. Thats a trail like you go out that doe. A row, see. They was in a big old cut a cotton all together, an one would be plowin, maybe some choppin. They'd git ta sangin.

Well now the boss man, he come ridin down on his hawss: an them colored folks be sangin, an he didn know what they was sangin about. The colored folks know, but *he* didn know. If he did, he would a shot us down.

Oh, we was sangin sumpm about "Hannah hurry up an go on down." Well see, we say "Hannah" fur the sun. But he didn know how da concentrate them words. The words was plain! But we was sangin in a way he didn understand what we were sangin about. We was sangin about *him.*

Sometimes a good songster would lead out, an boss man say, "Old Soanso, why dont you sang fur me?" He'd wanta hear you! But sometime he didn wanta hear ya, he say, "Hush up that damn noise an go ta work!"

I was out in the fields, oh long about nineteen-eighteen when I pickt this un up. Now this here's a feelin comin about, transacted on over to a song: a man loved so hawd, he didn know what ta name her, so he say, "Wooo! She's sweet as she kin be. I blieve she's a Angel Child." See, she left im the night befoe an aint come home. An he was sangin that song in the field, an you know the next mownin the woman come home? He sung her back! Thats what you call a soul down blues.

[From Mance's version of "Angel Child":

Wonder whats a madda wit my little Angel Child. (repeat)
She left home soon this mowning, an here its half past five.
All in my dreams, I could hear my doorbell ring. (repeat)
When I woke up this mowning, couldn see a doggone thing.
If you see my little Angel, please tell her ta hurry home. (repeat)
If she dont come back, people, I wont be round here long.]

First time I was on a train was nineteen-seventeen. I was comin out there ta pick cotton an ta hear Blind Lemon play on a Satiddy on the streets in Dallas. No, I never had been out no furthern Dallas when I met him. An I wouldn a went up there if I hadn been up there pickin cotton in the fall.

So I was pickin cotton on a week out in them country, in the creek bottoms. An some fella who lived around there, say, "Man, you oughta hear Blind Lemon Jefferson! He about a gittah player."

I say, "You reckon he is?"

"Yeah, man! An he a good songster too. Got a big loud voice."

Say, "Where kin I find im? He play Suppas round in here?"

He say, "Naw. He up in Dallas, man."

I say, "Well, I plays gittah a little. Maybe I kin find some kinda way up there an hear what you talkin bout."

An I had a first cousin that I was stayin with, an his daddy an mama. He knowed Dallas purdy good. We called im Son Pratt. His name fur a first name was Louis. We never did call im by his real name.

An Satiddy, about nine o'clock, we would git our clothes on an take a bath, an catch the interurban up ta Dallas. Go up there til it was six o'clock that evenin, an come on back down where I was pickin cotton at a little old place called Fletcher. Nineteen miles outa Dallas.

See, when Blind Lemon was playin on the street, them lectric caws was still in the place a runnin to an fro. Catch that interurban every hour. It was like a little old coach? Had this here lectricity wire on, it'll lectricoat ya? Trolleys. Thats right. Dallas an Ennis was the headquotas. They went on past Fletcher an all them little places as fur south as Waxahachie, an on outa there east ta Ennis. Thats somewhere long about fifty miles.

An when we got ta Dallas, we hung around where we could hear Blind Lemon sang an play. Not only me an Son Pratt, it was a whole lot a people's alibi: it was jest hunnuds a people up an down that track. They went fur that. Country people, an a lot a town people. So, thats where I got nated ta him: nineteen-seventeen.

M-hm. He hung out round on the track, down on Deep Ellum. You cross Deep Ellum Street, an turn go down on the H&TC railroad track. Central track run right through Ellum.

They forbidded im right in town, but the law would let Lemon stay out of town. Cause he's a big loud songster, an he'd have all that gang a people gatherin round im so fast, an they wouldn clusterate inta town. Certain distance in town they would allow him ta play an sang. Then he wouldn be botherin the people in town. Some of em went fur it, some of em didn like it.

So, they give him privilege ta play in a certain districk in Dallas. They call that "on the track." Right beside a the place where he stood round there under a big old shade tree? Call it a standpoint. Right off from the railroad track: that was his gatherin ground. An people stawted ta comin in there, from nine-thirty until six o'clock that evenin. Then it gittin dawk an he git somebody ta carry im home.

Oh, I dont know how much money he made, but he made his livin that way. He was a big, stout fella. Loud voice. He played dance songs, never did play a church song. He's a blues man.

He had a tin cup wired on ta the neck a his gittah. An when you give him something, why, he'd thank ya. But he wouldn never take no pennies. You could drap a penny in there an he'd know the sound: He'd take it out an throw it away.

Well, I couldn count the numba a times I seed Blind Lemon. Cause when our cotton would give out in this part a the country, why, the cotton was openin up, briefly, two months later up there in nawth. See, its cooler up there'n it was down here.

Well, we got our crops gathered down here first. Somewhere long about September an August. An October an November, up until the next year, we'd have cotton ta pick in Dallas County. We wouldn be up there all the whole season, you know. Went out there jest fur emergency, ta pick up a little Christmas money. Maybe come a flood or drought or sumpm at home. We git fifteen or twenty-five dollas, well, we rich. We'll come back home ta Navasota.

Lets see now. In nineteen-seventeen thats the first time I seed Blind Lemon Jefferson. An I misst a year seein him, from nineteen-eighteen up until nineteen-twenty. Cause I misst a year goin ta pick cotton up there. See, the crop was good that one year, an I stayed home.

Yeah, he made some money in Dallas. People heard im all his life—where he was bawn in a place called Wortham? They would give im a little money around, his kin people was there. He'd set on the street an maybe make three or foe dollas, foe or five dollas a day ta the highest. Money was scarce.

An so, he lived there. An when he got big an learnt a lot mow about music an diffunt songs, why then, he commenced ta hearin people say, "You oughta go ta Dallas, boy. You git on the streets, you kin make plenty money." Which he did. Made a good career there.

He played all his life til he got somewhere along about foedy years old. He played around in these places like I played, an on the streets. An they discovered him, an they got him ta come ta Chicago like I went ta Berkeley.

An the last time I heard Lemon, he was goin ta Chicago ta cut his first record. I never did see im iny mow. Thats where he died, in Chicago. Froze ta death.

No, I never did go interfere wit im. He was a big husky fella. I was a country guy, you know. He had sich a variety a sangin. An people give him ta be the best songster around in the places an precinct. I stood my ground wit im, but I could hear all he's doin, an see what he's doin. He knowed what it was some few mow gittah pickas hangin there around. He couldn see em, but we was expectin that: catchin on ta what he was doin. An I didn wanta be the one ta tell upon myself that I was listenin an catchin on.

Well, I know he wouldn a liked it. Thats the reason I was stayin my distance from im. Now, he didn care about how miny people come near im who wadn playin gittah. Had them handicapted. But somebody who was jest standin round there listenin, an tryin ta figger out what he's doin an how ta play be like him or sumpm: You know that didn go so well wit im.

I never would ask im nothin. I jest stayed quiet an listened to im. Cause I heared a people drankin, say, "Aw, Lemon, I kin play that. I kin beat you playin so-an-so."

An he say, "Well play it." An give em a trial, an they stawted an couldn ever finish it an he say, "See, you lied!"

Then he take his gittah, an told em, "Git out the way, son. I'm makin my livin here. I aint got time ta worry wit y'all. You caint play my song."

Cause nobody in the world ever played none a Blind Lemon's songs. Nobody in the world ever played none a Lightnin Hopkins' songs. Never will play it. He say, "Why you say that?" Cause he's got his own way playin it. He picks up on his own style. An he knows his own time.

Music aint nothin but time. Its not no good music if its untimely. You know that? Course, people say rhythm, but rhythm an time are the same thang. You got ta pat yo foot or clap ya hands: rhythm. Thats music. An so I kin play some song about the crosscut saw an all like that, I kin change that an put it in the diffunt rhythm, see.

He say, "What you call time?" Well they got a new name they give it in two, three ways: time, an rhythm, an beat. Steady beat, ya see. You give it a unsturdy beat, why you missin time. You give it a rhythm in the wrong time, why you breakin yo rhythm. All thats connected the same thang. You talkin bout one, you talkin bout all three of em.

First thang somebody'll have in they mind ta call the thang, they called it. An you go down the road an twenty minutes from the time you left, somebody else got another new name. Rhythm is the proper thang you should call it. Its the easy way ta explain what you talkin bout. Then the next main thang: its nothin but time. See you caint take nothin an make it outa rhythm but time. Caint take nothin an make it outa time but rhythm.

An what you call the beat: jest like you beatin the drum, thats the time beat, see? Thats time right on. A drum aint nothin but a time beat: "Blum, blum, baddla baddl baddl," then come back an git caught up wit yo lead music. You kin feel good towards what you doin, when you got the right time. Cause you know when you break time. Jest break time a little bit, you goin feel that, you goin hear that.

Yeah, I have played fur over a million people in my sixty years experience. I never breaks my time. Cause I played all night: I'm watchin my dancers on the flow. I'm looking at yo movements of yo foots, an see ever move that they make. An if they break time, I'll be spankin their time. If they went a little slow, I'll go a little slow ta keep right up wit em. An first thang you know, we done got back together. Got the same time. No, I dont lose no dancers.

But if I dont watch *they* step, an jest let them git along—dont pick em up, you know in wit my music—why then, I'm doin wrong cause I kin throw you off. But I wait on em. I kin tell ever time you git outa time.

Lot a people that dance by motion. Now you settin in that chair right there: you settin still. An you aint got no motion, cause why? You settin quietly. But once you take yo second thought, say, "I blieve it sounds good ta me. I'm gonna motion," you see. Reel an rock then, in the motion a yo body. So you kin call there ary one of em: motion, an beat, time, an rhythm. An gait right in there alongside of em. Cause you stawt off a slow speed, an then run it up fast, well you aint got no gait.

Well now, I liked Blind Lemon Jefferson's playin an his kind a blues. He was a clair picka. He sung like he played an played like he sung. He had a good gittah an a good loud mouth. But the technicians was diffunt: it wadn no rhythm to it. He jest sung like he wanta, because he had his own beat. Now he had double notes in his music. You know, jest hit about in spots. Break time. Sometime he put too miny bars in his song: he sung foe or five beats befoe he turn his song an change codes. You couldn time his music. Jest rock up an down, an didn keep a steady beat goin, an give the people the motion while they was dancin. People would jest stand around an listen at im.

That jest like you aint got no instrument at all, you jest in the field workin. An if you aint got no time at all, you jest got yo mind made up you sangin sumpm ta pass time. Jest like you thank if you sang, the sun go down quicker or the days go shorter. But when you git out ta sang sumpm in a mood with time: one two three, one two three, thats what music made out of.

See, I play straight time. Straight straight strictly time. Cause thats the way I learnt. Once you learn, son, an been at it long as me, you caint veer away from it. Cause you feel it. An then when you stawt, you gonna stawt right, an stay wit a certain speed, an diffunt gittah codes. Good music is time. You kin hear all the codes you want, but you got ta keep that steady beat in there. Thats why I git by so much: people wanta hear me cause I'm makin my music come right back in the order a makin that time, to an fro.

Now you take that song "Blues in the Bottle." It come up in nineteen-fifteen. If you gonna dance out on the flow, this here'll make ya move cause its got all the time an all the rhythm to it. See you kin jest git out there an then make like you dancin, if you jest keep this rhythm goin wit yo feets.

Jest like sometime, I had another musician or two playin together at them Suppas an thangs. Lemme see . . . Isom Willis, he was one. An A C Sims, that was my nephew by my sister Lilly's only child. We called him T Lipscomb fur a go-by, what people would reckonize im by. I heard people say T was the best player, after me learnin im. Cause he would sang an I'd do the playin. He been dead now, somewhere long about nineteen fifty-two. Died with sugar diabetes, had ta cut his legs off wit it.

Now we played fur all the Satiddy Night Dances an programs in diffunt places. An they gonna say, "T an Mance play, you well as ta close up if you had sumpm else goin on." Cause thats what make the music go good together, when two people face playin together. One dont quick ta hurry the other one. I keep right wit im, an he stay right wit me. I'm watchin him closern he thank I am. If he a little off, I come right back an connect wit im. See, we nated ta one another, played together. We keep that music goin to an fro together.

We was ta learn how ta play music in the style what we come out with: thats the reason they call it folk song. We learnt how ta play music wit sumpm that you could feel good, after you heard it. Or while you was hearin it.

We wadn goin jest out fur noise an hootin an hollerin. We had sumpm that we wanta put wit that music, ta brang yo attainsion. You kin be studyin ta what I'm doin or not, but you gonna pay attainsion to it if you like the sound of it.

Yeah fur a little while, I was strummin along backin Daddy up. An thats what I'm doin now. If I was goin by my age an what I done done, I'd be dead. But two thangs car- ryin me: this head remembrance. An these fangers have got good reaction in em. But these old fangers here, if some- body cut one off, I'm done.

The people that stay here an see me ever day: they dont thank I could play no music. Cause I never did carry my gittah ta town an try ta git on the streets. Only way you catch me, I'm playin at some club.

What you call a club now, we called em Satiddy Night Dances. Dance all night long. I had three crews ta interpe- tate with: The first crew was eight o'clock. I played a hour fur them. They had everthang in the bloom! Long about twelve o'clock, here another crew come in there. Fresh crew! I fan them outa there. Played all night til foe o'clock in the mownin, sometime eleven o'clock on a Sunday. Set- tin right in one chair.

Now when I gits ta playin, I go out a the bounds a rea- son. Cause when I stawt, I dont like ta stop. As long as it look like they payin attainsion ta me, I kin jest play all night fur em.

Finely, somebody had ta die ever Satiddy night. Somebody gonna git kilt. An I had ta git up under the bed ta stay safe. Git ta shootin over my head. Long bout twelve or one o'clock, you hear a gun somewhere, in the house or out the house: "Boom!" Somebody died.

One night I never will furgit it. They had me settin up there in a house winda: you used ta build them houses in the bottoms so the concrete'd be high, so the water couldn float in em. An wadn no lectric lights, had old lamp lights. No lectricity. No fan. An I'd git down there an set by that winda ta git a little air. Lot a nights I played all night long, didn have nothin on but my pants. No shirt at all. Jest sweaty as I could be. Tryin ta stay cool.

An this fella had done got drunk, an he stawted shootin iny whichaway. Had everbody duckin an crawlin behind does an under the table. One a them shots went right through my hat. Hat jest *flew* off the top a my head an I fell out the winda an crawled under the house befoe the next un git me show nuff.

An so, Mama heard them shots. An she knowed I was playin over there. Direckly, here she come arunnin, say, "Where my son at?"

Say, "Mama Janie, Courtney went ta shootin an Mance fell out the winda. You didn see im out there?"

Mama say, "Ohh Lawd! They done kilt my son!"

An so, the fella what done the shootin—name Charlie Thornton, we called im Courtney cause he was raised in Courtney—he say, "No, Mama Janie. I jest creased his hat. You know I wouldn kill yo boy. We's great friends, Mama Janie."

"Ohh! Aw Lawd! My boy's dead! Done kilt my son!" an all like that.

An so, I heard ever word they said, but I kep alayin right there, under the house. I wadn gonna move til they had thangs settled down. Cause I knowed Courtney wouldn a done it fur a purpose, but aint no tellin what a man do when he gits ta drankin.

Direckly, I say, "Here I is, Mama. I layin here up under the house. I'm all right."

She say, "Whynt you tell me you was down under there? An me out here, hollerin an goin on about my boy's done died!"

Yeah! I was playin all my life, but right round in my precinct. An them Satiddy Night Dances, it wadn preferred until Satiddy night. Cause we workt five days an six days a week.

Then I was ready ta come home an git ready ta take my little old gittah: walk five miles, ride five miles, cordin ta how fur I had ta go. But they gonna git me there some way or other. Ta hold that gang.

Yeah, them people would do all kinda dances behind my music. Waltz, slow drag, two-step. An then the one-step, swing-out, ballin the jack, buzzard lope, wringin the chicken's neck. Cakewalk come in somewhere in the midst a all that. Caint furgit that Charleston in there. Oh, buck dance was a little like that buzzard lope. An then, we had the blues.

The blues was an original type a dance, see. You was out there in the woods dancin. An when I'm playin them, we called em breakdowns: hurry up an dance an hurry up an be in the moods, swingin—used ta have a dance called swing-out? But now that wadn no kind of a blues dance.

Blues is something you should be payin tension to it. You set an listen ta the verses that you sangin the blues about. Some a them verses you put in there will reach somebody's feelin, what done hapm ta them. Some a their people that they know. Yo loved one, place you wanta go an caint go. Thangs you wanta do an caint do it. You got ta set an concentrate on the blues. It puts you ta thankin. Study slow. Thankin over thangs.

Blues is a slow step. Take it, an jest move around on the flow. An you caint dance it fast, cause blues not sposed ta be played fast. Jest be swingin around, an hold on ta yo podna, she holdin on ta you. An go around maybe two steps thisaway, an turn around, an dance back ta this forward step, an turn around an go back yonda a ways, to an fro. Blues is a slow motion.

I dont like ta play blues until somewhere along about twelve or one o'clock. Because, I'm got a blues feelin along about that time a night. An I kin memorize all a those verses. I kin sang blues, an put maybe fifteen or twenty verses inta one song.

Well now, if you wanta know what my sangin is, jest folla me from the stawt. Ever song I sang, I put verses in there ta reach somebody's feelin. See I conadick, in my mind, how ta make you feel sad or happy, with the words I place in my mouth.

Then you got ta take a song an itemize yo verses so they comepair—make a connection together. Aint no connection, aint nothin. You got ta place words wit a pencil, you dont git no suction outa it. Cause you jest write it! You dont feel good behind that writin.

An then where I could git so much kick outa it, an the people git so much kick outa what I'm doin: I got them words paired an stuck together. I got sumpm that'll match up ta ever verse I sang. Will fit in there. An I got some meanin ta ever verse I match up.

Jest like I said, "Baby, please dont *go*. Back ta New Orleans, cause I love you *so.*" You see how they sound? Sound like I'm sayin the same thang if you dont watch.

Then I say, "I blieve my man done *gone*—an I say that two three times in the song—"Back to the county fawm he's got his shackles *on.*" See how that sound match up? Ta them verses?

Call that song "Baby Please Dont Go." I pickt that up off a Vick Torrey, long about foedy or foedy-two. We called em juice boxes. An I had about fifteen cents in my pocket. I walkt up ta Brenham, an heard that played, it was jest about near finisht. An I liked it. I put another nickel in there ta play it, from stawt ta finish. See I didn git the chance ta play a song over once or twice. Twice ta the highest befoe I learnt it. An when I come home that day or night whenever I got home, I got the gittah an played it.

Well now peoples, they git me on the stage, they look in my face an say, "Thats a man looks like he sincerely in the way he's doin." I'm is! People kin tell yo expression. Say, "Now I like ta look at that man. What he sangin is jest as pure as he'd spittin it outa his mouth. He caint be makin up them verses, unless they was truth." An you kin hear it.

See, all my songs are what you call True Story Songs. Life Story Songs. That music was jest in my mind ta learn it, cause I like it. If you like a thang, it'll folla ya. If you jest pick up sumpm as a habit, you kin soon furgit about it. Thats how most music oughta be workt up: if you play sumpm the way you like it, somebody else gonna like it, cause its comin direckly from you. Then its gonna run through ya, see. It means sumpm to ya, an you kin hand it ta the individual.

But now a song if it dont have no feelin: well, you dont feel nothin from it when the fella hands it to ya. Its kind of dead. I been playin my songs maybe foedy years. An when I go, there wont be the blues that you hear me play on my issues. It wont sound like me. They'll be mostly writin. There's mighty few people gonna have the feelin—the worryin—because people dont take worry now. They git through what they gonna do right in a minute. They rush theyself. Its so fast movin now. They dont take time ta learn the feelin a what blues is.

Well, you might say blues wadn nothin but a cow huntin fur a calf. She lowed down in the field somewhere, jest bawlin ta brang her calf back around her. Well, she look fur her calf, she's worried about im. She had it inside a her she wanta find her calf. Thats a feelin she had. Thats what you call the calf blues. Not the people blues. When she find that calf, why then she satisfied. You got ta be unsatisfied ta have the blues.

PART TWO:
BLIND SEEIN'S—GRAVE MARKERS, BLIND WILLIE, BLUE BRAKEMAN, AND MOJO HOODOO...TIME

Did I hear a Jimmie Rodgers? That yodellin man? Show! I coulda went up wit im, I blieve it was in 1922. Come through right down there in my town. Did a show. They wanted me ta go off wit im cause he had the T B. He give out sangin in about twenty minutes an he's all in fur his show. But I sided it wadn none a my time ta go off like Hamp an Richard Dean done.

Say, you heard a Leadbelly? He served his time right out in Sugar Land penitentiary, below Houston. No, I never did see im. I was scared a that man. He was down there, an I passt through there like a bird in the air! Cause I didn wanta meet them convicts.

Now, this fanger pickin—like Hamp and Richard Dean done—it goes this way. He that plays a clear music, sumpm like Elizabeth Cotton, she plays clear: "Freight Train"— thats pickin fangers. An Mississippi John Hurt: "Stagger Lee" an "Candy Man." He picks that, jest clear. He was a good little thumb picka like myself. See, all that Mississippi stuff, [he had it behind] jest like I had that music here.

Its a very few fanger pickas. Its a lot a people kin code an strum an make notes an sang. But they caint correspond that sangin with they playin. Fanger pickas are: gittah say what yo mouth say. Yo mouth say what yo gittah say. An they kin be playin what you hear, an you kin hear it plain from the strangs as well as you kin from their mouth.

You hear me do that song "Rock Me Mama" in the old style? Me an a boy in Dallas composed that song. It is varied in a whole lot a ways. Some people would tempt playin it, but they's not playin it.

Now you see this slide here? Watch me. [Mance plays slide guitar style, similar to his technique on "Motherless Chillun Sees a Hard Time."] I put all that there myself. I'm movin about up an down on that neck. See, you've got ta feel these thangs. If it aint in you, it caint come out ya. Them boys look at me an say, "I wouldn play a gittah hawd as you fur nothin."

Thats where I git rid of em. See, they caint bass an lead ta save their lives. They got ta have a bass gittah, an a lead, an a man ta sang like I'm sangin. I'm three man deep. An aint but one man doin it. An then I'm foe man deep cause I'm keepin my beat goin, on them bass strangs jest like they got anothuh man beatin the drum. I'll do all of it. See, I plays lead wit my fangers an bass wit my thumb. Well, you got ta learn what you kin transact yo fangers, do diffunt thangs wit yo fangers. Its a whole lot a ways ta play that gittah.

You git out here an hear these people thats out makin big money. They really kin play, but they not doin what I'm tellin you. They usually leave off one part of it. They leave off the playin an sang better, or if they playin good they caint sang good while they playin.

You might have a record here by B. B. King. He is the best songster, of a *man,* that ever you heard. He got a clear voice. Change his voice high an low. See he practices that, an then he's united in it. It is inbred in him. Some people was bawn fur good songsters. Some people was bawn fur good players.

Yeah, he's as good a songster as I wanta set an listen to. But when he's sangin, his band is playin. An when he's playin, why, he's not sangin. You dont hear his mouth at all. You hear the gittah makin codes. Then he come right back an go ta sangin, an his gittah is in his hands. You dont know where they's at, but they's not on the gittah. An he got a way a doin that: if you dont know whats goin on, you jest guessin at what he's doin.

But now that Blind Lemon Jefferson, he sung what he pickt an pickt what he sung. When I was out there hearin im play, I was gittin some lowdown on what he was playin, try ta estimate how he was doin it. He played broken time. An you know what I learnt about Blind Lemon? How miny verses he would add to a song. I wadn crazy bout his music, I was crazy about the verses he had in there. See, I'm goin straighten them verses out an brang some time back ta the people.

"See ta My Grave Kep Clean"—thats the one I wanted ta learn, an I learnt it. That was the best song that I ever got in the foe years I go up there, to an fro ta hear im play. You say Dylan had that on his first album? M-hm. Well, I'll say.

So, I went ta listen at Lemon in Dallas. But he come up in a little old country town called Wortham. Up there tween Corsicana an Ennis. Maybe about fifteen stows in it. In the cotton country.

I played fur his tombstone mawka, when he was buried foedy-two years. Foe years ago [1969], people in Austin state git it ta him. Gold grave mawka, about that high. An I sposed ta play fur Leadbelly's sometime.

I dont know how they got holt a me. But they knowed me over my reputation. Publicity. An people say, "We heard that you could play some a his numbas." Which I only knowed two of em: "Out an Down" an "See ta My Grave Kep Clean." I knowed those two songs perfect.

An there was about five hunnud whites, an somewhere about twenty coloreds. An they had a mournin tent from here ta that road over there. It was rainin all that day.

Mista Lomax—John Lomax, Junior—sent by here an

got me ta go wit a man an a woman up there. I didn know where I was goin, but they had done sponsored me ta go up there an play over his grave.

So, well I went on inyhow, an they said, "Dont be no slacker. You knowed Blind Lemon, an they know that. An they want you ta play one song: 'See ta My Grave Kep Clean.' " See, he didn play it like I plays it. He had foe verses in there: Says, "One kind favor I askdid you. When I'm dead will you please, see ta my grave kep clean." Next one say, "Two white hawsses side n side gonna take me on my farewell ride." Now say, "When you hear that church bell tone," he compete that twice. An in between time he makes the gittah say "Blum, Blum, Blooommm" like a church bell sound. An say, "You know by that somebody's dead an gone." Well that the completement ta that verse. An then the foeth verse say, "Want you ta dig my grave, both wide an deep. An put a tombstone at my head an feet."

An he could show sang that. He wadn a gittah picka, he was a good songster. He could pick his voice inyway he wanta, jest like Lightnin Hopkins. See, his mouth carries him.

Now, I'm got about ten mow verses, so I kin keep asangin it. Then I'm got the time, an the time beat, where somebody kin have a motion. They dont hafta dance, jest set there an motion.

See, I put "Aint it hawd" as the first verse. Thats the name Chris Strachwitz give it on my first issue. An say, "Aint it hawd, but its true, that you kin love someone dont love you."

An make it stretch out long as I wanta. An comepair every verse. If I dont comepair em, I aint made nary verse: "I got a mother an father, both dead an *gone*." Thats the beginning. Say, "An left me here in this wide world a*lone*." You done made em match up. You not ended a verse til you went an make a comparement to it.

Blind Lemon put it out in nineteen-seventeen. He sung it

in his way, but he played it in a C code. He played most a
his music in C code an E. An I tuck thisun an rearranged it,
an put it in the A code. Wit a sad sound to it:

[Mance plays his arrangement of "See ta My Grave Kep
Clean":]

Aint it hawd, aint it hawd, aint it hawd,
Aint it hawd, everbody know its true.
Aint it hawd, aint it hawd, everbody knows its true,
You kin love someone an they dont love you.

Sometime, sometime, sometime,
Sometime, I thank my girl's too good ta die.
Sometime, I thank my girl's too good ta die.
Then again I thank she should be buried alive.

Wonder where my friend done gone?
Wonder where my friend done gone?
She went away, in the fall, didn come back home at all.
Where you went away, an you stayed so long?

Got a mother an a father both dead an gone,
My mother an father, both dead an gone.
Got a mother an father, both dead an gone,
An they left me in this wide world alone.

An the last word I heard Mama say,
The last word I heard my mother say,
She's layin down, on her dyin bedside,
Says, "Son, I dont want you ta weep an cry.

There's one mow kind favor I'll ask of you,
Just one mow kind favor I'll ask of you,
When I'm dead, Son, sleepin in the ground,
Will you see to my grave kep clean?

Want you ta dig my grave, wide an deep,
Want you ta dig my grave, Son, both wide an deep
Please dig my grave, son, both wide an deep
Put a tombstone at my head an feet.

When I'm dead an gone, dead an gone,
I want you ta dig my grave wide an deep

Then two, threes foe, jest ta let me down
An someone to sing a song."

An I played it right over Mista Woody Guthrie's birthday, about a year ago. I didn know he knowed me. But he
wrote about diffunt people in some a his scrapbooks. An
after he died, his wife went through the scrapbooks, an she
called me through by a fella who stayed at Oklahoma City.
She says, "You heard tell of a man called Mance Lipscomb?"

An he says, "Well, Mance done played here foe or five
time."

Said, "I lookt over my husband's papers, an seed
Mance's name on there. I'd love ta git him ta come up here
an play a song, an give Woody a birthday party. Kin you
git in touch wit im?"

An he got right on the phone an called me. Told me said,
"Miz Guthrie wants you ta come up here a certain day.
She'll pay yo way up here on a airplane. Plus yo airplane
ticket you git a hunnud an fifty dollas."

I said, "Well, I dont mind comin up there," cause I
knowed the fella what I was goin ta see. I hadn never seed
Mista Woody.

An she was late gittin there that Sunday evenin. She had
about eighteen people playin in a band. Givin him a birthday party. An I dont know fur show but the people told me
she was out a nine hunnud dollas on that birthday party.
Food, dranks, an passpoats an everthang gittin em there,
to an fro.

See, Woody made so much money, in the go-along she
never will give outa money. An they tell me he died in
sixty-six. He's well thoughta man. Everbody likes im.
Least I did, an I never met im. He could make a dog laugh
at im. He crackin some jokes an says thangs over the radio.
I hear people laughin fur an near.

But I was up there ta the house eatin dinna, an carried

215

my gittah up there. Ta meet her. She had a showfur drivin her. He show got a nice-lookin little wife. Yeah, she come ta me an say, "Is this Mance?"

I say, "Yes."

Say, "I want you ta play one a them old sad songs."

I say, "What you wanta hear?"

" 'See ta My Grave Kep Clean.' "

I sot there an got about midways of it. An the water jest comin out her eyes. She's facin me jest like you are. An I was right down on it, I knowed I gonna give it a best I had.

An got so sad she walkt away. An she stawdid into her room, a fella caught her about her awm an said, "Miz Guthrie, dont cry."

She turnt right round, snatcht loose from im an said, "Let me cry! I come here ta cry."

An she come right back an facin me, an when it come the last verse I played, she's there ta end it. She said, "Mance, thats all I wanta hear." She wanted a one specialfied man ta play that one song fur her.

Lemme see. Was another blind fella, retcht in here an played on the streets in my hometown: Blind Willie Johnson. I got some a his songs. Oh yeah, I was a kid, in the teenage, maybe in nineteen-sixteen. He come from Marlin or Houston or somewhere.

Cause he was travelin, an he come ta Navasota—him an another blind fella follad one anothuh—oh, he was a dawk fella, I furgit his name. But I knowed Willie Johnson. He could sang all those verses, but he couldn play the gittah: he'd put it outa tune, an I'd tune it up fur im.

An they give him a privilege ta go ta play, make his nickels on a Satiddy, on the streets. Now if he wadn a blind man, they wouldnt. Like I'm a man who was workin out on the fawms? If I played inywhere, it'd be out in the bottom or out in the woods.

See now, people could say Lawd was cruel an critical.

But I dont care, you caint prevail against God Amighty, did you know that? Who put him on the street? God Amighty put im there. He didn know whether he gonna git there, but he askt permission: Could he sang on the streets? Where people could hear im? An if he wouldn playin spiritual songs, religious song, the Lawd wouldn let im git on the street.

An they say, "Well, yeah. You blind. You kin have the corner at Tex's Radio place," thats what they call it now.

Why they done thataway? You figger yo own mind, an reaction: If you find a fella blind an couldn see ya, you felt sorry fur im, wouldn ya? Well. Thats why they was better ta him, because they felt his sympathy. Couldn a done no other thang but jest say, "Well, he caint see how ta walk, caint see how ta work. Caint do nothin but jest talk an eat. We'll hafta allow him a show."

Yeah, I found im at Tex's Radio. Across from where the bank used ta be at. Right there where he was standin ever Satiddy, until he moved away from here in a diffunt town. He sided he could do better, an he moved up.

He'd come right there on the corner, an he had people from here ta the highway. Jest hunnuds a people standin right there on the streets. White an black. Old colored folks an young ones an all. Listenin at his voice.

An how he got nated ta me, he ask, "Was inybody here could play a gittah?"

An lot a them people pickt me out say, "Yeah! Here's Mance Lipscomb. He kin play purdy good gittah."

Say, "Tell him come up here an tune up my gittah."

An so, I went over there an squeezed through the gang. He couldn see me, he jest hear me walkin. An I walkt up an touch im, say, "Mista Willie, I'm the boy come ta tune yo gittah up fur ya. If you will let me."

He say, "Come on! Yeah! Who is you?"

An I told im my name; he never did furgit it. I didn play

much, but I knowed how ta tune it up. An ever Satiddy, if I was late gittin there, he'd ask people where was Mance Lipscomb at.

He had a old rough gittah. It was rusty as a terrapin. A old piece a gittah wit holes all in it. Somebody may a give it to im, he jest out tryin ta make a livin.

An where he's made it then is sangin an playin. People put nickels in his cup an give im a little pocket change. He had a wire around the neck a his gittah, wit a handle on it. You'd drap a nickel in there, an then he'd play anothuh song, people'd go up ta him drap their nickels in there. An when he'd git some mow in that cup, he'd reach in there an git it out an put it in his pocket.

He was a real good songster. He wadn a gittah player. Ooo yeah, loud voice. Lookt like he was wholesome, he could hoot so. I done hear im sang so miny times I jest look fur im when I'd go ta town, cause I stayed there in the country, a mile an a half outa town where I was bawn.

The reason I know he musta been travelin: he skipt Satiddys. Cause he need be in Hempstead, twenty-five miles from Navasota this Satiddy, an come back here the next Satiddy. He jest moved about. People'd carry him, put im on a train, wadn miny caws. He go over where he wanta go. He went fur half fare: blind, mm-hm. An sometime they'd let im go fur nothin.

An so, he had that other blind fella travelin wit im. Yeah, they'd caught holt a one anothuh an walk with sticks. An then they'd ask people when they'd stop. "Which a direction that I'm goin?"

An somebody said, "Well come on, I'll carry ya there." An they'd lead em about. Sometime one be holdin this blind man, one on this side holdin the othun. They had a great respect fur im.

Johnson put out "Motherless Chillun." An I pickt it up from him. An then he sang other spiritual songs, but all his songs didn blong ta him. He got em from somebody else, see.

Like that song *"Titanic:* God Moves on the Water." Well, I heard him first in sangin it. That where I learnt it from. But anothuh blind fella from Houston put that song out. An I didn know that til about ten years ago.

He jest sung "Motherless Chillun" an *"Titanic,"* an this song about "He's a dyin bed maker. Jesus gonna make up yo dyin bedside." Now he sung them three.

Now I give you the understandin ta what I'm fixin ta play: "Motherless Chillun Sees a Hawd Time, When Yo Mother's Dead." Nobody treat you like yo mother did. Yo mother is the best friend, young man, you ever will have. Cause see, aint nobody in the world, *out* the world kin take Mother's place.

Now listen. That song is true: an say, "Yo father will do the best he can. But its so miny thangs Father caint understand." Is I'm tellin you right? Its so miny thangs a father caint answer as a mother. He kin go so fur as a father's wills an reaction. But he caint be nothin but a father. An this song is tuned in Spanish:

[Mance plays his version, in D tuning, of "Motherless Children Sees a Hard Time":]

Motherless chillun sees a hawd time, when their mother is
    dead,
Motherless chillun sees a hawd time, when their mother is
    dead,
Wanderin round, doe ta doe, jest dont know which way ta go.
No one else kin take yo mother's place, when yo mother is
    dead.

Yo wife or ya husband may be good to you, when yo mother is
    dead,
Wife or yo husband may be good to you,

Wife or yo husband may be good to you, nobody treat you like
  yo mother do.
No one else kin take yo mother's place, when yo mother is
  dead.

Some people say yo sister will do, when yo mother is dead,
Some people say yo sister will do, when yo mother is dead,
Some folks say sister will do. Soon as she married turn her
  back on you.
No one else kin take yo mother's place.

Some folks say yo auntie will do, when yo mother's dead,
Some folks say yo auntie will do, when yo mother's dead,
Some folks say yo auntie will do. She'll make a stawt, an prove
  untrue.

Yo father will do the best he can, when yo mother is dead,
Yo father will do the best he can, when yo mother is dead,
Father will do, best he can. So miny thangs father cant under-
  stand.
No one else kin take yo mother's place, when yo mother is
  dead.

Jesus will be a father fur you, when yo mother is dead,
Jesus will be a father fur you, when yo mother is dead,
Jesus will be a father fur you, through pain an sorra, lead you
  through.
Motherless chillun sees a hawd time, when their mother is
  dead.

Yeah well, I didn *steal* it. But I learnt that from Blind
Willie Johnson. An I got other pieces I learnt myself: *"Titanic."* Course, he played it.

But where I got it: was a diffunt blind man lived in Houston. He couldn play a lick. An he couldn read, but his wife
read it off a newspaper, he would rememorize it, an he
made him a song out of it. Cause he got the schedule of it
an made the verses comepair. An he made a record of it.

I never did meet im. I met his wife, after he was dead. An

we had a hootenanny goin in Houston? In nineteen sixty-two. An Mack McCormick, he stayed in Houston an he knowed this woman.

So he carried me down there, an I didn know the setup. I played around on the stage, an Mack McCormick come up an say, "Mance, I want you ta play 'The *Titanic.*' An when you stawt ta playin, I'm gone represent his wida an his daughter ta git on the stage, an set side a you an let you play it so they kin hear it."

I say, "Well, git em up here."

So, he pronounced that I was fixin ta play "The *Titanic.*" Here they come up on the stage an one got on one side an one got on the othun, I'm in the middle of em. I tuned up the gittah, an stawted ta playin, I knowed ever verse. An knowed ever angle on the gittah. An *she* knowed ever verse.

An she sot there an cried like a baby. She knowed her husband wrote that song, by his mind, an what she read it off to im. So here's "The *Titanic.*" I'm gonna show ya all them good codes:

[Mance plays his version, in D tuning, of "God Moves on the Water" ("The *Titanic*"):]

On the foeteenth day of April, year of nineteen-twelve,
When the *Titanic* struck a iceberg, almost too sad ta tell
God moves, God moves,
God moves on the water. Oh, the people had ta run an pray.

Titanic was sankin. They put lifeboats all around,
Says, "An save the women an chillun, Jesus let the men go
    down."
God knows, God moves,
God moves on the water. Whoa, the people had ta run an pray.

When the lifeboats got ta the landin, the women rusht around
Sayin, "Look out on the ocean. Look at all the men go down."

Mance in Houston, 1962, with Hootenanny poster. *Photo by Ed Badeaux.*

God, God moves,
God moves on the water. Oh, the people had ta run an pray.

Captain he was layin down, asleep cause he was tired,
Woke up in a great fright, cause aminy gunshot was fired.
God moves, God moves,
God moves on the water. Whoa, the people had ta run an pray.

(Spoken: Millionaire on that boat. He didn know what he's
   doin, he thought he knowed.)
Jacob Astor was a millionaire. Had plenty money ta spare.
When the *Titanic* was sankin, Lawd, he could not pay his fare.
God, God moves,
God moves on the water. Oh, the people had ta run an pray.

Now thats what you call spiritual songs. But a ragtime player is a git in the mood, we'll git ready ta dance purdy briefly. Its not no slow motion. They really dancin fast with that ragtime player.

That ragtime come in here in a cawnival. Barnum and Bailey? They had a clown ta git on the stage, an sang an play like that song "Hesitatin Blues"? An "Alabama Bound." See, I jest pickt up my gittah an strum along til I got it, oh, ranged where I want it.

Because all a my songs dont estimate in the same style an the same sound. See, thats why I jump back an maybe I jest play me a song from Blind Blake's: Everbody likes that song about "Keep on Truckin Little Mama." Thats a dance song. He playin it in a ragtime style. Well I'm feelin like somebody's gonna dance behind me, I aint *got* no blues.

Thats right. Now, you take Lightnin Hopkins: he's a E man. He's a great friend a mine. That rascal kin sang. He gonna run you crazy with that E stuff. He kin play E code good as he wanta. An everthang that have iny kind a sense to it, in a way of a git by, he gonna play in E. An maybe sometime in A.

He kin play them songs an he mix em up so bad you'll thank he playin five thousand songs. But you know how miny songs he sangin? Dont y'all tell im cause I might see im, an he'd kill me. He's sangin two songs! Cause words dont mean music: music got ta be changed by diffunt codes. See. You git the song, by sounds a the ear, you kin listen to em.

Ohhh, I first met Lightnin in nineteen thirty-eight, I blieve. In Galveston. Mm-hmm. My sister an brother, who is a twin ta my baby sister, they live in Galveston maybe thirty-five or foedy years. Call em Coon an Pie. Willie an Lillie fur a real name. An my brother got some kids, they my nieces an nephews. So I go ta Galveston very often.

An so Coon run around an he loved ta drank, say, "Lets go out an hear Lightnin Hopkins."

So I went in the place where he playin, I blieve it was on Thirty-third Street. They had the house loaded up.

So I scootcht in there an sot down right by im. He had heard a me, but he didn know me. I didn say nothin to im, an he didn say nothin ta me, cause too miny people fur us ta git ta talkin an goin on wit one anothuh. An I didn want him ta know me nohow. So I sat, catcht on what he was doin.

He had a lectric gittah that you plug in. Had his boots on. Had one a his legs down in his boot, the other one was down here. Had nice clothes, an he made a lot a money. They's payin im somewhere long about one hunnud dollas a night. That was real good money in them times.

So his sister was standin there an lookin at what he was doin. She's a tall woman. She lookt at me, an somebody told her who I was.

She told Lightnin, "Brother? You got ta play this gittah. You settin beside a famous man."

He lookt around at me, said, "Who's—what famous man? I aint scared a nobody."

Say, "You liable ta be scared a this man. Do you know who he is?"

He said, "No, I dont know who he is an damn if I care."

She say, "Thats Mance Lipscomb."

He jumpt up out his chair an shook hands wit me. Said, "I'm sorry I said that about you. I'm gonna let you play a numba."

I said, "No, I dont wanta play. You gittin paid."

An a boy from my hometown here in Navasota—raised up wit me—he said, "Lightnin? I'll give you a dolla ta let Mance play his Bumble Bee."

An so Lightnin got mad, cause he know he couldn play it. He said, "You oughta be walkin while ya talkin. I aint gonna loan Mance my gittah."

He say, "Well, I know you aint gonna loan it to im. But I'll rent it."

"I aint gonna rent it to im. Now when I git through playin here tonight, if Mance wanta go home an stay all night wit me, I'll let im go home wit me."

I said, "No, I'm right across the street here wit my sister." So thats the first time I seed im. We remained good friends from then on. He come from Centerville, an drifted in over ta Conroe, that was on the direction a Houston. Then he stawted playin in Houston an got a big name out there, cause he had put out one or two albums.

How come he knowed me? Cause he got wind a my reputation. I played music around home: fifty miles. Twas nineteen fifty-nine, I believe, when I quit playin music way from home. You couldn git me no farther from down to a colored settlement called Whitley Bottom. Fifty miles away as fur as I reacht, until I went ta Galveston.

But I'm well experienced now. I've had fawchun-tellas wantin ta tell my fawchun. First thang he done, look in the palm a my hand—know what he said? Say, "You got a lot a sense. You hawd ta fool." Not one. Might near everone I've been round.

I blieve I jest had been married, aw bout three or foe years, when I seed a lot a people comin up an down the road in wagons with tents on em. Sometime you could see thirty or foedy wagons. You know what we called em? Called em campers. But they was fawchun-tellas then. They got by tellin fawchuns fur foe bits or a dolla or whatever you had. But we never did deal wit em. We jest pulled em out a bog. Wit our mules.

An Mama would go out ta the road we stayed on, an they'd git talkin ta her. First thang you know, they'd look at her big heads a greens in the gawden. An they'd ask fur greens, Mama give em a croakasack. Everbody knowed her: if she was at the position, she'd divide inythang. She was the successfullest gawdna ever I been around.

Roastin ears. Irish potatuz. She had cushaws, them old big squashes? Everbody had greens ta go away. She had some kinda greens from one end a the year ta the othuh. Them campers, they'd come by there week ins an out. Maybe the same people that went around, come back the same way. Had borried or beg her out a some greens.

So I was grown an my boy he was somewhere along about seven or eight years old, when I got nated they was fawchun-tellas: I was ridin a little old gray hawss. An we had ta work in the road, free. If you twenty-one years old, you hafta give two days' work a year on the road. Ya didnt, they'd charge ya so much; you know penalty. That or either hire somebody ta work in yo place.

[From Mance's version of "Rocks and Gravel":

Rocks an gravel, make a solid road.
Takes a do-right woman, ta satisfy my soul.]

So I was goin up the railroad track an met them campers. They had some hawsses an thangs down in the right a way, that was the old public highway, An they come up ta the railroad, an cut me off on the hawss. And askt me where was I goin. I didn know what they's up to.

One say, "Gimme a cigarette."

I never will furgit it. I hand her my Prince Albert can, an while I give it ta her: See I'm talkin to anothun an she tuck it an put it in her bosom. An I'm lookin right at her.

But I hadn had sense enough or I couldn protect it—she had me hypnotized, ya know. I was watchin one from the othun, but I wadn watchin the right one. But I see her where she put that bacca.

An she say, "I kin tell yo fawchun fur fifty cents."

I said, "Well, you caint tell it because I dont *have* fifty cents." An I had a fifty cents in my pocket.

An she knowed it. She said, "Yeah you got some money."

An she hit on the side a my pocket an I told her, "Dont! Dont put yo hand on me. Thats what I got is mine!"

An she said, "Yeah, but you better let me have that piece a money. All I wanta do put it in my hand, an that'll wish ya good luck."

I said, "Well if I got inythang I'm goin ta work an I'm gonna go buy me a lunch wit it. I aint got none fur you."

An, I stawted ta ride off, an she caught the bridle a the hawss. You know it had reins on it. An helt me back.

An I got mad then! I say, "You caint hold my hawss up an, an I got ta go ta work!" An I spurred the hawss, an pusht her down.

An went on up the road. An the people we was workin fur say, "You a little late, but you got a full day comin." See the other boys was workin when I got there.

An I said, "Well I got tangled up with them campers."

They said, "Them's fawchun-tellas, man. You dont know their ways? You got by lucky. Wonder they didn put their hand in yo pocket."

I said, "But I spurred my hawss an made the bridle pull them down, an left there lopin."

"I wish I had a been there. Halted you on the road like that? Yeah, I jest wish I had a been there fur that." Thats the white fella talkin. But what he wish fur I dont know. Say, "Them thangs aint no good. I'm gonna stop em from comin through there. I caint block the state highway. But I kin keep em off the place. They're tricky."

She knowed too good that that fifty cents was in my pocket. But she already seed it in her *view*. Called em a gypsy. They wouldn work. They go around tell fawchuns fur some bread in a paper sack, or whatever they could git. I reckon they was from Texas. They comin towards Dallas when I saw em. See, they didn stay out on that fawm cause wadn nobody let em stay on the fawm. Cause they'd steal everthang they could run across. Now thats what the first fawchun-tella come about wit my remembrance.

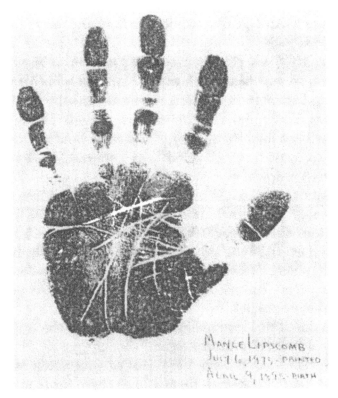

Mance's handprint. *Lipscomb/Alyn Collection, Center for American History, University of Texas at Austin.*

An then after I got grown, them kinda thangs com-
menced in here again. From people goin ta diffunt towns,
diffunt places: ta git the Mojo, what you hear that song
Lightnin sangin? "I'm goin ta Looziana an git me a Mojo
Hand?" An now you tell me if this dont sound sumpm like
Lightnin aplayin it:

[Mance plays his version of Lightnin' Hopkins' "Mojo
Hand" (also called "Goin to Looziana"):]

I lay down thankin bout a Mojo Hand,
I lay down thankin bout a Mojo Hand.
Fix my woman so she caint have no other man.

Dont let yo woman fix you like mine done me,
Dont let yo woman fix you like mine done me.
Mine got me crazy, I'm a fool as I kin be.

I'm goin ta Looziana, git me a Mojo Hand,
I'm goin ta Looziana, git me a Mojo Hand.
Gonna stop my woman from foolin wit anothuh man.

My Mojo's workin, my Mojo's workin,
My Mojo's workin, my Mojo's workin,
My Mojo's workin, jest wont work on you.

I'm goin away, wont be gone long,
I'm goin away people, wont be gone long,
Git a little Mojo Hand, brang my woman back home.

My Mojo's workin, jest wont work on you.
My Mojo's workin, jest wont work on you.
Woman, you aint done nothin in this world I told you ta do.

Now, if rocks was my pilla, green grass was my bed,
If rocks was my pilla an green grass was my bed,
That wadn no place fur me ta lay my head.

I hate ta see the evenin sun go down,
I hate ta see the evenin sun go down.
Put me on a wonder, I thanks about my brown.

Well, I'll explain it best I know how. Now a Mojo, they call it sumpm like a Luck Hand. Luck Chawm. Go git a Gamblin Hand. I know where they go git em at. But now what they look like, I never went an got nary un. I seed people talk about they had em. I've seed the reactions of people change, when they commenced ta usin those thangs on em.

Lot a people go ta some parts a Looziana, caint walk, an come back walkin. People would ride away from Houston an Navasota an places like that, by the cawloads. Sometime it take em two days an nights ta git there.

Them people in Looziana, they bawn with that kinda stuff. From generation ta generation. Old people died, an trainin them young ones up. An next old people die, train they young one up.

I heard tell a people could go ta Looziana an git a Mojo Hand an do myaculls wit it. An some of em went there an didn git nothin but got their money tuck from em. It never did work. They may a not went ta the right place. You know Looziana a big state. Now what they doin I dont know, cause I never did deal wit em.

See, everbody try ta play two-headed over there. But you got ta go ta one is who able ta *do* those thangs. Well, befoe you git there you may meet a man, an said, "Is this the way to a Mojo place?"

An he say, "Yeah! I'm a Mojo Man." Or Mojo Woman. Well, he wadn that, but he take yo money off ya.

Well some people in Looziana kin do those thangs. Sometime it'll look like season. You kin put it in yo dranks. Put it in yo food. Thats the only way they kin git next to ya. Or sprankle some in yo hat or clothes. Call it goofer dust.

Thats when it take effect on ya: you wonder who put it on ya then, an they know about it cause they kin handle ya. Make you do what they say.

Whats that? No. You couldn git me ta blieve nothin

wrong about Jesus Christ. No, he didn have no Mojo. Thats unjest. Say fur an instant: yo got yo solid mind— listen good—got yo solid sense. An you an yo wife gittin along fine. An you say, "Well, I blieve I wanta git a Mojo on my wife. I kin handle her like I wanta, an she caint quit me. I'm goin ta Looziana an git me a Mojo Hand."

Well, if you set out ta go an somebody carry you the right direction, an to the right place, it *could* work on *you*. Its always somebody in the world kin do sumpm you caint do, an you kin do sumpm fur the next fella that I caint do. Jest like that woman in New Waverly. I dont know whether she got a Mojo, but she kin *act* like she got one. She got too miny clients comin ta her. A thousand people come ta her: she do her biggest operation on a Thursday, an when you got out ta her house, she might have somebody there. Wait-in on her. But you caint come in there until that un come out. An one right behind anothun. Thats from sunup til sundown.

You go over there, about two hours east from here, in the piney woods? She got a white house, sets in a clearin aside a the road back in there. Pine trees comin in all around there. An she got a sister, call her Estella, who *kin* see. She the one registers you. You give her a ten-dolla donation, an if you need inythang else, she'll tell ya then.

Yeah, me an another fella was settin out there amongst all them caws on the road an in her yawd. Some settin at the gate. He say, "If you leave here in the same shape you come here, I'll eat this caw."

An told me bout a man he knowed, was down an wouldn even come there. Couldn do nothin fur hisself. Wouldn let nobody do nothin fur im, wouldn do nothin but jest go on gittin worser an worser. An say, "You know, when a man feel thataway, its jest hisself."

I say, "I reckon it is."

An so, direckly it come up my turn. I went on into the house, an sot down in a little old room in there. She was on the bed an had a chair settin across from her.

I say, "You gittin along all right?"

She say, "I'm jest fine. You feel all right?"

"Aw, purdy good."

Well. The old lady kinda halfway hinted at what the cause was a this here irritation of skin I got. But she didn come out wit all of it, cause she had never completed her job. See, I got anothuh treatment over there. I done paid her fur three treatments, cost ya seventy-five dollas. Well, I let up on the last one.

An so, onlyest thang I tuck notice of was: she told me where my house was an how it faced. Say, "Yo house turnt east an west. You got a climber vine come up aside a yo winda where ya sleep. You got a live tree in yo yawd. An that fur as I'm goin tell ya."

Is it true? I'm tellin ya! There it is, comin in the gate: chinaberry tree. That give me some faith in her when she said that. Cause she must a not be guessin cause she aint been over here, an caint come over here less somebody brang her here cause she blind.

Well, she gimme some medicine ta take an some ta bathe. I didn git much results out of it as I wanted ta git, cause I didn have the space of time ta talk ta her like I wanta. Cause there's foedy or fifty caws settin in front a her house waitin fur my time ta come out so they could come in.

An fur her ta talk ta me like she *could* a talkt. She said, "You gonna have a whole lot a money comin ta you. You is a long liver. You is a real long liver."

An I says, "You reckon I'm Hoodooed?"

Settin there, she a two-headed woman. She laught at me. You know what she told me? She's blind as a bat: said, "They got ya, did they?"

I said, "Who got me?" An I couldn even walk!

She say, "But I'm gonna pull you through if its the last thang I do. You too good a man ta be in that shape. An when I cure ya, I'm gonna tell ya how it hapmd."

An she caint see a wink. She say, "Thats as fur as I'm goin tell ya. It gonna take some time. I caint cure you in one day. Cause its been on you about two years. Now its got ta work out, so I kin draw it out ya. An what they did: you was gittin out an makin money, an people went hawd a what you was doin. But I tell you one thang. When I cure you, they aint gonna have a chance ta do nothin else to ya. I'm goin cure ya fur good. You jest go ahead on an do like I tell ya. You caint walk now. But when you come back out here again, you gonna be walkin."

Cause next time I went out there, if I wadn walkin I aint talkin ta you. See, was a woman here in Navasota had done had a boy by me. A full-grown boy. An she died. An about two weeks after she passt, I went back an told her I thought *she* the one Hoodooed me.

Know what that blind lady done? Her name was Mawthy, she jest laught kinda like I didn tell her nothin she didn already know. An say, "Now listen, I work with the Lawd. I dont do no Hoodoo. I works wit God Amighty. He give me this gift. An I wouldn take it an spoil it, ta put no Hoodoo on nobody. Because God, he's not no Hoodoo. Now, I kin tell you whats gonna hapm."

An so, foedy-eight states jest a lot a places fur me ta go through with in this music bizniss, an got diffunt atmosphere ta hit you. Thats a lot a climates you done went through. You git in them high mountains, that air dont penetrate yo breath like it oughta. They call that: airritation.

An I went ta Los Angeles, an was a young docta there sposed ta be a skin special. I say, "You reckon I'm Hoodooed? Talkin bout goin ta Looziana an git me a Hoodoo Hand. Thats where it come outa, an moved on over into east Texas an places. May be sangin about the song, its already done hapmd ta me!

Its funny ta me they caint find nothin. So, look like ta my

knowins, sumpms hid behind em. Must be someplace they aint lookt, or either overlookin it, cause maybe you caint see it, I caint see it, doctas caint see it. But I kin feel it. Mm-hmm.

Yeah, the blind lady she really hinted my hat was dresst or could be dresst. Gots the Mojo stuff. Contactin yo skin or somewhere about yo body. If they sprinkle enough ta take effect on you, it'll make you sick or make sumpm hapm to ya one way or nother. Dust or grease or water or inythang what they wanta put in there.

What ya call Mojo. What kinda effect it take on ya: you in the habit ta let people put that stuff on ya, in yo feed, in yo dranks: you caint control yoself, caint hep yoself. You or nobody else. He not *of* hisself. Tamarra, he'd go the other way. He got ta do what *they* say.

See, they got they Mojo workin. It control him, like they want im. He got ta mind them, jest like one a my chilluns would mind me. He got ta dance round their music. Now understand what I'm talkin about? Once they git you hookt, you dont blieve what nobody tell ya. Its a powerful control they got on ya, man. They got the inside a yo mind an yo feelins. An yo head turnt, right the way they want it ta be turnt. After you git that stuff in ya.

But now, Miz Mawthy, she dont tell you everthang. You ask me these questions, dont you thank she know aaawll what we sayin? Right ta the table! You stawt ta tell her an she say, "Dont tell me inythang. You come here fur me ta tell *you*." An she says, "You been speakin about me. You an the fella you been talkin the tape on. But you didn say no hawm bout me."

Well, you dont blieve that. It look like I jest, dont it? You couldn pitcher that in yo mind that it was fair, that she knowed what we sayin an what we doin.

Well. I tell ya. If I dont git these doctas ta cure me, why, I got a treatment over there due me. She knows it. An she know I spoke well of her.

Cause you see, all my people worried me. Thought I wouldn git cured fast enough. What was happenin ta me, it didn hapm ta me yestiddy. It taken some time, ta try ta git rid of it, cause it tuck some time fur ta stawt it.

See? One mile from here ta Navasota. An one mile from Navasota ta here. Kin you pitcher that in yo mind now? It taken me two years ta inherit this stuff. Well now, I caint look fur it ta git rid a me in two days. Cause its taken jest as long ta git in it, an may take it the same distance fur it ta git out of me. Got ta work wit it. Give her the time, see. Nothin in the world beats time.

Saturday Night Suppers and Life Story Songs

$\mathcal{S}$aturday Night Suppers, also called Saturday Night Dances, were the seminal social functions where Mance created his unique style of country blues and where he developed a captivating, hard-driving blues style that was totally imbedded in dance steps and rhythms. Mance may have missed some notes in his guitar playing, but he never missed a beat. This sense of timing, partnership, and rapport with his dancers and audience, he shares with the best flamenco guitarists. The Saturday Night Supper was his domain and his training ground—and there he remained the top dog for a good thirty years. This "ace man in the precinct" also tells of his courtship of Elnora and of their marriage on December 13, 1913, the year of "the Over-flow," which flooded even Navasota.

In the sixth go-along, Mance geographically and musi-cally defines his precinct, or sphere of influence. He chron-icles the evolution of dance steps, from the barn dance or square dance era of his father to the rock 'n' roll "twist" era of the late 1950s. He describes every detail of the all-night social events where blacks cut loose in any way they could on their only night off: the music, dancing, food, sex, drinking, and gambling.

Up until the thirties, disastrous floods and near-death experiences were ever-present possibilities in Mance's pre-cinct. Ironically, while floods constantly endangered cot-ton crops and the people who lived in the Bottoms, they also replenished the soil with silt and maintained its fertil-ity and were, in that sense, the life of the community. With-out floods, the demands of cotton farming combined with poor soil management practices would have worn out the soil in less than twenty years. The cotton culture economy would have ceased to exist, as it did farther west where scant rain and scanter soil could not bear its burden.

"The Bluffs" is a hilly escarpment that runs for many miles, roughly between Giddings and Washington-on-the-Brazos, where the Texas Declaration of Independence was signed. It begins in the west where the Brazos River turns abruptly from its southward flow to nearly due east; the Brazos then curls south again and hugs the hills until the Navasota River runs into the Brazos at the southern end of Allenfarm. The section that faces Allenfarm is what is re-ferred to as the Bluffs or the Hill. This is where all the blacks living in the Bottoms would head when a flood wiped out the cotton crop and took their houses and worldly possessions, livestock—and usually some of their people—to the Gulf of Mexico.

Mance and his uncle Jim Oliver saved a few of them in their paddleboat. His wife, Mary, was Mance's mother's

Standing on the Bluffs, looking to the east over to Allenfarm, 1977. *Photo by Glen Alyn.*

sister. They will figure in a later go-along, where Mance relates how they helped free him from the status of non-landed peasant known in Texas as a sharecropper.

Until the mid-1950s, the Texas county prison farm system carried on a variant of the tradition in which a peasant was defined as a farmer who did not own land. Allenfarm was a county prison farm that maintained its own jail. Overlooked by the Bluffs, its fourteen-mile, nearly 20,000-acre plantation stretched along the Bottoms between the Brazos and Navasota rivers. At the heart of the three-county area Mance called his precinct, it cast a long shadow that weaves like these rivers all the way to the end of this book.

I PLAYED COLORED DANCES fur fifty-nine years. Listen, they thought much a me. I suited em. That was the people come up under me an little oldern me. Until sixty-nine. The time expired when the teenage commenced ta foolin around with that rock an roll.

Now fur all the people fur fifty-nine years, I was the big ace a this country. My wife'll tell you, if somebody couldn git *me,* they didn have no to-do goin on. Yeah, everwhere a Suppa was given: if I wadn there, it wadn no Suppa. They follad me, walkin miles an miles behind me, carryin that gittah ta play fur a Satiddy Night Dance.

Now the white folks, they had little parties an bahbe-cues out in the suburbs in the country. They'd git me ta play at bahbecues, an I'd play fur the white dances on Friday night. Mm-hmm.

A fella used ta come ta my house ever Sunday an play gittah all day wit me. His name was Rusty Black; he was Gus Black's boy. He was one a my greatest white friends. Til he went off in that war over there an got kilt. Never did come back.

Lemme see. They ended that first big war in nineteen-eighteen. Cause thats the first airplane I ever saw in my life, when they first had that awmy. We uz plowin right up the river, when I heard that noise comin. One a them little old light planes, ya know: "Shuhh-shudidl jiju jiju jijoo." It was maybe about thirty-five or foedy mens in the field, an all of us was lookin where that noise was an couldn see nothin. An when it come across the Navasot River an we could see it up in the sky, scared us an scared ever mule in the field! Maybe fifty mules run off. Yeah, I never will fur-git that. The mule drug the people by their hand down on the ground.

I had a pair a mules that I could corral purdy good. They lookt like they loved me. They broke ta run, an I hollad at em, "Whoa! Whoa! Whoa!" I could jest manage them. They didn drag me, but they run off where I couldn hold em. You could snatch on the line—that wouldn do no good, man. It broke the plows, an some a the mules got cut with the plows.

One plane would scare people ta death! You had ta be mindful how you was comin down the road wit a pair a mules or a wagon an team, or a buggy an hawss, a hawss an a saddle: when that plane would come over so scarcely once in a while, up in the air, man, you had some trouble on yo hands. They'd break an run, cause they didn know what that was. Til about five or six or seven years. See, when a caw commenced gittin in rotation.

First caw ever is run was a Model T. Henry Ford put it out. One doe over ta the right. The left side, wadn no doe over there. Stirrin wheel was over on the left side. I'm settin under the stirrin wheel, an a seat fur you ta sit over here ta the right. They had wooden spokes. Had twenty-inch rims. They put the air in the tire, an after that, that wheel was up above yo knee.

See it wadn no concretes them days. You go down the road, you run into a mudhole befoe you got there, why you stop that caw, put it in first gear. An give it speed, say, "Wwrdrdr drdrdr!" Man, it'd split that water wide open. Mud come on top a that doggone caw up there. Couldn stall that thang, man. It was built like a wagon nearly. But you had ta be in a hurry!

First caw I ever owned was a T Model. Mista Mobley, the man I went ta Courtney with, he sold me one, cause he goin git one a these here B Model Fords. He sold me that caw, I blieve, in nineteen an twenty-six. He done woe it out. Inyhow, I thought I was rich when he sold me that old caw.

He had done bought him a new one. About twenty-eight, here come the Model A. Thats the new caw come out; it'd make somewhere about foedy-five, fifty miles an hour. An boy we thought we was splittin the wind.

An this little old caw what he sold me, why, he goose up about thirty or thirty-five miles a hour. An, man, we thought we was show ridin.

Next one I got was a Hupmobile. They dont make em now. I'd say it was late twenty-nine I had a Hupmobile. Next one was Studebaker. Then from that to a twenty-nine

Mules and wagon pulling a car through a bog. *Photo courtesy the Marcus Mallard Collection.*

Buick. From that, I commenced ta gittin in a Shivolay.

An the next I owned, I blieve, I bought a late Studebaker. It was somewhere along in the foedies then. They commenced ta immigratin these caws in here, you know the people in furrin countries done woe em out an put em on caw lots. An we thought we was show gittin up in the air, buyin a caw was woe out. We didn know no better.

An that how I jest commenced ta gittin diffunt caws. What would hep me out so much: I always vouch around, play fur these Satiddy Night Dances. An make ten an twenty dolla sometime a night if they's white dances. An then I'd have that money ta buy them thangs.

But a man jest ordinary git out on the fawm, he couldn buy one. Cause he had ta feed hisself by what the landowner fed im outa. But I would git out an make purdy good money off these white dances, on a Sunday an Friday nights. An Satiddy night I was with the colored folk, makin five an six an seven dollas a night. That was a whole lot a money.

Yeah, I remember once, when I was gittin into the money: a white dance hired me at Courtney. An they passt my hat around ta pay me. Wadn no colored folks there but me, an I was playin fur em.

241

Thats the reason I know: it aint all white folks is mean. Cause a lot of em tuck care a me. I couldn went ta places if I didn have white friends. They would carry me ta play that music. An I always stayed in my place, ya see.

I tell y'all a joke on me. Ya know this is Texas. We have a divided line wit some of em down here. We couldn associate together. Cause if the white people had their dance, we couldn even come by there.

But I was one they *had* ta git come by there cause I was playin that music. One night they give a dance out in the place where they had a sign: "Dont allow no colored folks." An they come woke me up out the bed. It was rainin, an I didn know who it was. I was layin down, an this man had his daughter there. Now, jest like y'all young people wants ta learn how ta play this music, an you'd come ta my house? Well, they parents wouldn object to it, an they come over there: they comin ta my house fur two years while I learnt em how ta dance behind my gittah.

Well, they hired a buncha white people ta play in a band. They had a steel gittah an a fiddle an accordion. They wadn doin nothin but "Ohhhhahhh!"

"Go git Mance, Papa." The songs they was playin, them girls couldn catch on with they feets.

So he come over there an got me an woke me out the bed—the girl is settin up in the caw—I didn know, cause I wouldn a went out there in my underclothes. I say, "You all excuse me, I didn know who this was."

She say, "Thats all right. I come at you."

I say, "Well I caint go thisaway."

Went back an put on my clothes, an they carried me down there ta that deadline where they didn allow no colored people. Well they turnt that band off. An hired me settin up there, commenced ta playin fur em, an these girls commenced ta dancin. An they papa an mama commenced ta pattin, cause it was they party an they was glad ta see the kids enjoy it.

Well, those guys what they turnt off, they wanted ta break in the house on me. Run me away way from there. If I'd a knowed it, I might a been runnin yet. But they didn git ta me, them boys; they made em leave there. An man, we had a time there that night.

So, I come up under that ether. Didn know no better. An come a Satiddy night, we'd be at the Suppas. Aw man, you couldn never tell what them people was up to at them Satiddy Night Suppas. Everbody there little an low, big an wide's got em a half bottle a beer in their hand here, sayin, "Ahhhh! So-an-so an so-an-so!" "This an that! This an that!" "You bastud, you!"

Sometime they go ta fightin an shootin, I'd go ta gittin up under the bed. Sometime break a gittah over somebody's head. Break gittah strangs, tryin ta play so loud where all them people kin dance behind my music. Some of em out there tryin ta dance, an that drunk un out there pushin em off the flow.

They'll keep makin so much noise, they dont know whether I'm playin or not. An I tell em all the time, I say, "Y'all show do carry on to it. Ever since I been in the world wit you, you jest look like you git worser." When the crowds git so noisy, that culls ya down. But I've played places where you kin hear a pin drop. I kin play purdy briefly fur the people at those places.

Same songs you hear me play at folk festivals, nightclubs an thangs—where so miny white folks at? Well, thats same songs you'd hear me play fur them colored dances. Because these days they all nated ta the same thang.

Now when I first played fur white dances, I wouldn play no colored folks songs. Fur foedy years, I played all white songs: "You Got ta See Yo Mama Every Night, Caint See Yo Mama at All," an "Shorty George," an thangs like that. Love songs—"Shine on Harvest Moon" an "You Are My Sunshine." Oh, maybe foedy or fifty pieces I played was white.

Oh man, fifty an sixty an a hunnud white folks be there. Private home party. Uh-huh. Bahbecue hogs or goats. You give a party, next week somebody else give one. I wouldn charge em no certain profit. I made an agreement: "Would y'all pass the hat around? An take a collection thataway?"

Sometime they'd git foedy dollas. I'd have a hats full a money. They'd brang it in an set it down there aside a me, an here I been all that time, steady playin. All right, I git through playin, I empty the hat out.

I played, oh, it didn have no limit. From stawt ta finish. Yeah, they danced an ended up around one o'clock. They'd go home then.

But my Satiddy Night Dances, they'd last all night. An jest me an that gittah. I could set down there in this chair like I am now, play til tamarra mownin, ten or eleven o'clock on Sunday sometimes. Just gimme some coffee an gimme sumpm ta eat, an I'll set right here an play.

You caint give me out. I got too miny ways ta play. Learnt how ta rest my fangers, see. First thang I play in a G code. Next thang in a F code. An switch em around in a C code. My fangers dont never git tired.

But you put yo fangers in one position, you'll cramp ya hands up. When I first stawted out, I didn know but one or two songs: you git tired in yo wristiz an yo fangers.

Lemme see now. I was bawn on the Nickelburr Fawm. Then we left him an went ta Docta Emory on the same fawm. Diffunt people bought those planations. Then when I left there, I come ta White Switch over there ta Mobley. An them three pieces I've might near been in a ring all a my life: Washington County, Grimes County, an Brazos County. I filled in them three places, playin Suppas ever Satiddy night. An gittin a dolla an a half a night.

Left Mobley's an went ta Courtney. From Courtney back ta Washington County, where I stayed wit Johnny Sommers in foedy-five. All right, an then I stawted aplayin up there ta Mow Place, up until fifty-six: I played out there at Allenfawm. Ever Satiddy night. I make three an a half a night, an I thought I was makin money. I was at that time.

Yeah, colored folks, they want them there dancin songs, an blues. I'm the only one could suit the majority a people. Cause I played thangs that I knowed they like. I know what ta play an what not ta play.

But I didn mix up my songs with the white race, like I did the colored race. Cause they wadn no colored man in there but me. So I regarded myself on the way what the whites liked. They'd dance the two-step, an heel-an-toe polka, an waltz, an thangs like that.

Now a lot a people lately, dont pay attainsion enough ta catch on. Cause fifty years ago, it wadn none a they time. They jest caught a little whiff of it. All these songs is made up about somebody's life story. If its worthwhile listenin to it. That why I got people so straightened out on these songs, cause I know what they's all about.

I was jest about ten or twelve years old when that song "Ella Speed" busted out. See, she got kilt in Dallas. That was nineteen-twelve. Boy kilt her, true as I'm lookin at you. An then they made words up about that an put the song together: "When they all got the news, that Ella Speed was dead, they goes home an dresses up in red." An, "Now there's two white hawsses side an side, gonna take Ella fur her fare travelin ride." That when they carryin people ta the grave in hearses. Wadn no caws.

See, thats a true song. Its reasoned down about how she died. An one boy slow-trailed her an shot her down at the good-timin place, bout dancin wit anothun. An he jest broke an run, that boy what was dancin wit her.

We used ta call them thangs ballrooms, ya know. Where they fit an kilt an done everthang they wanted to. Them thangs come out a what we called a bawn dance. You know, where you see them women that got them little

245

aprons an them men dancin with them little old blue-jean britches? They callin figgers: "Hands up wit eight. Circle right. Swang yo podnas. Promenate."

Thats what we was doin: square dancin. My daddy used ta fiddle fur them square dancin. Because he was about as expert a fiddla if I ever heard it. He was the best fiddla ever I met in my life. Like when I was bassin behind my daddy, they been dancin breakdowns. An bawn dance. The Satiddy Night Suppa, see, it stawted from breakdowns. They give em diffunt names, as the world growed, ya know.

Then, when it quit from that, we called em Satiddy Night Dances. Dance an a Satiddy Night Suppa is the same thang. Then its a festival too. We always found anothuh name ta give it. An then they'd say, "We goin to a ball." I dont know how miny names they give it. But you talkin bout the same concern. Cause we were goin ta the same place, an doin the same thang. An under the same music, cause I'm the musician that was carryin on.

Its been a lots a dances I could remember went on in my lifetime. When Daddy was fiddlin, they'd just git out there an dance, an their feets would might near talk. An man, they could dance a "Six Months Trouble." They'd hit it three or foe times, an then sliiide an swang podnas. A woman an a man was dancin, face ta face. But them feets was jest hittin the solid flow. Jest like you pattin yo hands. We called that the old breakdown. Then they moved from that to a bawn dance. But they jest changed the name.

An then they changed the way a dancin. They left there an went ta cakewalkin. Sumpm jest like, you do mow walkin than ya did dancin.

An then left cakewalkin an went ta two-steppin. You hit two motion steps forward. Then you come back two steps. Its a to an a fro step. Lemme see. "Knockin down Windas, Tearin down Doze"? Thats a good song I play fur two-step. I played that fur aminy night. An thats where I learnt how ta play that song.

Very few colored folk kin waltz, did you know that? They know how da two-step, hucklebuck, an Charleston, one-step, ballin the jack, swing-out. Like that swing-out: man an a woman dancin. An the man have the hand over his shoulder an holdin the woman's hand, an carry his hand over her head. An they'd turn around an meet one anothuh an dance the one-step. Then go back an reach out an git her hand. But he dont turn it loose. Carry it over his head, he come round an swang her around near about off the flow. An she stretch the flow, dancin, hit a few steps. An then pull her to ya, an she pull herself to ya: him an her facin one anothuh. First thang you know, he done swung around, call it "swing out." Go round an round. They know what position ta hold the woman to so she wouldn fall. That a purdy dance, too. Lot a fun. Keep you lively! An its good exercise.

An then, shortly after that, the cawnival commence ta spreadin in our areas a town. Barnum and Bailey: They brought the slow drag, an ballin the jack. Maybe two clowns come out on the stage, man an a woman, ta draw yo attainsion. They'd come out an sang a little song. An direckly he'd grab her an dance a little with her. They was real good dancers. An they crack jokes then. They do much dancin an sangin, because you had about ten or fifteen minutes ta git onstage an explain thangs ta the people.

They say, "Well, y'all oughta come on in, cause half aint been told." See there was mow better ta come, inside that show. You should pay two bits or foe bits, or whatever yo admission was ta come see the other part a the show.

Now I could rememba when ballin the jack: thats mow done wit yo knees. You gather a good twist wit yo knees. Hit yo knees together, to an fro. Little bit like the buzzard lope, you know. That come in here way befoe that ballin the jack.

An then they called that the shimmy she wobbles? That shake yo behind thataway, jest: women could shake, jest

The lion wagon of Barnum and Bailey Circus in Navasota. *Photo courtesy the Marcus Mallard Collection.*

like a leaf on a tree! The womens an mens be jest shimmyin, man, all over. An they stawted a song behind that. Say, "Shake like jelly, roll like biscuit dough." I was jest big enough ta git out an be among people. I wadn allowed out until I got about foeteen years of age. Then I went ta playin fur Satiddy Night Dances. So it musta been somewhere, oh, in the fifteens an sixteens.

Well they left that shimmy she wobbles, an come on ta the hucklebuck. Then the Charleston. That a fast dance, work their legs fast. Well now, thats dancin with yo feet. So they done left the Charleston, an they jest shake they-selves, call it breakin the chicken's neck.

An now I'm playin some a them same songs, but I'm doin em in a diffunt way because the dancin come up in a new motion. After Chuck Berry an the Beagles an all them people stawted ta playin that rock-an-roll music, people dont dance with they feets no mow. They jest dance with their fangers, an with the hips an the shoulder. You git whole lot a forms an fashion. Cause you caint dance but one dance to it. Thats that git together, that twist. Work they-

self behind. Shake. But nothin in their foots is comparin
with what was when us come up.

Oh, its so miny dances come up. But I knowed, I played
fur all of em. When I got those thangs organized in my
mind, an knowed whats it like, well I kept that goin. Cause
I had my regular time made up—an thats all I had ta play
is: time.

I'm changin the pace so fast, an so miny diffunt songs
soundin so good til they hafta turn around an respect me.
Then I'm playin my songs that I sang em, same as I play.
You dont git nobody ta play no gittah hawd as I do no mow.

Oh boy, I had some hawd nights on me at these Satiddy
Night Dances. Dont thank I havent played fifty-nine years,
all night long. A few times I'd play all night an half the
day.

This time a the night, they done got me there on a hawss
or mule or wagon, some way away from my house ta where
I'm gonna play? At yo house if you give a party, I'm the first
man git there. Cause if they didn git me there, people
stawted leavin there. I hold the dance.

There at somebody's house, they had a whole hog settin
at a table, bahbecued. Maybe this poach wouldn hold them
hogs, an all the chickens or spareribs, cakes, an apples an
candy. They had a side table off away from yo meat: had
peanuts, apples, an stuff on it. An the meat was stackt up
there, big old hog ham jest as brown, you could smell it foe
you got ta the house. They know how ta cook it too!

An man they et there til twelve or one o'clock. Hog hafta
be a mighty big hog ta last there til eleven o'clock. Cause
there's five or six hunnud people there. An they gonna
come back an eat, then dance.

An the one who give that Suppa, he make a hunnud an
fifty, two hunnud dollas a night, an that was a whole lot a
money in them days. An if they didn git me, why you well
as ta not give no Suppa.

Cause wherever I was playin at, people would tell one

anothuh where Mance playin at. An they git on their way walkin, ridin. Do all like that til they git there. Some people walk out fifteen miles a night!

They heard that gittah befoe they git there: three or foe miles down through the fields, cotton patches, an through the woods: they stop an listen. Say, "I kin hear Old Mance." An Old Mance didn have no amp or nothin. Settin by a winda so that music'd come out an hit the open air. A lot a people say, "I heard you wayyy down the road. Man, I couldn git here fast enough."

An they gamble: caseena, dice, mawdy, kotch, an all kinds a games was there. Poker games. As miny there in the yawd—well they mostly tell ya, "You gamblas? Git on out ta the yawd!" Suppa was inside the house, an they'd jest gamble all the way around the house. Settin there, gamblin til eleven or twelve o'clock Sunday. Piled the money there jest like that. I never seed the likes a so much money when I was comin up. Wadn none a mine, but I could look out the winda an see it.

First man ever played "Jack a Diamonds" in the world is me. Set down at home an learnt that song, aw I bet fifty years ago. Played it fur the gamblas. An I named ever cawd in the deck. Ever one but the seven.

When I playin that, I jest stand up set ta the winda: the gamblas'd be on the outside on the ground, an them words'd connect with what was happenin out there. All right. They'd bet the jack in that deck. See, it would lose mown it would win. Cause jack a diamonds is a hawd cawd ta play.

When you play the jack against iny cawd in the deck, he'll fail ta come. Some of em had done played that jack that night. An say, "An I told you last week, jest as plain as a man could speak: I'm gonna send you to yo papa's, payday." Done got broke an throwed all his money away, they tell im, say, "You gonna send yo woman home now, boy!"

Hoorawin im, ya know. See, they'd say inythang, do inythang, ta git you losin an keep you losin. Try ta git you
hoppt up an mad so you couldn thank about what you was
doin.

So I made mow money out that song than I made off the
whole time I played, cause they heard me playin that song,
maybe they feel that viberation give em a little bit a luck.
An if they come through the winna, they come ta the winda
an give me a dolla an a half ta two dollas, each one of em.
Sometime I come home wit foeteen an fifteen dollas a
night.

All a my songs is all True Story Songs. Is a feelin. Well,
what you git out that writin if you caint sang it an dont
have no inside connection? If yo whereabouts aint come
across wit some a that trouble, why it dont sound right.
You got ta have troubles or sumpm ta thank about. The
music is inside of ya. Sumpm done hapmd ta you or somebody else.

It aint much viberation ta writin music. Much strength.
Jest take yo pencil, set down here an write what I'm tellin
you: if you dont feel it, why you caint make nobody else
feel it if its in em.

An so, I commenced ta playin "Jack a Diamonds Is a
Hawd Cawd ta Play":

Well I played him in the spring, an he never won a thing.
Jack a diamonds was a hawd cawd ta play.

Well I played him in the fall, an he never won at all.
Jack a diamonds was a hawd cawd ta play.

I fell down on my knees, tryin ta play jack a spades.
Jack a diamonds was a hawd cawd ta play.

Well I played him against the ace. He was a starvation in my
    face.
Jack a diamonds was a hawd cawd ta play.

Well I played him against the deuce, puttin the jack when it
  wont no use.
Jack a diamonds was a hawd cawd ta play.

Well I played him against the trey. It was on a fiver lay.
Jack a diamonds was a hawd cawd ta play.

Well I played the jack against the foe. Turnt the jack right in
  the doe.
Jack a diamonds was a hawd cawd ta play.

I played him against the five. That lay like ta made me cry.
Jack a diamonds was a hawd cawd ta play.

I played him against the six. It left me in a terrible fix.
Jack a diamonds was a hawd cawd ta play.

An I told you last week, jest as plain as a man could speak,
I'm gonna send you to yo papa's, payday.

An I played the jack against the king, an it made the deala
  sing.
Jack a diamonds was a hawd cawd ta play.

I played him against the queen, an it turnt my money green.
Jack a diamonds was a hawd cawd ta play.

Thats a mawdy game. Mawdy Carlo. See, you bet yo
money on ya ace, that the ace'll beat the deuce. If the ace
dont come first out that deck, well the dealer'll throw you
in. "I played him against the ace, an it was a starvation in
my face." Lost my money, an I didn have no money ta go
home ta feed myself an my famly. Whichever cawd you lay
yo money out on, thats the one you expectin ta come.

An so, thats what gamblin is, is guessin. Jest like ball
team. Hawss races. Everthang you dont know, you guessin
yo way through. An you be lucky enough ta git holt a the
right trace a thangs, well you win. If you dont git the right
trace a inythang, well you caint win because it dont come
up there like you guesst it would.

It aint easy ta win when you wit a bunch a fellas an y'all

all jest guessin fur the outcome. But when you git in a bunch of em got the deck mawkt against you, well you caint win. Dont madda if you the ace gambla in the precinct!

I had some friendboys do me thataway. I played purdy regular fur a while wit some boys out where I stayed at. An they all got together: "Aw, Mance got plenty a money. Lets mawk the deck an beat im out of it. He aint been playin long enough ta catch on ta what we doin."

So I come on down the road ta the gamblin shack, where we played cawds an dice at. An they was already in there playin, had the lamps lit. "Looka here's Mance! Set down! Set down! You want us ta deal you in?"

Yeah. Mawkt that deck an cheated me outa all my money. Wadn long after I retcht in my pocket, an didn have a penny one. They commenced ta hoorawin me, say, "You go on home an see kin yo wife teach you how ta play," an all like that.

Well, I never was a hoorawer. An I couldn stand fur nobody ta hooraw me. So I went on home. An retcht up over the doe. I had a six-shoota gun ahangin up there. An the old lady kep awatchin me.

An so, when I retch up over the doe, she jumpt out the bed an swung me. She jest grabbed me. She say, "Gimme that gun!"

I listened at her. So, she kep it in her hands. I wouldn try ta take it away from her. Cause I didn wanta hurt her, an didn want the gun ta go off an be shootin my wife.

She said, "Let me tell ya: if you go back down where the gamblin at, you'll be either killt or kill somebody. Dont you gamble no mow. Because I'd rather have you than iny gamblin money in the world." So, I tuck her at her word. An we been together ever since.

An so, two three days or two three weeks after it hapmd, the boys told me, "You know, you show did study up a good plan."

I say, "What is that?"

Say, "We happy you didn come back down there, cause we likes ya. But we knowed if you come back down there you gonna aim ta kill us. But we had you dead ta the right. You didn see us. But we coulda seed you. If you'd a come back down there, on the road from where you was stayin at: two brothers, one on each side a the road, was goin layaway you an kill you. One had a twelve-gauge shotgun, an the other had a rifle. Sot out there in the dawk, crimpt down in the weeds an bushes, an in a ditch so the shots would pass over em, an not catch them in their own doins. Tween where you live an the gamblin game. They was gonna cut you ta the ground as you pass by between em. Catch you in a crossfire."

Well I could see the light where they gamblin from near-about my house. But I couldn see them mens up in the bushes.

An so I said, "Well my wife kep me from comin."

Said, "You oughta rememba yo wife as long as you live. Cause you never woulda made it back ta the gamblin shack."

Oh, when I first met Myno—thats what the kids call her—I was playin the gittah. An we would go out an have us a big rangplay. Have a meetin, you know, on Sunday. Foedy or fifty girls an boys'd be together. I had done learnt how ta play about three or foe songs. I was given up ta be the best *young* player that they had round here in this community. An so they all dwelled around me cause I could play that gittah.

She was two years youngern I was. I didn wanta pay her no attainsion, cause I wanted a bigger girl than what she was. First time I saw her, she tried ta git right in front a me. Ta make me look at her. But I was lookin at a girl little largern her.

So finely she went an saw me once or twice, at a rangplay

or a Suppa where I was playin. An she told her aunty say, "He dont pay me no tension, Aunty."

Aunty say, "You just keep on. He'll commence payin you attainsion."

I misst seein her about a year—I wadn stuck on her nohow! But finely she grew up: purdy good size. An she had nice, you know, built an good legs. A girl had a good big legs, boys go crazy about ya then.

An so she had nice-built legs, an man you talkin bout a woman could dance. That woman you see caint hawdly walk? She used ta make me sorta mad wit her, cause she'd git ta dancin wit some nother boy. You know I didn like that. I'd take my hand an break a strang, git her off the flow.

That what you call jealous. Say, "You dont wanta git with that old nasty boy, he's drunk or ugly," or sumpm. But I knowed, if she wanta dance, dance wit me.

My wife used ta set down an laugh. I say, "What you laughin about?"

"I laugh about when you used ta break them strangs, fur a purpose an make like that yo strang was broke." I'd do that!

An so finely one day, she got purdy close ta me. An the girl I was likin, why, her name was Lou Cindy. See, Lou Cindy'd write a letter, an Elnora would carry it over ta me an tell me what she wrote. An I'd tell her sich an sich a thang ta tell Lou Cindy, an she'd write it down an carry it ta her. Tell her what I'm sayin.

An so finely, a friendgirl a hers come up ta me an says, "Lou Cindy gonna git at you if you git close ta that girl over there." Talkin bout Elnora.

I say, "Well, this is a girl too." But I wadn courtin my wife. She jest tryin ta squeeze in edgeways.

Finely, they passt a few words. An Elnora said, "You like her. Dont ya?"

I say, "Yeah. Purdy good. What you talkin so much about Lou Cindy? You better be talkin fur yaself."

She tell me thats all she wanted me ta *say*. When I told her she oughta be talkin fur herself, then she went hawd at it then, talkin fur me ta like her.

So, I built a foundation wit her then. An I went wit her about, maybe, three years. We'd meet at Sunday school or a rang dance, jest inywhere we could meet, you know. Cause she was still wit her mother then.

An I was wit *my* mama then. Out on the Nickelbuck Fawm. I stayed wit Mother til I married. Foe I was nineteen, on back about sixteen weeks: married nineteen an thirteen, thirteenth a December. On a Satiddy.

I never will furgit that. Cause the nineteen-thirteen Overflow come in there, December. We had a seven or eight overflows. But this first overflow: I married in the time bein when it got us ta all move out. The river come up an spread it all over the Bottoms. Water got up, an we lost our crop an lot a hogs an cows an chickens. I moved ta the Hillside, where the water couldn reach us, an campt over there.

We used ta didn git no rain here but til we have a overflow. Yeah its wet now, these late years, in bout foedy years now. An you kin grow thangs, wouldn pay you ta grow in my time comin up. But when I was a boy we'd git about three rains a year.

But nineteen-eighteen, twenty, twenty-one, an all like that we had overflows one right after anothuh. Drowned out all the crops, so I went up around Dallas an Waxahachie ta pick cotton. Yeah, same years I was tellin you bout seein Blind Lemon.

I used ta paddle boats. Right down through this country here. In the fawmland. Houses was afloatin in that high water, an people be settin up on top a their houses, hollerin fur help. An sometime, we'll hear em a mile. Comin down, an the water was comin down. Hogs! Dogs! Chickens! Turkeys! Floatin on the water, some of em be on a log, goin down the river.

Jest the water was so high! An what water wadn in the river was out in the fawm. You know where Allenfawm? Tween the Brazos an the Navasot, it aint nothin *but* bottoms. Shuh, man! It wadn nothin but water from Valley Junction, Waco: an come on down through here an hit that current in the Brazos. An the Brazos on into the Navasot. Plumb on into the Gulf a Mexico when they come, them overflows.

Last flood we had I blieve was in twenty-six. Used ta have one ever year, or two or three a year. An it didn hafta rain! Jest like you had a drain: it rained up above there, an it drains off of Waco to us. Come on down here. An jest filled these countries full a water.

Sometime wadn nothin but a little old knoll where you could stand, maybe about a mile. An then everbody'd huddle up on that knoll, wit water washin all the way around ya.

I've paddled aminy a boat up an down, about six miles from here. Me an my uncle Jim Oliver. Savin people's lives. Gittin their thangs outa the overflow. Flood. You could hear em hollerin miles up an down this bottom. An hear it runnin like a train, that water: "Ssssshhhhccooo. Rrrrrrwww." You could hear that water comin. Try ta git ta some high knolls an save ourself.

Over where I stayed at on Sommers place, call that west side a the Brazos over there the Hill. Washington County an Brenham, all back in there aint nothin but hills. What you call the Bluffs, an the Hill, thats the same thang. They got a little bottomland the edge a there, reach from there down ta the currents a the river. An it got out some places down there.

An back in them low flats, thats the bottomland. Called that the Bottom. Nothin but flat land where we was at. Jest, you could roll a marble up an down the river bottom fur hunnuds an hunnuds a miles. Now White Switch, thats in the middle a the Bottoms—an in the middle a Allenfawm but wadn no part of it. An thats where we was livin when aminy overflow come. But, the one that boat got aloose from me: I was paddlin the boat, an me an my uncle was comin back in the Bottoms ta git some thangs that we left that we couldn carry out. Water comin in on us so fast. We put some a our stuff upstairs, an our hogs. We had a bawn, an had upstairs to it.

An me an Jim was comin back ta feed my hogs, an git some mow stuff ta carry back ta the Hill where we was livin. An the levee broke. I reckon you know what a levee is, wouldn ya? A high bump, where the water on the other side had ta be purdy high ta git over that levee.

An so we was paddlin the boat, an the levee opened up a break an made that water dammed up from it—jest shot through there "Wfooo," right through an whirl in there. An when we got straight, I was fur from here ta that high-way. Well, that water'll dig a hole through that levee, by its own self. It'll come through there so fast you caint count the minutes ta come through it.

An so we'd git a boat an take it which way they was, an git folks ta come off that house. A lot of em got drownded. An some of em we saved. Man, I saved aminy person's chickens an hogs, an people's lives. Paddlin them boats night an day. Some of em dead an gone now.

Them convicts made them levees befoe Mow bought that place over there at Allenfawm. White Switch is right nearby that planation. It used ta be a convict place up there in Allenfawm. You know, like people comes from Huntsville? The best ball players, best dancers, best song-sters—best inythang went ta penitentiaries.

Its some good songs come from the penitentiary. Like you sang some songs when you was workin on a prisoner fawm, that sometimes they'll make ya hurt. When the cap-tain feel like he wanta hear you sang, why he'll say,

"Whats a madda, old nigga? Whynt you sang?"

They say, "Yessuh, Capm." Then he go ta sangin.

An so, that fella come from the penitentiary. Yeah, he was choppin cotton fur us. He come out sangin about a prisoner fawm: "Askt my captain, what time a day. He lookt at his watch, an he walkt away."

An say, "Went all round the whole corral. An couldn find a mule wit his shoulder well." A corral, thats a lot where you keep yo teams at, yo mules: they have em penned up so they couldn git out. An they workt the mules so hawd, an done em so bad til they had sore shoulders. It had raw meat, under that collar?

I dont guess you know much about mules an hawsses an cows. But now, if you put a collar on a mule, it should be a collar that would fit im. If it didnt, it would make his shoulder sore.

So this here's a convict song:

[Mance plays his version of "Captain, Captain":]

Askt my captain, "What time a day?"
Yes, I askt my captain, "Tell me what time a day?"
He lookt at his watch, an he jest walkt away.

Got ta work so hawd, an my captain pay so slow,
Hafta work so hawd, an my captain pay so slow.
Sometime I dont care whether I work or no.

"Wouldn mind workin, Captain, from sun ta sun.
Well, I wouldn mind workin, Captain, from sun ta sun,
If you pay me my money, Captain, when payday come."

Went all around that old whole corral.
Yes, I went all around, man, that whole corral,
An I couldn find a mule, there wit his shoulder well.

"If you wake up in the mownin, I'll be seldom seen.
Wake up in the mownin, Captain, I'll be seldom seen.
You kin ask somebody else, Captain, catch my team."

Six months aint long, two years aint a great long time.
Six months aint long, two years aint no great long time.
Got a friend in penitentiary, doin ninety-nine.

Oughta been down on the levee, nineteen an thirty-foe,
Oughta been down on the levee, in nineteen an thirty-foe.
See the dead men, layin on ever turnrow.

Should a been down on the river, man, nineteen an ten,
Should a been down on the river in the year of nineteen an ten.
Women woe the ball an chain, jest like the men.

He jest come from the pen. Did some time in the penitentiary over there: Huntsville, foedy-five miles from here. An
when he got out, he weaved his way out, in the Bottom
where we was stayin. An he was lucky enough ta come ta
Mama's field. Mama was fawmin an I was a boy, heppin her
fawm. I was about eleven or twelve years old. An I was
comin out the fields an goin to the fields: totin water, you
know, I wadn big enough ta chop much cotton, but I'd be
the water boy.
    An he come an hired out ta Mama. Fur fifty cents a day.
They give her a hand ta hep her out, cause wadn nobody ta
hep Mama but me. Cause Papa an brother Charlie had
both left away from there.
    That man could sang that song an he'd chop cotton fast
as a mule could walk. He stayed there wit us that whole
year out. But I dont even know his name. But he stawted ta
sangin that song ever day along about eleven o'clock. An I
was gittin it out a him, an couldn play the gittah. An he
sung all those verses in it. Listen, he could sang! He might
make the hair rise on yo head.
    Yeah, he was free an footloose. See, if you do yo time out,
why they turn you out an give you little suit a clothes an
maybe five dollas in money, an turn you loose. Sign you
out. Yeah, he's a free laborer. Mama wouldn a hired im if
he was a convict. She'd a been scared of im.

An I made up that song in nineteen-twelve. Jest run across my mind until I got big enough ta play this gittah. An I rememorized it an went on an played it at these Satiddy Night Dances.

Did I do much dancin? No, man, I was always playin. Nobody else ta play but me. They wadn but about foe gittah players been in this country in my whole life. See, they couldn usually play over one or two songs, an they wanta gamble or fight or do sumpm nother else. An I jest tuck mine up in playin, you know.

An when I git off, the sun be up, man. Chickens done got off the roost, an lot a people done went ta sleep. In them houses where they give a Suppa: jest like yo wife was give out or you give out, they had beds where they didn take down, there in anothuh room. See, they usually hafta what ya call take down the house: move the chairs an tables an thangs out, an make room fur all the people whats gonna be there.

An then they'd say, "Well, you kin go in that room an take ya rest." Maybe foe or five, or six or seven people'd be in there asleep. Done give out. Babies! In the bed where peoples brought their babies there an put em up.

Man, you talkin about haddin a whole lot a good times an a whole lot a bad times. Jest like you git me tonight? This is the night, Satiddy night. An befoe I left that place, somebody would come talk ta me. Play fur him next Satiddy night.

When I agreed fur it, why then, they'd go ta talkin it out. Say, "Y'all come over ta my house, next Satiddy night. I done hired Mance Lipscomb!"

Man, they commenced ta hollerin, "OKAY! I'll be there!"

They used ta give Satiddy Night Suppas over there by Cole Creek, befoe I stawted ta playin in the Mow place. Me an my brother-in-law Robert Scales, we called im Paddycake. He played piana, I played gittah fur a while, over there in Washington. He was Pie's husband. She a good songster too. But she blong ta church now.

I learnt her boy—that maken him my nephew—how ta play gittah. We woulda been world's favors if we'd a stayed together. He could sang an I could play. We played all over Washington County an all in Brazos an everwhere. We called him T Lipscomb. Jest so everbody would know im, but his name was A C Sims. My sister Lillie had another husband, named Wallace Sims, an that was his daddy. An he was raised up under me. An see, the music was in him. That T could sang, man.

I had a sister oldern me, weigh about two hunnud an sixty pounds. Well, you oughta heard me an her together when we was kids. Playin gittah, an she'd sang behind me. She had a voice jest like that woman Mahalia Jackson.

People wanta know why people kin learn how ta play music. If there's nothin like that instain inside a you: somebody in that famly got ta play some kinda instrument. Then you kin have it estimated, inside of you got a feelin fur it. An it comes outa you. What you say, its in yo blood.

But now, if you aint got no music in yo blood, you kin play til you die: you wont have no talent in music. You caint git blood out of a turnip. Unless you put some blood *in* the turnip. See it wadn made in there.

Oh, I used ta play Suppas fur my sister. Last time you caught me in a drunk, I got over there an went ta drankin. Play a little while, drank some mow. An my sister's house was at the top of a little old hill.

After a while, I went outside. Git me a bit a fresh air an take a leak, you know. An my legs was sorta wobbly, I say, "Huh! Now, how you reckon that ground done got mounded up? I musta got lost. Be out on the turnrow somewhere."

An direckly, I stumbled an fell. Rolled all the way down that hill, into the ditch. An I found myself in that mud, water all on me. An couldn move.

So them people back in the house was waitin on me. One said, "That boy been gone a long time. He rested enough. Lets git some music goin here."

A Mexican was in there said, "Well, I'll run out in the dawk there an holla at im. See kin I find im."

He come on out off the poach: an I was down in the sank. Couldn do nothin but jest roll around down there. I say, "Hep! Somebody come hep me! Cause I caint hep myself." An he was standin up on top a the hill, an couldn see where I was at.

Finely, they fooled around an found me. Carried me up the hill ta my sister's place. An set me down in the flow. Didn put me in no chair! "Git out the way, you old drunken bastud! He's jest reelin an rockin an fallin down." Talkin ta me. Guyin me. Cause I couldn do nothin fur myself. Jest had ta lay there, take it.

I rememba everthang they done. An some of em I got even wit em after I got sober. Here they jest kickt me an walkt on me, they drug me an pusht, pulled me round on the flow. "That old nigga aint good fur nothin. Put im out the way! Roll that drunk bastud under the bed so we dont trip over im!" Throwed water on me.

Thats the reason I know a drunk man, he knows thangs but he caint govern hisself. But when you git half drunk you kin stagger around an git in misdemeanness. But as long as you drunk: I couldn git ta my knees ta save my life. Throwed up look like all night. Ever time I woke up, I was throwin up. An them people makin me out a fool, til daylight come.

An so I said, "Man, if I kin jest git on my feet, I aint gonna let them people do me thataway no mow." An I hadn been drunk no mow. I betcha thats fifty-five years ago. Oh yeah, I was already married.

Had little old bottle lamps at them Suppas. Them thangs I lit aminy one. You take a beer bottle an screw some rag down in it until you hit the bottom a that bottle. An put that half full a coal oil, what you call kerosene. An then pour a little kerosene out on the outside, so it'll catch a light.

An that thang'll burn, man. I used ta kill birds in the night with that. Yeah. We used ta blind birds right there around Breedlove's an Roberson's place, down there where Beck Wade an Ed Lathan at over there by Sommers' place? Back in them woods an hills an thangs, over on the Bluffs. You'll see lights lit up round in there, miles an miles when the robins was plentiful in here. They killed sacks a robins. Didn hafta have no gun, jest carry a plank or a stick an knock em out the bushes with that.

An some people'd git this old fat pine, an carry torch lights. You see some stuff come out a kindlin of plank, when it gits hot? Look like resin. An burn it. You caint hawdly blow it out.

Well, we had ta work in the day. Had ta hunt when you could. Yeah, jest wintertime. Robins come in here somewhere along in November an December. Sometime January, jest accordin ta the year an how cold it was. An them the sweetest birds you kin eat. You git a buncha them birds an pick em an cook em, they jest as fat as they kin be. But its against the law ta kill em now.

An so inyhow, you talk about eatin: them old Satiddy Night Suppas, they had peanuts. Candy, apples! An fish. Chicken. Backbone. An hams or meat, in a tub. Sometime it'd be two washtubs a meat.

Stawt ta cookin that meat in the mownin bout nine o'clock, an put it on a pit. It was some real good bahbecue pits. In the ground like you fixin ta bury a person. Wit a coffin, hear? Be a big open pit. An put some iron rods across the hole. An cut a hole in that raw meat. Maybe it was ham or shoulder: jest stake it through this side. An cut a hole over into this side, stick it through a hole that. An then them rods'll hold that meat up off the bottom a the fire.

Slow fire. They wouldn let ya cook it by no fast fire. They had a coals. They'd cut them oak trees down an have em there at the bahbecue eeevry Satiddy. An put enough fire in there ta keep that meat steady cookin.

An then they turn it over. An let it cook there so miny minutes, an put some sauce on a mop wit a rag around the stick where it wouldn git on ya. Catch a stick, an wrap that rag round it, an tie it wit wire either coil strangs. An then put it in a bucket. An put vinegar, butter, lemon. An you could smell that bahbecue five miles.

An boy you talkin bout some a the best bahbecue. Them people could cook that bahbecue so you suckt the bone! They was well done. Didn have no watch or nothin, they jest figgered it out in their own mind how long a piece a meat oughta be. Now them days is gone, but they not forgotten.

Well, music aint no count if you dont put no suction to it. Jest like a cook: if she come out here an dont have no salt in the bread, somebody gonna find out. Didn have no pepper in the meat. Its tasteless food. But long as she kin cook wit a season to it, why thats a good cook.

Well you got ta have a season ta this music. Jest like a cook. Then they'll git some viberation outa it. It make thangs roll across their mind: puts a pressure on yo mind because, "I believe that hapmd ta me or some a my friends." You put people ta wonderin about those thangs. I may be sangin about you. May be sangin about her. But some a these verses'll reach her mind an reach yo mind.

Now you take "Joe Turner Done Kilt a Man": people was sangin that in the fields, an I liked that song. But you see that song was sung round in my era, where I was stayin at, until I stawted ta playin the gittah. An I kept that in my mind an my remembrance, until I got ta play.

I pickt up a lot a my songs in open air outa the fields where we workin. On the fawms, ya see. People would come in there strangers an brang those songs in our community.

Yeah. It wadn no music in the field, you know. See, we was workin in brets. An brets a people: thirty an foedy people would be in one field. An they'd all git ta workin, pickin cotton, choppin, or plowin one. An somebody ahaul away an stawt ta sangin a song. An they'd git ta sangin, an he'd quit sangin. Maybe somebody else, about half a hour or maybe a hour, somebody blaze away wit anothuh song. An we'd be still workin. But somebody goin always be in the mood a talkin, or either in the mood a sangin.

Well you see, when they sang, that make em feel like the days wadn goin so hawd wit em. Jest like you walkin an you dont have no sound, nothin but yo foots on the ground: if you git ta walkin an movin around, it'll give you some kinda go ta keep the spirit up. See when you go walkin, well you keep a certain gait. You walkin steady, dont wanta give out, an dont wanta be worried. An you kin walk all day.

Well you could *work* all day if you had somebody ta sang in the fields. Say some jokes. Talk about somethang make you laugh, an lively. Well, you doin that ta sorta pass the time away.

We used ta chop cotton, by song. Jest like you—ever time you hear Lipscomb say a word an then you sung it back. That keep you in a motion. Keep you from worryin an thankin bout what time a day it was. I see songsters could git out ta the fields an raise up a big song, an it was a big thrill in there. Big thrill!

But you didn git that outa me. I'm listenin all the time. I caught on. An I caint sang, unless I'm playin the gittah. Now I havent remembered sangin a song in my whole life, dry along solo jest like. See, I sang what I play, play what I sang.

You dont see none a that now. Dont hear that no mow. They stoppt sangin, when they quit plowin mules an pickin cotton. Nineteen an foedy-five, you couldn hear no songs goin on in the field. Cause they use equipment like machinery. An you know you couldn sang much around on a tracta. People would set up there on a tracta; it would drown out yo voice. An it keep you always in a motion, thankin a what you was doin with that motor, you see.

All right, I give you some explaynation right now, bout this music. What you call a Life Story Song. I'm talkin bout a song was sung in Marlin jail. A man sung his way out a prison, like Leadbelly? It come ta my town, I blieve, in nineteen-nineteen or thereabouts. A boy come from Marlin, Texas. Thats a bad jail! Dont never go ta Marlin jail. They'll throw the key away an tie it on a rabbit's neck.

So this guy, he was named Freddie. He had a woman ta do something she hadn never did befoe. Maybe coulda been his wife, or his woman. An she didn care too much about im. He loved her mown she did him. She jest livin wit im, jest fur him ta take care a her. An he kep ahangin around her, an stayin there. Let her do him iny way she wanted ta do im. Jest ta git ta be with her.

So finely, she done im so bad: she went an put a man in his house, where he was livin with her. An put the man in Freddie's bed. An that was his home, an that was his wife an woman. She say, "If I make you a pallet on the flow an git in the bed wit anothuh man, then I'll git rid a you cause you got ta leave here."

See how I'm arrangin it? "Freddie's woman done sumpm she hadn never done befoe: she was in the bed wit anothuh man, an made Freddie a pallet on the flow."

So, he laid there. In the pallet. An the other man was in the bed with her. He said "Well, maybe she'll let me stay here tamarra. She done everthang she could ta git rid a me, but I'm gonna stay here inyhow."

Well, he was jest tryin ta stay there with her, by some means. He was layin there wide awake. An Freddie laid there tried not ta pay it no mind. Tried ta overcome it.

An so he stood it all, alright. Til what hapm to im: a while befoe day, the fella got in the mood an them sprangs got ta cryin. An he tuck much as he could, an he couldn take no mow.

He say, "Well, she done done enough ta me." He got tired a that woman layin up there in the bed talkin to anothuh man, an he was on the flow. Old Freddie got mad an he got bad. He got up an made a break fur his pistol. Yeah, he got up an got his big gun in his hand.

She saw him comin. An fell down on her knees. "Freddie, I know ya mad, but spare my life if you please."

An Fred jest lookt at her. Didn say a word. Throwed his pistol down an leveled it down on her an shot the woman. Kilt the woman! An the man broke an run. Out the doe.

So Freddie was goin down the road huntin the man. When the sheriff met im, he had his gun in his hand. An the sheriff say, "Freddie, I heard you kilt yo woman."

He said, "Yes, I'm lookin fur that man."

An so, the sheriff say, "I got a writ fur ya."

An he turnt around an said, "Looka here, Sheriff—"

Sheriff say, "What is it?"

He said, "How could you stand?"

"Stand what?"

Say, "Have a low-down woman aspendin yo money, an foolin round wit anothuh man?"

Sheriff lookt around at im, say, "I dont know how I could take it, Freddie. It makes a bad man, wit his gun in his hand. I tell ya: I'll play like I aint seen ya. You go ahead on, an try ta find that man."

An went on down the road, an he run across his papa. Papa says, "Son, here where you done wrong."

He say, "What is that, Papa?"

Said, "When you found out that woman wadn treatin you right, son, you oughta let her alone."

He said, "Papa, wouldn you a got mad? If you'd acomin home an found Mama wit anothuh man in yo bed?"

An Papa say, "Yeah son, I'd a got mad too."

He had a alibi ta git by, everbody but his mama. An Mama lookt at im said, "Son, you the only son I got. An I hate ta see you go." Thats all. He couldn conadick what his mama say. She hate ta see im go ta the penitentiary.

See? I'm showin you what the song sprung from. Dont thank now that wadn true. This fella sung his way outa jail. How he got out of it: the jaila was carryin food ta the jail. An Freddie was out in the jailhouse, playin his old gittah. The fella stood there on the outside, an it sound so good, he had the food in his hand waitin fur Freddie ta end that song.

He say, "You know whut? That fella show playin that song, jest straight out. Inybody woulda got mad, if he'd a come in found his woman with anothuh man in her bed. I'm goin back down an tell the sheriff ta come here an release this fella."

So he went on down the street ta where the sheriff at an say, "Looka here. Judge? Come down ta the jail. This man is playin a song, its true as he playin it. If y'all go down an hear that fella playin that gittah, with them true verses in it, I believe you'd turn him aloose."

"Oaww, I dont know I—"

"Now, you jest go down there an listen at im. He playin it, an sangin it."

So jaila went on back with the judge. Sheriff an the man was gonna feed im, stood on the outside, an Freddie didn know they was out there. He's still sangin that song. An they stood there, listened at im a while.

An the jaila said, "Well, what you thank about it?"

Said, "Open the doe an let that fella out. That woman *made* im kill her."

An he sung his way out on that. An went on about his bizniss. An if you hear this song, you'll thank he *ought* a been got out. Go thisaway:

[Mance sings his arrangement of "Freddie":]

269

Now, Freddie's woman done somethin hadn never done befoe.

She was in the bed wit anothuh man, made Freddie's pallet on the flow.

He got mad. He got bad. Went for his gun, in his hand.

Freddie's woman saw him comin, went ta fell down on her knees.

I kin hear her cryin, "Now, Freddie, spare my life if you please.

I know ya mad. You got bad. Oh, wit ya gun in ya hand."

Freddie meet the policeman, wit his big gun in his hand.

"Well, I heard you done kilt yo woman?" He say, "Yes, I'm lookin fur that man.

I got mad. I got bad. Wit my gun in my hand."

Freddie said, "Looka here, Judge. Judge, how could you stand

Have a low-down woman, spendin yo money, foolin round wit anothuh man?

It makes her bad. You bein mad." Wit a gun in his hand.

Freddie say, "Now, Mama. Mama, ya hafta let me go.

Cause the woman's mistreated me, an I had ta shoot her so.

You'd a got mad. I got bad. Hoo wit my gun."

Freddie's mama say, "Now, Son, you my only chile, I know.

But you shot an killt that woman. Now, boy, I hate ta see you go,

For bein bad. Bein mad. Wit yo gun in yo hand."

Freddie's papa say, "Son, here where you done wrong:

When you found out that woman wadn treatin you right, Son, whynt you let her alone?

You got mad. You got bad. Hoo wit yo gun in ya hand."

Freddie said, "Looka here, Papa. Papa, wouldn you a got mad?

You'd a comin home, an found Mama wit anothuh man in yo bed?

You'd a got mad. You got bad. Hoo wit yo gun in ya hand."

Freddie's papa said, "Yeah, Son. I'll tell you what I'm goin do.

If the judge give you foedy years, I'll have em apardon you

For bein a bad. Mmm mad. Wit yo gun in yo hand."

Freddie said, "I done laid down, Papa, tried not ta pay im no
  mind.
But a while befoe day, I was woke. Heard some sprangs acryin.
I got mad. I got bad." He wit a gun, in his hand.

Now he sung his way outa the jailhouse. But when I
learnt that song I hadn never heard Freddie sang it. How I
got the words, an got em rhymed together: a boy brought it
ta Navasota from Marlin. Thats near about Waco. He was
whistlin that song an sangin it, but he couldn play a gittah
one.

An this fella come ta me. He sung that song, maybe foe or
five times, where I was playin at a Suppa. An I rearranged
that song, an then I come ta playin from that night, until
right now. Ohhh, Lawd, I wisht I could thank back there. I
reckon say it was somewhere long about, in the twenty-
second year. Nineteen an twenty-two. Playin right here in
town one Satiddy night. Cause it couldn a been twenty-
one, because I had done come back from Dallas, where
Blind Lemon was at, when I heard Freddie.

I'm the only man played "Freddie," but the man was in
the jailhouse. An he wadn on record. But see, I made a
record outa it, on my numba one issue: "Freddie." Its jest
as true as I'm talkin ta you. Thats a True Story Song.
Nearly ever song I sang about somebody's life. Even it
might be by *my* life. An everbody show liked that song
cause its sech a straight, straight song.

Caint ta Caint and Walter Mobley in De Pressure

In Navasota, African-Americans worked and lived under "De Pressure" all their lives. It manifested itself in the daily "caint ta caint" work cycle, from predawn to twilight (from "caint see" to "caint see"); in the five-and-a-half-day workweek, capped off by the roaring Saturday Night Suppers and the Baptist church penance and religious ecstasy the following morning; and in the seasonal cycle of the agricultural year. Except for 1945, all of Mance's years before his "discovery" ended with his facing Christmas either further in debt or just breaking even after an entire year's work on ten to twenty-five acres of land. When the Great Depression ("De Pressure") arrived in the thirties, it is no wonder that Mance paid it little heed. For a decade, whites got a taste of "the blues" that blacks had been savoring ever since slavery times. "De Pressure" may have left a bittersweet taste of irony in Mance's mouth.

From the Allenfarm and other county prison farms, which drew their labor as much from minor offenders as from felons, to the use of dogs in the fields for infant child care, to infant and disease mortality, to out-and-out murder on the turnrows, "De Pressure" was a way of life. It was a constant blacks could depend on. Out of "De Pressure" came "de blues."

The sharecropping system replaced slavery as a means to maintain productivity on the cotton plantations. Mance was born and began his turn behind the plow on the Michelborough Farm. By 1922 he had found Walter Mobley, who became Mance's "boss man" and one of his best white friends. This relationship lasted until 1944, when Mobley gave Mance a team of mules so that he could move up from sharecropping "halvers" (giving half of every crop) to the rent-farming stature of having to give the landowner every third bale of cotton and every fourth bushel of corn. "Thirds and fourths" became a synonym for rent-farming. Finally, Mance worked for Johnny Sommers from the end of World War II until 1956, whereupon Mance ended his career as a farmer when he moved to Houston to get free of this system—only to return to Navasota two years later.

Walter Mobley was an anomaly in the midst of this way of life. Respected and loved by blacks, but run off his farm by his brother-in-law, Mobley never fit the stereotype of the brutal, exploitative landowner. Balancing him out, though, were Tom Moore and his brother Harry, who came to own Allenfarm, the largest prison farm in Mance's precinct. Some would argue that Mance's downright refusal to play "Tom Moore's Farm" in Navasota was unwarranted, but none of these folks had experienced during their childhood the lynching of an "uppity" member of their race, witnessed the shooting of a fellow worker in their twenties, endured the framing and hanging of their best friend in their early thirties, and had a cousin whose bones were found in a cotton field long after he was shot and left for dead. Through it all, Mance was steadily working with his mules, his hands, and the earth. Studying a way to survive. Studying how to get through and out of his circumstances. And playing the Saturday Night Suppers nearly every week.

Mance saw himself as a farmer first and a musician second. Farmwork occupied most of his hours. He excelled at this tedious, risky, time-honored occupation, and he excelled as a musician. He had more experience leading a team of mules than he had leading a floor full of dancers, a house full of listeners and eaters, and a yard full of gamblers and lookers-on. It wasn't the work itself that dissatisfied him. He loved his relationship with the animals and the land, but he was never given financial credit for it. The world recognized him for his musical skills, but he was never rewarded for his farming expertise.

LIKE WE SETTIN HERE, I'm jest happy as I kin be. Because it used ta be I had ta git up an go ta that field, from caint ta caint. An boooy, when I'd git out that field, this time a year be so hot. July, August. Bathin didn hep you at all.

I used ta be walkin along, had my leg jest wide open. Chafed it. Followin them mules. Heat rash. I seed people had it so bad til blood, had it ta pulse—viberation in their thighs—while they was walkin.

My brother had it so bad, he keep his leg over this side an one over here. Tuck a bode an heist that winda an let the wind blow in on im, an first thang you know, he'd be gone ta sleep. They put some powder between his legs. An that thang would git raw again the next day.

Boy, talkin bout pullin some hawd days, I pulled em. I

workt so hawd in my lifetime, look like I dreams about it now. An I wake up in the mownin, thankin I got ta go ta the field. I lay there an git myself reckomasized. I say "Aw, the devil! I aint got ta go ta the field this mownin."

Fifty-nine years! How in the devil I'm gonna git rid a that jest soon as I stawt out with this music bizniss, about twelve years ago? You caint furgit it in twelve years. Gonna take some time fur me ta furgit the way I had been perfawmin an actin in the field, an cuttin cordwoods an diggin ditches, an aliftin rocks an totin spools a wire from here ta downtown an back. An all that kinda stuff.

You know what? We used ta git up in the mownin, it was foe o'clock. We had ta git up when ya hear that bell rangin. You seed that bell out at Mista Tom's, hadn ya? Well now, he aint the only one had the bell, but he got the one cost mown iny average person on the fawm. Them other people had a little bells. Mista Tom's bell cost ya somewhere long about a thousand dollas. Kin hear it five an ten mile!

You know what the first bell is? "Blaing! Blaing!" Git up. An git ya breakfast. An then anothuh hour, it'll rang again. That be five o'clock. Lets go ta the lot. Mules hemmed up in there so you could catch ya mule an git yo gears on em an go ta the field.

You better be in that lot, five o'clock: everbody catchin them mules. An when they git the mule caught, put the hawness on em, then they jest strung out a there an headed on down the turnrow. You'd plow two mules, I plowed two. We'll have em tied mouth ta mouth.

An we'll go ta the field. We're sposed ta be there when daylight come. Standin on the turnrow. Then hookt up yo plow. Sometime you couldn see down the rows no furthern a mule ta where yo plow was settin. Til the sun rose an you kin see way down the road: may be twenty people right down side an side on the turnrow. My plow side a yo's, next one side a the next one.

An then we say, "Come up!" Ever one a them mules was

275

trained so when ya say im ta come up, you done said come up ta all of em. One mule is the lead out. Jest say, "Come up there!" Maybe the mule's name was old Ada or old Beck or old Manny. Named after people. An them mules knowed their name, did you know that? Show they knowed their name.

One thang, you cannot take a mule an say, "Well, I got a mule colt." Ta be a pure mule, he's part hawss an part jenny. Jennyjack. Got a little body, little legs, an got a big long head an long ears. You seen them little old thangs look like a little old rabbits hoppin around. "Aank! Aank! Aank!" Jack got biggest head you ever seed. You take that jack, an breed im to a mare: he'll mate wit a mare an git a mule colt by that mare.

Now a jack git a jenny by a jennyjack. But the mule caint breed. When he come in there bein a mare mule, thats fur as he'll git. Cause he's bred, crosst up. He's half hawss an half jack.

Well you never hear that bell no mow until twelve o'-clock. That bell was at the place where you come ta feed yo mules. An git yo dinna? You call that a corral. That bell would rang, an then you come in an git you a little food, an throw the mules a basket a cone or hay or what you feedin em on. An one o'clock, it'd rang again.

Five ta twelve? Plowed an choppt an raised the devil! Thats what you'd do! Yeah, talkin bout what you do, you better be workin.

First cultivator I ever saw was nineteen an twenty-two. You dont know what a cultivator is, do ya? It had two handles, an a tongue. A mule is on this side, mule's on that side. An it had a breast yoke hung on the mules, ta hold that tongue up. Put a breast chain in it, an that hold them mules apart. That mule take one part of it: as he walks, it would go to an fro. All right, you hook that chain down the side a his back, to a iron singletree. Thats a iron bar about that long. Hook that up ta the left-side mule, an say, "Come up!"

Then you put sweeps on that. Sorta like a big blade, cuts the ground up. An you git between them two handles. An you could carry them handles to an fro, cut the grass, an git back off the cotton. I'm the onliest cultivator man ever stawted ta plowin wit a cultivator. One row.

When we stawted ta plowin, we didn have but one sweep an one sweep stock. Sumpm like ya pushin these here plows down in the gawden. Well, our plows was biggern that. One plow was hookt up ta one singletree, an a pair a lines. The mule was learnt ta git up side a the cotton, an you hold the handles up aside the cotton. An go to an fro, see, it would cut the cotton up if you wadn steady drivin.

You ever seed a plow? A turnin plow had one side, an it throw dirt ta the side. See, you'd put that plow so deep in the ground, an then you say, "Come up, mule!" It broke that dirt'll throw way over here, about six or eight inches over ta the right. Then you drove up one side, an come back on the othun, an lap that dirt. Take two full drives, an that row was finisht. Jest like you kiver up a ditch? That plow would kiver that up. Thats a turnin plow.

Then the cultivators come in; you didn drive but one row was all you had ta do. An count. Cause it was two sweeps: one was on this left side, one on this side, an a handle. You walkt between em. See, we done that when we was makin the cotton. You know, cultivate? After it come up, well we was keepin the weeds an grass outa the cotton.

We had a strain on little bitty cotton, cause be careful or we gonna kiver up that cotton. We knowed how close ta git to it. Everbody couldn use the cultivator. An when it got up knee high, we could git away from it a little further, why it wouldn be worryin us so high that way.

An if you got dry an wanted a little drank a water, well they had water on the turnrow. In wagons. One mule had a

Ed Lathan with mule, plowing his garden, 1978. Ed and Lilly Lathan were good neighbors of Mance's while the Lipscombs lived on Johnny Sommers' farm. *Photo by Lucy Loscocco.*

thang on em jest like you'd hitch up the hawss to a buggy? Had two wheels on it. An then it had them shavs went through it, an a barrel settin in that thang. You take yo mules down into the field, an ever time you moved back up ta the turnrow: well, you call fur some water, it settin right there. You go there an git you a drank, or maybe a water boy brang you some. Then turn yo mules around an go back the other way. It moved as you move. Right down the turnrow.

This kinda weather, you know how miny days it take cotton ta come up after you plant it? You planted it wit a planter. It sumpm in there got a gear, a little old clog goes over an over, an got one wheel.

An you had one mule up on top a that row, an he's pullin that planter, an you's right behind that planter, it goin "Cuhhrr ludlu ludlu ludlu." Had two little bitty old sweeps on it. An when it go ta the end, them little sweeps would kiver them cottonseed up.

A lot a people planted earlier than others. Now you take a fast fawma: they had plenty a seeds, an a lot a time they would plant early, hopin for a early crop. Yeah, Mista Mow an them would plant in March. It was cold then. Most times it'd git sumpm or nother where it couldn come up, an it'd lay there too long in the ground an them seeds would rot. Because it was too much cold weather on em. Come a frost or the ground still be cold. An then you couldn do nothin wit it but let it lay there or either plow it up.

But he had plenty a seeds ta waste. We didn have no seeds ta waste, little old cheap fawma. We'd take our best shot. We'd plant first a April. When its warm. We git our first seeds down, so we'd come up with a regular right time. In three days that cotton was comin out the ground. Never did miss a crop.

An then noontime come: they had a lot boy ta feedin the mules. All you had ta do is go there an pull the bridle off the mule, an he go over ta the trough an commence ta eatin.

Was a lot boy a boy or a man? What you thank a boy gonna do out there wit all that kinda stuff? Better be a man! He couldn lift up them baskets an put that feed out there if he wadn a man. Had ta see to it the mules had enough feed in there, or too much feed. You seed a trough? They carry that feed along there befoe the mules come out the field. An then thats all the mules had ta do, jest back their ears an go up ta that trough. Go ta eatin.

Thats what that lot boy was out there: he was trained ta that. Befoe he ever stawted, they come give him, in request. Said, "Do you know how ta feed mules?"

Say, "Yassuh, I know how, but its accordin ta how miny baskets you wanta give em. Dont wanta give em too much, an I will give em enough."

Said, "Well, I want twenty mules fed. An I want you ta give em a half a bushel to a mule."

Well we would give em a half a basket a cone, an they had enough.

I never was the lot boy. I didn work on them big fawms where you hafta be estimated how much ta give yo mule. They had maybe a hunnud head a mules in there. That estimated to a hunnud head a people. But a smaller fawm like I was on, why I jest had a pair a mules ta feed. An caught our mules an went ta the field.

I went ta several fawms I was workin. No, I never did have my own fawm. I was workin by the fawm arrangement. Out at my fawm, we had about twenty famlies. Thats about five-hunnud-acre fawm. If it was twenty men on that fawm, an I was the landowner, I had twenty famlies ta care fur, an twenty teams a mules ta feed.

Jest like you stayed in that house over there, somebody else stayed over there, an on down til you counted maybe fifteen or twenty famlies was on that fawm. An them houses, some of em lookt good as this one, some of em was raggedy. Accordin ta yo family: you had a big famly, you got a big house. An if you had a little famly, jest you an yo wife, you didn need no big house. But you had a lot a chillun, you needed a whole lot a room fur em.

Yeah, we planted cotton. Planted cone. An we choppt cotton. Choppt cone. An plowed it an pickt it. Cotton an cone what I was raised up, until long about in fifty or fifty-one. Then we went ta raisin feedstuffs. You know, bail hay an plant some feedstuff fur cows. Up until fifty-six, thats when we left the fawm.

An so, you come outa the field at twelve. Eat yo dinna. All us settin round the table, eatin peas, diffunt thangs. I dont know what my mama'd cook, but she was a good cook. An my wife too. I see people kin stop eatin an do sumpm other else, but man, my whole hawt an mind's in it: I want eatin when I eat, an holla stop til I git through. Then I kin do sumpm else.

My wife cook all kinda diffunt mixtree: pie an meat, an soup an sumpm. Conebread. Ham bone. Ham hocks. I likes that. Now I tell you what. If you cook the ham hock: boil im in the beans, black-eyed peas or sumpm like that, I'll eat it. I'll know it if they come cookt in the same water, at the same time. Cause I was raised that way. Thats how I got nated to em. You brang a piece a ham by itself, well I dont want it.

An when the bell rung at one o'clock, you hafta go back ta the field. They didn hafta rang no bell fur you ta come out at night, cause you couldn quit til the sun went down: thats caint ta caint. Thats right. The sun was yo bell. You know the sun down when it sposed ta be turnin into night. You dont sposed ta work at night.

So they was cryin fur, "Hurry up! Hurry up, let the sun go down." An we'd sang that song about, "Hurry up sun! Go down, an hide yoself behind the western hill." See the sun go down in the west. Maybe five or ten people git ta sangin that same song. Tryin ta make the day go away.

M-hm. Inythang come up in our minds, we sang inythang we wanta. Man, we sung diffunt songs all through the day! We jest walkin alongside a one anothuh. An, we talk sometime. In amongst the row, you know. An first thang you know, say, "Whynt you sang a good song?"

"I blieve I will." An bust out an go ta sangin that song. An then ever one of us is sangin the same song, same verse. Us close enough fur us ta hear one anothuh. Jest like if you like a song, you'll sang it, wouldn ya? An sometime it'd make ya feel better. Sometime maybe it'd worry ya. Songs estimate on ya mind. Make yo mind wonder. Blues near about the same thang. Why? Because blues make you have bad, or a good feelin. You first be happy. Or maybe you git sorry first. Whatever concentrate in yo mind, you gonna do that. Git rid of it. You wanta git rid a some good feelin, you turn it into some sad feelin. Blues is jest music wit a feelin.

Yeah. We had a lot a fun, an a lot a worrynation. Its a whole lot in fawmin. If I was able ta fawm, thats the happiest life ever I lived in my life, even if I didn git nothin outa it. Because, see, I was nated ta fawmin. I knowed exackly what steps ta take ta make a fawm.

So like I was tellin ya, when that sun go down, you had ta go ta the lot wit yo mules. If you couldn ride yo mules, you walkt out an drove em out. Some mules would pitch, an you couldn git on em.

Man, plenty mules would throw you an kill you. Shuh man, yeah! I had a little old mule called Caesar. I broke him. He was about, aw, a little mule colt. An he wouldn let nobody catch im but me. He'd kick ya. An they wouldn let nobody ride im.

I couldn ride im. Nooo, Lawd. I didn hafta do but put the gay on im, tied ta his mouth wit a strang, you know. Caesar jest walk right up alongside that little mule I was ridin. Followin me, I didn hafta tie im.

An then go up ta that plow. I got off that mule I was ridin, an Caesar'd be standin up side a there. An I hook im up ta his iron singletree. An then tie his mouth together. An put a line over there on im, one on this side. An then he'd follow that mule into the jumpin-off place.

But you couldn catch im. It was about maybe thirty or foedy mules in that lot. We'd catch mules by lamplight. Couldn see how ta catch em. Maybe I done got yo mule, an I oughta had my mule. But when we git ta the field, an daylight come, if I found out I had the wrong mule, why then, we changed mules.

But you could see what they was doin wit my mule. I never will furgit that little old mule. The boss man knowed sumpm was done happenin between them thirty or foedy mules in that lot. An I could walk up to im, an he'd throw his head down an I put the bridle on im. But when some-body else walk up to im, try ta say, "Whoa, Caesar!" Man, he would paw ya. Kick ya.

An then I had me anothuh mule, never did stay in that lot. Dawk come, out he jump. Ever mownin I go ta the lot, jest as well head fur the woods cause thats where he at: hidin an eatin. Til I done found me anothuh mule, an here he come back ta the lot: gonna eat up all the feed in there. An no use goin off in the woods huntin im, cause I look high an near, couldn find im nohow.

It was months on end befoe I discovered his where-abouts. Finely, me an my friendboy Beck out huntin one evenin: I spotted that mule back in them woods, by a big old oak tree. I say, "Hht! Now what in the devil you reckon he doin, standin there facin that tree like he study starin it?" Lookt like he was lookin right through that tree nearly.

I sot there, sot there. Direckly, he move a little bit this way. Then he move again. Ever time he moved, he line up with that tree jest like a hand on a clock. Say, "Now this sumpm I aint never seed befoe."

Direckly, a twig snap an the leaves rattle over yonda. An here the mule move again, but then I seed what he's alook-in at. Here Beck on tother side a that tree, an he still aint seed that old mule. He'd move, mule move right along wit im. A deer pull the same trick, did you know that?

I say, "Well mule, you purdy smawt. All this time you been akeepin from me, hidin out an keepin out a day's work. You knows considable well. But, one thang you dont know: they's two mens in the woods this day."

An Beck, he jest keep movin, had his eyes out fur a bird or possum or rabbit or sumpm. Old mule sidle around that tree til he lookin at him an I'm lookin right down on his tail end.

Level that shotgun down on im, an poppt im wit a round a buckshot. That mule honkt an hollad an lit out fur the lot lopin! An jumpt the fence into the lot. Didn even break his gait! Ohhh, I didn have near the sturbment outa him after that.

I was on the Mobley Fawm then. I was a showfur on that fawm. I did that from nineteen twenty-two up until thirty-one or thirty-two. An my boss man, he liked ta let me drive fur im. He'd give out, an I drive him hunnud or two miles. Ta Foat Worth an buy a carbox a mules.

I'd git in the caw, an they'd leave here at night: maybe midnight we stawt out. In the mownin, we'd be in Foat Worth fur him ta git a bid on them cows. An they got mules in them lots, call it the shippin pen. Wild mules, all kinda mules. Some of em you could handle, an some of em you had ta break em. Had never seen nobody. See, they raised them mules out in big pastors out in West Texas an places, an shippt em in there by cawloads, an auctioned em off.

They out there in them old corrals an pens an thangs, jest ahollerin an pawin an carryin on. He'll look at em an pick out a certain amount a mules or cows. Jest like these old wild longhone cows: durn, you could ride on them hones if you could set up there. Hone what they hook with.

An when they give im a price on em, he'd have em load em up in the cawbox. Buy fifty an sixty head, sometime a hunnud head. Ship em back here on the train ta Navasota an Brazos Bottom, an sell em.

Walter Mobley. M-hm. He was the best white man ever been in Navasota. Ta colored folks. He never did come out in the fields, talk about fightin us an kickin us around. Nah. You could always look ta him: he's a friendly man, talk to im, realize wit im.

An somebody tell him sumpm bout his hands, he said, "Well, did they do iny damage on yo place? I pay you fur it."

Say, "I'm goin beat it out im!"

Say, "I'll pay you fur the damage if they done some damage."

Walter Mobley in the 1920s. *Photo courtesy the Marcus Mallard Collection.*

A lot a time, they tell lies on us, an he knowed it. "Aw, his damn dog got in my henhouse an kilt all the chickens." "Nigga broke in the lot an rode one a my hawsses til he's sweatbackt."

He say, "Well, I'll pay you fur the damage fur how much he done over there." An we aint done nothin.

An when we'd git behind that fella's back, I'd say, "Mista Mobley, that man there beat you out a yo money. We didn do that."

He'd say, "I done that ta protect ya. I know you didn do it. If I hadn a paid it, he'd always had a grudge against ya. Catch you off from me, he wanta beat an knock ya."

I said, "Yeah, you right."

He'd tell me, some old mean men say, "YOU LET YO NIGGAS HAVE THEIR WAY! You dont do em like it oughta be done. Hafta be mean ta those damn niggas. Beat em an knock em."

He said, "Well, you do yo's thataway. I'm gonna treat em Right. All I want em ta do: ta tell me what they need, an if I kin git it to em I'll give it to em, an then when they work fur it I'll pay em." Man, they hated im cause he wouldn fight niggas.

Now Walter Mobley, he even partly raised me. He stayed on Fuqua Prairie. You leave my house, an go right on up the road ta where he was bawn an raised. An I workt wit im somewhere about twenty-eight or twenty-nine years.

I follad him from Doc Emory's to a place called White Switch down there, befoe you git ta Allenfawm. Nearby the Navasot. A little old stop-by, you know, ta git off the train an load cotton or mules an thangs.

I follad im from White Switch into Courtney. That was nineteen an twenty-two. Stayed in Courtney twelve years wit im. An I stayed wit im over there in the bottom at White Switch, about two years—that was foeteen years. Then I was workin fur Mobley back in that direction on the J. T. Lott Fawm. Musta been along in thirty-foe, cause Little Mance's first wife had her first chile in thirty-five, an we was at Lott's place then. But that baby died not too long after it was bawn. An I stayed wit Mobley there in Washington somewhere long about eleven years. Til foedy-five.

Oh, I got grown an he kep me with him. Until him an his brother-in-law got up ta this place: they owned a fawm. Least his wife an his wife's brother, they inherited a fawm between they papa an mama: an her brother was sorta mean. No sort in it. He didn want his sister's husband be on the same fawm! He wanted ta take all the whole thang on his shoulder an do what he want.

So Mobley told his wife, say, "I'm gonna move my fawm an my people off the place, an I'll go somewhere else. Cause I dont wanta kill yo brother, an I dont want him ta kill me. He got a ways I dont like. Now, you caint git yo part untangled from yo brother, an divide the land up where you have yo part. You jest let it stay like it is, an I'll go rent me a place ta put my hands over there."

An so we went ta Washington, an stayed over there twelve or thirteen years. He stayed in Navasota. But he would go ta Washington ta fawm.

An then his old brother-in-law tried ta come over there in Washington. Tell him what ta do.

He said, "Let me tell you one thang: I dont come over there an tell you what ta do. You got me ta leave the place over there in Courtney, an I give Courtney up ta you. Now I've got me a fawm rented over here in Washington, an you stay away from here!"

Oh, the Lotts owned leagues a land back in there. Jest like the Mow brothers. You couldn never tell which is which, cause some little youpps didn blong ta the Lotts, an some little youpps didn blong ta the people what was callin theirself ownin it. Youpp a land: you know, little corners. Thats a shawt way we called it when I was comin up.

Jest like you hear me say a while ago about mules. Podna, when the sun go down, you lead that mule back into the lot gate. An the lot boy had the key, he lock that gate. An you went home when you left the lot. Go ta yo house an feed an try ta git a little sleep.

An only way you hunted is in the wintertime when it'd rain or be cold, an somebody had a possum an coon dog, you go ta huntin with him. Or we wadn workin the next day. You couldn hunt an work man, shit! Where you gonna work an hunt? Gonna hunt that bed! Cause listen: ten hours a day, you done made it. Overmade it. Man, you'll fall dead out there walkin an huntin at night. Tamarra you got ta rest, man.

An so, thats kep us under a mood a tryin ta be of ourself. Take care a ourself. I had ta go ta bed, when I eat suppa. About no latern nine o'clock. Catch up with that hawd day's work I done done. So I could meet the Man the next day.

I rememba one time, I was on Sommers' place an Johnny Ewing was my neighbor there, an pickt cotton fur me sometime. Lemme see, he had a little old whelp, called im Blue. He's a dog but he's a blue tick. We went down there in Sommers' place an fained a possum down on the Brazos River one night. Jest as you drop off that hill. An she trailed that possum plumb over there, down on Mow's place. An he shot im, the old possum's in a nest an musta kilt im. Cause he laid down an wouldn look no mow.

Now T Roberson, he had old Sam an old Coon, an a black-an-tan dog, Ransom. Well he'd git there an lay his leg cross like that. Then Sam git around there, he set there an lay there, an after while he bawk an he rap on that tree, an if they dont go ta fallin on the ground, he was up there. That old rascal could show slay a coon.

Well, I been aware a dogs all my life. Mother, she had a bunch a us kids. An the least of us workt in the fields. All a the little kids, like babies on down ta three months old, they carry em ta the field an put em under a tree.

An its three of us raised up under one dog. That dog wouldn let you come up ta that tree ta save yo life. An when one baby done stawt ta walkin an big enough ta git around an protect hisself: Mama an Papa back on an lay the second baby out under a tree. Put im in a old blanket or sumpm there, where he wouldn git in the sun.

An that dog was layin right there at that tree. An the rows what we was workin was purdy good long rows, you know. A lot a people was in the field; they'd git ta talkin an sangin an goin on. An you couldn hear, oh, fur enough fur discover that baby was hollerin. But that dog go ta bawk-in, jest like sumpm anothuh comin up ta that tree. An that baby would holla.

An if you come up there an wadn none in that famly, you couldn come near that chile, or man you'd hafta kill that dog.

Befoe I come over here in Grimes County, we had a old bobtail dog, called im Old Jack. Well, he look like he had part bulldog in im, had a big head. My boy over there raised im. Old Jack been nated to a bunch a kids. That boy a mine had foe wives an ever one of em found kids. Quit one, an marry anothun, they'd have kids!

An we'd go out in the field, an put Old Jack out there under a tree, an throw a tow sack or sumpm there. An he lay on that sack, an that baby was right there by a big old shade tree. He laid right there wit his foots crosst. Never would catch im wit his foots straight out there.

An he'd look at that baby until we went an come back ta see about that baby. An a snake: we seed foe or five snakes a day. You know a lot a snakes is on the river, an they'd come up there under shade cause that baby's in the shade. That dog see them snake come acrawlin up there, great big old moccasins an pilots.

An we'd git there an have two or three snakes: he done kilt em. Shook em an had the guts out of em. He catch im right in the middle a his back, an commence ta slangin im. When he git through slangin im, he's dead.

An Little Mance had a second wife. Them kids be playin outdoze or sumpm like that, Jack wouldn let nobody come in the yawd. An when she git ta whuppin one a those kids, you know she couldn whup them kids? When they git ta hollerin, Jack come in there an see about them chillun. If she didn shet that doe quick, he gonna tear up that girl's dress off! Jest flat off her. Alice hated Old Jack. He come in that house an make her let them kids alone. Now you tell me a dog aint got sense? He just caint talk.

One a the best friends you got is a dog. People say people. Listen, I say a dog is the best friend, cause sometime people go ta sleep. That dog if he's outdoze, he stay awoke an smell that scent fur sumpm comin up towards you strange, or too much noise: he gonna let you know. Podna, he gonna take care a you. Thats why I say he's the best friend, because you aint got no friend when people sleepin in the house like you are.

Five or six miles, if they's a stawm or sumpm comin, nawth, them dogs an hawsses kin smell that wind five miles befoe it git there. I know that cause I was raised up with the hawsses an cows an dogs. Jest like its a big cloud come in the nawth, an the hawsses an mule out on the prairie or out in the woods: when that stawm git nearby, them hawsses an mules an cows an dogs commence ta rowin an runnin, it wadn long befoe a stawm comin.

The wind is a powerful thang, an a dog know sumpm another by scent. They caint talk, they kin bawk, but they kin know they masta by scent. An know a stranger. An how they kin figger that out? Well I oughta know now, cause I had over about a hunnud dogs in my life.

I'm got a pen a dogs. Been pairin em a purdy good while, greyhounds? I got em all scattered round diffunt places. Since I been in this music bizniss, I dont have a chance ta hunt much. But I still love them dogs an got a nice pen built out there.

I got one, I couldn keep im in that pen. I blieve it was seven foot high, an he come out there some way, I dont know how that dog would git outa there. An that dog didn have but three legs. Coal black, his name was Coaly. He broke his leg runnin a jack rabbit, an fell in a hole? Wadn a rabbit on earth could outrun that dog. He might outduck im an git away. But jest stay where he could see im, Coaly jest run that rabbit so fast he could outrun the rabbit.

So this man bought him fur a breed dog, an I hunted wit

290

Mance with greyhound, 1971. *Photo by Bill Records.*

im. We was out here by Fuqua Prairie one day, an that dog
was runnin a rabbit. I was off from im. An he come ta me
totin that dog.

I say, "Whats the madda wit old Coaly?"

An he might near was cryin, cause he loved old Coaly.

291

White fella, Mista Johnny. He said, "He broke his leg. Mance, could you kill im? I thank too much of im ta kill im."

I say, "Well, what you thank? I love im too, an he aint none a mine."

He said, "Well, he aint gonna never be no mow good."

I say, "I aint gonna kill im."

Well, he toted im onta the truck. His leg was jest limber. In three places broke his leg right up where this second joint up here. He was bleedin.

Brought that dog here, ta my house. I said, "What you want im here fur?"

Said, "I dont wanta see im. You wont kill im, an I caint kill im. Jest put im out here."

An you know what I did? I bandaged that dog's leg wit some sticks ta kinda brace it. Done purdy good til them sticks come off one night. An then it bent back again.

So finely, we went over here ta Mista Beard, he was a vetenarian. Try ta save that leg cause he was a real good runnin dog. He say, "He got too miny bones broke in there. I'll charge ya seven dollas. You take pity an have it cut off."

Now when I done pickt im up, I said, "Mista Johnny, I got Coaly's leg cut off."

He said "Well, he's yo dog. Whatever it cost ya, I'll pay ya fur it."

An I kept that dog round here, I reckon, two years. Maybe three years. An you know what that old three-legged dog would do? He would catch a jackrabbit with them three legs. A jackrabbit! Mista Johnny didn blieve that. You might not blieve it.

One day, I had three or foe other dogs an he had five or six dogs. He went down towards a big prairie. I said, "Mista Johnny, you aint got no dog." I hoorawed im all the time.

He said, "Whats the madda wit my dog?"

I said, "Old Coaly outrun yo dog. Three-legged Coaly."

He lookt at me jest as funny. He said, "Man, that dog caint run."

I said, "Well, I'm gonna brang im next time I come. An I got some money ta put up he'll outrun yo dogs."

He said, "Well, I aint gonna bet ya, but I'll tell you this: Coaly caint catch no rabbit."

I carried old Coaly out there one day, an all those dogs runnin loose an he's hoppin on that front leg.

An after while, Mista Johnny say, "Yonda he goes!" That old jackrabbit was up.

Old Coaly beat all them dogs ta that rabbit! An he stoppt jest considable an lookt at me. He said, "You know that old, three-leg bastud done beat my dogs up aside that rabbit? Mance, he'd a caught im too!"

But he couldn balance hisself with that one leg, you know. An when he got up ta the rabbit ta retch at im ta grab im, he turnt a flip wit it.

An when he got up an straightened up, the other dogs had the rabbit an gone. He didn know which way that rabbit went.

Oh, I had greyhounds fur a long time, fifteen or sixteen years. I had five or six greyhounds befoe I went ta Berkeley. Well inyhow, inybody like dogs bettern me, they hafta stawt ta eatin em. An I feed my dogs jest like I will my people. My wife told me one day I was out there—soon one mownin tuz still cold—seein how my dogs was. She say, "I blieve you thank mow a them dogs'n you do me."

Its a funny thang, that you wouldn blieve some a the thangs I kin tell you about went on in my lifetime. I have went an parcht cone: aw, you'd dig a little hole in the ashes, an kiver the cone up wit em. But its got ta be hot. Cone'll swell when it git hot til it pop out them ashes. It git on ya, an you kin see cone flyin all over the prairie nearly. An I've put ashes all around my mouth, eatin that parcht cone fur make-a-day—fur a meal. Cause it was the ashes had a good taste to it. I had as miny ashes in me as I did cone.

Ashes'll wash you out. Clean ya inside out. Thats right. We wadn sick, in our days. No docta didn hafta come see about us. We had grapes. Three kinds a grapes: mustang, an old post oak grapes. Next was these thangs what you make wine outa: muskydine. Find em in these ravines.

Cows on these pastors might near keep the grapes et down. When it was aplenty woods in here, you could go down that creek over by Sommers' place, called that No Man's Land cause nobody ever did come possession of it. I hunted back there; its dawk in the daytime. Big old wood rabbits, we called em swamp rabbits. They big as a coon nearly. They's the best eatin rabbit in the woods.

They used ta have, well, it is three kinds a rabbits: I already called swamp. An then its a shawt one called cottontail. Next one is jackrabbit. I hunt all of em.

An then its three kinds a M's, did you know that? When you go ta the commissary, they furnishes so much food an allowance to ya. On a fawm. All right. People used ta have a way a gittin back at their boss mans, ya know. Colored folks had a lot a sense, when white folks thought they didnt. They could talk about they landowners an their men who works em, an say sumpm that they didn know what they was talkin about.

So one colored fella say, "If you dont watch yaself, I'll send ya where you kin git ya three M's at."

An the other fella say, "What three imz?"

Say, "If you dont watch me, I'll send ya where you caint git nothin but them three M's furnisht to ya: meat, meal, an molasses."

So this guy stirbd up a big word he could slang on that fella. An they went ta fightin bout that three M's. Cause the fella in the know was hoorawin im, an the one didn know got hisself stirred up over gittin put in the Dozens nearly. So they kep that goin I reckon, since seventy-five years ago.

But now that pellagra, that was ragin in here somewhere, nineteen thirty-two it come in here. Its sumpm like the influenza. That thang invented from these planations. Pellagra is sumpm jest like the diabetes. Well, these people out here in these fawms wouldn give the colored people enough break ta have no flour an diffunt ingredients. You heard me say them three M's? Jest raise cone cone cone cone cone. Fed em up with cone.

It tuck a inside nature, inside a yo stomach? You couldn commanacrete. Mannacue yo food, it went down, that old husk stuck to ya. Its sumpm like cancer. They jest wouldn let ya have no food. An a lot a people commenced ta takin down with pellagra. An so, from one to anothuh taken down. They jest git sick, an you caint git over it.

Now what my daughter-in-law, Little Mance's first wife, come down in the bog wit, it was a diffunt sickness than that. Lemme see, we called her Little Sister Odom, an call Little Mance Brother. She come outa Odoms famly. She got down wit kidney trouble. An she done got near about blind, her eyes swelled. Yo kidneys, you know, got a whole lot effect on yo eyesights.

An Docta Hansen come ta her right back in the Lott Fawm. That was when the docta come ta yo house; you didn hafta come ta hisn. He waited on my famly. An she was in the madda nearly dead. An he doctored on her when he first stawted ta practishun.

An so he brought his bag in there, lookt down on her in the bed, an she was all swole up. Come on outa there, say, "You git two tablespoons a this down her, an do it three times in a day. If you hafta pry her mouth open, you git her ta swalla it. An if she'll take that medicine, she might pull through. I give her about fifty-fifty. But you dont, aint nothin ta keep her from dyin."

295

An my wife say, "Well, how long she go ta takin that medicine?"

He say, "You put a big pan underneath a her bed." See, in them days, we all slept on shuck mattress. Take pilla tickin an stuff it full a cone shucks, an that made us do fur a mattress. Dont be talkin bout no cotton mattress, man. An say, "You hear a water runnin in that pan, you know she done loosened up. An that swellin'll go down, an I blieve she'll be able ta see again."

So they done like he told em. An show nuff, it was late in the night next night or two, we heard that water come from beneath that bed where she's layin. Droppt down through them cone shucks into the pan. An so, he knowed he had struck some a the complaint with the medicine he was givin her.

An so I couldn pay im in money. I had somewhere along about ten or eleven cows, an I give him a cow ta pay her docta bill. An I been square wit im ever since I knowed im. I blieve he would say a good word ta inybody about me.

He raised Little Sister up til about eight years after he doctored on her. She got up an found two kids. An then she was drankin beer an whisky an all that sweet soda water. That was against her kidney. An then it tuck back on her again, an she died.

An that hapmd over in Washington on the Lott's. An so I stayed in Washington until years ta come. Then my boss man Mobley, he sided he would quit fawmin. He give me foe mules, a cultivator, an turnt me aloose rentin: thirds an foeth, thats the same thang, m-hm. Fur inybody I could rent from. Jest turnt the mules over in my hand an told people I had done workt an paid fur em: "If you wanta rent him some land, why he got the team, an he kin show cultivate. An he got a famly."

An havin my own team, that brought me up ta thirds an foeth: ever third load a cone, ever foeth bale a cotton, well that was the landowner's. An the rest of it was yo's. See, if

you didn have ya own team, you hafta give him half a inythang you raised. That was called halvers.

Yeah. They rented me land, cause I had my mules an
team an they didn hafta buy me no team. All they had ta
furnish me was some ways ta make a livin fur ta make that
crop. Go in an borry some money at a bank. An when the
end a the year come, my crop would pay fur my indebtments, ya see. If it didn pay this time, I pay so close to it,
why they let me have some mow anothuh year.

But I jest couldn git lucky ta make no money on the
fawm. Raised on it all my life. I like fawmin. Cause I understood it, an knowed how ta fawm. Ever near cut in a fawm,
I knowed how ta take that right angle on it. Knowed when
plantin time come fur cotton, cone, an thats what we was
raisin.

An I know what month ta stawt ta plantin, an know
what month ta lay by our crops, quit workin em? An scoop
up the dirt on the roots an stems? Call that layin by. An
gittin ready fur the cotton ta open ta pick: when you lay
by, you see a boll a cotton here an yonda open. An bout
eight or ten days after you see one boll open, you stawt ta
pickin an you got maybe half a bale ta the acre openin. An
then you go to a gin, have it ginned. An had it hauled ta
town an sold it.

Man, I was at home on a fawm. But I was treated so bad
on it, that I never could inherit nothin. Ever year I'd git in
debt, a little deeper an deeper. They jest kep me in debt so
they could work me, you know.

An how miny years I done that, its hawd ta tell. You
hafta figger that out wit a pencil, near about it. But I
stayed in Washington eighteen years. I rented from Mista
Mobley up there, two or three years befoe he give me the
mules. From thirty-six til sometime when that next big war
was stirrin.

After he quit fawmin, then the land wadn cultivatin
enough. It takes foe acres ta make a bale a cotton, might

297

Allenfarm cotton-loading dock, circa 1920s. John D. Rogers is on the right in jodhpurs. *Photo courtesy the Marcus Mallard Collection.*

near, on that poe land. Didn make me have no accumulation like I could make some money.

An my boss man, he never did fawm no mow, an he got sick an died. Somewhere long about nineteen sixty-three. Thats the reason I quit im. He quit me cause he quit fawmin. I'd a been fawmin with him I reckon right now, cause I liked him an he like me. Walter Mobley.

Then I drifted from Lott's, in Washington again, on the Bluffs. Upriver a few miles from where I was at. But I was on the riverbed. I stayed right in that precinct up the road, in foedy-five. On Sommers Fawm.

They had strong land round the riverbeds, ya see. We call them the bottoms. That land would make a bale or a bale an a half ta the acre. But I couldn git enough land up there ta suppoat my famly. If I coulda got about fifty or sixty acres, why I coulda inherited sumpm. Well, I couldn git over ten acres. That wadn but fifteen bales ta the highest that I could raise on that fawm.

John Sommers. Well, I reckon he was good in his way, but he wadn good ta me. Tuck all I made an robbed me. You know, when he was comin up in the world, he was lookin out fur hisself.

Listen: I was bawn a slave an didn know it. Yeah. My daddy was eight years old when slavery time declared freedom. The white people never did change it.

I call myself a slave until I got somewhere along about foedy-five years of age. I had ta go by the landowner's word. Do what he said ta git a home ta stay in. An then when I make my crop, why he sold the cotton, an figgered it out his own way. An brought me out in debt. I didn clear no money til nineteen foedy-five in my whole life.

An then the man what I was with, I cleared, I blieve, five hunnud dollas. An he wanta keep my money an give it to me if I needed it.

I told im, I say, "Mista Sommers, I thought you say I done paid you? An when I pay you, the money you owe me is my money. Not you keep it."

Say, "Oh, you gonna throw it away."

I say, "Well if I do, its mine."

See, after I done made five hunnud dollas, an cleared an paid the indebtments ta him what I owed im, was I out a debt? But he didn want me ta have it, unless he give it ta me like *he* wanta.

But thats all over now. I tuck it until I got tired, an run off an went ta Houston. Oh, I workt fur John Sommers somewhere along about eleven years. Never did git outa debt but that first year.

Well, how we gonna do when we didn know nowhere ta go? If I put you in this house an fasten you up, you caint git out. Well, we wadn fastened up in the house, but we was fastened up on their fawms. An we had ta go by what they said. Not only me, all the colored folks was in on that fawm arrangement.

You see, planation, thats a big fawm. They wouldn specify bein a planation unless you had about twenty famlies on yo place. Five or six people on yo place, you wadn no planation owner. But they git about fifty or maybe sixty hands on they place, an houses old piece a houses built. An they furnish you a team. You hafta work their team, fur halvers. An they shawpen the plows an keep the mules fed. An thats what they would put out: mules an feed. Then they'd git half the money outa that crop.

All he furnisht was mules an the tools. He'd git his free! Other than you jest workt their team. They bought thirty an foedy an fifty an sixty, seventy mules a year if they needed em. An hire you ta plow em an work em. An then you paid fur yo groceries an what clothes you woe outa yo half. Yo docta bills, whatever you got.

Sometime we come ta town, git some thangs at a stow. An sometime they haul em out from town in a wagon an put em in a commissary. An issue em out to ya. Commissary, you know what that is? A wayside house. It would stay lockt up, until Satiddy. Satiddy, you come up there an they brang maybe fifty or a hunnud sacks a flour. So much a this, so much a that, accordin ta the hands they had. Distribute amongst em. If they had a hunnud hands, they had a hunnud sacks a flour an a hunnud sacks a meal. Hunnud-pound sacks. An little black syrup, you know, molasses.

Oh, most you would git: cordin ta how big yo famly was. Thats five or six in the famly, you'd git a big sack. See, they wadn but two in the famly, like me an Elnora when we first stawted out, you'd git a small sack. Well you was charged with that. Entered it on a book. An you hafta pay that indebtments at end a the year, what you tuck up out that commissary.

How you gonna do iny better when aaall the colored folks was doin the same thang? An all of em went fur that. Wouldn nobody dispute the white man's word. We couldn—only time we had some, come privilege: on a Satiddy night. Go ta these Satiddy Night Suppas.

You know you was bosst, man you wouldn have that yoself. You know what boss man is? Tellin you what ta do an what you not ta do. A pusher an a shover. Well, we called em overseer. Thats the man what lookt after yo work an seed you was doin it correckly, or uncorreckly. What he say, why, it went.

An we was scared ta do sumpm he didn want us ta do. Is two thangs gonna hapm: you either got ta git whuppt or leave the place. If you didn do like the boss man say.

One man ridin his hawss, he could corral a hunnud people. One word spoke a hunnud times! He say, "I want you boys ta git this cut a land done today." Or tamarra.

Whatever the time he estimated fur ta git it finisht: a hunnud people agreed to it. No word back, say, "I caint do that." It wadn no caint.

Say, "Yassuh, I'm gonna try." Then you suited him.

An if you couldn do it, he'd fuss. Cuss you. Whup you. Kill you. Or run you off. Least you'd run yoself off. Keep from gittin into trouble. Lot a people jest went on off somewhere else. An never did see em no mow.

A lot a people that went off, they went an got em an brought em back. Jest like you had hogs git out yo pen, an you found out he's out, you go catch im an put im back in there. See what I'm talkin about? An thats the way people was estimated on.

An there them rascals all dead an gone now, an I'm still livin here. Man, I workt fur some haaawd men. Ya know, bein a fawma all my life, I seed stressful thangs hapm on a fawm. Now, I wadn grown when this hapmd. I was courtin Elnora then.

We had a fence divide fawms. See, like I was on this side

301

Tom Moore's farm overseer Elijah R. Curry on Allenfarm in 1946. Curry was referred to in a Huntsville prison song. Mance was playing on Tom Moore's farm during this period. *Photo courtesy the Marcus Mallard Collection.*

a the fence, I blong on this fawm. I wadn allowed to go cross that fence. Unless I had permission ta go over there.

Fawm I was on, they had a thousand acres on it. An the next fawm had three thousand acres. Next fawm over there is a bunch a people over on the other side a the fence plowin cotton. Well see, we couldn mix up, cause we was doin diffunt thangs. An we was under diffunt boss mens.

An so, one day we was choppin cotton on the fawm I was on, somewhere long fifty or sixty hands. In a bret. Thats a lot a people in one bret. Way we'd git through out of our worrynation on a fawm: we'd sang it through. We was doin the same time, but by our sangin an be merry, that consumed the time wit our minds.

An first thang you know, we hear sumpm over on the next fawm, jest a wire fence between us: the people is fixin ta take out fur dinna. The mens was last people would git outa the field. Womens'd go out at eleven-thirty. Go home an cook fur their husbands. An twelve o'clock, the mens would be outa there, eatin dinna.

So this man was goin home. You know, me an him was plowin side an side, me on this side a the fence an him over yonda, up until time fur the womens ta come up outa the fields. An wadn but the one man mongst the womens. Mens wadn allowed ta go out when the womens went out.

So the old boss man was ridin a little gray mare. An he rode up an askt im, "Where is you goin?"

Well the old man was the boss man, he was hawd a hearin. An he didn understand what this man say. An he rode the hawss up ta the man ta cut im off. Away from the women.

The man had his hoe on his shoulder. He said, "Mista Burl, I'm goin home ta cut Hattie some wood." His wife named Hattie. "She aint got no wood ta cook."

He still didn hear im. An he rode his hawss ta cut im off again. Ever time he'd go around, overseer ride the hawss in front of im.

An he caught holt a the hawss's reins ta keep im from steppin on im. Pusht im off at his mouth wit the reins.

Boss man jest out with the thirty-eight an shot im right here in the neck the first lick. Next un, he hit im right there in the hawt over on his breast. "Boom! Boom!"

We heard it an we lookt up. An he was fallin then. An he wadn no further from us than from here ta that road. I said, "Whoa! They shot him down."

An his wife commenced ta screamin an hollerin. An the women, some of em they run an some of em went back ta git over him, you know, cause he were dyin.

An so he laid there. He had a hoe file in his hand, an he fell with that awm out thisaway. Man, they jest went there an lookt at it. His back was under other awm. An he was dead. His tongue was stickin out. An his eyes was open.

So they sent fur the law ta come an investigate. What they call the inquest. It was eleven-thirty when that hapm. They had ta git the law outa Bryant, twenty-five mile an they rode hawsses an little old caws. An taken em a hour or two ta git there.

They kivered im up wit a old blanket. An he was swintled up jest like that, you know. That hot sun was makin him swell up.

An so when the law come, his people was settin round. Cryin an worryin over the dead man.

An the old man had his hawss tied to a gary post. The old man what shot im, the overseer. An the law askt him—he knowed he's hawd a hearin—say, "How'd that hapm?"

An he told his story. He said, "Lonzy stawted up on me, wit a knife. An I shot im cause I didn want im ta cut me with his knife."

An the law says, "Well, where is the knife at?"

He say, "He had it in his hand when he fell."

He say, "I dont see no knife."

You know it was over a hunnud people standin there. Didn but one man see that knife, an I lookt over there an seed it way over away from him. An I say, "Yonda a knife."

An the law said, "That man couldn had that knife in his hand an fell wit it that far away from im. You got ta give an account a sumpm else."

So his wife say, "That man got off his hawss an put that knife in my husband's hand. Lonzy couldn a had it in his hand enough fur him ta go ta kickin an then throw it way off over here. My husband had no knife. He had this file in his hand." Died wit a file clampt in his hand. What you shawpen hoes with.

[From "Key to the Highway":

> Shoulda been down on the levee, nineteen an thirty-foe,
> See the dead men layin, layin, on ever turnrow.]

Well. That was over in Brazos County. That passt up. That overseer didn go ta jail. An didn go pay no fine. An that show ya how people was criticized, in the colored race: his word wadn Die-Die.

So when they kilt a colored man on a fawm, they'd say inythang an git by. You know, they used ta have a little go-by, they'd say, "Kill a mule, buy anothuh. Kill a Negro, hire anothuh."

Nawsuh! Jailhouse was built fur Mexicans an colored folks in my town. White folks done what they wanta. An might near do what they wanta there now. Everbody's the law there. Them big bankers. An them big landowners. They make their own law.

An if you could read about what kinda law they have, its a wrong kind a law: Jim Crow law. Call that Klu Kluck, where all them people got the same mind an everbody git together an side on the same thang. An you know that Klu Kluck was still around here, killin folks an scaryin the people til, oh, about on up ta nineteen thirty-two, I blieve.

Shuh man, colored folks had ta dig the white folks' grave up until a few years back. An sometime I'd throw a rock or piece a dirt or sumpm in that grave, befoe they'd kiver it up.

Well, ever year somebody got kilt. When I come up. An that was the last man was shot down, right close ta me. Did iny colored people try ta say inythang an do inythang bout that killin an goins on? No! No. We had two mens ta fight back. An they got lyncht.

We was hemmed up. We wadn gittin nowhere. An I commenced ta lookin fur somewhere else ta go. An I quit fawmin an left Washington County an went ta Houston. In fifty-six. An stayed there til part a fifty-eight, doin part-time jobs round in Houston. I found out it was a better life.

An then, I got hurt at a lumbayawd down there an come right here an bought this place. An thats why I'm here now. They discovered me as a musician. An they sent fur me ta come ta Berkeley at the university. An I made it whole, ever since then. See, I been movin about, man. I didn stay in no one place, I always lookin fur better.

Ever town in the world is named after some big leadin man. Houston: Sam Houston, its named after him. Ever time you git to a town, its named after the man got mow money'n inybody.

Well, the old man owned White Switch, his name was White. It used ta be a convict fawm. White Switch an Allenfawm too. Thats nawth a White Switch. Where they kilt aminy man, an put im in the wagon an dug his grave out in the field. Shot em down, jest like dogs.

You know what a county fawm is? Its like a penitentiary. Had prisonas, but they wadn no convicts. You know, people go ta Navasota. Catch a drunk stealin sumpm, they put im on that county fawm. An make im work that fine out.

See, the man owned the fawm, make him a great big old house an put iron bars an fasten it up at night. An shackle them people ta the bed. An pay yo fine, ten or fifteen dollas or no fine at all, but he'd work ya long as he wanta.

But ya see, the govamint broke up these planation fawms. In these times recently. Made Huntsville penitentiary. Wouldn allow the people ta work you like you was in the penitentiary. See, these big mens that owned all this leagues a land, they made they own penitentiary. An you git in jail or kill a man, they git you an work you on the fawm til you work ya time out.

An then we call that good time. You know what good time mean? All right, if I go ta the penitentiary an git them ta release you, befoe yo time is out. See, I'm puttin myself as a parable, well, I would pay so much money ta the penitentiary you was workin fur. Then I hafta give an account a what you was doin, so miny times a month. An if you was doin right, why, I could keep ya. But if you got unruly, I had ta send you back ta the penitentiary. Then they'd give me my money back.

You take Tom Mow—listen at me good: his papa had plenty money, plenty land. He could build inythang he want at them times. An he could put you in a pen jest like a fattenin hog. If he wanted to. You wadn in the pen when you got here, but you was worsen in the pen.

See, they couldn protect all these places. The govamint, you know, is rulin an rulin the world. Been rulin it all a my life. An they kin predict that you caint have these thangs ta go on out here, unless you lawflee could do it.

Never did work on the Mow Fawm. No, an I dont thank I will. Now I played gittah on the Mow Fawm. Ten or eleven years I played Satiddy Night Dances over there. All the while I stayed on Sommers Fawm. From foedy-five til I left an went ta Houston.

I got the "Tom Mow Blues" on one a my albums, but you know what it is? A-nonymous. First time they tuck some tape a me, they sent it across the water. An I begged em not ta put it on the record.

I blieve it was somewhere along twenty-seven dollas the first check I got. I dont know how miny checks I got until they quit broadcastin. But they didn put my name on this record, til they got ta England. They jest sold it over there. So they dont come back here no mow, ta who was doin it.

You wish I'd play that song? You want me ta go home wit my eyes shut?

I played it up here ta Roy Mow's. Played at that boy's swimmin pool one night. He is in Houston, study a lawya practice. Sot up there like I'm is now. Kids aswimmin out there in the pool.

After while, here come Roy Mow. Say, "Mance?"

I say, "Yassuh."

"Play, the 'Mow Brother Blues.' "

I say, "I caint play that song."

"The hell you caint!"

An I said, "Mista Roy, y'all got me wrong."

He say, "Mance." He come out there an I was settin in a chair. Backt up against the wall. He said, "Dont be afraid. You kin play that Tom Mow."

I said, "Now look. I'm gonna tell you straight. I kin play it, but I dont wanta play it. An I dont thank its right fur me ta play it here."

Say, "This aint Tom's house, this my house. Hell I'm a Mow too, did you know that? Clarence is my daddy."

I say, "Yeah, but who gonna carry me home? I got ta go home!"

He said, "Well, nobody gonna bother you."

Man you oughta heared me put in some nice verses about them Mows! An them bad ones, I left em out.

Said, "Now you playin it!"

I said, "I show is," but I knowed I lessin the worse ones out. Because I knew, had I sung the song like it oughta be sung, it'd hit him purdy briefly how he did. Talkin bout, "Hit you cross the head wit a singletree." I left that out. "Tom Mow tell ya he's yo best friend, jest stay away from the cemetery, he'll keep you away from the pen." Huh-uh, that wadn in my mouth. Had fifty verses I left out.

An he says, "That show is a good song."

See, where that song sprung from: some a the verses would come from the people who workt out there. The boy who made that song up, he's workin fur Mista Mow. Plow-in mules. He died about a year ago. His name Yank Thornton. He had a good voice. An he didn have no music in it, because he couldn play no music. But he could sang good.

His home was in Courtney. Lets see, he come in there, I blieve in twenty-nine. Little befoe that first big freeze come here an made ice over the Brazos. An he made up some verses an put the verses together an made a song about it.

An I'm playin Satiddy Night Dances. He come in there one night. An said, "If I sang a song, reckon you could play it?"

I said, "I dont know."

He said, "Well, I'm gonna sang the 'Mow Brothers.'"

I said, "Boy, you better not sang that thang over here."

Said, "Man, this is over in the Bottom. Mista Mow at home asleep."

I said, "You reckon he is? He may be asleep, but somebody here listenin."

He said, "Well, I'm gonna be the one sangin. You jest play."

An that old boy commenced ta sangin that song an puttin them verses in there. An eeeverbody, stood around him. Cause everthang he said in them verses, estimated what Tom Mow would do an what he had done. Ta you or somebody else.

So then I got in a act a playin it, off in the certain places. I'd knowed the song a long time, but I never did wanta fool around playin it. See, they sung the song out in the field, when it wadn no white mens around. But he got it in me, in the knack a playin it.

That song never will be ended. Because you kin find mow verses ta put in it, what done hapmd an what Tom Mow had done. Cause he doin sumpm ever day new. An next week or next day or next month or next year: sumpm done hapmd ta somebody, why, you make anothuh verse.

You wanta know mow yet about the Mow brothers? Well you know, if you got iny sense an dont use it, you a fool right on. You caint say everthang an do everthang, because it'll git back ta hurt you sometime.

Now these books'll be sold. An you dont know who goin buy em. If they reach back ta him, in iny book: if Mista Tom dont buy one, somebody else have one near by im say, "Looka here, what Mance Lipscomb wrote a book about you."

Come up ta my house an be shootin me down.

You say "Well, Mance got shot down. Mista Tom shot im down. I hate that." Then you dont know nothin about what that book done.

An you say there's a lot a people caint blieve these thangs hapmd ta me? Show they caint blieve it. Why? They never been ta Navasota. Dont know what its like here.

Jest like Doc Bowman, the one fixt my teethiz? He come here an ask me did I want sumpm ta eat at them cafays downtown. An I told im, say "Doc, if you hongry, I'll stay out in the caw an you kin go in, git you sumpm ta eat. Else we kin go home ta my house, an Elnora kin cook us up some dinna. Cause they dont allow no Negroes in there, except if they cookin."

An he wouldn blieve that! Thought I was hoorawin im.

So, we went on in there an show nuff, they didn serve him or me one. Wouldn look at us! An we left from there an aint been back. An that was in, long about nineteen sixty-eight.

So you see what I'm talkin bout? I still aint dead. But a lot a people try ta seek out, ta find out yo bizniss. But still: long as I live, I'm subject ta git some bad thangs done ta me, if I say bad thangs about people. See. It aint what you do, its the way you do it.

An so, that song you was talkin bout Tom Mow, I heard

it out in the fields. A boy plowin. An he sangin about "Mista Tom'd whup you and dare you not ta tell. An be at the lot in the mownin, when the lot boy rang the bell."

See? It combine it right there. All right, say, "Soon in the mownin, you'll git ham an egg. An dinnatime come, you git yo beans an bread." Thats the second verse. An then, Yank combined them verses together, an I set it ta music so the people could dance behind it. Oh, man, I told you that song it never will end. See I kin place verses in there, an I aint never put in there.

But they didn nobody tell Tom Mow I put it out, cause that wadn on one a my records. He say, "Lightnin Hopkins, from Houston. If I see that bastud, I'm gonna kill im."

An I could hear a little breeze a that. Said, "Mance, dont you play 'Tom Mow's Blues' around here. They mad wit Lightnin."

"Let em stay mad wit im. He aint mad wit me. Cause I aint gonna play it around here. Inybody ask me ta play it, got ta be in Califownya somewhere." So I kept that song hid, maybe thirty years. Still kin play it.

Now Tom Mow, he was the daddy a all the Mow brothers. An his daddy was a Tom Mow. See, it was five Mow brothers now—you count em. The oldest one was named Walker Mow. An Clarence was the second boy. All right, the next one ta him was named Steve Mow. An then Tom, he was the foeth boy. An Harry Mow, I blieve, was the youngest one. They used ta call em foe Mow brothers. But it was five in the family. I reckon I know. I know em jest like I know the day from night. Knowed em all my life. Them boys, some of em was oldern me an some of em was youngern me. Raised up around em.

Nooo, I tell ya what: I jest see em in passin. I never did deal wit em. Because I didn stay on their place. Understand, I didn stay on nary one of em's place. Jest played on their fawm. They had such a rough name, an I was sort a scared ta git in tight wit em.

311

Robert Moore, "Mista Tom" and Harry's daddy, circa 1895. *Photo courtesy the Marcus Mallard Collection.*

See, that stays well: when if I find you's a bad fella, I jest kinda vary away from you. Keepin me from bein bad treated or hafta do bad thangs.

Well, they didn like colored folks. Do you see what I'm talkin bout? They didn communicate wit colored folks, fur a long time. If you didn need sumpm or they didn want sumpm you had or want you ta do sumpm fur them, they wouldn talk wit ya. An fool wit ya. Unlessin you stayed on their place. If they didn handle you like they want you ta be handled, why they wouldn take up no time.

Why they had that kinda reaction? I wisht I would know. I tell ya one thang: I reckon they was bred up ta that, from the ooold foeparents. They was tot that: a Negro wadn good enough fur em. An they didn want associate wit no Negro.

That was back in slavery time. An when segregation [integration] come out in Navasota—that was in nineteen sixty-five—people was tryin ta communicate together, but some a their old people kep em apart.

Well I played on Harry's Fawm a while. An I played two years on Tom Mow's. Somewhere along about thirty-nine or thirty-eight he was workin a place called the Baker Fawm. Then he bought Allenfawm, somewhere in the foedies cause I was over here in Washington. An it was still a convict fawm then. But it left from John Rogers ta Tom Mow. Ever since I been hearin the name of its Allenfawm.

Mance and Elnora at home, 1971. *Photo by Bill Records.*

Well, there's people been kilt on Mow's fawm, I'm jest tellin y'all. I wadn out there. Shot down in the cotton patches, an they didn know he was dead until they pickt cotton.

Heat stroke, thats right. The boy what they kilt was a cousin a mine. An they misst im; they didn know where he was. He was dead. They shot im, an he drug off in the cotton patches an stayed there. I didn go ta his funeral, cause I didn have no bizniss over there.

Some cotton was tall as, oh, near about touch that lamp up there on the ceilin. An they found him, but he was already dried up. A woman pickt up on im in a cotton patch: out there in the cotton with the bones, awm, an everthang on im but his flesh. An them eyes was out. Them big eyes there an then that woman run up on im an seed im in the cotton hill, an she jest fainted. Wooo, tell me they had ta take that woman ta the docta!

Elnora Myno Lipscomb "Thats the Life We Come Up Under"

If Mance was "the heart of the family," then Elnora would have to be called its rock. Called Myno, Sister, Elnora, and wife, she tells her own story in this pivotal go-along placed between Mance's accounts of his years in Navasota and of life after his discovery. However far he traveled, first in his neck of the woods and later all over the United States, Elnora was always there when he returned to the home she created. After their only son's birth—called Little Mance and Brother—Mance and Elnora gradually came to support sixteen family members, including their two invalid mothers. By 1973, their only son had provided them with four daughters-in-law, twenty-six grandchildren, and thirty great-grandchildren. The members of this interdependent extended family learned to work together and to count on each other. Without them, Mance and Elnora would never have been able to grow and harvest thirty-one bales of cotton one year.

Chronologically for the most part, Elnora takes us through the moves from one plantation to another, and through seventy-five years worth of anecdotes from her life. Through the farms, work, sickness, love, and perils, she defines with a light heart what the family, the food, the Saturday Night Suppers, and the church meant for her.

Elnora's mother, Annie Dillard, was an exceptional cook. She passed her talent on to her daughter. By the 1930s Elnora's "cookswomanship" and Mance's musicianship combined to form a winning economic partnership in the Saturday Night Suppers they hosted. Elnora cooked the food, looked after its sale, and provided the location, while Mance provided the music and attracted the ravenous crowds. On occasion, she graciously shared her husband with other people eager to raise extra money by means of these Suppers. This diplomatic behavior cut back on the jealousy with which some looked upon the Lipscombs, but not entirely. Meanwhile, Mance Junior grew to be the man they could depend on to perform the duties and the chores necessary for them to maintain their place as sharecroppers in the farm system. This freed Mance to travel with Walter Mobley and extend his musical career into a broader precinct—all activities that increased the family's earning power.

Signal events for Elnora were two floods (they lost almost everything they had in one), a tornado that split their house in half, with Elnora on one side and a mother-in-law and a sister-in-law on the other, and a fire that destroyed everything but their lives and nightgowns and a pair of overalls. Mance was present only for the last of these disasters.

Elnora's fresh and laconic narration rounds out the

word portrait of their intertwined lives. She offers a woman's perspective that lets the reader discover details that Mance left out of his life, and adds nuance to the accounts of certain events, usually complementing but sometimes conflicting with Mance's version of those same events. Elnora's voice adds the depth of relationship to the story of their lives. Theirs was a love that extended beyond the grave.

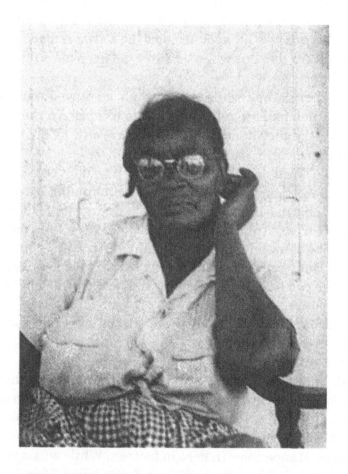

Elnora Lipscomb on the front porch of her new home, 1961. *Photo by Ed Badeaux.*

You come in here an stawted a conversation wit me, I didn know you was gonna put me on this here tape. Well, Mance knows what ta talk about an I jest, see: he been somewhere, an he knowed sumpm. I was jest tellin bout our back life, how we come up an how we lived an everythang.

My name is Elnora Lipscomb, an Mance Lipscomb is my husband. We been married fur fifty-eight years. An never have been apart—not, you know, through madness—since we been married. Never have had a nickel, undivided. If I got a dime, he got a nickel. If he got a dime, I got a nickel. An didn care how he went an come, he's always made home pleasant fur me. But when he leave, he keep me a full cupboard.

An so eruh, one while, he went off an stayed a month. Thats when he first got in this music bizniss. An they told me, say, "Mance done went somewhere, now he done seed some a the world. He aint comin back here."

I said, "Well its one thang about it: if he dont come back, I'll be here. Somebody gonna come. I aint gonna leave. He got ta come one day. Whensever that day come, I'll be here waitin fur im. An if he dont come back, I kin tell you one thang, he show left me a livin. I dont hafta worry bout that part." Dont care how long he stayed: his home is happy, when he come back. From round about sixty years, back up until today.

FATSO! Come in an git these. Brang me some summa sausage, Baby William!

You wanted ta hear what I sayin ta the chillun too? Well, I reckon you *do* like ta hear jest iny old thang then. I got enough of em ta talk to now: twenty-six head a grandchillun. M-hm. An thirty-some-odd head a great-grandchillun. An jest one son!

Little Mance come in here in foeteen. While we stayin in Navasota. Call him Brother fur a famly name. Mance was out there workin on Docta Emory's place. An we moved on out there the next year. Had a straw boss out there over-seein the place. He was workin fur Royal Lott. Well, I dont know what was his trouble.

They was plowin, an I said, "Mance, I blieve I'm gonna plow."

He say, "I know you dont know nothin about no plow-in."

I say, "I kin learn." You see, I was up on the hill an they in the bottom. Nobody be up on the hill but me, an I'd be so lonesome. I say, "I rather be down there tryin ta plow than ta be settin up here all day by myself."

He say, "Well if you wanta learn, thats you."

An so we went on out there, an the old boss man, he come out there, you know. Shoes shinin like gold. Pistol in his side. Legs stiff as this here chair leg: had on them jodhpurs. "Elnora? Git on up ta that cotton an plow it right!"

Mance says, "Mista Jowls, my wife hadn never plowed befoe. She's jest out here ta learn. An inythang you got ta say ta her, say it ta me."

"She better plow that cotton right, boy!"

Mance say, "Elnora. Take them mules out. Take em out an go on ta the house."

"By God, you better keep that mule ta that plow, you darkie, you. Goin on down the row."

Now Mance say, "I said take him out."

An I tuck them mules out, an he say, "Now you an the mule go on ta the house. Cause you dont have this ta do. You aint made no trade with him. I'm the one who—"

He come over there, chawgin at Mance about what he'd do wit Mance, an my mother-in-law was there.

She said ta him, say, "You white son of a bitch, you! I want you ta know you aint got nary nigga chile out here in this field! Did you understand me? That my boy, it aint yo boy. If you put yo hand on my chile out here, me an you'll fight til we git it an blow it up to our neck! Jest touch me if you wanta. I'll kill you, or else you kill me."

319

It come jest a minute: "Aunt Jane, Jane, I wadn gonna—I was jest gonna try ta scare im, I wadn gonna do nothin to im."

Mama Janie said, "I know you wadn gonna do nothin to im! Less you kill both of us."

So eruh, comin on the next week, it rained that night, an it was too wet ta go ta the field the next mownin. An so my sister-in-law tended ta my baby fur me. She didn git back in time enough fur me ta go ta the field.

He come aridin up there. "Elnora? Why you aint in the field?"

An I told im, I says, "Habm got nobody ta keep the baby. Pie an them went off this mownin, an they habm got back."

"By God, you coulda carried im out there an staked im under a bush."

I say, "When I stake *my* chile, it'd be by somebody *else* stakin im. He aint no cow an he aint no mule an he aint no hawss. Long as the blood run warm in my vein, I'll never stake im."

"You git you a hoe an take that nigga an stake im, you black so-an-so. Else I'll whup you out ta the field." An cussin me an all like that.

But he didn raise his hand against me. I told im, "I'm jest stawted well washin, already got on my apron an thangs. I'll go out ta the field when these thangs git a chance ta dry."

Then he told the folks I didn have good sense. Now quite a few people would take their chilluns out ta the field an tie a rope round em, up under a tree or big bush where it was some shade. An he tellin me ta stake my one chile where a snake or who knows whut'd come up on im. Nawsuh, I wadn doin none a that! Mance didn know nothin about that part, til some time after. Cause he was already in the field plowin.

An it wadn too long befoe that straw boss come round there again. A fella named Henry had a house up the road from us. An so that straw boss was tellin his wife the same stuff he'd told me ta do.

Well, Henry heard him cussin an his wife yellin to an fro, an come up there ta see what was the madda. Told the overseer dont cuss at his wife.

He said, "You keep talkin, an I'll wrap this whip around yo throat."

Oh, they was a big crowd gatherin round em. Mance had done come up out the field ta see what was the commotion. An all at once, Henry pulled out a knife an went fur that white man. Pulled his gun out his side an was gonna shoot Henry. Then Mance pulled a singletree out from one a them plows, an knockt that gun from off his hand. An cut him *down* off that hawss, ta the *ground*.

Henry was gonna stab im, but that crowd pulled him an Mance both off im. An he was jest ahollerin, "Git away from me boy, I'll kill you," an sich as that.

Mance was hollerin, "I'm a grown man, jest like you, even if I am a nigga."

An the people said it wadn no use killin im, cause then the white folks would come round an kill a whole gang of us.

So Mance come on in the house, headin fur the fireplace. He always kep his huntin rifle over the mantel there. There wadn nothin but me in between him an that gun. If it hadn been fur me, he'd a shot im.

So Mista Jowls, he throwed himself back up on his hawss an rode away from there.

An Mance says that night, "Elnora?"

I say, "Uh?"

He say, "Wake up."

I woke up. Say, "What you doin wakin me up this time a night?"

He said, "I'm gonna leave here."

I said, "Where you goin?"

He said, "Somewhere. Cause if I stay here, I'm gonna git kilt or else kill that man."

So I got up. He went bout two miles up ta his sister's that night. An stayed away from there, til that straw boss Jowls left away from there.

Then the main boss man come ta ask Mance ta come back. "You oughta come an told me about whut it twas about."

Mance say, "No, I thought it was the best fur me ta leave. I left, til *he* left."

An say, "Now, you didn do nothin ta him, an he didn do nothin ta you. I told him go hunt him a job somewhere else. An I want you ta come back an finish out yo crop."

So thats the life we come up under. Wadn too long befoe Mista Jowls got kilt. Yassuh, went somewhere an bosst, an a Mexican laid im down, they say. Oh, we have lived a life in this world.

Well, that was Mance Junior there. Thats the father of all these chillun. Yassuh. Now when he was eleven years old, he was pickin bettern two hunnud an sumpm pounds a cotton a day. An he didn hafta make it.

An when he was bout fifteen or sixteen, he jest had tuck over the house. Jest sich as plowin, raisin hogs, raisin cows, an diffunt thangs like that. An when he git through gatherin the crop in the wintertime, he'g go out an cut all his winter wood. Ever bit of it up. He wouldn hafta git out through the winter. See, way back yonda we didn have nothin but wood. Wadn no gas an nothin like that.

His daddy'd be goin diffunt places, drivin his boss man Mista Mobley around Dallas an Houston, to an fro. An Brother be there takin care a the home, ever since he's been nigh on sixteen years old.

Yassuh, then we'd have ta thrash puckawns, an help live outa them puckawns. Cause we wouldn make nothin outa his crop. I rememba one year we made our crop. Thirty-one bales! Five hunnud an sumpm pounds.

Five-fifty is a bale. When you put sixteen an seventeen hunnud inta cotton, an when you gin it, well then it'll make five-fifty, sometimes five-hunnud-pound bale. But when you jest gatherin cotton, they puts it in a big old wagon. Well, when they puts sixteen or seventeen hunnud on that wagon, they'll call it a bale a cotton.

An they'll carry that ta the gin. They'd gin it out an bale it up in some kinda bag look like a croakabag. When they'd stuff that all in it, well, they called that a bale then.

No, Mance Junior wadn big enough ta do nothin then. But it twas Mance an me an his mama an his sister, two brothers. Well, we made thirty-one bales a cotton that year, an the Man said we'd made a clear receipt. Thats the reason I never did like no gambla. I say a gambla is jest takin his chance. He's jest like a fawma. He got a mow chance ta lose than he is ta win.

Yassuh. Our water, we hafta used ta git it out of a creek. Jest, runnin water. Now they dont hafta go out the *house* ta git water. These young people got it easy an dont preciate it.

M-hm, Little Mance is the only chile I birthed. The first and the last. We didn have no hospital in them days. You find a chile, then you find im at home. You didn hafta pay but five dollas. To a midwiver.

HIHAH! I'd be tellin a lie if I told it was an enjoyment. Mmm-hm! Well, I always did wanted two, up ta the least. I wanted a boy an a girl. But I didn git my wants.

My sister had foe. An my son done had twenty-six. I reckon he went wayyy back. You know they say you kin take after yo older head. Now my papa, he had eleven. An my grandfather he had thirteen, so I reckon thats the way the water run under the bridge.

Oh, far as I kin tell you bout my famly, they all comes

from Washington County, in a place you call William Penn. Thats right over cross the river there. Brazos River? You know I fell in that river when I was a kid.

I jest hear Mama say I was bawned in Washington County. If you wanta know what year it was, lemme see Mance was bawn in eighteen ninety-five? Thats the way I keep up wit it. Well, he's three years oldern me. An one month back, I was found on March the eleventh. That'd brang me here in ninety-eight, wouldn it?

An I was transferred from Washington County ta Hempstead. Well, Mama an my daddy, so they say separated when my sister Rosie was about seven months old. She was a little behind me in the age. An Mama say we left there when I was about three years old, an went ta Hempstead.

Oh, Daddy stayed over in Washington County, that was his home too. He was fawmin cotton crop an cone crop wit some man, I dont know who it was.

My mother, call her Mama Lulu, see she was named Annie Dillard. But after she married my father, she was a Kemps. My daddy was Wes Kemps, an she was Annie Kemps. Now she was tall an brown-skinned. Some would have it she was red. Had long hair. It wadn say curly an it wadn sayin nappy, jest ordinary hair.

Her mother was part Indian, I reckon she had some in her too. Now my grandmother, she was jest a low dark woman wit long, curly hair. Coal black. Her name Camelias Dillard. M-hm. Thats fur as I kin git at it.

My grandfather an her? What kinda people they was? I thank they was the sweetest old people, look like ta me I ever seen. Because I never did hear em argue, never did hear em call one another a tale, a lie, or nothin. If they did it, they always would wait til we be absent. They always had a smile. No. Wadn none a them slaves. They come in here free.

My daddy had six brothers. Junior, Sammy, Wilson, Daniel, Walter, an James. They was all Kemps. An I never did have but one whole sister, an that was Rosie. An then had three sisters an six brothers on Daddy's side. Fanny, Klassy, and Bird Kemp, that was my sisters. An Charlie, Hubbard, Henry, Buddy—called im Buddy but he's named Wes—an Buster Kemp, that was my brothers. They stayed from around us, all the time. See, my old papa had his second wife. An thats where all them halfs come in.

An my mama, she stayed hired out cookin all the time. Thats the reason where my grandma ta Mama raised us. Out to a big planation, they called it Stone Bottom. Everwhere we stayed on a planation, in the bottom somewhere. All but in Navasota. But I didn stay on no fawm til me an Mance married. I stayed in Navasota an Hempstead in my come-ups. Mother stayed in Hempstead town. An eruh, she was a chef cook. She'd go from town ta town ta diffunt white people. Plenty white people demanded fur her ta be present in the kitchen. Paid her by the week. They didn give over: when she got foe dollas a week, that was gittin top price.

An finely, some white people moved from Hempstead ta Navasota, an she follad em up here. An we stayed at Stone Bottom wit our grandmama bout two three years, an then Mama come got us. When I was about eleven years old. Brought us ta Navasota, an thats where I've been ever since.

Thats where I got grown at, an thats where me an Mance married at. When I was fifteen years old. December the thirteenth. Nineteen an thirteen. Right over there on the place they call Graveyawd Hill. Then I was livin over there wit my mama. You know over there where the cemetery at? Right cross the tracks.

M-hm. Caint nobody say we didn have all the love we need in our famly. There aint nobody now but me an my husband. I thank he got a sister an a brother livin. Down in Galveston, we calls em Coon an Pie. An I aint got nary sister livin. Well I got some halves, but we wadn raised together. So his famly done got down ta three. His sister an brother an himself there. So we jest livin fur each other now.

An I done all a my work right around Navasota. Cookin. No, I didn work in the fields hawdly. Well, not til a good while after we was married. I pickt cotton an choppt cotton, much as you wanta. Much as I could! That was up ta *you* what you wanta pick. Yessuh, I've pickt high as two hunnud an sixty an seventy like that.

Thats all the kinda work ta be done in them days. Cause white folks didn hire ya like they do now, where they hire ya ta cook or wash an iron, work in stows, an all like that. Well nothin like that wadn in style in them days. Hm-m.

I cookt one time fur a white woman. That was Miz Crutchfield, she's dead now. Well, I didn go ta cook then, she got me as a helpa. Ta wash dishes, ya know? An so, she'd go off sometime an tell me ta cook sich an sich a thang. An I'd cook it.

She told her husband one day, said, "Well, I'll blieve I'll jest hire Elnora ta cook. She kin cook so nice!"

But shuh! In them days, when you made two dollas a week, you was doin good. Some of em cookt, they wouldn git but a dolla an a half.

Yassuh. We all had it tough. I rememba one time a boy was walkin along the road, out in the fields an thangs. It was a weekaday an a white man come ridin by on his hawss. An he askt im why he wadn in school.

An that boy said he wadn gonna go ta no school.

He said, "If you aint goin ta school, git that hoe an git in the field!" Well, he was tellin im right an he *wadn* tellin im right, ta my way a thankin.

Cause the boy said he wadn gonna do none of it, an when he said it, he tuck a rope off a his saddle an whuppt that boy to his knees.

So the boy run off, an a bunch a white mens went ta look fur im an they couldn find im, an got his brother an beat him fur the other boy. Cause he didn do like they say.

Well I tell ya, we always did have shoes ta wear, but now, we had em but we didn *wear* em. See, all the chillun would go ta school barefooted through the summa, an springtime til school was out. Til on a Friday, then our parents'd let us put shoes on. Now through the winter we kep shoes on our feet. You could git shoes fur a dolla an a half, sometime a dolla. Work two, three days fur that.

An them houses we lived in, chile, I dont know what they *didn* look like. Some had two rooms, some had three. Nothin but wooden windas, an they opened from the outside. An shet from the outside, you hafta pull em in an latch em wit latches; didn have no glass windas in them days.

No poaches, nothin. No, we set out in the yawd. That was our poach. Didn nobody set out like I'm talkin ta you now. Mm, sometimes you'd catch a few houses with trees in the yawd. Mighty seldom.

Yeah, we had stoves an fireplaces, didn have no heatas in them days. Burn wood in both of em. I cookt on the stove. Never did cook nothin on the fireplace.

An the walls: jest one piece an some of em had cracks in em big enough ta put yo fangers through it. They'd keep you warm come wintertime. Jest tape em up with newspaper. Hep stop up the cracks.

An them walls come right down on the ground. We had blocks it set on, about like that: up on yo knee. Sometime, water be so high, it gits right along at yo kneesiz in the houses. They'd have a shangle roof. Them old wood shangles? They'd keep the water out of em.

Yeah, we kep a gawden. Thats what they live outa in them days. Gawden an chickens an turkeys an hogs an all like that. We didn git no beef, like they do now ever day. We'd git some on a Sunday mownin.

What we didn raise, we git inta town here in Navasota. They'd give us so much a month. How much they give ya, accordin ta how large yo famly was. If you had a small famly, like me an Mance when we first stawted ta makin it—well some of em'd give you what you tell em you thank it'd last you a month.

An it would last you because you wouldn hafta buy nothin ta amount ta nothin but sugar an coffee an bread an stuff like that. Cause we'd kill our hogs an make our meat an lawny sausage an diffunt thangs like that.

We kep it in the smokehouse. They have a little smoke-house built outside. Well it wadn no take carin ta *do* ta that smokehouse. Jest like hog-killin time was up in the wintertime, an hung it up in the smokehouse. They smoked meat in them days.

Salt it down when you first kill it. Jest sprankle salt on it an rub it in good. An let it stay in the salt about two or three weeks. Then take it out an wash it, an hang it up an smoke it bout a week or two. An thats all you had ta do ta eat it. Leave it hangin in the smokehouse. An it'd be jest the same as salt bacon.

Well see, we had sumpm they called hickory in them days. An we'd put that in there in a big tub, an see to its not blazin. An thats the way we'd smoke it. M-hm. Some of em'd really last. We killed so miny til they'd be rank on us, sometime two an three at a time.

Shuh, since I stoppt raisin gawdens, I caint know nothin. All I know is lay down an git up. Thats what gits me when I go ta sit down an git up. In these knees, jest so stiff. But I dont guess there's nothin a docta kin do about it.

When we married, I was stayin here in Navasota town. Mance was fawmin on Docta Emory's place, under his mama. An I didn move in at his place, fur a while. I stayed wit my mama bout, oh, a solid year. Jest because I wanted ta stay, an Mance he wanted ta stay cause it be in town. Well, we *went* together but not in a *house*, you know. He didn stay so far from me. An he'd come visit me at my mama's place ever night an carry dinna.

Aw, it wadn like that so long, cause he finely left the Bottom an come ta where I was. An finely, his mama give up fawmin, an he went back ta the country. An I went wit im. Yassuh, we would have a good time out there. On a Sunday they'd have a ball diamond, they'd play ball.

An so when we left from out ta Docta Emory's, we moved back ta town cause of a high water runned us outa there. An so we jest stayed in Navasota, I reckon til Little Mance was about eleven years old [1925]. Mance'd go back an forth to work. Jest two miles an a half. Yeah, in them days we would jest work as one famly. We'd have fifteen acres a cotton, an thats all we'd fawm. Well see when we's fawmed fur ourself, we would tend ta our own *books*.

Well we was workin fur Mista Mobley when we was at White Switch an he left there an went ta Courtney. An we went an moved on down there with him, reckon long about thirty-two or thirty-three. See he married a Lott girl, an they made him overseer, workin fur the Lotts. Old man Jimmy Lott called hisself ownin all them places. But we didn work under the Lotts. We workt under Walter Mobley, his son-in-law. An seem like him an his son had it in fur Mobley.

An they hired Mance ta keep book when everbody's out, pickin by the hunnud. Well Mista Mobley would hire so miny hands a day, jest whosunever wanta pick. See, he was what you call the counter. Oh, I reckon about two falls, you know you didn hafta pick cotton but once a year.

Well them two falls, I'll tell ya how that run: Mance would weigh from, oh, I reckon, about twenty or twenty-five hands a day. Call it "keepin book." Keepin everbody's weight straight? It'd take a person ta know what they's doin. Yeah see, he could count it all up an write it down in the book. Jest like you pick three hunnud a day, an Betty'd pick foe, an I'd pick five an all like that. Well see, he'd keep that straight an give it ta the boss man on a Friday evenin.

An that boss man brang the money out Satiddy mownin.

Aw, we was down there I reckon bout seven years. An then we left Courtney an went ta Washington County. Over to a place they call the Lott Bottoms. An when Walter Mobley give that place up, he jest come ta town an went ta runnin the bus stop. An so we jest got us a place over in Washington. That was in the fifties we were in Johnny Sommers' place. Thats when our house got burnt down, I thank in fifty-one. Left his place out there on the Bluff they call it. We went ta Houston in fifty-six. Stayed there bout, fur two years. We come back ta Navasota an rented a house right down here on the Washington road. Out there by the West End Grocery. An we stayed there until we bought an built this home, where we at now. An, we ended up with this *home*. In Navasota.

Oh, when I first seed Mance, he was playin fur a Suppa. An he's playin the gittah out from where he was bawn. He was stayin on the Brosig place, I blieve, when I met im. That was right cross the fence from Docta Emory's, which they used ta call all that Quinn Fawm. Well, they moved over ta Emory's after that flood washt em out.

An I told my auntie, I say, "Oooo, he's nice lookin! I like him."

She say, "Whynt you say sumpm to im?"

I say, "No, Mama'd kill me if I say sumpm ta him."

An so it rockt on, an I guess it was about a year after that befoe I seed im again. Then I met im at Sunday school. An I was transferrin words from him to a girl what he called hisself coatin. Carried it over wit me an brang him words back. Well I dont know exackly about him goin wit her, how long an thangs sich as that, cause I wadn allowed out much. You know they said that was Mance's girl.

An at last one day I told him sumpm what the girl had said.

He say, "Beats you talkin fur her, you better be talkin

fur yaself." An then I thank I growed about six inches when he said that.

An so, we stawted from that. Well, occasionly we'd meet one anothuh at Sunday school, an thats when we'd git ta talk our little talk.

Poppin off at each other, an finely my mother sent me ta my grandma's down on ta Stone Bottom. An I stayed down there two years, befoe my mama sent fur me ta come back ta her. I'd wake up at night an say ta myself, "Well I dont guess I'll ever see *him* no mow."

An so, finely Mama sent fur me an my sister ta come home, over where she'd moved ta Navasota. An I got in touch wit Mance again. We stawted ta coatin one anothuh, call ourself coatin.

An Mama didn allow me ta take company nohow. I wouldn tell im ta come ta my house, cause I knowed Mama wadn gonna let im come there.

An so he askt me could he come up ta see me.

I told im, "Yeah." An I told im what night an everthang.

Chillun, that night come I had left *home* cause I knowed Mama'd *kill* me if a boy come up there. Went an stayed all night wit anothuh girl! Yassuh!

From then on, we seed one anothuh in spots fur about two years an six months. So we slip around thataway an coated til I was about fifteen, an he askt Mama could he come ta see me. She told im, yeah, he could come.

An finely we decided we'd marry. Married in nineteen-thirteen. December the thirteenth. So we become husband an wife an been that up until today. I'm tellin you, we have had some hawd times together, but we still stuck there.

We had so miny floods, an I dont rememba the years. But one flood, that was the December flood, now I know exackly when it come. Cause thats the same year we married in. Yassuh, a big flood, jest wadn nothin could stop it. Jest had ta hapm. Yassuh.

An eruh, we used ta move out the floods, jest every year we'd have a big flood. But nothin like that! Course it was *deep* floods, but you wouldn hafta move out lessin you stayed in the Bottoms. Cause it would stop in them low places. Oh, the banks didn used ta run so high on that river, an it didn used ta be so wide.

An when it come, it jest come all over the Bottom an you jest had ta git out. We'd hafta move to a place you call the Hill. Thats over on the Bluffs.

They have some waste houses up there sometime. Well sometime it'd be high as sixteen an seventeen jest stayin in one house. Done moved out ta high water. Jest like me an Mance jest man an wife, we couldn git nary empty house, we'd all hafta pile up together. Be so miny there, wouldn have no house an had ta stretch a tent fur em ta git under.

An we jest stayed an waited, up on the Hill. Well, accordin depend on how long the water stay out. Sometime the water stay out a week, an sometime you'd hafta stay out two weeks. Til it dry up so you could git back in there.

An it put you on a wonder? How we lived in them houses in the Bottoms, an it be floodin so down there? Well that beats me! All I know is stayin on the fawm, an everbody stayed on the fawm in them days. They didn stay in town like they do now.

No. It wadn no white people stayed out there. Jest like, this place blongs ta Mance: an he would hire you ta see after it. An they would be the onliest white person out there. They called him the straw boss, the overlooker. He'd come out ever mownin an go back ever evenin. Sometime he'd stay out there a coupla nights an go back.

Well, sometime we would be lucky enough ta be done planted or jest gathered or sumpm anothuh like that. Jest like we'd done got all the best a the cotton, an they call that scrappin cotton. When it git down ta where you could jest scrap up on fifty or sixty a day. Well they would come along about that time: December, November. Like that.

Jest sometime it'd come up in the summatime when the crop would be in a bloom. Maybe it was peakin long about the last a August, here come a floodin. An we had ta leave away from there. Never would know jest exackly when they'd come on down the river. Mostly they'd come in the fall an wintertime befoe you went ta plantin, but sometime they could fool ya an jest come when they feel like it.

Well see, *some* years a overflow'll drown this crop out, probly down here. An up yonda—Dallas or maybe West Texas somewhere—well, somebody'll have a big crop a cotton, an they'd go up there an pick. You know, when Mance was goin up ta Waxahachie an run into Dallas wit his cousin, one they call Sonny Pratt? I didn hear him say a word about Blind Lemon an sich as that. I jest dont know why he didn say nothin ta me about it. I reckon he's knowin too much a fast time. HHM! Cause everbody knowed he was out there.

Well inyhow, the way we got a notice of it be a flood: jest like they tellin you now, "Its floodin here in Marlin," or somewhere like that, "an it be comin on down south at so miny miles an hour." An then we'd git ready ta git out, an we'd be lookin out fur it then.

An that was jest how that un run, in nineteen-eighteen. Me an my husband's auntie Mary Oliver? We was goin a piece away wit some woman had been up ta our house. Sun was shinin out, bright as the kid shined.

An, we kep ahearin somebody holla, holla, holla. An I lookt back.

"Aunt Sweet!" I say, "Sweet, that man yonda jest keep arunnin in behind us hollerin! Do you know him? Look like he hollerin at us."

An we all stoppt an lookt back, an he throwed up his hand at us.

An we waited.

An said, "Y'all better come on here an git outa here jest quick as y'all kin. An git yo thangs packt. Water come runnin, so miny miles an hour, an it be here about sundown."

I say, "An the sun shinin thisaway? An aint rained?"

He say, "It show is comin."

An so we turnt round an come back. An when we got back there, Uncle Jim, Mance's auntie's husband, he got out an caught up an hitcht up the wagon, an we was out.

Mance was in town here, workin over here fur his boss man what had the fawm we was on, Mista Walter Mobley. He didn know nothin bout it til he comed out there.

An so Jim said, "Well I'll take my load a thangs out, Sister, an I'll come back an git a load a yo's."

An got a load a his thangs out an come back ta git a load a mine when he got back, an we stawted back out, that water done come up ta them axles! An the sun shinin jest like it is now. Couldn git back in there no mow. So there was part a hisn out an mine was in there. Didn have much nohow in them days an the water had ruint that.

I dont know where that water come from, but they say it's a cloud busted way up above somewhere. An that water jest come on down here. Jest that quick. It was a week befoe we could come back in our homes. Never did rain. Not in that whole week. Jest water water water. Had us anothuh high water in twenty-eight. Cause see, from then on they went ta puttin all the houses up on the hill.

But that flood we had in nineteen-thirteen: shuh, we was stayin over here in Navasota by a creek, they call it Bowmount Creek. An that water jest backt that creek out.

An so, Mama come off the job one night. She said, "Woo!" Say, "Sister!" They all called me Sister. Say, "Y'all settin up in this house playin dominoes, an the water is comin up on the poach."

Which it was! An we had ta move out there that night. Got about that deep in the flow, bout deep as my hand. Mance was stayin out in the country. An now thats the biggest one we ever had ta my knowins. An peoples had ta

The 1913 Overflow in Annie Kemps' neighborhood, when Elnora was living there with her mother, Annie. *Photo courtesy the Marcus Mallard Collection.*

move out the Bottom then. Git out the way a that water ta the high hills an everthang. Well, it last about two weeks befoe we could move back home. That Brazos an Navasot too, they all come up outa the banks. An all them little creeks backt up.

An I rememba one time it kep arainin an rainin, an a big wind come along an I was on one side a the house, an Betty Jean an Mama Janie was on the other. Split that house down the middle. That was a stawm, that wadn no flood. It was when we was stayin on Johnny Sommers' place.

Oh, water an fire is sumpm, I'm tellin you. But water is a little powerfuller than fire I thank, cause water kin put out fire. An so eruh, it was in fifty or fifty-one, we was on the Sommers place. We got burnt out. Lost everthang we had.

I jest dont know exackly what caught it ablaze, but it was some great big wood rats. An see, they didn have no thin matches in this time. They didn use nothin but these here nickel boxes a matches. An I thank that rats musta caught holt to a match. You know, they kin strike a match jest like folks. An I aint used a box a matches since. I always git them penny matches.

We had a upper loft ta the house. An they'd tote ever-thang they kin wreck an scrape up that loft. An so, I was layin there one night. I say, "Ooo. The rats done stawted ta draggin stuff now." We had a tin-top house. "I aint never knowed em ta be this bad here."

An so I kep ahearin sumpm pop like popcone. I said, "That must not be no rats. I better git up an see what is that happenin."

An I raised up my head an lookt in the eaves in the east room, under where one a my grandgirls was. An jest when I got up ta: I said, "Whooo, my Lawd! Looka there! This house is on fire!"

So I jumpt up ta run in the kitchen, ta git some water ta come back an put it out? Got in the kitchen an it was worser in the kitchen. Didn come back in the room where the little girl was ta put it out.

An I commence ta pourin water in the kitchen, didn have sense enough ta wake Mance an the boy up. I was in there tryin ta fight the fire by myself.

Mance heard me an he come in there. He say, "Give it ta me. Let me hep ya, Elnora."

An I handed it im an I said, "Git that bucket up there, Mance."

He got that bucket, an me an him was throwin water. Lookt like the mow we throw, the bigger that blaze would git.

An that time, my grandson woke up. He said, "Give me the bucket an let me go ta the well." That was the one called Junior Boy. His name Ernest. Thats the oldest one.

An so befoe he could git back from the well, Mance say, "Come out! Come on Elnora! We caint make it. Lets git out!"

An we stawted out the front doe. An jest as I went ta step off the poach, I said, "Woo, Mance! My grandbaby's back in there!"

An the house is jest in a blaze. An thats where I got burnt: when I run back ta git Ruby.

She was kivered up a head an ears an ever time I grabbed, I couldn grab nothin but the kiver. Couldn find no hole ta catch holt to her.

An the fire was gittin so hot ta me, I said, "Woooo, Lawd!" I screamed, I said, "Lawd have mercy! I caint make it. I caint git my chile."

An when I screamed I guess that woke her up. An she commenced ta fightin the kiver an I got a chance ta grab her by her awm then. An pulled her on out. Oh, Ruby was about seven years old. She got burnt a little bit.

An Bozo said he heard it but he thought it was a stawm roarin. Said he heard that roarin, an jumpt up an run out the back doe. An he was jest standin there hollerin, "Ohhh, my Mance! Ohhh, Daddy Mance! Ohhh, Mynora an Daddy Mance!"

"Bozo!" Called im Bozo but his real name was Clarence. I said, "Here we is, around here!"

He said, "Lawd! I thought y'all was in that house."

I said, "Well its good you was large enough ta look out fur yaself. Because I had forgot all about *you* was in there."

An so we went on up ta Little Mance's. He stayed bout quota mile from us, maybe not that far. I didn know I was burnt til I got halfway there. I said, "Woo, Mance, I'm show is burnt!"

He said, "Burnt?"

All across from this right elbow here, on down ta the knuckles. An all across my foehead. Woo, I reckon if I didn had a rag on my head, it'd jest singed all a my hair off. Jest wheresunever that hanky stoppt.

An we went up there, we didn have on nothin but a gown. Didn have a piece ta our body. Mance had one pair a overhauls. An he wouldn a had them if I hadn a washt that day, an they didn git dry, so I left em on the line.

I don't know what'd a hapmd if there hadn been a road twixt our house an the crib. Cause that grass jest burnt til it got ta that road. Then it stoppt. If it had a been grass all the way across there, why, it'd a blowed up the crib an all, because Mance had two fifty-gallon barrels out there in the crib. Loaded wit gas. Ta run the tracta. I said, "Lawd, I'm tellin you the truth: the Lawd show was powerful."

An eruh, in the wintertime, long bout December, we'd buy all our groceries. We'd buy foe an five big sacks a flour, three sacks a meal, lard, an sugar—hunnud pounds a sugar. Jest everthang we could thank of, you know. Well, that would last us til May or June one; we didn hafta buy no mow.

An I had that in the smokehouse, jest right out there in the back yawd. An jest had kilt three hogs. An I betcha ever one of em weighed right at three hunnud. An had my lawny sausage an everthang in there. Had so much meat hung up in that smokehouse an sausage, that you go in there in the daytime, I had ta light a lamp it be so dawk in there. An I guess I had about two hunnud jars a diffunt food put up. Ever bit a that got burnt up. We didn have nothin.

An so, I saved that ta say this: had jest pulled my teethiz. I had sold a hunnud an sumpm dollas worth a turkeys. We sold some fur Thanksgivin, some fur Christmas.

An I had decided, "Well, when Winsday come, I'm goin ta have my mouth made, gonna git me some teethiz."

M-hm. That Tuesday night that was when the house got burnt down, the money an everthang. I didn have a penny one. An from then on, hawd luck struck us, an I never would be able to no mow.

Until Mance got into this grabblin wit the musics proposition. An I said, "Well, I dont need none now. No mown ta meet the people. Cause I kin eat inythang I wanta eats. I aint lookin fur nary anothuh husband. I'm done without em this long, I kin do without em *on*."

An so, thats turkey money I was gonna have my teethiz made of then. Oh it was in March when that blaze stawted. Yassuh, so thats the way the cookie crumbled in them days.

An I went ta Docta Hansen. He said, "How you got burnt, Elnora? Went back ta git yo pocketbook?"

I say, "Nawsuh, I didn go back ta git no pocketbook. I wadn thankin about nothin but tryin ta git my grand-daughter outa there."

He said, "Well, lots a the people goes back ta git the pocketbook. I'm gonna give you a treatment fur nothin."

Well, I didn stay burnt so long. Jest this place stayed tender a long time. I tell ya, when you have a burnt house you jest—me, I dont know about nobody else—I kin smell a rag now an I jest git all ta pieces til I find out where its at. Jest upsets me. An so, thats the way it was.

Well, you jest keep alivin. Luck'll strike ya. Had stawted out wit nothin. Left Sommers an went ta Houston; well that was in fifty-six. Then we come back here in fifty-eight, an went ta rentin over there on the Washington road. An Jim Oliver—thats Aunt Sweet's husband—he sold us this piece a land where we at now, so we built on it an moved up here.

I said, "Well Mance, I tell ya whut we do: we be's payin twelve dollas a month down ta where we's rentin at. We kin move up there, an take that rent an sorta hep finish the house, an take what you do. That'll make enough."

An when we moved up here, this house was jest a big bawn. Wadn nothin in there but jest a top. An windas an doze. Wadn no rooms divided at all. We had one chair an one homemade table which is mate with the other one. An old wood stove. An we couldn hawdly stay in there fur it smokin. An so, thats the way we stawted out. An ever-thang we got now, we cumulated it since Mance been into this bizniss.

An first time they come there ta check up on me: big old

339

white man come there an was German. We was stayin
there aside the Washington highway where the West End
Grocery at? That was in sixty.

An he said, "This where Mance Lipscomb stay?"

I say, "Yeah, thats where he stays."

"Well, where's he at?"

I say, "He on the job."

Say, "What time he be in?"

I say, "He quits at five o'clock. But I dont know, it be
somewhere about six or six-thirty when he make it in."
See, I wanted ta throw em off cause I didn know whut they
was lookin fur.

An he said, "Well, would you mind us comin back speakin to im?"

I said, "No, I wouldn mind it."

An jest bout time they git back, I said, "Well, there come
my husband now."

He said, "That yo husband?"

I said, "Uh-huh."

I said, "Now wonder what these here persons lookin fur
Mance fur?" An I jest knowed Chris—he was his manager,
ya know—was a lawman, so I said, "Now I know Mance
aint did nothin. I caint wonder what they'd look fur im
fur."

An let me tell you one thang, they come back that night.
An they played an they played an they *played*.

An I was layin down cross the bed, an I sturbd one a the
chillun in the bed. I say, "I dont care how come they dont
go on away from here. Boy, they times is past due an done
got mine too. Bout like a Irish gives an everthang you pays
fur."

An so when they left, Punkin—call her Ruby—said
"Mama, that man give Daddy Mance fifty dollas!"

I said, "You dont blieve none a that."

"Yesm, he did cause I seed it."

An you couldn see nothin but these gums! I didn hapm ta have two cents!

They askt Mance could they come back that Satiddy. An they come back that Satiddy an stayed about two hours or a hour an a half, an give im fifty dollas. That made him make two hunnud dollas, cause they'd done give im a check fur anothuh hunnud.

Mance say, "I'm goin right on now an spend this an git me a top put on my house." An I never will furgit the top a that house. Nawsuh. Then the chillun was hoorawin me a long time, say you couldn see nothin but Mynora's gums.

An so, after he got in this music bizniss, one while he went off an stayed a month. Way up nawth, outa state somewhere? He wrote an told me, say they begged im so he overstayed his time.

I say, "Well that was all right"—course I didn miss im so much then in them days, cause I was up where I could git around an see ta my bizniss, an all a my grandchillun was prackly grown. An when I didn feel like goin, well they could go.

But you know Mance wont hawdly complain. Dont care how much botherin him, he dont let on ta nobody. Only jest once in a great long while. But I know his reaction, cause see, I know im. An I know how he oughta act an when he's all right an when he's all wrong. He tries ta hide it from me, but he caint hide it from *me*.

Well, he'd done been music biznissin about three weeks. He didn stay quite til his time was out, cause he got sick. I'd told my grandson, I say, "Its sumpm wrong. Now I dont like the way this here letter reads."

He said, "I thought you'd be proud ta hear from im."

I said, "I am. I'm proud ta hear from im, but he aint talkin right on this letter. He aint even askt about the dogs an nothin. An thats near about the first thang he wanta know about is his dogs, when he gone away from home."

An so direckly, about two three nights after that, some-body walkt up on the poach an my granddaughter say, "Daddy Mance?"

I said, "Ah-oh. I know its sumpm wrong now."

We was all settin there in the livin room. An he jest walkt in an stood there an lookt! He didn say a word.

I said, "Mance? Whats wrong?"

He said, "Nothin."

I say, "Well, *sump*m's wrong wit ya. I been wit you too long ta dont know when sumpm's wrong wit you."

An I kep on askin, he say, "I been a little sick. I had ta go ta the docta while I was out there. He couldn fine nothin wrong wit me."

I say, "Well I aint no docta, but I know sumpm wrong wit ya."

So I called down there that Satiddy, an they told me ta brang im in that Monday. An I carried im in there Monday an I said, "Docta Hansen, what seems ta be the madda wit im?"

He say, "He jest got cold. His blood got chill. But if he do like I tell im, he'll pull through."

Fur about a week, he jest couldn even write his name. Jest stawt that M, an jest like a little chile begin ta learn how ta write, jest make E's an all, down the line.

I said "Mance, you caint write."

He says he jest didn have no feelins in im. No kinda ways.

An he say, he come out a buildin one night, up there in Seattle, I blieve, goin somewhere an his feets began ta git cold. An from his feets up ta his knee. That was sixty-eight or nine, somewhere along in there.

You know, whenever yo feets git cold, thats gonna chill yo whole body. So, he done all right after the docta treated im, up until he had this here pickin at his face like that. An he done been an been an been. An aint nary a docta seems ta kin reach it.

Oh, that was about three or foe years afterward, when that itchin commenced over im. M-hm. Cause you know, *one* sick person is contrary. Jest one. He want everthang his way. Cause I know how my husband was. Sometime he jest—didn nothin suit im.

I told im one day, I said, "Mance, I never did thank you'd turn out like this. As nice an kind as you was."

An he'd look over his feet. Sometime he'd say, "Well Elnora, I dont mean ta be like that."

Yet an still, I guess it was hawd on him bein down so. Cause all those years he never would stop an take his rest. But you know, Blue always did tell me, from a chile on up said, "Myno, when Daddy Mance git where he caint go like he used ta, he gonna be sumpm ta handle." Yassuh.

An eruh, two or three doctas done told im it was his nerves. An they give im some nerve tablets an told im ta take that medicine. An lay down an take ya rest. Then about the time he'd take em, they'd put im ta sleep.

Well see, he wont do that. Talkin bout he aint got time ta sleep. He got ta go! An he been settin up so long. Sometime I'd agree with the docta, because he been settin up ever since I knowed im. An probly befoe I knowed im.

When he's little like that, he say he used ta play behind his daddy. I imagine he didn set up as much, but after he got ta be his own man an his own boss, I *know* he sot up.

When he stawted out with that gittah, well that was befoe I seed im. His daddy played the fiddle, an he was acomplementin behind his daddy, bassin behind im. Ever since he was eleven years old.

No, Mance wadn playin a bass. He playin them low strangs, on a gittah. An his dad'd go ta Suppas, sometime he'd be there fiddlin. When I first seed Charlie, he was fiddlin.

Oh yeah, Lawd! I heard him aplenty time. He was fiddla outa his hawt, I'm tellin you the truth! He could make that fiddle pray, jest like you say, "Our Father Who Art in

Heaven." Father's Prayer. He could make them strangs say the same thang. Yassuh, he was a fiddla.

Well I thought his daddy was all right, ta my ideez. He was jest a jolly old man, jest blieve in hoorawin all the time an kept you laughin. An diffunt thangs like that an didn bother nobody. His bizniss was yo bizniss. He didn make him no diffunce. If Charlie seed it, you neednt worry bout him sayin nothin about it. I thank he was a nice peaceable man.

Now Mance kin play most iny little thang. Sometime I used ta say, "I just caint understand how he plays like that." Oh, they'd hire im ever time the bell rang, when he played fur ten or fifteen dollas. But I tell im, "I wouldn look back at sech as that. When you were playin fur that little amount, you had it ta do an hep make a livin. But you aint got it ta do now."

Thats what his manager told him, say, "Dont play under a hunnud dollas a night. If they don't give you that, jest furgit about it."

Now you take me an Mance: we dont hawdly ever have a conversation wit each other. Its got ta be sumpm mighty stressful fur us ta set down an talk together. We'll pass a few words at each other, an thats that. Hm-m, I dont mind that. Done lived wit im so long, see I know his ways an he know mine.

Yeah, when we first married, he used ta haul hay ta diffunt places. An I'd always cook, an wait fur him ta come in an we'd eat together.

An so the last one time I waited on him ta eat, I say "Well, I'm gonna lay down here across the bed. When he comes, I'll git up an fix the suppa an we'll eat."

When I woke up it was twelve o'clock, I say, "HHM! He aint made it in yet. I'll wait a little longer."

An I went back ta sleep, an when I woke up again it was day. Mance still hadn come. I say, "Well, come this day on, everbody got ta eat fur theyself."

Well he eat fur hisn an I eat fur mine. An I aint waited on im no mow. No, I was waitin all the time so we could eat together, but he fooled me that time. He say he's about got in a scrap game, thats what he told me. I dont know where he was.

No, I haven waited on im since an I haven et to the table wit im since. Its jest a habit I've got. Oh yeah, I aint never stoppt cookin fur im.

An then lemme see, it was a drought comin through here, I blieve it was in twenty-five. An they was runnin this highway through here that year. An Mance workt on the highway. Well, thats the onliest work was done. Cause it didn make no crop. An so we all, everbody was runnin fur ta git on that job.

Now when he was wit his mama, the landowner would talk ta her an whatever she agreed with, why thats what we workt under. It was halvers, an then rentin third an foeth when Mobley give im his own team a mules. Aw, I seed the times we'd pick until January. M-hm. I've pickt a hunnud pounds a cotton in January. Chile, you'd a been glad ta git it in them days! Yassuh, now I've pickt cotton fur foedy cents a hunnud, an thats low as we ever got. Oh yeah! It was too low then! But we lived bettern we live now. Because thangs were so much cheaper. Big sack a meal costin thirty-five cents, an a big foedy-eight-pound sack a flour costin a dolla to a dolla an a half.

That was years ago. About in the early foedies, I reckon. But you know, we aint never had ta buy no food wit no stamps. Like they give out in them wars? We jest had ta git sugar with them. Thats all, an flour. When we couldn git these sugar an flour an thangs too, was in that Depression times what they call it. Cause we'd raise hogs an chickens an turkeys. Milk cows, so we had butter an all like that. Cotton stayed about the same. Yeah, it wadn so hawd. I didn hawdly miss nothin but the sugar. That ta go in my coffee.

345

An so, I was talkin about some mules Mance had. Now he brung two on ta Johnny Sommers place, one was Lawra an one was Sara. Cause Walter Mobley give him that team a mules after he quit an went ta runnin the bus station in town.

Well we left Sommers, cause he fooled around an hired im a straw boss. An we couldn git along wit the straw boss. They called im Skeeder, but I never did know his right name.

Well, I tell ya what decided we'd move. I got sick up there: I got ta the place I couldn walk. Jest like I am now, but I didn stay that way but two weeks up there. See, he built us anothuh place after we got burnt out, an it was on a cement slab? An I blieve that was what made my legs give out, walkin on that cold slab all time.

An I told Mance, "I'm gonna leave. You kin stay here if you wanta. I'm goin ta Houston where my chillun at." Where my oldest grandson was down there then. An I was sayin, "You here workin day an night. Both of us'll be down direckly. An then we'll be in it. You caint take care a me, an I caint take care a you. So, you kin stay here or go, it dont make me no diffunce. I'm goin."

An I guess Little Mance moved, cause we moved. An so we tow off down there ta Houston.

When I first went there, well, thats when the tale was told. Said, "Lawd, I done come down here now. I know I'm got ta use gas." Cause I done all a my cookin on a wood stove. An let me tell you, I burnt up pots an pans, chile, an my awms so when I first got that gas stove. I dont know what I burnt the most, my awms or the bread!

So the grandboy come in that day at dinnatime. Brought a stove. Hookt it up.

Come off a work at eight o'clock. He said, "Mama, aint you cookt?"

I said, "No, son! Mama's jest waitin til you gits here so it wouldn be so cold." Scared ta light the stove!

An so, it come the wintertime, he brought the heater in an hookt it up. An Mance an I were show cold, settin up there aside the winda in the sunshine.

Purdy soon he come there again, "Mama, you aint cold?"

I said, "Hm-mmm, Mama's aint cold." It was so cold I didn know what ta do!

An so, he lit it. I said, "Now Roy, aint no use in you waitin til the boys come off the job ever evenin ta light the stove."

An so, one Sunday mownin wadn nobody there but me an Mance. So I went ta finely do light it. I got me a piece a newspaper about that long, twisted it an lit it. Jest standin in the bathroom, I lookt down there at that hot water heater. Say, "This thang here must be fixin ta blow up. Cause that blaze is curlin up there. I'm gonna git outa here!"

An I went there an I told Mance an he said, "Put it out!"

I said, "I aint gonna put nothin out! Whynt *you* put it out?"

He said, "I dont know how ta put that out."

"Well I dont either!"

An so, I went back in there ta peep again. I wouldn go in the bathroom, went ta the doe an felt. Heater had went out, but it was still hot. An it jest stung me! You talkin bout somebody runnin over a chair!

An Punkin, my little grandgirl, said, "Whats the madda, Mama?"

I said "That thang in yonda. It lit up!"

She said, "What?"

I said, "That hot water heater. I dont know whether it done busted or what."

She said, "Mama, that stays lit. All the time, unlessin the wind blow it out."

Oh, some funny thangs have hapmd ta me. Yassuh!

When I hafta turn mine on, I have a long enough paper there so I wont burn myself. An ta this day, you dont find no hot water heater in this house.

So thats what I cookt them hogs in fur them Suppas, that wood-burnin stove. I'd do all right in the summatime, but when it git ta rainin, that wood git wet. Yeah, I used ta be a good old cook, but I done played out now.

Oh, chile, I seed the time I could dance but—you heard that song bout "I'm done got too old ta cut the mustard"? U HN HT [laughter]! I seed the time I could git on there at eight o'clock an stay til God break his day. Danced my feets off, an I'd say I done workt it off. Cause I danced one night in the week. An work ever day. I have workt an walkt a mile an a half. Three times a day. An cookt fur sixteen head a people.

Well, it was two famlies together, my part a the famly an Mance's part. We stawted off at Lott's wit nobody but me an Little Mance an Mance. An everone heard tell of us, they come right there til it made sixteen head.

Well his mama, she got sick. She had ta come there. An Daughter had died an left a grandbunch. That was Mance's sister, she left three. Then, later on, my mother come. An her daughter. An some mow grands, an there it was.

Sorta like the song, "I done had my share a workin." Mance used ta sang, "I done had my fun if I dont git well no mow." Well, I done had my share a workin if I dont be able ta work no mow.

Lawd, foe in the mownin, I'd git up an fix breakfast. We'd all git up an eat, an the mens would all go ta the field. Then I'd wash dishes an follow them out. Cause when God break his day, we gonna be at the end a that turnrow. Walk back ta the house at eleven. Well, we ate dinna at eleven-thirty, an noon we better be ta the field again. An stayed there hoein or choppin, pickin or plowin til a little befoe sundown. Well, then I'd come out the field an git ready fur suppa. So, thats the way it was.

See, the womens would all pick cotton up until Friday. An the mens would work Monday up until dinna on a Satiddy. Well Friday after dinna, we'd wash. An then we'd clean up the house Satiddy mownin an from that ta town. Come back home an make fur the Suppa.

An we had sich a hawd time, we'd give Suppas. Come Friday night, up until Sunday mownin I was stirbd. We'd kill a whole hog. Sometime turkey. An jest some peanuts we'd parch them. Soda water, three-day beer. Candy. Cakes. Pies. Well I'd have aaalll that ta cook.

An we'd set up all night Satiddy night, an sell that out. From this time, oh, little befoe sundown on a Satiddy evenin until about Sunday mownin little befoe day: that hog'd be gone! We wouldn have a thang.

An then I'd be killin chickens off the yawd. You may thank I'm jokin: I have sent ta the stow, an got two cans a salmons. You know what salmons is? They in a can. Call em Eatwell. An I have made ten dollas outa two can a salmon ta mens they call gamblas. Where they done gambled all night an done sold outa everthang Sunday mownin. Then I'd make salmon balls, an they'd buy em, fifty cents apiece. So thats the way we come up.

You know, back yonda you used ta didn wait on yoself. You'd tell the clerk what you want. An they'd git it fur ya. Now, thats what you'd do wit a Satiddy Night Suppa.

Mance's aunt Sweet give em fur years an years, an I jest clerkt behind the table. Til they left an moved up there ta Waxahachie. She an Mama Janie were sisters. I'd sell sich as candy an peanuts an coffee an all like that. An long about, I reckon somewhere back in the thirties, they stawted ta worryin me about givin Suppas. So they'd have somewhere ta go. So I jest pickt it up, an went ta givin em fur myself. That was at the Lott Bottoms.

We'd slow down a while, an we'd stawt back up again. Wouldn hawdly give em, though, til in the fall a the year. Cotton-pickin time. Because then it'd be mow money in circulation. We'd stawt along about August. Thats when this cotton would stawt ta openin. We'd give em til about the last a November. Whenever it come ta gittin too cold fur the gamblas ta set out an gamble, thats when we'd slow up.

When it be rainin an cold an like that, why I wouldn make over fifty or sixty dollars, cause it wouldn be but a few come out. But this time in the year, gittin into summatime, when it was a good night I'd end up wit me sometimes eighty, ninety dollars in the clear.

Oh, chile, I jest dont *know* how miny peoples would come there. Cause it be mow outdoze than it would in the house. Oh, there would be about foedy or fifty, jest one crowd go in an anothun come. Like that. Til broad daylight.

Them what could dance an them couldn dance was on the flow. Jest ta make the crowd bigger. Some were jest out there havin fun. An I hawdly ever did dance then, cause I'd be waitin tables, ya know.

Wouldn hawdly be nothin in the house but womens, an girls an boys what danced, an all the mens'd be out around the gamblin game.

An the womens inside the house be jest settin down lookin at the girls dancin. M-hm. They would be talkin, but I always would be off in anothuh room, clerkin. They'd have a table cross that doe, an whenever they'd want sumpm, why, they'd come up ta that doe an ask fur it, and I'd sell it to em.

Sometime that table be near about long as this room is wide. Well, I'd have cakes an custards, apple pie an tatuh custards an meat. I had candies an apples an oranges an peanuts. Ice cream, jest everthang on that same table.

We'd buy ice cream in a big freezer. Fur ice cream cone. You could git a big five-gallon can fur about a dolla an a half. Two dollas ta the highest. Git a big bag a peanuts like that fur a dolla. Two sticks a candy, big sticks fur a nickel. Thangs was cheap in them days.

No, I didn charge. They could come in free, an jest buy what we had when you git in. We'll have a hog an sometimes chickens; I'd run out an go out there an catch the chickens off the roost an kill em.

Hog aweighin bout two hunnud pounds over, you could git it an kill im on a Satiddy mownin. Had me big washpots where I could pearboil im, wit salt an black pepper an red pepper. An season it. Then take im out an put im in a great big stove pan, an bake im an mop im. Wadn no bahbecue in them days, you know, jest bake it. In that wood-burnin stove I had.

Like I'd cook a ham, git it done. I'd take that out an put it in sumpm. Git anothun an cook it on til I cook it all up. No, it wouldn take so long! I stawt on cookin on em Satiddy mownin. Well see, I wouldn have nothin ta cook but my hogs, cause I be done cookt my cakes an pies that Friday. An I'd have all my meats ta cook that Satiddy.

Yeah I'd make up jest so miny cakes an pies, accordin until I git tired. Sometime I'd have nine an ten, an foe to the lowest. Cause they didn care too much fur cakes, but that pie an custard: they want that with the meat. Oh, I'd cook fried apple pies an all like that. An come Sunday mownin, they done et it all up.

Says they'd stawt ta gatherin bout foe o'clock Satiddy evenin. An they gonna stay there all night Satiddy night. Til God break his day. An sometime til nine o'clock that Sunday mownin. Me clerkin by my table in that room, here in this room Mance may be settin on that divan: he playin an they dancin.

Oh yeahhh, they was everwhere. Out in the gamblin shack an everthang. Like that old house out there, nobody dont live in it: they'd make it a gamblin shack outa that. Gamblas would stay all day Sunday. They'd break up long

Elnora's kitchen on February 1, 1967. *Photo by Burton Wilson.*

about nine o'clock Sunday night, cause they'd know they had ta meet the Man Monday mownin. Yassuh, jest like me, I was a man, you was a man, an you done got me off in a loser. Well, I stayed right there an try ta win my money back.

Aw, the last one I give on Lott's place was in thirty-six. An I'll tell ya why I quit em up there: see back then, there wadn no beer joints. An peoples would make that bootleg whisky out in the woods an keep it hid, an they'd sell it ta the Suppas. You'd tell im what you want an pay im fur it. He'd go out in them woods certain distance an brang you what you want. Mighty seldom you'd see laws out there.

Well, I had my bizniss clerkin in the house. I didn have no bizniss ta look outdoze fur. I wouldn never see em sell no whisky. Til the next mownin somebody may tell me. An they may not. Well, I guess some was like this: they'd be lookin out ta see whats happenin.

M-hm. Some folks know me, now I dont know them. Cause they'd come up ta the table an everbody knowed I was Miz Lipscomb. An this one fella kep acomin round there an, "Oh Elnora, you oughta sell that whisky an beer. You show doin good with these Suppas." An I didn know im so well.

An direckly the law come out an askt me, "Are you Miz Lipscomb?"

I told em, "I'm is." I said, "How come them ta know me, an I aint never seed them befoe?"

An they said, "We heard you was givin Suppas out here."

I told im, "Well, they got so rowdy. An I decided I wouldn give no mow, because sumpm else might a hapmd."

He said, "Well, they tell me you's sellin dranks out there, an fightin out there."

I said, "Well, I dont know nothin about that. Because I was inside the house."

So the next Satiddy night he come around again. Crow Baker. The same man was urgin us ta give a Suppa, thats the one was tellin the law all that mess. Why is that? Jest, some people aint got no hawt. See, some people wants ta see you do good, an some dont. Jest jealous a us making that money, all I kin see. Aw chile, some people dont care what they do!

An you know, it twas my own mother told them laws how ta run up on me. Yeah, I jest went visitin, an I'd always tell her where I was goin.

An she said two white mens come there an askt where-abouts I was at, or either my husband.

She said she told em, "I jest dont know."

An kep on askin her, an she told em where I was.

I dont know what was her vision fur tellin em. I jest told her, "Dont never tell nobody where nobody at. Because you dont know what they want."

Yeah, that broke me from givin a Satiddy Night Suppas. The law commence comin out there an bustin thangs up. Lookin fur that bootleg whisky, what they said they was doin. Then too, the peoples had done got ta scufflin so, I jest said, "Enough's enough." I didn give anothuh one til, oh a good while after we'd moved off a that place. An it lookt like ta me it wadn so bad where we moved, an I went ta givin em again.

Til beer joints come in. Then that was what made away with the Suppas. Let me see, them beer joints come in about fifty . . . earliern that. I rememba now, cause I was operated on in foedy-two. You know I never did git over a hunnud an foedy in the wintertime, up until that time. But I done got stout now!

An so, them beer joints was in then. An everbody's talkin bout the Big Wheel, the Big Wheel. That was the name a the beer joint. An I said, "Lawd, I'll be glad when I git able ta see that Big Wheel."

It was right there on the highway as you comin from Lott's place toward Washington. Its gone bad now. It was jest an ordinary buildin. Like a little stow or sumpm. An anothuh little old house settin up above it, on a little hill like.

Yeah, we quit givin Suppas about two years befoe we went ta Houston. Well, they git loaded at the beer joints an come out there an raise saind an fightin, everthang, so I sided I'd jest close down.

M-hm. Befoe them beer joints was round here, we'd git us some soda water an make a big old crock a that three-day beer. We'd git some yeast an some diffunt kind a syrup. It been so long I done forgot. An so much a sugar an so much a water, an let it set three or foe days. Til it come jest workin backud an forward. Then you take it out an strain it, an put it in the bottle an cap it, you know we had a beer capper.

Sometime you'd pull the top on one—HMP!—an it'd shoot clear up ta the top a the house. I could drank that *good,* but these days its too bitter fur me. Mmmm-hm! It wadn too sweet but jest good enough ta drank ta me.

Why would the peoples go ta the Suppas? Ta have fun. Ta eat an dance an drank. Gamble. No, if they couldn git a musician ta come an play, well they wouldn nobody *give* no Suppa.

Mance was the onliest musician around. It wadn hawdly no musicians in here in them days. Mighty few. I tell ya the way they bidded back: cause I'm gonna give a Suppa this Satiddy night, well somebody else would give one the next Satiddy night so he could git ta hire Mance ta play. An on an on an switcht about like that.

An later on I jest give em ever Satiddy night, cause I had the musician. An its a cinch they's comin ta where music was at. They'd ask me ta give back an let them give a Suppa, so that Mance could play fur em. An sometime I would, an sometime I wouldnt.

An so, Mance'd be settin there, jest playin. Now he'd eat his suppa long about nine o'clock Satiddy night befoe he stawt ta playin. Long about twelve or one he'd come an git im a cup a coffee. An he wouldn even come up til the next mownin. Mmm-hm!

I tell ya how Mance would play. He knowed how ta keep *time* with the dancers. Now if they'd git slow, he'd git slow. An if they'd stawt ta dancin fast, why he'd play fast music.

Aw chile, when I met im he was playin Suppas. You heared im play that song "You Got ta Reap Jest What You Sow"? He sangin it when I married im. I couldn tell ya how miny songs he knew back then, cause I didn stay there long. Cause in them days young folks wadn allowed out like they is now. But now Mance, he could learn so much mown me because he was playin music, an he *had* ta go out.

Oh, them blues numbas, some of em is slow an some of em aint. Blues ta my idea is sumpm fast. An then if you take somebody, settin down: maybe they listen at that blues song about, "Dont yo house look lonesome, when yo woman's packin up ta leave." Well, thats truth. An all at once, sumpm done passt over you. Slowly in yo mind. Thats the reason I say some fast an some slow.

An you take a man: reason I know the blues, they say? "When a man take the blues, he'll catch some train an ride. An when a woman take em, she'll hang her head an cry." Well, thats true. So its six in one half I'll say an half a dozen in the other.

Aw, some a them Suppas would go til day. I'd sleep til about eleven o'clock an then I'd git up, fix dinna. An go ta church. Yeah, Sunday was church day. Biggest majority of em went. See, we didn have church every Sunday. Jest once a month, an that be on the first Sunday or second Sunday or third Sunday.

Until long about August or September they'd have sumpm they called revival meetins. Jest like, was a buncha sinners out there, see, they'd come in the church, an the Christians would pray fur em. If they felt like they was changed, why they'd come in an jine the church.

Well they'd run that meetin fur about two weeks. Some-time they'd have ten an twelve an fifteen ta babtize. Me an Mance's daddy was babtized together. An after I fesst ta hopes in the Lawd, well I jest furgot about the Suppas an went ta goin ta church.

I didn jine the church til after we was married. Oh, by him talkin bout he got kickt out, jest cause he got out an went with the world, I reckon. Playin the music an playin fur dances, an all like that.

He never would hawdly go ta church. After we married no mow than carry me there. An jest a buncha mens would

stand outdoze an laugh an talk, til the service was over.
Then they'd take their wives an carry em on home. They
wouldn take us in there, jest brang us ta the doe.

Church wadn too far, bout a half of a mile. Walkt most a
the time. Mighty few buggies was here. Yeah, be a bunch a
folks jest walkin up an down the road goin ta church.
Mens an womens, kids an everthang.

Sometime I'd fix dinna befoe I go ta church. Well, if
tamarra was Sunday an I knowed that was my church day,
I'd do my biggest cookin on a Satiddy. I wouldn have so
much ta cook that Sunday mownin.

Wouldn have time ta cook nothin through the week,
cause we'd be in the field. We hafta cook the quickest little
thang we could git through the week. Til on a Sunday an
we could cook inythang we wanted ta cook. Then I'd cook
foe or five dishes. Sometimes greens, sometimes beans.
Chicken. Steak. Sometimes I'd cook a cake, an maybe a
tatuh custard. Dewberry pie an peach pie.

Mmm-hm! When I could git around, I thought I was the
best cook in the world, an I done seed em all. You know,
when people is settin down eatin yo cookin, an act like
they like it, look like you kin enjoy it better.

Well I never did care nothin about no awmadella. We'd
cook coon sometime, possum sometime. The fact a the bizniss, Mance hunt so much til he didn care nothin about
nothin like that. No, he'd give it away or sell it one.

Yeah, on a Sunday we'd have a crowd gatherin in here.
Come afternoon, Mista Mance play us a piece. An then
from there they stawted ta dancin. In the yawd, on the
poach. Jest inywhere. Til a certain hour an then they had
ta go in; they couldn stay out like girls do now. Hafta be in
by dawk. So, thats the life we come up under. Wadn no
stories to it. It was the truth!

No, Mance wouldn play no place through the week. No
mown settin out on the poach an practice fur hisself. Sometime he wouldn pick it up in a run of a week. Lessin he'd go

out somewhere an hear a new song. Then he'd come back an sorta practice that song. I reckon he'd be too tired ta play ever night. Yeah, if it was in the summatime, he'd be out on the front poach. He wouldn hawdly play in the wintertime, lessin somebody come in there an ask im ta play em a piece or two.

Well they liked us all right, but you know, some people jest dont wanta see you do good. M-hm. Now jest like when he's fixin ta build up here, they "Aw, he aint gonna move up here, he aint doin nothin but talkin, he aint gonna be a—"

Jest like when he first stawted ta goin off. Some people said he didn have sense enough ta go off an make no music, he aint had enough education fur that.

An when he come back, an was showin his pitchers an thangs an the write-up about im: oh, they jest thought that was wonderful.

Aw, they come an tell me about, "You gonna look fur im one a these days an aint gonna see im. Some woman be done tuck im."

Mance's gravemarker, January 1993. *Photo by Tad Hershorn.*

I'd tell em jest as quick as I could open my mouth, "Well he makin my livin. Thats all I care." So they couldn make nothin outa that. Cause they knew I had a answer fur em.

Never did worry about him findin some other woman— after he got up in the age. Aw, if he *did* inythang in his young days I didn know nothin about it, cause he's goin so miny places playin music. I dont know what I woulda felt like. I dont *spect* its all right, if I *knowed*. But I never did hear tell of it, an I didn see im wit nobody. An I didn have nothin ta worry over. I'm tellin you the truth, cause I never did experience that feelin. It aint but one time I'd worry over Mance, thats when he'd go off an tell me he'd be back in sich an sich a day an didn come back.

Well, they dont *know* nothin bad about Mance. I been knowin im aminy year, an aint but one bad thang I kin say about him: he jest was too good ta people. Cause I tell ya, its all right ta be nice, but you kin jest give away yo earnins.

Some people tells im, say, "Mance, if you had a got this opportunity when you was young, what would you'd a done?"

He say, "I dont know what I'd a done, but I know I got it when my time come. Cause if I had a got it when I was young, probly I'd a been dead, or I'd a been separated from my wife or sumpm nothuh. Now I know what ta do wit it."

[Elnora survived Mance by two years. These last two conversations occurred after his death.]

Yeah, I tried ta git one *here*, but the man what was makin em he had got so old. So I went up ta Bryant an I said, "What is the cheapest you kin make one outa?"

He said, "Well I kin make you one fur three hunnud."

I said "Well, go ahead on an make it then. Its his money, an I feel like its all right. Because he's payin fur it hisself, even if he *is* gone."

An so eruh, I had his pitcher put on it. An had em ta put

on there that he was the Master a the Music. An a coupla mow thangs: had his age an the day he was bawn an ever-thang.

I askt em, could they have it ready by Father's Day. That

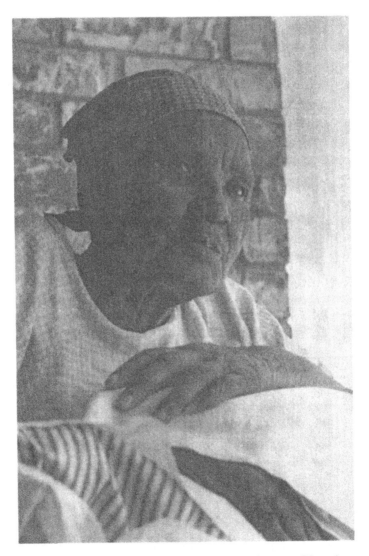

Elnora Lipscomb shortly before her death, in 1978. *Photo by Glen Alyn.*

was jest two weeks from the time I went. He said he couldn git it ready by Father's Day. An I told em, "Well I'll jest put some flowers on his grave then."

Yeah, look like ta me I was settin by the doe, jest like I always set an watch the TV in that chair. An I hapm ta look up an I glimpst Mance. I said, "Umm, there's Mance!"

Comin an he's jest smilin hisself down. An I was smilin, I dont know who would beat the smilin, me or Mance. I sayin, "Look at you! How long you been walkin, Mance?"

He say, "Oh, two or three days."

I say, "An walkin jest as good as ever, too!"

He say, "Mmm-hm."

When he got, first step an he vanisht. Come up on the poach steps, an I didn see im no mow after that. Thats about sometime last month. September.

Oh yeah I've had sorta like, *feelins* he was nearby but not like *that,* though, cause I'd jest imagine I'd be gittin back in the bed so he could git in the bed wit me. But thats the onliest dream I had how he was talkin ta me. Yeah, thats the onliest one I seed him in that vidgion, that night.

It was nice. Ta see him so jolly. Oh, I was so happy he was walkin. I said, "Thats him!"

Out of the Bottoms, onto the Bluffs, and into the Big City

Through a bizarre set of disasters and escapades, Mance and Elnora managed to break free of sixty years of economic bondage, bearing out Mance's adage "Sometime when a thang hapm to ya, when its hurtin ya its fur ya." In the 1951 fire described in Elnora's go-along, the Lipscombs lost everything they owned, including Mance's guitar and Elnora's teeth money. By 1956 they had come out ahead in one year's farming, with a net profit of $500, and they had managed to acquire a dozen cows, thirty-five hogs, and a hundred chickens. Mance was sixty-one and facing old age, armed with his wits, a small herd of livestock, a Social Security pension, and a rented house, working a few acres of land he knew would rarely (if ever) bring him any profit.

That's when they hightailed it to Houston. The circumstances of the Lipscombs' move to Houston and Mance's encounter with his former overseer of Sommers Farm provides a down-to-earth context to the national political arena of 1956–57, when another Texan, named Lyndon Baines Johnson, was working to maneuver the first civil rights act since Reconstruction through both houses of Congress.

Through a narrow escape, Mance's nimble fingers and his courage, a family support system, a way of carrying himself with integrity and skill that befriended blacks and whites alike, an accident, and a chance meeting on a street corner with an ambitious lawyer's hawker, Mance and Elnora wound up in a very unlikely place: they became landowners, with absolutely no obligations to a bank or an overseer. In 1960 Mance and Elnora moved into their own home on three acres of land, a stone's throw away outside the Navasota City Limits sign. They had managed to beat the system.

Meanwhile, in Houston, Lightnin' Hopkins made a cameo appearance on his home turf while Mance backed up yet another old fiddle player and attracted an urban audience to his music. Mance had converted to electric guitar in 1949, and was playing electric while in Houston from 1956 to 1958.

In 1958 the blues historian Sam Charters sent Chris Strachwitz a postcard from Houston. "I've found Lightnin Hopkins!" Sam reported, knowing that his fellow Hopkins devotee would be excited to hear the news. The Englishman Charters documented American blues in the fifties. Europe had demonstrated a strong interest in the blues, and a popular question being asked in France was "What state is Lightnin' Hopkins from, and is he still alive?" While in Houston, Charters either did not notice or never encountered a "Mance Lipscomb" backing up an old-time fiddler named Bill. By the time a local musicologist named Mack McCormick took Chris around the beer joints of Houston in 1959, Mance was back in Navasota, and Lightnin' was in California with John Lomax, Jr., singing at the Berkeley Folk Festival. It was a near-miss.

This adventure is the demarcation line between Mance's former life as an indebted farmer and weekend musician heralded as "the ace man in his precinct," and his future life as an internationally acclaimed country blues artist who played most of the folk and blues festivals of the 1960s. This uncanny series of bends in the river and twists in the road left Mance poised for his discovery in 1960. Aint it funny, how time slips along?

So I HAD IT HAWD all my days. But dont never give up. A quitter loses. Jest keep on. Doin the right thang. I lived so hawd, til I cried, an I studied, an I sweated an give out. Tryin ta make a increase. I buried my mother, my daddy, my sister's kids. Still I was behind. I fooled around an paid all their debts. I thank I buried about six of em in the famly. They didn have nothin. I got it up on the credit. Workt it out. I got ta the place where I paid it. I dont owe nobody inythang.

But now when I run off an slippt off, I was in Washington County. See when I was workin fur Mista Johnny Sommers, he always kept me in debt. Ever year, my debts run up higher an higher. An I was eleven years, an never did see daylight. No mown when daylight come.

He was what ya call a absent boss man. Stayed up in Dallas, didn hawdly come down here. He an his brothers got that gin up there on the Bluffs? On past St. Matthews Church, goin towards William Penn an Independence? An you kin set up there, look right down on Allenfawm. Mow brothers got that planation too. An when the wind come outa the nawth? You kin hear that Tom Mow bell come rollin along them Bottoms an on over the river, then up the hill: "Llun. Lllun-lummm."

He got somebody ta sell im a tracta up there in Dallas, an they bought anothuh tracta. An he brought it down here an sold it ta me fur five hunnud dollas. Wadn no count fur nothin but ta haul wood an cut pastor. I'd cut pastor fur him, an try ta make a crop. I couldn git the durn tools on that tracta ta work right.

So when I went ta his place, I had eleven head a cows. Herefords. Whiteface. I had foe mules. He made me sell the mules an buy that tracta. An then he tuck mortgage on my cows. Five hunnud dollas. An then when I found out I wadn gonna pay up, I jest slippt off an left the cows there. He done increase since then somewhere along about eighteen or twenty cows.

An thats his fawm up there where we was workin at, an me an my boy make the crops. He would have Little Mance ta see after his cows. You know, when the calves come in he would docta on em. An mawk em an brand em, keep em goin. An we was keepin the fence up together. You know, buildin fences an puttin diffunt new wires an diggin postholes. When we wadn in the fawm.

An I was give out. Man, I done so much hawd work fur them its apitiful. That man used ta have us totin spools a wire: he was on this side wit a stick through it, an I was on this side. Totin it from there down ta the Foe Fawks. An then we stretcht that wire wit wire stretchers.

He had somebody doin it fur nothin, you *might* say. Oh well, he paid me fur our cotton. An then the little daywork we done, we got a little money outa it, a dolla an a quota, a dolla an a half a day. What was a dolla an a half a day? You couldn do nothin wit it hawdly.

He had him a overseer, same as what ya call a straw boss, by the name a Mista Skeeter. Lived down in old Washington. Well he issue us out in a check. That check was cut so little that we couldn buy much wit it. That was in fifty-six, cause we kin buy mow then than we kin now. But we didn git no mown twenty-foe dollas a month he's allowin us. I thank it was me an my wife, an I had two grandkids wit me. Little Mance next ta me, he had seven or eight. Well he'd git a little mown me. We couldn live outa that. So, I would skip around an hunt. An pick up puck-awns an try ta make my income, ta take care a myself an my kids an Elnora.

The least that I made there a year was twelve bales a cotton. An come out in debt every year. Aw, sometimes I'd git a hunnud an twenty or a hunnud an twenty-five dollas fur a bale. Cordin ta what sort a year. A wet year or a bad year, you got yo cotton all entangled up, wouldn git no good staple outa it. It valued down to about eighteen cents a pound.

He would buy yo cotton. You couldn sell it. An he jest give you what he want fur it, ya see. So I jest kep acomin out in debt.

Then, we got burnt out an he built us a fine house: concrete flow. Concrete front. An the back was concrete, they jest put concrete all over the whole place. It had double windas there.

He say, "This is yo house. An when ya git so ya git old enough, you draw yo pension." Well, I wadn near ready ta draw pension when I was there. An he said, "Then you kin tell the people that you payin me rent fur the house. An that make yo pension come higher." He wadn tellin me nothin! I was figgerin a way ta go all the time. But I didn tell *him*.

In fifty-six, I say, "Ya know, its time fur me ta make a change. This man takin everthang I kin inherit—my crops an cows—an they brang me out in debt mow an mow ever year. I blieve I'm gonna move up." Talkin ta myself.

One night I laid down, I jest rolled an my wife woke up an says, "You sick?"

366

I say, "I'm sick inside."

She said, "What? Inside?"

I said, "I'm studyin my way out."

Say, "What you talkin bout, yo way out?"

Them days, when you go off an leave a man on a fawm: owed him a nickel, they would try ta come git you. Make you come back. An if ya didn come back—cordin ta where you was—he'd whup you an *make* you come back.

Now my daddy was a sensible man, but he wadn no good provider. But I listened, tuck what he said: "If ya caint pay a man in the full, well you pay im in distance." You know what distance means? You kin walk out of it. Slip out of it.

I went an studied that night, an that whole week. I didn eat much. I say, "I'm tired a this man takin my earnins, an treatin me jest like I'm a child. I'm gonna move."

My wife say, "That man goin come an git you."

An I say, "Thats what he'll hafta do."

That Sunday, I wrote my grandboy a letter. I raised a grandboy an he went ta Houston an had a job. I say, "Git a traila, an come up here next Sunday evenin befoe night, an load my thangs up, an move me ta Houston. Cause I'm tired a doin what I'm doin an treated like I am."

An so, I played ever Satiddy night an Sunday fur a beer joint fur a dolla, or whatever I could git outa it. About five o'clock that evenin I was settin there, seed a traila an a fifty-five Shivolay truck: stranger. He turnt off at the beer joint.

Somebody said, "Who is that comin yonda wit a traila?"

I say, "I dont know." When he got closer to me, the mow I could realize who it was. But I didn want the people ta know what the boy comin up there after, cause the talks gits out.

I said, "Ohh, thats my boy Sonny Boy. You know what he huntin?" He was huntin me. I throwed em off, I say, "He huntin some cone. Iny a y'all got iny cone around here ta sell?"

They say, "No, we aint got none ta sell." See, I knowed nobody didn have iny cone cause it wadn the time a year fur it.

So, he liked ta drank beer, an he stoppt there. Come in say, "Aw, here's Daddy." They all called me Daddy. That was my sister's boy, Louis Coleman. One they called Alice?

I say, "Well, you wanta go up ta the house?"

He say, "I . . ."

"Wait a minute. Dont say 'I' nothin. Jest say you wanta go up ta the house. You say sumpm I dont want ya ta say." An I pulled im on outa there, befoe he let sumpm slip out.

I didn have no caw, an he had the fifty-five Shivy an the traila hookt behind im. I say, "Boy, you wait til night." I stay about foe miles from the beer joint, William Nolan's place. "Then you go up there, stawt ta loadin me up."

Sundown come, we drove on up ta my house. My thangs in there ready. My wife had packt up what she could, skillets an lids an dishes. Had over a hunnud chickens. Had about thirty-five hogs. I give some a them away an then staked some mow out wit Jude—thats my boy's wife. An I said, "Now when you sell em, you give me some a the money. I'm gone!"

[From Mance's version of "Key to the Highway," by Big Bill Broonzy (circa early 1950s):

You wake up, in the mownin, I'll be seldom seen.
You kin tell my captain, let someone else catch my team.]

I had few people I could trust. I had some hogs weighed two or three hunnud pounds. Two three sows are goin find pigs. Chickens. I kilt about fifteen hens, an put em down under. It was kinda cool you know, night. Carried em ta Houston put em in the deepfreeze. Thats what I lived offa about two weeks. Them chickens.

Man, I had buckets an pans on the traila, loaded up jest like cotton. Put them pans an lids an rockers an cans on the traila an we had thangs wasted all the way from Washington ta Houston. An ever time I hit a rough place, a pan or a bucket'd fall off, an I said, "Keep on." What we got there with, why we got there with that. I didn stop. Cause I was runnin off. The Man liable ta overtaken me, ya know.

Mownin come, we was settin in Houston. My grandboy couldn git in the house he rented fur us til day, so they could come there an git the key fur me. We sot there on the truck.

Direckly, Sonny Boy come an sot out there wit us. Said, "Well, I tell ya: I aint got no place fur y'all ta stay here tonight, but yo thangs'll be tuck care a. Aint nobody gonna bother em. I'm gonna carry you over here ta some people's house an let y'all lay down."

Day come, he open the doe ta the house, an we moved the thangs in there, an that where we stayed at. On East Thirty-eighth Street. In nineteen fifty-six.

In Houston. I didn know one street from anothun. But I know I done left that fawm. Couldn find no job. There I was: stranded. I had foeteen dollas, I never will furgit it, in my pocket. That foeteen dollas didn last over two days. I been buyin little bits an thangs toward them chickens I kilt. Said, "Now I got ta git me a job somewhere."

So finely, this music is one thang all ways got me by. When I got ta Houston, about the first week I got there, colored guy heard me. An you know news gits around.

Say, "You know, Lightnin Hopkins around here." He was a famous player in Houston. He had all the places he wanta play. Places he didn wanta play. The most money where he's gonna work at.

Ohh, they was talkin bout "Lightnin Hopkins, Lightnin Hopkins!" I had seed him two or three times. He didn worry me, cause I had sumpm in my fangers fur Lightnin. He couldn never play the music I play.

They said, "I want you ta play wit Lightnin."

I say, "No, you want me ta play wit Mance. Last night he played wit hisself."

Say, "Aww, I heard he coulda beat you."

I say, "Well, he's got sumpm ta do an I got sumpm ta do. He's doin his numba, I do mine."

Lightnin dodged me. He didn wanta mix up wit me, he saw me in Galveston. Nineteen thirty-eight, first time I seed im down there. I was seein Coon an Pie. They's twins, last ones bawn in the famly.

Finely, one night, a fella he say, "I'll tell ya whut. I like yo music. I'll give ya ten dollas a night ta play at my beer joint." Oh man, that was a lot a money in them days. Thats mown I ever made in my life, ten dollas a night.

I went there on a Friday night, he say, "You kin come back Satiddy night. Man, you make twenty dollas in two nights!"

Well, thats what I lived outa: twenty dollas, fur about six months. Now my boy, he follad me everwhere I go. I caint lose him. So he come on down an stayed wit me about a year. Up until fifty-eight. He got a job, an my grandson he already workin there at a fillin station. So they kep me goin, wit that twenty dollas.

Finely, old fella playin the fiddle, I was playin fur his son had that little beer joint right on the street. He played some real good fiddle. Old-time fiddlin. His name Bill. An he got stuck off on me, playin that gittah behind that fiddle.

An the police had that beat, you know. An they come up an down, check on thangs.

First thang ya know I seed two polices, lookin in the doe. I said, "Now, sumpm gonna hapm here." An I checkt up playin.

Two polices walkt in. I said, "Uh-oh. I'm gonna git arrested here."

He say, "What yo name, fella?"

I had ta tell em, said, "Mance Lipscomb."

Say, "We been listenin at you out there, on the street."

I said, "Listenin at me fur what?"

He say, "Boy, you play some damn good gittah."

I say, "Show nuff?"

Say, "We had ta come in here ta see how you look. We aint never heard no gittah played like that. We'll walk that beat, up an down. An ever time we hear you playin a diffunt song. This is our beat: go ahead on an play."

I said, "Thank ya. I didn know what was up."

Said, "Whats up: we like ta hear you play."

Oh, them people jest dug in there, little small place hold about a hunnud people. That boy did well: in a week's time, all them joints around in that precinct broke up. Comin down ta hear *me* play. The people had them little bands come over there, an some of em liked me an some of em hated me, cause I broke their joints up.

Finely one boy said, "Mista, where you come from?"

I say, "I come from Navasota."

Say, "We show do like yo music." Thats one a the band boys.

Othun walkt up an say, "Aww, he aint nowhere." That was one a the band boys criticizin me.

An the othun say, "Man, he *aint* nowhere. He's somewhere! We caint touch this man. Thats the reason we aint got nobody over at our place. This man done drawed all the people over here."

An the boy's name Milton what hired me, say, "Well, we got thangs in the bloom, aint we? You doin right."

I played there fur him about six months. An his daddy joined in, commenced ta rehearsin wit me. See, that fiddle was sumpm new to em round in Houston. An I would jest bass im, backin im up an that fiddle would sound out so good.

The policies was dancin out on the street. Said, "Boy, you got sumpm goin here! Where you git them people at?"

Milton said, "My daddy playin the fiddle, an Lipscomb is

playin the gittah." I was playin lectric gittah then. Since about foedy-nine.

Say, "Well, you doin good, since you have no fussin an fightin here. Man, we caint hawdly quit comin up an down this street, listenin at that music."

I stayed down in Houston long about two years. An all the while, they up in Navasota, scratchin round fur me. Ohh, he was huntin me like a dog huntin a rabbit. Honey, he said I owed im five hunnud dollas, an I dont owed im five cents. A bridge is trust: if a man owe you some money, you jest trusted him with that. Long as you dont take no mortgage an stuff away from his place, he caint come say you owe him nothin!

See, they put that book on ya. An then, "There, you done well this year. You may do better next year." Thats what I got *made* ta do better. I was doin worser ever year.

An when Johnny Sommers found out I had slippt off at night, people would write an tell me, an people moved up from Navasota, jest dwell in diffunt places in Houston: they all said, "Man, Johnny Sommers an Skeeter Stolz, they lookin fur ya." Thats how the news got ta Houston.

I said, "Let em look down here. They'll find me." I had some good backuz. I got the white folks on my side. Colored folks.

They say, "Dan comin at you!" Thats the devil, you know.

Now I got satisfied. Finely I come back up ta Navasota one day, an he had a overlooker: Mista Skeeters was lookin fur me. He was mad an wanted ta know why I left, an sent his word, "Come on back!"

News got out that my boy come up there an talk about killin the overseer. Some fella had done moved in on his place, where he stayed below me over there on the Bluffs. An maybe he got ta drankin, come an say, "Mista Skeeters, Little Mance done come up here an beat me. He say he goin come back an kill me, an when he git through wit me, he comin ta kill you."

An Mista Skeeters say, "I tell you whut: if I lay eyes on him inywhere in Washington County, he goin be one dead nigga!"

Somebody told me about it. I got on the bus an come up there one Satiddy. I said, "Well I aint got but one son, aint got but one time ta die. I'm gonna try ta keep him from killin my boy. I know he hadn been back down that road since he left there. There's a false repoat went out on my boy, an then the Man wanta pick it up because we left there."

I come up town that Satiddy mownin, I was standin on the street talkin. Colored fella say, "What you doin up here?"

I said, "This is my home, aint it?"

"Yeah, but man, Mista Johnny Sommers an Mista Stolz lookin fur you."

I say, "Well I'm here."

"What ya come up here fur?"

I say, "I come up here ta protect my boy. I heard Mista Skeeters totin a Winchester in his caw fur ta kill my boy. Now I'm gonna talk ta Mista Skeeters if I kin find im, which I aint goin out ta Washington. I'm here in town."

Talkin ta this colored fella, he leaned ta my ear, "There Mista Skeeters now!"

He come up an stoppt his caw right on the street. An he was lookin around, I was lookin im right in the face. I walkt up ta the caw, put my foot on his caw fender. He lookt around in my face, said, "Uuht! What the hell you doin here?"

I said, "This my home, Mista Skeeter."

He said, "What kinda damn stunt is that ya call yoself pullin? Slippin off an owin Mista Johnny Sommers all that money?"

I said, "Mista Skeeter, that aint what I wanta find out from you."

He said, "What you wanta find out?"

I said, "I heard you was totin a gun ta kill my boy."

"You damn right! I heard he's totin one ta kill me."

I said, "Thats the biggest lie ever was told. My boy aint got nothin against you."

He says, "Well I'm damn show aint gonna let him kill me."

I say, "He aint gonna try ta kill you. Looky here. You got a boy?"

I knowed he had a boy, he say, "Yeah."

"Well you love yo boy, dont ya?"

"You damn right!"

An I said, "I dont cuss, Mista Skeeters, but I damn show love my boy. He aint done nothin like talkin against you. You let that boy alone. Now, you kin kill my boy an I kin kill yo boy."

He say, "Whut?"

I say, "It goes two ways: dont you kill my boy, cause you dont want me ta kill yo boy."

He say, "You damn right I dont want you ta kill my boy."

I said, "Well you damn right I dont want you ta kill my boy."

He say, "Mance, I thank you talkin some straight talk."

I say, "I know I am. If you love yo boy, I love mine."

He drappt his head, say, "Yeah, you right. Well, does yo boy got sumpm against me?"

I said, "Not a thang. You treat us nice. An my boy likes ya an I like ya. Lets git this thang settled. As long as my boy live, he aint gonna do nothin against you, cause you aint done nothin ta him, an I aint got nothin against you. You told us when we first moved there an you stawted ta bossin me, Mista Johnny wadn gonna let us have no settlement ta clear no money offa him. An I watcht you fur foe years, an everthang you said come out true, didn it?"

Said, "Yeah."

Say, "Last year I was there I made sixteen bales a cotton. An you say I was gonna make some money. My boy was gonna make some, an he made twenty bales. An Mista Johnny aint give us a penny, did he?"

Say, "You right."

I say, "An you told us us oughta leave there. An I tuck ya at ya word."

He knowed its the truth. Say, "You stay away from here. Hell, he aint no good." He tuck a reflect, say, "Mance, look there at back a my caw."

I say, "Fur what?"

Said, "There's a Winchester. I'm gonna unload it, an I'm gonna treat you an yo boy right. You come up here when ya git ready."

I said, "Well I thank ya." Thats the way I got ta goin back. But he was gonna shoot my boy. On hearsayin.

Now, befoe I come home: this fiddla, he was a handyman at the lumbayawd, been workin there about ten or twelve years. An he likedid me, cause he wanted me ta be wit im ever Satiddy night. Say, "Do you know inythang about the grades a lumba?"

I said, "No. I dont know one piece a lumba from anothuh."

Say, "Well I'll learn ya. I'll come by an pick you up, an I see if I caint git ya a job."

I didn know much about no lumba deal, I was jest workin tryin ta make some money in Houston. I got a job there a week pickin up scraps a lumba, pilin em up out the way a the trucks. The boss man come out—I didn know one from the othun; it was a great big lumba compny. An they watch ya out the winda an all round, see how you reactin.

An I hired under him, as a fella had done had his recess two weeks, an I work til he come back.

So I went up there an say, "Well yo man done come back off his vacation. Thats far as I'm lowed ta work."

The boss man aint said nothin, I said, "I'm talkin ta you, boss man."

He lookt at me an said, "I hear ya, but its goin in one ear, comin out anothun. Boy, you tend ta yo bizniss. You works good, an I like yo ways a gittin along. I'm gone vouch fur you some kinda job around here, til you catch on."

An they put me as a helpa in a cawbox, unloadin lumba up on the truck. I workt there seven months. Man, I was makin fifty-eight dollas a week when I stawted! That was gittin into the money then. An all the boys commenced ta likin me, cause they heared me play on Satiddy nights, an I talk wit em an all.

First thang I was doin, handin up lumba ta the truck driver. I was on the ground, an the truck driver was on top a the truck, stackin lumba. An I was jest as crazy as a cricket.

Truck driver says, "Man, hand me this two-by-foe."

I'd git a two-by-six or a two-by-eight.

He say, "Put that down! Thats not a two-by-foe!"

I workt myself down, pickin up the wrong pieces a lumba. Three days, I caught on. An finely I got the truck drivers all on my side, an they wanta git me on the lumba piles an unload lumba. Oh, them people was crazy bout my work, cause I hold up a whole lot a their laziness. I was thrifty, I was a good man them days, I had plenty strength. Yeah, I was goin on sixty years of age.

So, thats where I got hurt: Houston Lumba Compny. One Satiddy mownin, somewhere long about nine o'clock. An I like ta got kilt ta git where I am now. But ya know, when sumpm gonna hapm ta ya, when it *hurt*in ya its *fur* ya. Good or bad. But my *bad* bill made me *whole*, ta git *good* thangs ta hapm ta *me*. I was in the hospital about two months, wit fractured neckbone.

I was standin there, loadin two-by-foes, I never will furgit it: one Friday evenin, the boss man say, "Lipscomb, I dont blieve we gonna git this cawbox unloaded befoe the day's out. An we gotta have it emptied out by tamarra when the switch engine come in here, else we hafta pay a penalty on it. Wonder could you come up here an hep these boys out an git it unloaded? I know you dont sposed ta work on a Satiddy, but I'll pay ya a little extra."

I said, "I'll be down here."

So I got up there Satiddy mownin: three trucks was there, one behind anothun. We'd load this truck, an move the othun up. We had two trucks an workin the last load. We were gonna finish up by ten-thirty, an we done done our day's work, we got full time fur half a day.

An finely, the last truck driver pulled up ta the side a the doe, an I was slidin the lumba off a that roller pier to im. We had a big old foe-by-foe nailed cross the cawbox doe, holpin the weight up. We had a dolly pier inside a the boxcaw. An we pull the lumba down, two or three pieces at a time, much as we could lift. We had a jack ladder inside on the flow, that we could pick that lumba up. From that dolly pier you shoot it out the doe ta the truck helpa. Jest slide it up, an that thang had rollers under it. An then he'd catch the end an whup it round in the truck, an load it an stack it.

Direckly, the boy say, "I done loaded the front end, Lipscomb. Wait a minute. I'm gonna pull the truck up, so I kin load the back end."

An I had foe pieces a numba two-by-foes, one on top a the othun, an I helt it wit my hand on the dolly pier until he moved the truck up, so I could shoot it back out. An the end a that lumba, I stoppt it inside the cawbox. But the roller pier, when he pulled up, was stickin out too fur: The truck hit it, goin by. An knockt that five hunnud pound dolly pier down, in the flow. An that thang cockt up, an all that lumba—foe pieces—flew up the top a the cawbox: a-lllLLAM! an shot back by me, an cut me on the leg

377

an hit me on the awm, an knockt me out the bed. An fractured my neckbone. Didn break it, but knockt it outa
place.

An then the boy what drivin the truck went on down
about ten steps further, an say, "Well, we ready." I could
hear im.

An the man what handed some lumba down to me, he
heard the truck pull up, an that lumba hit the back a that
caw: a-llLAM! Now I'm layin there in the flow. Out. Man
lookt around an say, "HEY, MAN! COME HERE QUICK!
QUICK! This man in here dead!"

I was dead out, but I could hear everthang. But I couldn
move. Thats the last thang I rememba him ta say.

They commenced ta gittin under that plank an comin in
there ta git me. Grabbed me in the truck, an they resht me
ta the first-aid place at the lumba compny. Wouldn hafta
go ta the hospital unless you was really injured. An I was
show nuff injured.

So when I woke up, I was layin on the operatin table.
There I'm layin up there wit my leg buckled down, my
hands buckled down. I commenced ta twistin. An was a
lady standin on this side, an one on this side: nuss.

I opened my eyes, said, "What I'm doin up here? Well,
wheresomever I'm at."

An they smiled at me. Feedin me ice, an ice was comin
out my mouth fastern you put it in, cause my mouth was
closed. I was in a way of out. They was pushin it in my
mouth ta keep the fever outa me. An they says, "Oh, why
you in good hands."

I say, "Well—good hands where?"

They smiled, said, "We jest takin care of ya."

I said, "You show is takin care a me. What all this water
down in my bosom?"

They laught. They knowed I didn have no bizniss knowin where I was, cause a patient git scared when you find

out you in a critical condition. An they tryin ta keep it hid from me. They did have it hid from me.

I say, "Well I'm gittin up from here."

One nuss lookt at the othun. "You reckon you is?"

An I commence ta movin an tryin ta git up an say, "Y'all got me hampt down here. I caint git up."

Say, "Well, I coulda told ya that. You caint git up, until we *let* you up."

An I felt my legs, an they's tied down, bolted down, my awms was stretcht out. I said, "What y'all doin to me? I wanta git off this thang."

So they said, "Mista Lipscomb, you got a little minor bruise on ya. You had a accident. But you doin all right now."

Two doctas was there an they was disgussin: see what was wrong, had iny bruises. I had a awm cut, bleedin. Leg was cut, where that lumba scaped by me. They had them wash that blood off an bind it up. Put my awm in a slang. An they come in an say, "Lipscomb. He kinda realize where he is?"

Nuss say, "Yeah, he done come to."

Say, "Well, I blieve he's all right. We done tuck X rays on im. He bruised, but I dont feel no bones broke. You wanta git up, Mista Lipscomb?"

"I show do!"

Say, "Well, git up."

I say, "I'm tied down!"

Nusses laugh, said, "Well, try it again." An unbuckle them thangs off my awms an legs, an I sot up on the table.

I said, "Kin you tell me where I'm at?"

Say, "You's in the first-aid hospital."

I say, "Yeah? Well I wanta go home."

Say, "We'll let ya go home. But you caint go by yoself."

Then I got up an stawted ta stagger around. An they holpt me, say, "Well you git back on the table. You aint ready ta git down."

I said, "I know I aint been drankin nothin."

Say, "No, you jest got a little bruised up. About ten or fifteen minutes, you'll come back an reckomasize again."

I lookt, an I says, "Know this jest a place I aint never been befoe. An sumpm hapmd ta me, I didn know how it hapmd."

Well, all my friends—oh, about thirty-five or foedy people was workin there—had done quit their work on the job an comin up there ta see whether I was dead or how much damage was done to me. An the docta wouldn let em in.

I had a real good friend, he stayed there. He said, "I'm got ta come in there ta see about Mance."

Docta said, "Now—"

"Listen. I hear his voice in there."

Docta said, "Well, you kin come in. But, one at a time. He's recovered, but he still not hisself."

An so he come in, an he come in cryin. He said, "How you feel, Lipscomb?"

I said, "I'm doin all right. Whats the madda?"

Nusses stawted ta nod their head to im not ta tell what hapm to me.

He come on out, an two or three at a time come in an them boys say, "Well I'm show glad you didn git kilt. We thought you was gone."

I said, "What hit me?"

Then they commenced ta disgussin what hapm to me.

I say, "Yeah, I rememba that now."

Say, "But you all right."

So about a hour one a my friends, the one was acryin over me, he say, "Let me put im in the caw an carry im home. It'd be easier fur his wife ta take it, wit my caw than a ambalance run up there."

So it was a Satiddy mownin about twelve o'clock when I got outa that first-aid place. My wife Elnora was sweepin up the house when they drove up in front a there, jest as nice an quietly. Thank two or three a my friends was wit me. An one was drivin. An here my awm was bind up in a slang, an my legs was bind up where ya couldn see my leg. I was cut on the leg an I didn know that.

Myno come ta the doe, an I was gittin out the caw, an two men was on each side a me. My wife says, "Ohhh, Lawd! Look at my husband!" An she commenced ta hollerin an goin back in the house.

Kids an the folks commenced ta comin out, wanted ta know whats the madda.

So finely, they assisted me in the house. I said, "Where is the wife at?"

"Last time I heard her she say her husband is hurt an she went out the back doe." She didn come back in a hour or two.

An I said, "Tell my wife dont worry, I aint hurt."

An direckly she come in the room, they had put me in the bed. An come ta the doe an lookt at me. Say, "How you feel?"

An I told her, "I'm all right."

The docta told em ta put two pillas under my head. If I had some bruised blood, he didn want it ta come up ta my head. I never will furgit it: I could lay an look out on the streets, jest like I'm settin up here in this chair.

An after I laid there an got correckamasized, then I went ta sleep. It was somewhere long about five o'clock in the evenin when I woke up. People was around my house: jest like a funeral. They was talkin low; I could hear em out there talkin. An they didn bother me at all.

When the news got over Houston, a whole lot a people was there, day an night. I was well cared fur. They come there an brang me fruit an orange juice. See, I had a good reputation all my life. I had mow friends in Houston might near I did in Navasota where I was raised. Cause I carried myself that way.

About three or foe days, I commenced ta movin round in the house, I thought I was all right. The docta had done told em ta git me up there the third day, so here a caw come, an carried me up ta the first-aid place. I walkt in.

Docta say, "Walk around a little, Lipscomb, an lemme see how you reactin."

I walkt around.

"You doin all right. I wanta dress yo awm again." I had a big cut on my right awm. An they peel that off, an put a little mow medicine on it, an bind it wit a new piece, an put it back in a slang. An he say, "You kin go back ta work, in about a week."

Well, I wanted my job cause I was makin seventy-five dollas a week! But they give me half a my wages ta live on, til I could be able, you know. So I said, "Well, I blieve I'll go back ta work. Cause I'm makin mow money workin."

An so, foe or five days, I could walk a little. An I walkt down on the streets ta pass the time. I stood on the corner ta catch me a way home. An I didn see nobody I knowed.

After while a stranger come by, pulled ta the side. "Whats yo name?"

I told im.

He said, "How'd ya git hurt?"

I told im.

He say, "You been back on the job?"

I said, "No. They gimme a certain limit a time ta come back."

An he told me, said, "Man, you dont know what you kin do!"

I said, "What you talkin about?"

Say, "Yo awm's in a slang! You crippled in yo leg. If you got hurt on the job, an then went back. . . . I works fur a lawya. I kin git you some money outa that hurt."

I say, "How'm I gonna git iny money outa this?" I was green, ya know.

He say, "You let me take ya ta my lawya. An this case you got: if you aint been back on the job, you kin show git some good money outa that. Dont you go back."

I tuck im at his word. I said, "Okay."

"Monday, I'll be on my way down Houston, see my lawya, an I kin put yo complaint in, an he'll vouch fur ya."

I said, "Well I aint got no money ta pay no lawya."

He say, "You dont need no money."

So he carried me there that Monday mownin. I didn know where he was carryin me. Houston's too big fur me. An his lawya was upstairs; we went up on the elevator. It was windin round, jest go up slow too.

Finely, here his lawya settin up there in a chair, wit his foot up on the table in front of im an his legs crosst. I said, "This man's fixin ta shoot pool. This idn no lawya." Thats what I had in mind.

An the colored fella knockt on the doe. He was workin fur that lawya. Git them clients ta come in.

"Come in! Come in, Come in!" Lawya looks at me, an tuck his foot down off the table. "Oh. . . . You got a good patient here." Talkin bout me. Say, "Yeah, well—whats his name? Set down! Set down!"

I sot down, told im my name.

He said "Yeah! You's a good fella. You a whole lot better tern these fellas what I been takin cases, jest mudjured an makin me lie an do thangs."

I said, "Now this aint the right place."

He lookt at me, said, "When did you git hurt?"

I said, "I got hurt on July the seventh. Ten-thirty. On a Satiddy."

He never stoppt writin. "M-hm, so you aint been back on the job?"

"No."

An askt me a few questions, he bookt em down. An I give all those thangs straightened out. That was nineteen fifty-seven.

Said, "Well, if I take the case, its fur a certain percentage."

I say, "Well lawya, I dont have iny money."

He say, "Listen: I dont need no money. I got a case ta win. An if you need iny money, tell me now an I'll loan ya some money."

I didn say nothin.

So he told me ta go to a real hospital, so they could verify I was hurt. I stayed there three weeks. Then that made that lawya had a strong case.

An about two weeks after that, the compny lawya came. Ta take a checkup on me. An I had ta go through coat again, wit my lawya an the compny's lawyas.

My lawya, he settin there in this office, he say, "Now you jest tell the laws, jest what you told me. I blieve you kin tell them cause I got yo book down."

Its two lawyas: one is askin you one question, one is askin you anothuh. Cross-examine ya. Thats confusion, ya see. No, it would dont confuse me, cause I'm ware a them thangs. People try you out. I been tried out miny cases. Ask me some questions over. Yeah, they tried me a lot a times ta double-cross me.

Cause when a lawya, somebody like a jailhouse man, is talkin ta you, or the judge: he'll fool around, liable ta ask you sumpm nothuh, an make a fool out ya. Cause you dont understand him, an he dont *mean* fur you ta understand him. He'll catch you lyin, twistify it around.

So when he's cross-examine me, my lawya git up in front an say, "Pardon me."

An the judge say, "I'm not talkin ta you."

Say, "Yeah, but you talkin ta my client. Listen: he dont know what you talkin about. But I do. Why dont ya come clean wit im? Speak out, where he'll understand what you sayin." Yeah, that lawya you got kin always take care a yo situation.

So my lawya an them got it all straightened out, an they laught it off, you know, an drankin coffee. Guyin one ano-thuh. One of em told my lawya, say, "You got this boy

Lipscomb trained. You gonna make a lawya outa him."

An he said, "Well, I hope so. But I aint gonna let you cross-examine im."

So I stayed away about two months befoe I heard from im again. An I thought probly they was gonna come across, in two weeks. Well, they first offer you a settlement. An if you take that bid, they pay you off.

But that lawya sot out ta git something. He called me, says, "Lipscomb. I got a offer fur seven hunnud dollas on yo case."

I said, "Yeah?"

Said, "But I wont take that. I told em I hear em an dont hear em: go an come again. He'll come back. They got three times ta come here, an if they dont come ta my requirements, then I kin sue em. They aint gonna stand no suein. It a big compny, an got good lawyas. They tryin you out, gonna see what would you accept."

I said, "Well, you the lawya. I'm jest the patient."

So they stayed away a certain length a time, an offered him eighteen hunnud fur it.

You know what he told em? Said, "I hear ya in this ear but I dont hear ya in the other ear. I wanta hear in both ears." So when he got ta hearin em in both ears, that was the third time.

About six months: I was broke. But I tried ta hang on, wit my grandkids an thangs an let them tuck care a me. Til it was purdy well gittin ready fur Christmas.

An I had it ta telephone my lawya, I said, "I need a little money. I'm behind in the rent. An I dont have a job."

He said, "I told ya you could git some money the first day you come here."

I said, "Yeah, I done without it up until now, but I need a little Christmas money."

He say, "How much you need?"

I say, "Oh, about a hunnud dollas."

He say, "Oh man, that aint no money! A hunnud dollas wont go ten minutes wit ya."

I say, "Yeah, but I aint got the hunnud! I'll take inything."

He laught, say, "Lipscomb, why dont ya git you foe or five hunnud dollas?"

I say, "Oh, no man! I dont git no foe or five hunnud dollas in yo debt."

He say, "Thats yo money I'm payin ya."

I said, "Well I aint got no payment yet."

He said, "But you got a case. You jest as good as got some money. Christmas, man! Git ya some money."

Well, I didn see what he was feelin at. See, he had a win case an I didn know it. I coulda got a thousand dollas, good as I did the hunnud. I said, "No, a hunnud'll do."

He said, "Well. Why dont ya take a hunnud an fifty, inyhow? Fur Christmas?" An he fooled around an made me take a hunnud an fifty.

That last me up until I went back ta Navasota an went ta work. An thats all I got outa that man in about a year an six months. I done tuck his advice an come back here somewhere in August.

Cause he say, "Dont stay in Houston, cause yo Social Security'll show up you gittin paid here. But you go back ta Navasota or some other place, it wont tell on ya so quick."

An they sunt me word of a man had some tractas wantin me ta cut the highway. They knowed I could drive tractas purdy briefly. An I come up here makin a dolla an a quota a day, an I rose up ta five dollas a day an I was gittin somewhere. But ya know I always had someplace ta play on Satiddy night, little a much. An sometime I lived purdy good outa it: seven dollas a night.

Yeah, I workt under Old Man Bingham. He was the straw boss. You talkin bout his famly, I knowed his son. His granddaughters. Known his daughter-in-law. Wife.

Two a his brother-in-laws. Thats far as I could stretch out an know em.

An I was the head man over them eight tractas, befoe he come where I was at. Call that overseer: man seein you be on the job at certain time a mownin. Seein you bein there ta quit the right time a the evenin. Thats what you call a fawman: man carried the time into the owner, then he would pay em off.

Owner's name Mista Pascal. An he bought two tractas first. Me an my boy was drivin one apiece. By next year the compny bought im six mow. An he paid so much ever month from the highway, til he finisht payin fur his tractas. He makin good money.

So I had, wit myself there was eight people ridin in my truck. I was haulin hay into the truck, ta where we stoppt the tractas off, like this evenin. An go back the next mownin. You had ta greaze them tractas, put oil an gas in em, jest like you do a caw. I tried ta keep that man's machines in good shape. Cause when they was sumpm wrong, I stop an fix it back. A flat was on a tracta, I git the truck an go ta nearby town, an have it mounted back on the wheel.

But I seed I was gonna head into some trouble wit all them young boys, an they wouldn mind me. An I wadn tryin ta fuss at em. Lot a colored folks caint work under colored folk like they oughta, would work fur a white man.

So I went ta the tracta owner, I said, "Looka here. I'm gonna still drive my tracta, but I dont wanta be no overseer over these boys, cause they gittin so rowdy. An I caint tell em nothin. You hafta git somebody else got a little mow voice than I have." See. He made demand on what had me in front of em. Fault me fur what they was doin.

An so finely, he hired Old Man Bingham. An then he wouldn *take* off the boys like what I tuck off em. He would turn em off an git new ones.

An I kep aworkin on that highway. Said, "Well I jest as well furgit about that lawya. Blieve I best keep on workin, git me a little money on a Satiddy night, playin that gittah. An make it howsomever I kin make it." Couldn hear from im in a year!

So finely one Friday evenin, when I come offa work, a man come down there wit a bicycle wit a telegram.

An I was spyin it, said, "A lawya something wants you." I furgit his name. An say, "Come at once."

I say, "Now I wonder what he want in a year's time? I'd go through a motion in talkin ta the other lawyas, an I'm tired a that. I aint gittin nothin outa it."

But I tuck his advice. An the next mownin, I caught the seven o'clock bus an went on down ta Houston.

An went upstairs. He settin at the same table where I first found im at. Lookin out the winda. By hisself. An I knockt on the doe.

He say, "Come in!"

I opened the doe, he turnt around, said, "Well doggone! Here's old Mance!"

I say, "Show is him. I come ta repoat ta see what you wanted."

He say "Boy, I'd a *flew* down here if I'd a been you."

I said, "How'm I fly down here? I aint no bird."

He said, "Git you a airplane."

"Nooo, man, I aint comin up here on a airplane."

Had a big old envelope layin up on the table. He said, "Well, here's a present fur ya. Open that envelope."

An I lookt over it. Opened it, an that check was thirty-five hunnud an five dollas in there. Made out in my name.

I said, "What I'm gonna do wit it?"

He lookt out the winda, downstairs say, "Go right cross the street. There's a bank over there. I caint cash yo check. You cash it, an you come back an pay me what ya owe me."

An I went on over ta the bank. They didn give me no static. An come on back up ta his office.

He counted up his money: owed im a hunnud an fifty dollas, an owed im fur that lawya fee, an the hospital fee.

That checkt me down from thirty-five hunnud ta seventeen hunnud an five dollars.

No he didn do no purdy good job, he done a good un. Thirty-five hunnud dollars! Yeah, I appreciate what he done. He done sumpm fur me that I couldn do fur myself. An then I didn git all the money. But, it hadn been fur him bein a good lawya, an knowed his grounds, I wouldn a got nothin. See?

An that caused me ta be right at the house I'm at now. I been livin there since about sixty. Wadn nothin there but dry land. I bought that place from my aunt Sweet. She raised me partly. She dwelled around wit my mother's chillun, an call em her chillun cause she nursed us all. She had a pick in the famly, an I was her pick. An so she went ta Waxahachie, an she had bought the lot an she didn wanta stay there.

An finely she got behind in the tax. Then I commence ta thankin, wonder could I own that lot. An I wrote her a letter. We'd write maybe once a week or once a month.

It was hawd fur me ta try ta buy a lot then. I say, "I want the lot, but I'm not able ta pay fur it."

An she kep awritin. She say, "My husband Jim an me want you ta have that lot. If you kin pay the taxes, then we'll give you the deed."

So my uncle had the fellas write out the deed, an mail em to me. An I had ta sign in Anderson, thats the county seat a Grimes. I went up there an the people knows me; I workt fur the county collecta, Cooper Dies. He showed me the way in an out, when I bought the three-acre hawss lot fur taxes.

An he say, "Well, you *did* sumpm fur yoself."

I say, "Yeah."

He say, "Well ya know, that foedy sumpm dollars cause you ta own that lot. You sign these papers an its yo's."

Then, I got my accident money an bought a old house, an it was a better of a house than you kin buy at the lumbayawd now: six-room house. The walls of it was eighteen foot high. Old out-a-dates house, way back in the ancient days. They plankt that wit two planks.

Had it moved an I tuck that lumba an pulled the nails outa it in my spare time on Satiddys an piled it up. People stole a lot of it. Still I had enough ta build this house, all but the studs.

Well, foe or five cawpentas robbed me outa my money. One got a hunnud dollas fur about one day's work. But he did a hunnud dollas worth a work that day. Quit me an went an got anothuh job.

An, I let a fella have a hunnud dollas ta git his caw outa the shop. He did purdy good: got the frame up, an the windas an the doze all cut. Put the top on it. An the sidin. Still wadn no dividation inside the house.

I said, "I'm show gittin somewhere now." Soon as I commenced ta braggin on him, *he* quit. No doze!

I said, "Well I'm gonna leave here, an nail some doze an windas ta the house. I'm gonna move up there. Thats *my* house." See up until then, I was stayin out on the Washington highway, where the West End Grocery at when you pass inta town? An I moved up there ta where I'm at now, on the Piedmount road.

My wife an Frank—my grandboy what plays the lectric gittah?—they finisht operatin that house. Put up the walls inside, put all that sheetrock an newspapers up on em. That was befoe I went ta Berkeley.

That fence right round my house: I got it put up on the credit, from Old Man Bingham's boy. He was a interest in a big hawdware stow here. Used ta call it Turner Pierce an Bingham.

So he come here an steppt it off, an figgered it out. He said, "It cost ya a hunnud an eighty dollas. You kin pay me like ya wanta. Monthly."

I never misst nary a payment. An then I commenced ta makin this music, an gittin them plays purdy briefly. An in two months time I had done paid him every nickel I owed im. An so I had it made with Mista Lloyd.

But some clerk didn know me, say, "Well, sorry."

Here come Mista Lloyd, say, "What the trouble here?"

Clerk look at me, say, "Mista Lloyd, this old . . ."

"Let him have what he want! Dont ever turn this man down fur nothin!"

So, I go git inythang I want in there. Long as he was livin, you know, on a credit. But in other words: when he spoke, the big guns was firin, ya see? I waited til I caught *him* in there.

An I fooled around an cut that one album, an in nineteen sixty-one I commenced ta goin out an playin music, in all diffunt states an thangs. Least they come ta me. That album caused me ta be right where I am now. So you never know whats gonna hapm to ya. Bit I kin tell you sumpm: some a y'all is young, an some a y'all is old. You jest try ta live right. One a these days a little right come comin to ya.

Discovery and the Berkeley Adventure "Gittin Outa My Precinct"

Like so many innovative country blues musicians throughout the South, Mance could have returned to Navasota, passed the remaining years of his life as an aging farmer whose old-fashioned music had seen its heyday, and faded into oblivion. In 1949 he had switched to the newer and, for him, more unfamiliar sound of the electric guitar, and was playing electrically right up until a certain evening in 1960. That night, a remarkable bend in the riverbottoms changed the course of his life. A couple "out of town" white boys stuck an acoustic Harmony guitar in his hands that he'd never laid on eyes on before, and recorded him while he flawlessly performed over two albums worth of songs on the first take.

Mance's discovery produced in him a transformation in perspective and self-image. The first airplane he had ever seen so frightened his mules that they nearly dragged him across the fields. After his discovery, Mance would fly on airliners, where he flirted with stewardesses, brushing against them while remembering a recent past where brushing up against a white woman was a potential lynching offense. The airlines took him to lucrative gigs and fame, where white fans would idolize him and white women would fawn over him. Mance had to spend some time adjusting to this kind of treatment. Unlike his old friend Jim Thomas, who, as Mance has related, was hung in 1926 for having a love affair with a white Jewish woman.

Outside his home state after 1961, fans would call him Mr. Lipscomb, while in his hometown he was still required to address all white men as "Mister"—whether they earned his respect or not. One loyal fan and friend was Carol Ottosen (now Maya Spzakowski), a Berkeley socialite and chef during the 1960s. She named Mance her son Vion's godfather. In the early 1960s, she and four of her husband Jack's friends, Wayne and Alice Pope and Bruce Bratton and Lorie Cornman-Bratton, helped Chris Strachwitz paste Mance's and others' pictures on some of Arhoolie Records' early issues. She often cooked Mance multicourse dinners at her house when he played in the Bay area. (While several months pregnant in the Vietnam era, she also placed herself in front of a troop train and was saved at the last split second by a black employee of the railroad.) Mance's wife had cooked for the white folks. Now the white folks cooked for him and literally waited on him hand and foot.

When Mance looked through the telescope at the convicts of Alcatraz, he said they looked so close that he could have shaken hands with them. Yet he was standing on the concrete near the Golden Gate Bridge, miles and an ocean bay away from them. Considering that the Allen prison farm lay at the heart of the land Mance called his home precinct and that his half brother Gainesville had spent time in the state prisons heavily populated with black prisoners, I have always wondered how close or far Mance felt to or from those prisoners he could safely view through a telescope. What turned over in his mind as he experienced the freedom that his mastery of his guitar and his discovery at age sixty-six gave to him?

The tenth go-along could be viewed as a study in paradox. After Barry Olivier's invitation to the 1961 Berkeley Folk Festival, with the help and support of Pete Seeger, Jean Ritchie, Sam Hinton, and Chris Strachwitz, Mance transformed himself from feeling like an outsider to knowing he was an insider. Overnight, he won the respect and admiration of musicians of national stature, all of whom considered Mance their equal. Pete Seeger, folksinger nonpareil, associate of Woody Guthrie, and captain of the *Clearwater* on the Hudson River, whose activist singing career has spanned over four decades, and Jean Ritchie, the "real McCoy" Appalachian dulcimer-playing folksinger from Kentucky, were just two of countless musicians who welcomed Mance with open arms. And by 1962, John Lomax, Jr., and his wife, Mimi, along with their sons John III and Joe, had formed a friendship with Mance that lasted until John's death in the early 1970s. It was John, Jr., who helped finance the award-winning Les Blank/Skip Gerson documentary of Mance, entitled *A Well-Spent Life*, filmed in Navasota in 1970.

Mance had seen the large Texas towns of Houston, Dallas, and Fort Worth, but in the context of a hired hand whose skin color forbade him to experience most of what those towns had to offer. Mance's three-day train trip from Navasota to the wilds of Berkeley, California—seedbed of liberalism and political activism of the sixties—took him from one sort of world to a distinctly different one. Mance's ability to survive and thrive in both worlds was a feat Marco Polo could have admired.

As evidence of his adaptability, Mance refers to just a few of the dozens of nationally prominent gigs where he performed from 1961 through 1973, including an anecdote from one of the Monterey Pop Festival's earliest dates (probably 1962 or 1963).

By the late 1950s a small group of "race" music enthusiasts were scouring the countryside in search of its roots. In Europe, this sound had been identified as distinctly American. Both exemplars of an important category of that sound and contemporaries with similar country blues finger-picking styles, Mance Lipscomb and Mississippi John Hurt invite comparison. Tom Hoskins remembered Hurt's mention in one of his old recordings of his longing to return to his hometown of Avalon. To rediscover Hurt, Hoskins had to ask around for directions, drive to the end of a dirt road, and cross a river before he found Hurt sitting on his front porch in the Mississippi Delta heat.

To find Mance in 1960, Chris Strachwitz and Mack McCormick went searching through the Brazos Bottoms for the real Tom Moore they'd heard Lightnin' Hopkins sing about with such fervor. Their quest led to Mance Lipscomb's front porch in a two-room rented house on the west side of Navasota. Local cooperation was no doubt encouraged by the fact that the Moore brothers were under investigation around that time—once again—for alleged acts of physical harm to a black man. Many residents treated Strachwitz and McCormick with kid gloves, because they were not sure whether they were really undercover federal agents or just loco outsiders.

McCormick and Strachwitz were two wholly different men thrown together on a mission with fate. McCormick was an erudite folklorist from Houston with a near-encyclopedic knowledge of the blues and its roots. Strachwitz had first heard American pop, jazz, and swing on American Forces Radio while fleeing Germany for the U.S.A., near the end of World War II. After hearing hillbilly and rhythm and blues on California radio stations, he became an avid fan of Lightnin' Hopkins. Of all the people they recorded, McCormick considered Mance the best find. He so convinced Strachwitz of Mance's authenticity and historical value that Chris overcame his initial impression that Mance's delivery was too soft and melodic and chose to launch his new record label with Mance's release (Arhoolie no. 1001, *Mance Lipscomb: Texas Sharecropper and Songster*). That choice led to a whole new life in these United States for Mance and Chris alike. What follows is Mance's story of how they opened the doors to those lives.

Now Y'ALL DONT BE FRAID a that tape recorder settin there, cause I furgot about those thangs in sixty-one. But I was jest crazy as a frog when they come up there. Man put all that equipments on my table.

Couldn keep em out the house or let em come in the house, cause my wife had done told off on me where I was goin, what I was doin, an when I'd be home. They had done been ta my house, an I didn know nothin bout that cause I was out on the highway, workin. Cuttin grass under Mista Bingham.

An so, that was in sixty. An it was way long in the summa bout, I reckon, end a July or August somewhere. An come home sweaty. Dust all in my clothes, an "Hht! Now thats a caw I aint never seed befoe. Got outa-state plates on it." Settin out in front a my house.

Elnora settin there on the poach. Got two white mens settin alongside a her. Say, "Now what in the devil? Two polices layin fur me at my own home, an I aint done nothin?"

Mance on the front porch of his own house, 1961. *Photo by Ed Badeaux.*

Finely here one come ta meet me, say, "You Mance Lip-scomb?"

"Yassuh, I—reckon I is."

A big un an a little un there. Big un settin by the poach, an the little un talkin ta me, say, "We heard you was a musician. Could you play us a little piece?"

Say, "Well, I jest have come off from workin. Aint et nothin, aint had time ta clean up." Try ta throw em off, see. Cause I dont know what they doin comin round ta my house.

So, we talk to an fro a minute. Finely, he says, "Well, we aint had no suppa. Gotta git us a couple little old thangs out the stows. I blieve we'll go ta town an git us a little snack. An while we eatin an thangs, why, you kin eat an take yo rest. I come back down here tonight. Reckon you kin play us some numbas then?"

That was about six o'clock in the evenin. I said, "I dont know. I'm workin. Hafta git up, bout foe o'clock an git a truck ready so I kin carry my hands. Oil an greaze up the tracta. I'm head tracta man. I dont wanta stay up too late."

"We wont keep you up late."

I said, "Well you kin come back down here, bout a hour inyhow."

So here they come back, when they went ta town an got suppa an got six cartons a beer. They thought they had me hookt. But I didn want no beer.

An I was watchin im an he said, "Now you jest set down an relax."

I said, "I'm gonna relax an all this goin on on *my* table an you kin tell me—whats goin on?"

An he's hookin up wires onto—look like a long rod standin in the air, had some kinda club fastened down on it. Call it a mike. An had this box: all the wires leadin into it. Two little wheels goin round an round, you could see through em. An I'm still standin there, an he said, "Set down."

An I stawted ta set down, I said, "Looky here! Tell me what y'all doin!"

Said, "Oh, we jest gittin thangs owganized."

I say, "Fur what?"

"So you kin sang an play."

I say, "I got ta sang an play wit all these wires?"

He said, "Well, thats goin through these wires. Now, you set down an relax. An git ya gittah. Jest play like you aint noticin us. Dont pay us iny tension."

Wadn but two there. But I was knowin their reaction, the way they were doin. Lookt like they tuck over my house. They jest come in there an told me ta shet my doe— an didn have but two rooms in the house: "Shet yo doe."

"Now what they call theirself wantin me ta shet my own doe? Hem me up in here," I said ta myself. "Aint no man in the world know mow about their own home than the other fella know. I got chairs an poke irons, an everthang in this house. If they stawt sumpm, I kin git one of em."

I say, "I'm gonna git the big un first. An then I know I kin handle the little un." One was way up over me. Tall you know, about six foot. I lookt im over, I said, "Oh well. I dont know what I'm doin, but they treatin me right, I'm gonna try ta treat *them* right." But I'm still watchin their reactions.

Said, "All right, Mista Lipscomb! Play us a few songs, so we kin let you go ta bed." So finely he got me sorta settled down.

An what got me: see I dont drank much. I might take a drank a whisky once a month or nary time a month. No beer, nothin like that. My head's always level.

An I was watchin those guys when I sot down, an he said, "Now, you jest play like you played at these Satiddy Night Dances."

I said, "These people dont know about where I played at no Satiddy Night Dances. Somebody been talkin."

An one lookt at the other, said, "Yeah, we got yo reputation."

I said, "You got mown a reputation, talkin bout I'm playin out on Satiddy night. Thats where I stawted ta playin."

See Chris Strachwitz an Mack McCormick—that was the little one—they had been into Navasota, askin fur "Who is the best gittah player in this precinct?" Stoppt along the highways where people workin in the field, an ask em the same question. Even went up ta Mista Tom Mow an askt him. An you know what ever one a them people answered? "Mance Lipscomb."

Say, "Where he live?"

"I dont know. Blieve he stay in Navasota somewheres."

So finely they stoppt at the railroad depot, an found a fella named Pegleg knowed where my house at. An he brought em by here. An thats where they was waitin fur me. When I come off a work.

Man, they was drivin up an down the road, followin my tracks where that tracta make a sweep in that grass. Couldn find me nowhere! M-hm. Chris Strachwitz. He's the one made that Ahhoolie Records.

So inyway, they had a six-carton cans a beer settin down on the flow.

Say, "Take a can a beer!"

Say, "I dont want iny beer."

"You dont drank no beer?"

Said, "Mighty little."

Said, "Well, we brought this here fur you."

"You musta brought fur yaself. I dont want none."

They say, "Well take one! Its cool! We brought it right out from off the ice."

Well it was hot in the year. I was cuttin highway. I wanted some cool water an I couldn git to it, an he insisted me take a can an take a little bit out of it. Said, "You got a icebox?"

I said, "Yeah, there's one right in the corner."

"Well put em on ice. An pull one, so you kin relax."

So I said, "I blieve I dont want nary un," an when I said that, its open.

I didn wanta be no slacka you know; I turnt it up an tuck two little soups outa it. An man, my head commence ta gittin swimmified. See, I caint stand much alkyhol. About half a can a beer gonna make me near about drunk.

So when I got the gittah, I say, "I caint play this gittah. That man dont know he done made me half drunk." See, I prefer my head ta be always level.

Finely the beer kinda died down, an I commenced ta stretchin out diffunt numbas. I went ta *town* with that gittah, an they was lookin at me, smilin. Ever song I'd change, they'd laugh. "That was a good un." An I'd watch em, they eyes movin on me some. They's watchin me, too.

But I didn git plumb tilted. Only two swallas. But you know that alkyhol hit me up on top a my head, an I thought I was goin wild. Doin sumpm I didn know I was doin. An I played twenty-odd numbas befoe I quit playin.

An then they askt me, "You wanta hear it back?"

I said, "No! I dont wanta hear it back."

Say, "Man, you dont know what you done done!"

I say, "I show dont. But I know one thang: I done played, an I dont wanta hear that back no mow."

Said, "Jest hold ya gittah. Aint no need aplayin it."

He pulled the plug out from me, an done sumpm after that, an here it come! "Sugar Babe, Sugar Babe" I'm sangin! That was the first song, an the next one about "I'm Goin down Slow," I rememba all them pieces. An the sound come back an everthang I played—I know I had played it cause I know my voice, know my music.

"How y'all do that?"

An they commenced ta laughin again.

I say, "Well what is that y'all operatin? What is that on the table, makin my music go right back like it was an I done already done it? Man, all the songs I sung here, over that thang, done pickt it up."

Said, "Oh, yeah. How ya like it?"

I said, "Well, I'd like it good if you'd gimme one a them thangs what y'all got sangin like me."

They stoppt. An turnt the tape out an said, "Now listen, Mista Lipscomb. This is a tape recorder. An we goin try ta cut you a record outa there."

I said, "Cut a record outa it?"

He said, "Yeah. We'll arrange it some way where we'll give ya one."

I said, "Tonight?"

He say, "No, caint give ya one tonight. We gonna carry it off an have a record cut out of it. Once thats passt, why, you'll have a record made."

An I said, "Where you gonna carry it?"

Said, "I dont know. We liable ta carry it ta Germany, or either over New Yawk or somewhere. Git it ta operatin."

I said, "How long thats gonna be?"

Said, "Well, we'll give you one after while. Could you sang a little mow?"

I said, "Yeah, but I wanta know you gonna gimme one a those thangs." I'm tired a sangin fur nothin.

Say, "We'll give you one when ya git through."

I say, "Oh God, these people say they jest tryin ta hep me—they aint gone do nothin, else they'd done done it right now." So they didn know what was on my mind.

After a while I got through sangin, an they commenced ta gittin all those wires wrappt up an takin this tape off the table. I say, "Well looks like you would leave *sumpm* here, an I done *sung*."

Said, "No, we caint leave it here, but we'll send you one back."

I say, "How long befoe y'all send it back?"

Said, "Oh, I dont know. Maybe a month."

An I furgot about those fellas, I said, "Well. They come here an got me ta do all that playin an got my tape. They're through wit me. They aint gonna never send me one a those thangs."

In the go-along, one boy says, "Well, we'll thank ya, an here's a souvenir." Now, I dont know what a souvenir was til that night.

Piece a paper wrappt up an folded up. It was in the night, an I kep it in my hand an went out ta the caw, holp em load the quipment.

Finely, one of em said, "Well, we'll be back down here in about two weeks."

An I said, "Two weeks?"

Say, "Yeah."

An I said, "Well, try ta make it on a Satiddy, cause I'm workin up until then cuttin highways wit a tracta." See, I knowed the old lady was mad wit me, keep her up late fur a little a nothin.

Said, "Well, we'll jest do that."

I said, "Well, here's the souvenir you told me ta keep."

Said, "Well, I meant fur you ta keep it."

I say, "What in the devil is a souvenir? Nothin but paper." I went ta the doe an opened it. The old lady was layin cross the bed, all thought up. You talkin bout fire: I could smell it befoe I hit the doe. I didn know how ta git in there without jest walkin in there an let her fan me out wit her mouth.

First word I got: "I'm show is sorry I married a old gittah player."

One foot was on the step, I was scared ta put the othun up there. I couldn say nothin cause I done played the gittah about a hour or so now an kep her woke. I say, "Well, you sorry you married old gittah player?"

"Yeah! You aint got no sense. You play all night."

I said, "Well I got ta go ahead on, in the house."

An a little old light was over the bed, she still layin across the bed. I went ta go ta the light.

An my little granddaughter, about foeteen years of age, she beat me ta the light. She seed me wit sumpm in my hand. Like a paper. So she snatcht the light over my wife's head an tuck that paper from out my hand. Unfolded it. "Woooo, jest look here, Myno! At the money Daddy Mance got!" Talkin bout me.

So my wife raised up, said, "Lemme see." Argument was over with then, she saw that money. She commence ta unfoldin it, an counted it there's a twenty-dolla bill, a ten-dolla bill—thats thirty—an a twenty-dolla travla's check had my name on it. No mow fire then!

I said, "Wait! Let me see it. An old gittah player made it!"

She said, "Hand me that money." An I was scared too, cause thats a big woman. I didn wanta test her.

She say, "You reckon them people give you all that money?"

I say, "Yeah. They told me ta keep it cause I offered it back to em. I thought they was jest puttin me on."

Say, "You know you got fifty dollas in here?"

I said, "What?"

Said, "Yeah."

The girl said, "Ohhh, Daddy show got a lot a money."

An I'm proud, but I never could git the money no mow. You know what she did? She tuck that money an counted it out, an I dont know whether she put it in her bosom or under a pilla. I aint seed it since.

So man, that thang went along. An I was jest as crazy as a frog. I didn know what was happenin, an she didn know what gonna hapm.

An show nuff, in two weeks they come back. You know

what? She had the tables all fixt up an clint off an the chairs settin there.

I say, "You gonna play fur em?"

Said, "No. *You* gonna play fur em."

I said, "I thought you was tired a old gittah pickas?"

She said, "Them people'll be here in about ten o'clock."

Show nuff, about ten-thirty they were there. Well, when the big man come back, here they come wit im a woman an her husband bout this tall! Little little low fella, an a little low lady. But they grown! Lookt like midgets ta me, ya know. I said, "This woman got on this long dress, an she aint no mown about three or foe foot high?"

I lookt at that woman, an she was talkin some kinda talk. They couldn talk words that I could understand. They come in talkin, they drankin, an I was settin there, listenin to em find out what these people say or what they *was* sayin.

An the man what brought em there first, that was his auntie an uncle. An they come in an talkt ta the fella who could understand me, an I could understand him. The way I got information: he would tell me what they say, an then tell them what I say. So, he handed word from one ta the other.

An I was jest amused, watchin them people "Blib-blib-blib lib-blib-blib."

I say, "What in the devil these people doin? This a big mess here. I blieve I dont wanta play here, cause I caint understand them people."

Finely, she said ta him, ta tell me ta play.

He said, "Well, she ready fur you ta play some."

I got the old gittah. The old lady she, show nuff, was thrifty around the table. Gittin thangs straight, cause she done got fifty dollas an she was lookin fur the next fifty. An she had everthang handsome.

Finely I got ta playin. Sot down an played a few numbas, an she lookt at me an the man lookt at her. Husband an wife. See, Chris brought them from Germany. An they was talkin Germany. I didn know what they was, til I got in the midst of em from time up until now.

An finely I played fifteen or twenty mow songs, an they told the man what I could understand, "Well, blieve they would go." That little low woman give me fifty *mow* dollas. Oh man, I'm rich!

My wife was peekin round, out the hole somewhere sees everthang went on. I couldn hide that! When I got through wit em, she said, "What did they give you?"

I said, "They didn give me nothin—"

"Yes they did! I saw em give you sumpm!" A hunnud dollas I had—the old lady had it, I aint got nothin!

Course, I didn *make* no money until I got ta Berkeley. At the university. An I didn wanta go out there. Califownya was a place I aint never been. I aint been outa Texas in my life til sixty-one. An I didn know how ta meet those people, an I tried ta git out of it.

Show nuff, about three weeks after Chris an them gone again: here come a letter back. Askin me would I come ta Berkeley, Califownya. Said, "We'll give you three hunnud dollas, come out here fur foe days." I read the letter over an over, an lookt at it an let it run on.

An I thought that was a lot a money, like it is here. But still, its a long ways ta git up there. I said, "I dont know about nobody from Berkeley."

I told my wife, I say, "Here's a letter talkin bout comin ta Berkeley. Play up there to a—university."

An Elnora said, "Well you liable ta be missin yo best break if you dont go out ta Berkeley."

I said, "I dont thank it is, cause I aint goin from here ta Berkeley."

So I wouldn answer the letter, an here come a record. My first record. They sunt me two issues. An I tote them thangs round up an down the street, didn have no record player. Everbody what had a record player, I'd carry it up

Mance, Elnora, and grandchildren on the front porch of their home, 1961. *Photo by Ed Badeaux.*

there an play my records on theirs. Man, I had a strang a people—about thirty an foedy—up an down the road might near ever evenin at night, hearin that record. Wadn no sound on there when I got through playin it. Woe it out.

Til finely I said, "Well I blieve I'll write em, I aint got enough clothes ta come out there on. They jest offered me three hunnud, an so I aint got that. I hafta have some money ta go out there."

So I answered the letter, told em I wadn sufficient ta come up there. I said, "I aint got sufficient clothes, an I aint got money ta come out there." So, I thought I'd git rid of em.

An so, me an my wife was livin over there on West Wash-

407

ington, you know, goin west towards Washington town? Well, it was about eight or ten days after that I went ta the mailbox. It was right at my house: a long letter, from Berkeley, from the university. There was a check in there fur three hunnud dollas in one sheet, an the next sheet said, "We'll give you five hunnud ta come up here an play foe days. An here's three hunnud dollas advance. Either you kin send that money back or—go."

I said, "Here, here's a big check here, wife. Three hunnud dollas worth. An it wrote out in my name."

An I read on down ta what they say ta do wit it. Say, "Now you could git you a hunnud dollas worth a clothes. It cost about a eighty or ninety dollas ta come ta Los Angeles. An you kin have enough ta come on ta Berkeley. Berkeley's foe hunnud miles from Los Angeles." An I had about fifteen or twenty dollas left, an bought some clothes too. I had clothes, but I was tryin ta git out a goin!

So I hate ta send that check back, cause I need that money. I said, "Well, I'm gonna makin up my mind ta go up there, an tough it out."

But I wadn goin on no airplane. I said I catch a train an go up there, an have em ta meet me. I went ta Houston an cot the train, twice: two years outa there. Goin ta Collarena an Minyapples an Los Angeles, an San Francisco. Yeah. I rode the train til they starve me ta death. Couldn git me on a airplane fur two years.

So here come one a them old long trains in Houston. An the man carried me ta the train depot, he done all my writin on the back a my first album. Mack McCormick? An it had all the background—my father an where I come from an what I had been doin.

Yeah, they called it sharecropper. I didn know it was nothin but jest a fawma. I was raised in my remembrance a what I could git outa it in my mind, is a fawma. But ya see, they had it all ranged: sharecropper an a fawma is all connected. So I jest rejected that in my mind, I still feel like a fawma instead a sharecropper. But they had a new way a callin it, on every album I got: "Texas Sharecropper."

An I was on that train, three days an nights foe I got from Houston ta Frisco. An didn have a mouthful ta eat an not a drank a water. Course I didn know my way around on that coach. An everbody was eatin an goin somewhere I didn know what—but they'd come back eatin sumpm, I say, "Where y'all git this food at?"

An say, "Up here ta the dinin coach."

I didn know nothin about gittin up an down on no train. I thank it was bout thirty-six coaches long. I'd stawt up there an git lost an come back. Way I could find my way where I was settin, I'd leave my coat or sumpm or hat, so I'd know where ta git back ta.

An all I et was jest a little old Coke or sumpm another, an some little old cheese on it. Its a push thang on the train. You push that button an whatever you press, why it comes down. Right or wrong: if you push the wrong button, you dont git what you wanted. I couldn operate that thang. Lot a thangs I leave settin there on the thang, an go on back an set down.

An I was slow bout askin people fur information. An I sot there, sot there an git up—only thang I could figger out: cause I saw them people go into the restrooms. But the dinin coach, I didn know where it was.

Thirty-six coaches long. An that thang go down the mountain, you could git off an light a cigarette an git back on it. But dont you wait til its straightened out. Boy, that thang come out there would make like a hunnud miles an hour when its straightened out. Taken me three days an three nights gittin up there.

An I quit them trains. An you go from Houston ta Califownya on them airplanes: about hour an foedy minutes you is in Los Angeles. Same time from Los Angeles ta

Houston. An when I go ta catch the bus ta go home, taken me foe hours ta git a bus outa Houston. I could walk home if I was able.

I was up there in a stawm one night. That airplane lookt like it was gonna turn over, an the bottom was ashakin. An so, I'm lookin up there in the front, watchin them little old stewardesses, they was together. When you see them git together an talkin ta one anothuh quietly, its sumpm goin wrong up there. An they kinda scared too, but they wont let on. An one come by me, I said, "Girl, whats happenin?"

She said, "Well we in a stawm. We soon be out of it direckly. They gonna predict how fur they got ta go befoe they git out it."

After while that old man up in the front said, "Will y'all lay wit me? We in a stawm, but I'll see ya safely through."

I say, "Hell, I caint do nothin *but* lay wit ya, I guess. I tell ya one man gonna lay wit ya until it falls, cause I aint gonna git out a this airplane."

Yeah. You know what I done at the airplane two or three times ta them stewardesses? Yeah, I studied a prank on em: so, I went out an got on the airplane. Went back, an the girl showed me ta my seat. I sot down. Stretcht back ta the back seat. An you hafta fasten yo seatbelt. I know it wadn fastened.

An the girl come by an they watch ya, you see. Said, "Mista, you aint got yo seatbelt fastened."

I said, "No'm, I caint fasten it. Come here an fasten it fur me." An she done what I told her. She got behind me— right back here behind my shoulder—an reach over. An anothuh stewardess knowed me; she lookt around an said, "What you doin?"

Said, "I'm fastenin this seatbelt on this man."

"Let im alone, that man kin fasten his seatbelt. He tellin you that fur a purpose!"

But she had done stawted then I done leaned back. An my back, hit her little titties, they was soft, you know.

She said, "Oh you—you mashin my titties!"

Yeah, them people have a lot a fun outa me what know me. My wife told me, says, "Them people gonna whup you up there if you *is* up in the air."

I said, "I aint doin nothin. I jest gittin service."

So finely, I made it ta the Frisco train station, in Berkeley. I didn know where I was. An I was lookin fur a man who cut my first record? He knowed me, I knowed him. He sposed ta meet me there. It was foe o'clock.

An the train was so long, an so miny people comin up. An they was walkin all up an down the coaches, lookin fur me, an I was lookin at them. I didn know nobody. Everbody lookt diffunt. Never did see Chris. An he's lookin fur me, the one they call Chris Strachwitz?

Finely, here two ladies comin up aside the train. An had a paper. Lookt like a newspaper they had. She's lookin all around, say, "I dont know where he is." I could hear what they were sayin an see what they was doin, out that winda I was settin by. She look again, say, "Here his pitcher."

Finely, she say, "HERE he is!"

An anothun say, "YONDA HE IS!" an pointed at me.

Man, I had a old suitcase settin down on the ground. Say, "Yeah, an here he go too, cause I'm jest from where yonda is an you dont catch me." An I stawted ta leave there. An she come awalkin purdy briefly, tryin ta catch up wit me an I reckon she commenced ta runnin an she overtuck me.

I said, "What you want?"

Say, "Well I been tryin ta catch you. Is this you pitchered in here? We come here ta meet you." An lookt back—man, it was foedy or fifty people strung out, tryin ta git up there ta say hello ta me! I'm wild, I dont know whats goin on. All them people jest comin up there, an knowed who I was by my pitchers all in a poster.

An right direckly Chris discovered me. He knowed what was goin on in all that commotion an I didn know what was goin on. An he say, "Hey! Here I am!"

I lookt around, he's a tall fella. I say, "You better come on here, cause I'm fixin ta leave here."

He say, "Git in the caw!" Had a old Volkwagon.

An I say, "Where the caw at?"

He say, "There it is. Right there. Git in! Git in!"

I say, "Chris, why you hurryin me so much?" An man, I lookt back: about fifty or a hunnud people mow, strung out tryin ta catch me ta shake hands wit me, an I didn know nothin bout that. An I got in that caw. An they strung out behind me where I was goin ta room at, in they caws.

So when I got in the Volkwagon, two polices is in there. Man, my hawt was beatin, an they was lookin at one anothuh an lookin at me. They seed I was scared.

One of em says, "How're you, boy?"

I say, "Doin purdy good." Didn let on they had me rattled. Them old big guns, them stripes up an down.

One police say, "He's a purdy good old boy. Why dont ya pay his fine? He goin play at that university. He'll pay ya back."

An he said, "I reckon what his fine gone be?"

Other policeman say, "Well it wouldn be over about foedy or fifty dollas."

I said, "What y'all talkin about?"

See, they laught say, "We talkin bout you."

I said, "What I want a fine fur? What have I done?"

They say, "Ohhh, you aint done much. You was jest standin in the wrong spot. You stoppt in the wrong place when we found ya."

"I stoppt in the wrong place? I sposed ta git off here, ta Frisco."

Say, "I aint talkin bout Frisco. You in the wrong spot a land. You an the people all messin round, you stood right there where it'd confuse people."

I say, "I was jest lookin fur a fella: this man drivin me." An Chris, he knowed all about the low-down. He drivin, kinda smilin. Cause they had me dead to the right. I didn know what was goin on. An he laught.

I said, "I'm in this here caw, y'all got me arrested?"

Said, "Well, in a way. In a way we aint. But we aint gonna put you in no jail." Jest guyin me, you know. Man, my hawt got bigga then, talkin bout jailin me. Cause I aint never been ta no jail in my life.

Police said, "I'll tell ya what. You is gonna play at the university. We'll let you by, an you kin pay me back. I'll pay ya fine."

I said, "Well I aint got no choice. Whats the fine gonna be?"

He said, "Oh, it aint much."

I said, "What ya call much?"

An Chris said, "Dont guy im. You got im scared. He dont know what y'all mean."

An the police bust out laughin, say, "No boy, we escoatn you ta where you gonna stay at."

I dont know what escoatn was. I say, "What ya call 'es-coatn'?"

"Seein you safely where you goin."

I say, "Ohhh. I thank ya."

Finely, they pulled in a big old concrete driveway an drove under a shed. Some grape arbors was crosst up under the shed. No top on it but grapes. Provided that shade fur that driveway in there. An I didn wanta git out. Didn know where I was, til they told me.

Direckly, here come a little boy about eight or nine years old, say, "Mama! Mama? Mama! Here he is!"

I said, "Uh-oh, I done got ta the wrong place again."

The little boy say, "Here he is!"

An she say, "Tell him ta come in!"

Little boy said, "You Mance Lipscomb?"

An I said, "I show is."

Say, "Come on in."

An the police say, "Well, I tell ya, Lipscomb. We gonna

let you off here. Tamarra, why you kin play maybe the next day, an you kin pay us back. We'll pay ya fine."

An Chris told em, says, "Dont guy im no mow. He dont know what y'all talkin bout. Let him off. He's worried ta death."

I say, "I show is worried. Talkin bout payin em back, when I aint done nothin."

An he said, "No boy, we jest brought you here safely. Now you in good hands. This is where you goin room at."

I said, "Thank you, suh."

An so, the little boy opened the doe, an I went in the house, an he say, "Set right in here."

I said, "I show aint goin no further." Where I lookt, there was glass here, turnt around an Mance was over here. Say, "How miny Mances here in this house?" Could see Mance everwhere I turnt, man, that glass would show me up. I said, "Show is fancy here. I aint got no bizniss in this place."

An when he opened the doe, I was hongry an they was cookin dinna fur me. An I smellt that food. Scent comin out the doe. I said, "I dont blieve I'm at the wrong place, boy. That food show smells good in there. I'm goin in if they put me out." Had been done without sumpm ta eat, three days an nights. Only that little old half a sandwich.

An so, when I got there the little boy say, "Come on! Come on in! Come on in!" He knowed my name. He said, "Set down, Mista Lipscomb."

I sot down.

Say, "You tired?"

I say, "I show is, son."

He say, "Rest yo foots! Lemme pull ya shoes off!"

I said, "Ah-oh, I'm gittin soft preferment here." He was handy. So I did jest like he said an pusht em up on some-place there, an sot there an relaxt.

An the boy pulled the shoes off, said, "This is yo room." All them glasses, everwhere I lookt I could see Mance. I got ta lookin around. All decorated an everthang straightened out. He say, "How you like it?"

Say, "Its all right." You know, its foe thangs I'm aware of: smokin, drankin coffee thats two. An playin music, thats three. An eatin is foe. An I commenced ta smellin that scent comin through the doe from some other room. I say, "Who is that over in the room there?"

Say, "Mama an a colored lady cookin dinna fur ya."

I said ta myself, "I wish they'd hurry up an git it done." Man, they had ham, turkey. The best food ever I saw in my life. It was about five o'clock in the evenin we stawted ta eatin suppa. I thank I got ta Frisco about foe o'clock, an about twenty minutes out ta where I was gonna live at.

There was about thirty-two people at the table wit me. Thirty-two! Sixteen on one side, sixteen on other side. An they put me at the head a the table.

The colored woman, she cookt me some conebread. Said, "Well I know you from the State. You likes conebread, I betcha."

I said, "I show do. Like iny kinda bread."

She said, "Well here's some conebread I baked." Sot it on the table alongside a me. Jest like a cake, had a little sugar in it. An I commence ta eatin ham an chicken an turkey. Oh man, I was pusht out this way!

So there they all come in anothun room, after they got through eatin. An there I was surrounded wit people I dont know nothin about. Askin questions. Where I'm from. See, they had been playin my record up there an had all my publicity. An finely, I sot down an commence tryin ta talk to em. Couldn talk ta one fur the othun. An, bout this time a the evenin, that house was loaded up. Everbody I blieve in Berkeley was there, could *git* in there.

An the police had ta stop the caws from comin in the driveway. An I lookt out the doe, I seed all them people an police. I bet it was over a hunnud caws done follad me up there. An they had ta git em off the streets. I said, "Now what in the devil is this goin on up here?"

So finely, Chris, he said, "I'm goin home, but dont you set up too late. They gone stawt you ta playin. An I know how you is: you'll never stop when you stawt. Jest tell em you tired."

An then he talkt ta the people, askt em would they release an let me go an take some rest. Cause I wadn goin be on the program until the next day, but they wanted me ta git plenty a rest.

Finely them people aint said nothin about no rest. An I wadn goin ta say nothin about no rest among strange people. Ever time they say, "Play this, play that"—here I go. An I was so sleepy an tired, man, lookt like I was jest sick. An they stayed there til about foe o'clock that mownin. An then I couldn go ta work the next day, cause I'm give out, ridin up there. Give out playin that night.

I slept I reckon about three hours. It was about seven-thirty, eight o'clock I got up. I'm a early riser.

An so, the next day they wanta git me ta go down ta see some sights an scenes, you know. So I went around, purdy briefly around San Francisco. An boy you talkin bout scared when we crosst that Golden Gate Bridge: all that water an all them bridges an thangs man, I shet my eyes! I aint never seen nothin like that. Until nineteen sixty-one.

An then they scared me again out there: Applecress, where them prisonas out in that water? Is a big place out there. No, they didn carry me out there where them prisonas was, but they carried me where I could stand on the concrete. They had some thangs you could look through like a microscope: you could see everthang they do. I said, "Man, I'm tired a lookin out there. Look like I'm shakin hands with them prisonas out there." So I got drunk lookin up out through there.

But, man, you talkin bout the first day I was playin there: I had foedy-one thousand people lookin me in the face. They wadn lookin in my face, cause I had the head down, had my hat pulled down over my eyes. An I never did look up, cause I was jest chilled through.

Stage shy. Jest like a kid would git out on the stage an say his speech. He got it allll figgered out good, til he gits over that stage befoe all those people. Then sumpm gonna go wrong if he aint mighty strong. He got ta have a mighty strong conscience. Dont, he'll miss out.

But now listen, you got ta be ware a these thangs like I am. See, I been filled in with that thirteen years. What you call aware: I'm used to it, nated to it. I dont care if its one person, I play jest as hawd fur one as I would fur one thousand. See I'm broad-hawted. Got a open hawt cause I'm not fraid a those people, cause I'm done it enough ta git used to it. An it dont fret me or bother me at all. I stay myself cool ever since I was out on the program two years.

So they wouldn put me on til the second day after I got there. I got a scrapbook a that. An you'll see me settin in the chair like I am now, facin—foedy-one thousand people!

Mance before 41,000 people at the Berkeley Folk Festival in 1961. *Photo by Chris Strachwitz.*

Nobody but me on the stage—an the polices, an I'm show scared a them. An I didn know what they meant ta be behind me.

An ever time I'd play a numba, I'd look back an glance on em. I said, "What are these people doin up here wit all them guns on?" They was escoatn me, ya know. Keep somebody from gittin on the steps. Disturb ya.

Now you tell me that was where a sick man was. Ohhh Lawd, you talkin bout nerves, they gone gone. An the people couldn see my face. Jest could see my head down an I'm playin that music. Only way I could play it: feel fur it. I never could look yonda towards them people. Cause I dont need no seein ta play a good gittah.

An I sot there. I didn know whether the gittah tuned up or not, I jest blammed away on it an try ta git sumpm outa it. An I never lookt up. Played about three numbas. I was tremblin an nervous. I glimpst up to a few a the people, but it was foedy-one thousand facin me. I couldn take that, lookin at that there people.

Cause when you play sumpm the people like, they caint git up there, but they kin throw popcone up there at ya, an candy. One woman throwed her money purse up on the stage there. A great big purse! I dont know what she had in it, but I didn touch it.

Oh, there's some people! If you dont know what you doin, you git to a place where people likin you an put they hands on ya they tear you up. Fur you know, *friend*ly.

Tear yo clothes, take yo watches off ya. One lady had my watch. Pull it off an I had it hookt up. She said, "Its a souvenir. I'll pay ya fur it."

I said, "Miss, dont take my watch."

An she give it back ta me. If they dont have sumpm ta carry home, they jest had ta touch the entertaina. An they wanta carry a piece home, show em, say, "I had my hand on im." An that hand was too much hand ta have my gold watch.

An I aint had nary anothuh watch wit a chain on it
since. Its at home now. I dont want em ta tear it up. Cause
if they git round you, call theirself souvenirin you, why,
they'll tear everthang you got on, if them police dont carry
you through: one on one side an one on the other side, say,
"Let im by! Let im by!"

Say, "I wanta shake hands wit im! I wanta put my hand
on im."

You go through a lot a stuff wit people when you out on
the program an they like ya. But I thought they was hatin
me, I thought they was gonna kill me. An they act like they
gonna kill ya when that one git holt a you an the othun got
ya an the othun got ya.

But now, I done been in foedy-eight states, I done got
used to it now. I dont be fraid no mow, but that foedy-one
thousand liked ta kilt me. It was hot—an I thought I was
cold. Jest tremblin like a leaf on a tree!

An only way I got off that stage: the one old lady was
settin in the front tier. You know, they respect old people,
they give em the front seat. An let them set down, miny as
could git in there. See, I was foeteen foot above all them
people. An its about, I reckon, ten thousand a them: from
there fur as I could see, an all of em had them little hats on.
Little womens, old womens.

An done put the young people further back. A gang of
em settin on a big hill way out yonda away from me, an it
was mow wayyy back, in the woods. They had all kinda
loudspeakas on me. An that thang was sangin so: five miles
you could hear that sound post, from where I was settin on
the stage. Reason I know that, it come out in a paper, the
next mownin: "We could hear Lipscomb five miles downtown. Amongst the traffic. Sangin an playin."

But this old lady in the front, she had a little hat on, bout
big as this thang here. Settin up on top a her head. An I
glanced at her an she said, "Mista Lipscomb, kin you play
us one a them old gospel songs?"

I knowed what she meant was a church song. I say, "I blieve I kin."

She says, "Well, I wish you would play me one."

So I said, "Well, maybe I kin play you a gospel song."

I didn know whether I could play iny kinda song cause I'm scared. An I taken my knife out—I have a way a playin wit a knife, they call a slide? I kin tune that gittah an still keep aplayin it. Cause I wanted ta git off that stage.

An, I tuck my knife an tuned up the old gittah, an the people was pattin their hands, you know, befoe I got the gittah stawted. An I blazed away on "Motherless Chillun Sees a Hawd Time When Their Mother Is Dead." I was talkin bout me an everbody else. On that gittah.

I played about foe verses. An that lady, she got so happy. An that whooole regiment a people there commenced ta hollerin an cryin an goin on. An I aint never seed em, but I heared all that stuff goin on down in front a me.

An I lookt round, lookt under my hat, kinda had my hat down. Police comin up behind me. I heard im walkin, but I study played, I didn wanta stop. An he toucht me right in the back. Like that, gimme a tap or two.

An I lookt around, I said, "Oh, I'm arrested now."

He said, "Lipscomb?"

I said, "Yassuh."

Say, "You hafta quit."

I said, "Quit what?"

Say, "You quit playin that sad song. Look out there in the audience." I didn know nothin about no audience. He was talkin about the gang a people. Say, "You got the whole regiment out there confused. Dont you see them people there out in the front a you cryin an hollerin an goin on?"

I could hear em hoopin way back yonda. But I didn look right down under me: an there all the people was cryin an goin on, I said, "Stop playin?"

He said, "Yeah. That song is too sad. They caint take it. You hafta quit."

So, thats the way I got off the stage. Played about foe numbas—an I was sposed ta play thirty minutes. An, show nuff, they cut it off. But did he did me a favor gittin me off that stage! I was ready ta git off befoe I did git off.

I didn know it was goin that well wit em, you know, but its a lot a people was there. Some of em had jest lost their mother. That went over em. Some of em had lost their mother maybe a year or two ago; they rememba what I was sayin in the verses. An they jest couldn stand them verses I put in there.

Man, they didn know how glad I was ta stop. I quit about half a the song. So they got me off the stage, an I went towards the dressin room where the musicians go. An they met me at the doe. I never did git ta set down. I stood there. An they was round me jest like flies. I got em off me with that one song, or either got em on me. To an fro, til they got so miny people around me you couldn see me nowhere.

Askin questions. Askt me where that song come from. Where I learnt that song at. They had never heard that song. An how long I been playin. Everthang they could figger ta ask me, they askt me that. An I try ta talk ta this un an that un.

They say, "Thats a sad song. It woke up eeeverbody!" See, everbody was cryin. Them wadn cryin, they was rejoicin. Say, "Where you git that song at?"

I said, "Well, my mother used ta sang that ta me, when I was a boy. An I invented from what she said in her song, an I made music to it."

Said, "Oh, man, thats the best song we ever heard in our life."

An the police said, "Well, will you let im git by? We's tryin ta carry him ta the dressin room."

They said, "Well, we wanta git a autograph from him."

I couldn write, man, I'm tremblin. I said, "What *is* a autograph?"

They said, "Write yo name on this paper, on this pitcher."

An I said "Well, I caint write standin up." Couldn write settin down either, cause I'm scared ta death.

So the police jest told em say, "Y'all'll hafta git up off him. He give out. Y'all jest worryin him ta death. Now if y'all want inythang, peaceful, let him set down." An they put me in a chair an I signed, I reckon, over a hunnud an fifty autographs.

An I was stranded there one hour. I was give out. Signin the autographs. That learnt me what I was doin. But when I stawted I dont know whether I was writin it right or not, I jest doin sumpm ta hand them piece a paper, gittin rid of em. Jest a autograph, what is that? But when I got about half of it done, then they told me what I was doin.

Then finely, they carried me in the dressin room, where the musicians set down like we settin here. All the entertainas say, "Man, you know that show did sound good ta us." Talkin ta me! I'm a musician too!

I say, "Y'all like that?"

He says "Oh, man, how did you git that song? Where you arrange that song from?"

An while I was talkin ta the musicians, they pusht in the place where we was. That doe was open an they come in there, talkin ta me. Police had ta git them outa there. Where the entertainas may wanta change clothes, or drank some coffee or sumpm? Them people didn care nothin about if that was a dressin room or nothin.

An I didn play no mow that day. See, you only have one set a day. An the next day, I had people ta carry me around, talk ta me, an git me sorta brave. I was a man was lucky enough ta git with the big staws a that show: Sam Hinton, Pete Seeger, Jean Ritchie—an Mance Lipscomb. Us foe was together. Everwhere we went.

Now Jean Ritchie, she played some kinda little old auto-harp. What you call them thangs wit two necks to em? Not thrail it, she had thangs look like a fiddle. A dulsmer, thats it. She could sang, she's a Kentucky woman. An old Sam Hinton, Pete Seeger, they could play inythang.

An its the second day. I commenced ta gittin mow used ta what was goin on. Pete Seeger was my best man. An he know sumpm was goin on wrong wit me, an he jest stays right where I was. An somebody say sumpm ta me, he stop an see what they sayin. An rush me away from em so they couldn confuse me too much. But he knowed them people was gonna do that. An he would jest come up an tell me everthang about how ta do nothin but react ta myself.

Say, "Now you jest go ahead on, an they ask you sumpm, you give em a good answer. If you feel up to it. But you caint worry wit all these people, cause all of em gonna ask you some questions. So you jest stop wit some of em, an some of em you pass them by."

See, I didn know I was a big *man* until all this done hapmd. Maybe a year later. I thought they was jest runnin me down an doin sumpm they ought not ta do, cause I was scared ta death.

Oh, Pete Seeger, he estimated how ta git along wit em, cause he already had done got nated ta that. See, I was a new man: never been over there, had not been to a university in my life. Never played at a blues festival in my life. An he knowed all about it.

So, I was fixin ta face all them people out there, an he could see sumpm wadn set right in me. An he come up there an told me, "You in good hands. You played fur this miny people befoe?"

"Nawsuh."

"Well, I know you aint played befoe foedy-one thousand, but I done heard yo record. An I know you kin play that gittah. You know what you do when they call ya?"

"I show dont."

"All right. When you hear em tell the people who you are an where you come from, an announcin yo name an all like that, you jest walk straight out ta that chair an play the best you kin play. Dont be worried wit all them people out there. Dont even look at em. An when you git through, turn yo back on em an walk away. Dont look back. An you wont be scared of em, an they'll thank you got experience." Givin me encouragement, cause he could see I needed it. An thats jest the way I done it.

But now, him an Jean Ritchie an Sam Hinton: they tuck me as one a their buddies an carried me round, an we sot ta the table an et together. Foe days. He say, "Yeah, we gonna all eat at the same table, an drank the same drank if you want it."

An everwhere I went, they went: Jean Ritchie, an Pete Seeger, an Sam Hinton, an Mance Lipscomb. Jest us foe together. An so they didn leave me stranded by myself. An that give me a sorta thrill, cause I had some protection walkin wit me. Everthang I didn know, they was carryin me about, showin me diffunt sights an scenes. They was a great help ta me. Cause Lawd, if I had ta have been out there by myself, I know I'd a fainted. But once in a while you git somebody ta go along wit ya: show you the way around an hep you out, why, first thang ya know ya git mow nated to it.

Jest turn you loose by yoself, man in a big place—University of Berkeley is a big place. Man, thats the best place ever I been in my life. An I played at somewhere around eighty or eighty-two universities. An if inybody know their way around in universities, I know.

Lemme see, I been in Newport in sixty-five. Sixty-nine thousand there. I played Awkinsaw in seventy-three. I have two bookin agents: a man an a woman. Now you take the woman's named Sandy Getz, an the man's name is Richard Waterman. Thats why I dont have much rest:

when one aint got me, the othun is waitin on me.

Oh, I was playin in Houston. Call it a hootenanny. An we was all got nated ta sangin. John Lomax [Jr.] was there, an a buncha others doin diffunt thangs. Mack McCormick would come out an talk a little, an then we'd go ta sangin again. Musta been in sixty-two, cause I had done been ta Berkeley an come back. An then my name got out broadly everwhere then.

See, I been filled in with that twelve years. On the thirteenth year now, nineteen seventy-three. Inythang you ask me, I dont care how big the audience is, say, "Mance, play me Soanso." Maybe somebody done heard some a my songs that I'm jest playin while I'm on the stage, an they wanta hear em. I never turn around an refuse ta do it.

I wanta tell you a little joke on me, an I reckon I'm through now. I was in Monterey? Where I'm goin next week. I was up on the stage, playin an sangin.

An so, I got off. An you had ta step down ta the ground, on stairsteps. Here two ladies comin on: walkin an lookin at me an this police escoatn me. Here come two ladies all dresst up lookin at one anothuh, an followin me up.

So the police say, "Git back, git back." Well, they had ta tell a whole lot of em ta git back. Cause everbody tryin ta git in there ta shake hands wit me.

First thang you know, them womens come in there. An the police lookt back, an them womens had me stranded. One was on one side an one on the othun.

An I was froze. I was scared a them women. Cause they had me. An one boppt me on the jaw an kisst me on this side. An you ever seed me stompin a hole in the ground! Jest like a bull upset! The other one grabbed me on this side an kisst me. An their husbands was lookin at me, laughin.

Police say, "You all through in here? Will you git out? An turn this man aloose? You got him scared ta death."

I say, "They show *is* got me scared."

An the woman on the right said, "Noo. My husband told me ta kiss Lipscomb fur him."

I said, "Lawd, Jim Thomas I'm comin to ya—hangin right up alongside of ya direckly. Cause I'm show gonna be dead when I git through kissin here." Never has kisst no white woman in my life! Least I didn kiss her then; she kisst me. An man, you talkin bout tremblin!

An the police had ta drag me where I was goin in the place where ta rest at. An I had my check. An I had it might near tow up. Aholdin it in my hand. An the man say, "Come on in, Lipscomb."

An they shet that doe. Said, "What kin I do fur ya?"

I studied an I said, "Well, I reckon this the place where I git my check casht, aint it?"

Said, "Show. We cash one fur you inytime."

An there the check wadded all up in my hand—I was scared ta death. I sayed, "Well, I reckon its good."

An they unfolded it an say, "Yeah, its all right." That in Monterey. I oughtn ta not wanta go back there no mow. Might meet them same womens again.

Playing for the White Folks "This Music Bizniss"

From the 1961 Berkeley Folk Festival until his hospitalization on January 30, 1974, Mance appeared in much of the continental United States, and even slipped over the border into Canada. His appearances included folk, blues, and pop festivals at Newport, Ann Arbor, Berkeley, Monterey, Los Angeles, and Miami; the 1968 and 1970 Smithsonian Folklife Festivals, the 1973 Arkansas Bluegrass Festival, the 1962 Houston Hootenanny. In short, he played at most of the major music festivals of the 1960s and early 1970s and at over eighty colleges and universities. His walls at home were covered with mementos, ranging from oil-on-canvas portraits to blown-up photographs and posters. His scrapbook was as thick as a novel, even though it contained only a sample of the press notices he received. He was in *Who's Who in America*. Among the frequent guests Mance met in the Berkeley home of Phil and Midge Huffman were Bob Dylan, Joan Baez, Sonny Terry, and Brownie McGhee and others.

Mance appeared on stage with such diverse musicians as Pete Seeger, the Grateful Dead, Mississippi John Hurt, Mason Williams, Mississippi Fred McDowell, Earl Scruggs, Doc Watson, Jean Ritchie, Arlo Guthrie, Sonny Terry and Brownie McGhee, Lightnin' Hopkins, Muddy Waters, Buddy Guy and Junior Wells, Ramblin' Jack Elliott, Willie Nelson, Ken Threadgill, several of Mance's "students," and scores of others. He became friends with Robert Shaw, a Texas barrelhouse pianist from Austin who shared several stages with Mance. One man responsible for a portion of all these appearances was Dick Waterman, Mance's East Coast booking agent who booked scores of blues artists and Bonnie Raitt. Waterman now works with the Center for the Study of Southern Culture at the University of Mississippi in Oxford. Sandy Getz covered the West Coast for Mance out of her agency in Los Angeles.

A musician's musician, Mance included among his students Taj Mahal, Ry Cooder, Bob Dylan, Janis Joplin, Frank Sinatra, and countless others. Through these talented souls and his own recordings and documentaries, his musical influence continues to be felt worldwide, albeit often anonymously. The most notable documentary films and videos are Les Blank and Skip Gerson's *A Well-Spent Life* and the documentary made for the 1968 Hemisfair and still shown at the Institute for Texan Cultures, in San Antonio.

He even caught the ear of a president—namely, LBJ. Perhaps Mance's integrity, wisdom, and musical genius helped to remind Johnson why he fought fifteen tireless and pragmatic years for civil rights. Eight months before his death, he came to the first Kerrville [Texas] Folk Festival in 1972—expressly to hear Mance Lipscomb. That night, I was acting as security guard, a Vietnam veteran disguised as a hippie, watching a side entrance. In a sea of Secret Service agents, I opened the door as Lyndon, Lady Bird, Lynda Bird, and half a dozen others passed within a foot of me. Waves of paradoxical emotions swept over me as we exchanged greetings—from my mouth issued an awkward "Hello." As the former president moved on to take his seat directly in front of the stage, he changed for me from an archetype into a human being. Rod Kennedy's introduction to Mance during that weekend led to this book. An innocent abroad and a downright ignorant one, I'd never heard of Mance Lipscomb prior to Rod's introduction. A music enthusiast and promoter in Austin from the 1950s until he founded the Kerrville Folk Festival, which he carries on to the present, Rod Kennedy has displayed a consistent and eclectic appreciation for fine music in many genres.

Dr. Roger Abrahams was one of the first people to book Mance into a Texas university. Mance often stayed with the Abrahams family when he came to Austin. As I related in the introduction, Dr. Abrahams became my mentor for this book.

What attracted these people to Mance was his undaunted integrity and superlative musicianship, steeped in a tradition of entertaining country folk for over half a century. Mance was a walking, singing treasure chest of folklore and one guitar-playing son of a gun. He wasn't all that bad of a storyteller, either. By the time he entered the national spotlight, he stood on the solid foundation all this experience provided. At seventy-seven, he retained the endurance to play seventeen hours out of a twenty-four-hour period. That actually happened in 1972, on the day he played the Ken Threadgill Fourth of July Picnic, near Austin.

To date, Arhoolie has put out seven Mance Lipscomb solo albums. Reprise recorded three albums of material but issued only one of them. In addition, Mance shares an album with Lightnin' Hopkins, and he appears on numerous anthologies. He's been recorded noncommercially by dozens of universities and hundreds of home tape recorders. And finally, the Lipscomb/Alyn Collection resides at the Center for American History at the University of Texas at Austin.

The details in this go-along are a few drops in a very large bucket. Mance is refreshingly honest and disarming: he kept looking at "this music bizniss" from the grounded perspective of his front porch back in Navasota. He never seemed to get too impressed with either himself or the funny business he was in, though he was very proud of the recognition and the money he received from it. This go-

Mance with "fans" at Armadillo World Headquarters, 1970. *Photo by Burton Wilson.*

along offers a good overview of what this world was like for Mance.

Born on April 9, 1895, the son of a former slave, Mance lived on into the year of the Bicentennial, 1976. As a child he knew that just touching a white woman while passing her on the street could be a hanging offense; eventually he could watch his grandchildren graduate from racially integrated schools.

On January 30, 1976, I was sitting in a chair by the window in Mance's hospital room in Navasota, where I'd passed many an hour over the past six weeks. I was reading a biography of Gideon Lincecum, one of Texas' first botanists, who settled near Independence shortly after Texas won its independence from Mexico and who lived not far from where Elnora Kemps was born about sixty years later. At 6:30 P.M., I finished the last page of the book, describing Lincecum's death. As I closed it, I looked up right after Mance had taken his last breath. Elnora survived him by two years and two months. This concludes the triumph of Mance's life. Knowledge of his death might just free the reader to revel in what Mance accomplished against such long odds. I think that's the way Mance would have preferred it.

SEE, I NEVER BEEN OUTA TEXAS until sixty-one. An I went back ta Berkeley shawtly after they got nated ta me an my music. Cause they had so miny gigs waitin on me til, when I went back the second time—that was in sixty-two—I quit the highway. An I been on the road ever since. Daddy, they made me *whole* when I went ta Berkeley, first time I was out.

But now I done been all over Califownya. Sacramento, Sandy Bobra, Monterey, an Richmond. I been down on Long Beach. Highmonica Beach. I caint rememba all a them. But in the go-along, you kin jest name someplace that I aint been, an I kin tell you, "Yes, I have."

Its so miny places they dont know where I am, an wants my bookin agent ta book me in them places. Payin good money. But she wont book me until September. What she wantin me ta do, an what I should be doin: takin my rest.

Cause it dont do me no good, makin a thousand dollars an then caint enjoy it after I make it. Clump over in a field or sumpm, in reaction a my health. You dont hafta be sick all time; you kin be broke down. An these people aint broke me down in twelve years, but they right at it. I got a little fever somewhere. Appetite's kilt. Aint nobody gonna take my place after I'm gone. You kin set yo world all over, but you never will find nary anothuh Mance. Yeah, its a whole lot a ways out, whole lot a ways in.

An Sandy [Getz] told me, "Come home an rest." After I left Awkinsaw [in 1973]. She say, "Now, you jest go home an sleep an eat. You aint got ta worry about nothin. If yo money give out, I got some money aint give out. You my ace man!"

You know what a ace man is? All right, I dont care what you got in the deck, its no highern a ace. Thats the top cawd in the deck. An I'm not a cawd but I'm a man.

She got a lot a people that she book. But she dont put nobody over me. She makes me mow money'n ary entertaina she got befoe her. An I makes her mow money, see. Well thats what you call I'm her top man, ace man, highest man.

An I been lucky. Ta survive an come home safely. I didn know where I was, I jest give out an bound ta go. When they sent me a telegram or a phone: might say, "You hafta go catch a early flight, Tuesday." An when I git ta my destiny, somebody always waitin when I git there. They pick me up, an we eat a big dinna in San Francisco or Berkeley, or where I'm mounted to.

[From "Key to the Highway":

I got a key to the highway, billed out, an I'm bound to go.
Gonna leave here runnin, cause walkin most too slow.]

But when I git back here ta Navasota, I jest as well ta
hush. Cause they dont wanta pay too much around here, ya
know. I used ta go out fur fun. An I played hawda fur
nothin than I do fur sumpm. If it aint but one there, I play
jest as hawd fur him as I would if it was a thousand. I aint
lookin at the gang.

But my grandkids call me a old folks player. An I'm the
man stawted all the music, fifty-nine or sixty years ago!
See, I learnt em how ta tune their gittah up. Stawted em
off. But they got their way a playin, an left my way behind.

They thank they doin all the music in the world, cause
the Beagles showed em rock an roll was all the music. An
Elvis Presley, I thank he was one a them too. An this here
Chuck Berry. B. B. King. Jimmy Reed. An when they wind
up, the same music comin right back. Never change
nothin! They changed jest ta put you ta sleep or where you
deaf.

You caint hawdly find one man kin play all types a
music. I plays three hunnud an fifty diffunt songs. An some
people ask me, "How kin a man like you keep all them
songs in yo head? An dont furgit an dont cross em up?" Its
hawd ta do, an its easy if you done it a long time. First
thang you git yoself ta understand what you doin. Then
you kin figger those thangs out easy. Well thats the way I
nated myself. Which it tuck me about fifty years a learnin
what I was doin. An I done it bettern nobody could do.

Oh, I done made aminy person happy. So miny people
wants fur me ta play places: all they got ta do is put a paper
out wit my pitcher on it, says, "Mance'll be here sich an
sich a day." Austin an San Antone, Kirkville. An Califownya. Minnesota. Ann Awba, Michigan. Seattle, Washington. Boston, Massachusis. An foedy-eight states.

433

I was in Awkinsaw, in June the twenty-six, this year
[1973]. Eureka Sprang. I did two shows over there. Out in
the woods, an we had a canvas on top of us: tryin ta take
care of our lectric wires an amps an thangs. We had seventy-five thousand people lookin at us from here, fur as
you could look across the prairie an see em. An the first
show I stawted, I never completed it cause it come a rain,
an I went home.

The next mownin why, I was in town where I stayed.
People could jest stay out there, wake up, an they'd be out
there in the woods at foeteen miles from town. So they
called on me, somewhere long about nine o'clock. They
gonna pick me up. They had showfers jest regularly one
after anothuh, goin to an fro gittin the musicianists where
they stayed at in motels an then brang em out.

They had certain times a day they goin be on the program. An I was sposed ta be on the program at eleven o'-
clock, an they had me there. I saw Earl Scruggs, an Jack
Elliotts. Several people knowed me. I blieve Woody Guthrie's son was there too. Ahlow?

They show hated fur me ta come off the stage. I was
puttin it over the program so high an so good. An they'd
holla, "Mow MOW MOW MOW!"

You could see people wavin at me, hollerin an screamin.
So, second time they right me back: an man, everbody on
the ground, seventy-five thousand, opened up wit me:
"Gimme That Old-time Religion," everbody answered me.
You could hear me five miles over that mike! That was a
real good setup. Jest like I'm talkin now, you kin hear me
downtown.

I was home about three days, she called an say, "Mance?
You know who this is?" My bookin agent. Sandy Getz.

I say, "I'd know you in the dawk. Inywhere I hear yo
voice."

An she said, "Good. This is Sandy. You had a good time
out ta Awkinsaw?"

I say, "I thank so. I wouldn know."

She say, "You were wonderful! Them people didn want you ta git off the stage. I wadn there, but they sent me a repoat about you. Them people say if inybody ever mention yo name to anothuh festival, they show want you ta be the head man." They told her I was the staw a the show! Somewhere long about fifty musicianas was out there.

Well one thang, I'm nated ta the young class a people. They say, "You too old."

An I say, "No, I got a young hawt."

Oh, I'm the Hippie Man. I was given up ta be that, an I reckon I'll bear that. See I been among them people, when hippies really first stawted out. An ever time they lookt around: somebody tryin ta have their hair fixt like the Beagles. An it slipt up on us an didn know where it come from. I know when it come in here: one left-hand player an three others come over here hollerin an hoopin, an hoop the people outa all their money an left. An carried it back over ta Europe.

An here me an you scufflin here, helpin this state out. We couldn git a job here. Playin music. Here the Beagles: sold out tickets round a place in Los Angeles called Disneyland? One a my fans was down there, an I was playin at the Ash Grove. On Melrose Street. An so, he say, "Mance? How in the devil them durn Beagles got on ta one a yo songs?"

I say, "One a my songs?"

Said, "Yeah! They had yo verses in there."

I said, "Well I got a copywrote on my songs. An they caint steal it. I dont know which one they tryin ta sang." So I never did give it much thought.

But I talkt ta my recordin man, Chris Strachwitz? He gives reference about what I got on labels. So, he knows all about that bettern I do. Some copywrote fur thirty-three years. An they caint take them. Unless they buy em, an then own em, ya see. Pay so much a song, or they in trouble.

You know, people got twistified in mind about a song, they got a little sketch of it. An they say, "I wrote that song." A lot a people aint got credit fur the songs that they wrote. Somebody else tuck em from em. Whereas lots a time, they tuck a lot a my songs an predicted em in their lane.

Bob Dylan? M-hm. Rascal was a good friend a mine. But he got too much money offa one a my songs, an he wont say nothin about it: "Folla Me Down." Yeah!

I had a fella come here an told me bout Ramblin Jack Elliotts, I played wit im down there in Houston one time. He say first Elliotts heared a me, Bob Dylan set im down an played im one a my records.

Now its a great diffunce from the way I play it: he plays it in a G an a C code. An I play it in a A code. An he used diffunt verses so they wouldn know where he got it. Say the record compny git mow outa it that way? I guess so.

But he follad *me* down two *years* ta git that *song*. No, he didn come here. He follad me from Berkeley University. An when I went out there he was there. I didn know Bob from nobody else.

An when I went off a duty: he was settin round me, an hear what I was sayin, an pick up a lot a songs. He could imitate. But he wadn playin no gittah. Then. Takin you know, learnin from his head. He was a best songwriter ever I heard tell a.

Now watch:

[Mance sings two verses of "Baby Let Me Lay It on You" and adds a third verse, which is from Dylan's "Baby Let Me Follow You Down":]

> Let me lay it on you, Baby let me lay it on you.
> I'd do inythang in this whole round world
> Jest ta git ta lay it on you.   (1926 verse)

436

Baby dont ya tear my clothes, Dont ya tear my clothes.
You kin shove me an push me try ta take my life.
Baby dont ya tear my clothes.   (1926 verse)

Baby folla me down, Baby let me folla you down
Do inythang in this whole round world [God almighty world]
Jest ta git ta folla you down.   (Dylan's verse)

[From "Nighttime Is the Right Time to Be with the One
You Love," sung by Mance Lipscomb:

Dont the moon look pretty, shinin down through the tree.
I kin see my woman, but she caint see me.
Nighttime is the right time, be with the one you love.

From Dylan's "It Takes a Lot to Laugh, It Takes a Train
to Cry":

Don't the moon look good now, shinin through the trees.
Don't my woman look good when she's comin after me.]

I learnt "Baby Let Me Lay It on You" in nineteen
twenty-six. He loved that song. I say, "This is Bob's song,
what I'm fixin ta play," when he follad me up, you know, on
the program. Thats the same song I'm playin: he was listenin at me playin it two years befoe he learnt it. He got
the credit fur it. But he give me credit on his album slip.
Yeah, he's a great friend a mine. An I dont care. Because I
got so miny songs he caint git credit fur, cause lot a songs I
kin do he caint do. He's a cool-headed boy. I tell ya one
thang: he wadn nobody's fool. It wadn long befoe he got
rich. An he follad me from Berkeley to the UCLA.

An you see them old feets right here? I been right in that
soft mortar. Grauman's Chinese? A boy carried me up
there, an I said, "Where the cafay at?" There's a big old
place where they room an bode up there: its the biggest

437

hotel up in Hollywoods. It was right under there, where all that cement got on me at.

I got my name wrote wit a piece a steel. An they got a heister? It would kinda lift you over in that cement. It was Roy Rogers an Hoot Gibson, all their names in there. All them old fellas been dead, gone, fur years. Frank Sinatra, got him in there too. They call it a walk fur the staws, sumpm anothuh like that. Everbody's got their name wrote down in that cement, an got a big staw alongside it. Yeah, thats while I was playin at the Ash Grove, on Melrose Street. At Hollywood.

M-hm. When they find out who I was, they move me about so fast I hafta git the names a the towns. I been ta San Francisco so miny times I caint count the times. One time they had what you call a *dead* band playin. But they wadn dead, cause they up on the stage aplayin that loud music, you know. Lemme see, I thank they said they was Grateful *to* the Dead. An after they played out, I got up there an played. That was somewhere in the fall, long about nineteen sixty-eight, I blieve.

But you know, I got so miny thangs that a poe man needs. Dogs. Hogs. Chickens. Chilluns. Caws. Trucks. What mow could I ask fur? M-hm. Where I beat the rich man, a whooole lot: I got sich a friendly way an friendship. A rich man aint got what I got.

So one day, I was settin on the front poach, where it stay cool up under there in that shade. An direckly, here come a big shiny caw down the road. Had but the one man in it. White fella. He drive up alongside the fence an pawk his car under that shade tree out there.

Gits out his caw an walks on in the yawd. Say, "I'm lookin fur a man by the name a Mance Lipscomb. An I blieve I done found im."

I say, "Yeah, this is him. But how you know me an I aint never seed you befoe in my life?"

438

He jest laugh an say, "I hear you play purdy good gittah. Would you mind playin a few songs fur me?"

I went on in the house. Got my gittah an brung it on outside. Sot down. Tune it up an played im a numba or two.

"Purdy good." He say, "Kin you play a song called 'Freddie'?"

I say, "How you know I play that?"

"Well, I jest hoped you could play it."

An we went on like that fur about a hour. So finely, I say, "Mista? Looky here: we been settin here, an ever song you want me ta play, I kin play it. How you kin know ever song I do, an I know you musta not never heared me play?"

He smiled at me say, "All right, Mista Lipscomb. I jest wanted ta hear fur myself, cause I couldn see how one man could make all that music, an it comin outa one gittah."

An so, he carryin a case wit im. An he pull sumpm outa it, got pitchers on em. Say, "Well, this'll show ya: I got every record you made, up until now." Thank I had made three. He said, "Jest like that record sang an play, you played it right here today. Why dont you come ta my hometown sometime? I've been talkin about ya an playin about ya. An let my friends see you in person. You know I bought all yo records. I buy em so fast you caint hawdly git em there in Cameron. An they want some a yo records. How kin you git em?"

I hadn ever stawted ta orderin on em an I said, "Well I kin order some."

Say, "Well you order me three."

So finely, I sot there an he said, "Lipscomb, why dont you have you some dentures made?" He see I didn have no teeth.

I said, "Well, I'm not able."

Said, "What you talkin bout you aint able?"

I say, "Take money."

He said, "Thats the truth: It takes money. Well, I'll git

you some built, purdy cheap. You come up ta my home, I livin in Cameron. I'll take the measure a yo mouth an git you some set in."

I say, "You gonna take it?"

He say, "Yeah! I'm a dentist."

I say, "Well I didn know I was talkin to a tooth-bendin man. I blieve I got a way in an out. But how much it gonna cost?"

He say, "Well, you dont want no piece a dentist. Like you play music an goin out. You want them thangs be snug an look nice in yo mouth. It cost you round foe hunnud an fifty dollas."

I say, "Ohhh, Lawd!"

He say, "Dont talk about 'Oh Lawd,' an draw back. That foe hunnud an fifty dollas'll make you look younger, an you git on the stage you aint shamed ta open yo mouth. I'll tell ya: you come up there next week, on a Thursday, an I'll have em fitted. My name is Docta Bawman, an I treat you right."

I say, "Yeah, I blieve you will, Doc."

"I kin make it plainern that: I'll put em in a shape where everbody'll be lookin at ya. An I'll put gold in em."

I said, "Put gold in em?"

An so, I went up there Thursday. He sot me in a chair. Rared my head back, I didn know nothin whats gonna go hapm. He put some paste in there, you know, hunted all around in my mouth. An he knowed what to do and not do.

An he say, "Lipscomb, I got a lot a people askt me ta git you up here ta my place. I'm gonna carry you up ta the house an let you look at it. Hold about five hunnud people. Eat an drank out there, dance out there. Its right in my yawd. I built it an been had this thang paradin here fur diffunt people ta come in here, playin an entertain."

So show nuff, I went on up ta his house. His wife, he called her over the phone say, "Wife? How you feel?"

She say, "I'm feelin all right. You comin home, Doc?"

Say, "Yeah but, I'm got guest. Comin wit me."

She said, "Who is that?"

Said, "Mista Lipscomb here."

She say, "Ohh, Lawd! Is Lipscomb here? Gimme a phone, an let some a my neighbors meet im."

So she an about ten or twelve a her friends met me at the table. I et dinna, went on back ta the office on my way back home. I said, "When kin I git these teethiz, docta?"

He say, "Lipscomb, you come over here, day after tamarra."

I said, "Well uh, I'm gonna pay you foe-fifty?"

"Thats right."

I say, "Well. How much I'm goin hafta pay down on em?"

He said, "Jest play it out. At my patio. Cause I need ya."

An so, Doc fitted em in me, an in a week's time I went up there. Five hunnud people was there from Dallas, Austin an everwhere. I was playin that gittah, thankin bout them teethiz, you know.

I got there about eight. Tuz dawk. So I played, an I played. Direckly, about ten o'clock I askt em, "I blieve I'll take a break."

Say, "I thought you'd holla."

I said, "Now I aint tired, Doc. I'm gonna take a drank, git me some coffee or soda pop."

I commence ta meetin the people. They was dancin an carryin on. An I shook hands wit em an got a autograph. Said, "Mista, you is the playinest man I ever heard in my life."

Here was a cripple man, walkin around there an his crutch under his awm. Had his leg broke, he say. He said, "Would you play my gittah?"

I said, "I dont know. I might not *kin* play it. Gittah dont suit everbody's hands, you know."

He said, "Yeah, I heard that. Well try it."

I opened it up, there was a five-hunnud-dolla gittah—brand-new—in there. An he couldn play ary amount I was bawn ta die. Jest totin that round!

So, I played a few numbas on it. I said, "I'll tell you one thang, you got a real good gittah. But I dont wanta play yo's an break a strang." I didn wanta play his gittah cause I was nated ta mine.

Say, "Hell, its paid fur. Play it all you want. When you git tired of it, put it right in the case."

He turnt his back ta me. An walks from here ta that gate an stop. Seem like he was kinda in the midst: he's talkin ta somebody, an I got in a whiff of it. I'm purdy good listena. He say, "Well, I reckon its about time fur me ta go."

Somebody say, "Where you goin?"

Say, "I'm gonna catch that eleven-thirty flight outa here ta go ta Los Angeles, an see Mance Lipscomb. He playin at the Ash Grove."

Doc was walkin around, an he got a whiff a what this fella sayin. He laught, said, "You look around, you might see Mance Lipscomb round here close."

He said "Well, he's not here. But one thang: somebody been takin trainin from Mance Lipscomb, cause that fella playin now play jest like Mance Lipscomb."

Doc said, "Look over again. Would you know im if you see im?"

Said, "Oh hell yeah, I got his pitcher im my pocket." He look in his pocket. Put his hand on his crutch, he lookt. . . . Said, "Now if that aint Mance on over there!"

Here he come over ta the mike an say, "Well, you show play some good music. You done saved me a trip ta Califownya tonight." An slipt sumpm in my shirt pocket an hobbled on off on them crutches.

I never stoppt playin, I said, "Thank ya."

He say, "You welcome."

After while, Doc come back. He seed it. He see everthang goin on. He say, "Mance?"

I say, "What is it, Doc?"

Say, "You know I told ya, poe folks dont be around here much. All these people here is well-ta-do people."

I spoke right quick, I say, "You forgot about me. I'm a poe boy."

Doc walks up ta me say, "You might not be poe as you thank."

I say, "No, I dont feel like I'm poe in yo house. Now dont git me wrong. I feel welcome an rich here. But still I aint got no money."

He say, "Whats that in yo pocket?"

I said, "What pocket?" I furgot about the man put sumpm in there.

He run his hand in my pocket an come out with that bill, say, "Thats all right! You aint poe now, is you?"

I lookt at it an man, I said plain, I said, "Man, thats a hunnud dollas! That man didn mean ta give me no hunnud dollas."

He kep it in his hand an askt fur the man, he knowed im. Said, "Did you mean fur Mance ta keep that what you put in his pocket? He thought you jest guyin im."

Cripple fella say, "Hell, yeah. He's worth a hunnud dollas ta hear that man play."

An Doc say, "Well, its yo's, Mance."

So, that night, about three-thirty, I wind up playin wit Doc. Doc said, "Well, Mance. How much I owe ya?"

I said, "Doc, you say you gonna take it out in what I owed ya fur teethiz."

He looks at me an smiles. Said, "Mance, dont you know you done played over five hunnud dollas worth a playin here fur me tonight?"

I said, "You thank so?"

Said, "Hell, I know it! I had a whole lot a friends ta come here ta hear you. An they enjoyed it. An some of em sleep an some of em still tryin ta dance. An they et what they wanta, an its all on me. Now, yo teethiz is free now." An I

443

had a hunnud dollas clear, what the man gimme. Doc say his name Ben Vaughan the Third. From Austin or San Antone somewheres. Said he was a lawya, an a judge in the Supreme Coat a Texas.

So Doc put pure gold gittahs in the roof of em. You got a flashlight, you kin shine it in there an see em. An git my mouth all twistified an caint shut my mouth: lookin at the gold gittah. If they'd a put it on top a my head, wouldn a been no strain. But they had ta go an put it on top a my mouth. Yeah. Its got "M*A*N*C*E*" up in the top of it. An got some staws in there too.

An so, seventy-eight years of age now, I'm seein thirteen years a my life that I wouldn seed, hadn been fur the young people: preciated me here, an communicatin wit me. Settin at my house. An havin fun wit me. I'm enjoyin that. I'm goin inywhere I wanta go cause I know how ta treat people. Especially the young folk. I say in the radius a thirteen years I been havin it purdy easy.

Oh yeah, I've experienced a lot a thangs. Thats what I go out fur: ta learn the ways of people an reactions of folks. An how ta git along wit people. You got ta make friends

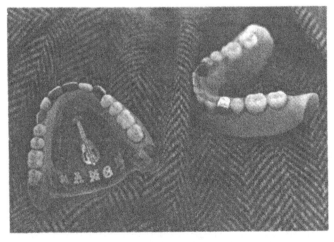

Mance's teethiz, 1976. *Photo by Glen Alyn.*

wit people. An let em know who you are, an you got ta find out who *they* are.

Now I've met some nice people, an met some bad people. So I went through wit both of em, the bad and good. An I haven had no trouble outa nobody in the whole twenty-foe states I've been in. So they didn fight me bout my ways an action. Because ever time they seed me I was the same man.

I mix whites up jest like I do my kids. I dont care what color you is. All a y'all got the same notion. All y'all dancin the same dance. An all a y'all is fightin fur me.

But now these people I'm dwellin wit, when I go out ta these places where I'm playin: I like as not ta go ta bed six-thirty in the mownin. See, I play better late than I kin when I first stawt. Now, about nine o'clock a little foe nine, I done got up an changed clothes an went outdoze an walkt around. Come in an drunk me a little coffee, they show me where ta turn that spout on. An I kin drank coffee an lay back down a while, an nobody wake. They snowin.

Once you git a certain age, it takes less sleep ta do ya then. I kin git two hours sleep, an wont git anothuh in a whole night. I'm the roughest old man ever been out. About settin up.

An so, twelve o'clock: They still layin there. An I'm ready ta eat dinna. They ask me, say, "You hongry?"

I tell a little white lie, I say, "No, I done had me a little egg, or sumpm anothuh you left in the Frigidaire."

Say, "Man, you kin go in there an git you what you want. Its free fur ya."

Man, but I have had some times out there in Califownya. Playin clubs an universities, an them folk festival gigs. Man, you go in that there dressin room where we's all git in there nated ta dressin. My time comin up, an they come there at the doe an call me out, maybe the next fella out. Room full of us in there. An ever one of em drankin sumpm or smokin them griefas an diffunt thangs.

One lady come in there, say, "Where is Mista Lipscomb at?"

An fella say, "You jest passt im. He right there by the doe."

"Mista Lipscomb! Will you do me a favor?"

I say, "I dont know. If I kin I will."

"Will you play me 'C C Rider' when you git back on the stage?"

I say, "Show will."

Said, "Why dont you take a whiff a my cigarette?"

I say, "No, I jest quit smokin."

She say, "Well you aint smoked like mine."

I said, "No I . . . I dont wanta smoke like yo's. I smoke like a cigarette I been nated to. But now dont git me wrong: I'm not refusin yo's jest cause you got a diffunt cigarette. You like yo style, an I like mine. Now we even up, aint we?"

She said, "Well, you made it plain."

Time I said that the law come in. An she put that durn long cigarette in her purse. That quick. Man, I had mow a them thangs offered ta me than a litter. I got a nice way ta turn em down.

Now, I been ta so miny parties I caint keep up wit em. An so one of em, you oughta been there, man. I was cryin myself. I thank I put all of em water leakin. I was tellin em a joke about Sonny Terry: he was a great friend a mine, him an Brownie McGhee? They work together. An so Brownie, he's a good cook. Inybody say Brownie caint cook, why, they dont know how ta eat. Inythang he wanta he kin cook—cake, all kinda foods. So, they set up a rig: "We gonna have a big dinna at Brownie McGhee's house." In Oakland, Califownya. That where Brownie lives. It was somewhere long about sixty-nine.

So finely we got everthang awganized. It was somewhere long about sixty or seventy people was there. Brownie had bahbecue, there was food ta waste. Oh man, a community dinna. A lot like them Satiddy Night Suppas I played at. Everthang cost them around fifty or a hunnud dollas. But them boys make plenty a money, you know. They spend their money, they have their pleasure.

So I talkt hawd talk ta them boys, cause they take it. See, I dont use much cussin in my language. But I say some thangs near about like cussin ta them. So finely, I said, "What y'all waitin on? Its around close ta one o'clock. I'm show is hongry. Caint you give me a sanwitch or sumpm?"

He say, "You coulda been eatin. But we're waitin on Sonny."

So everbody settin around, wonderin like I was whats so late gittin the food straightened out. Carry the tables all out in the yawd.

Finely, I heard sumpm ta "Bdrdrdr bdrdrdrt," here come two people on a motorsickle. Come right down toward Brownie's house. Sonny settin behind, an a woman was drivin it. An he's rared back, you know, holdin her.

I said, "Brownie, that look like Sonny yonda."

He lookt up, says, "That *is* him. Mance, give im the devil when he gits here." See I talk bad talk ta them like I'm mad wit em. He like that jive.

Here come Sonny an his girlfriend. She cut the motor off an Sonny commenced ta gittin down. An she give im a hand an leadin im in the yawd.

I said, "Sonny? You know you got everthang helt up?"

He said, "Yeah, I know it. But if I had been drivin myself, I'd a been here befoe now."

An I lookt at im I said, "Now how you gonna drive? You blind!"

The woman she lookt at me an laught. I hadn never met her befoe. She was a white lady. Thats his girlfriend. Nice-lookin woman.

An Sonny said, "Hey, Mance!"

I say, "What you want now, Sonny?"

He says, "Will you promise me you'll watch my woman? I

caint see good. Some bastud be talkin ta my woman, an maybe I dont want him ta talk to her." I know he's guyin me.

The woman, she smiled.

I say, "I show will watch her, Sonny. She hafta be kinda careful cause I got my eyes right on her."

Say, "Well, you do that as a friend, cause she's a purdy woman."

I say, "Yeah, she show is nice lookin."

So, we all go ta talkin, an he ets dinna. An he settin up there, he's noddin off into a sleep.

An we's jest a big way talkin. Lightnin Hopkins was playin the gittah, an Brownie McGhee was carryin out over Lightnin: "Lightnin, I kin play gittah better, over behind my *neck* than you kin play in the front of it." Boy, that made Lightnin mad!

An so, I knowed what was happenin, an I slipt up ta Brownie, I said, "Brownie."

"What?"

I say, "Lightnin caint stand that. He thank he's the best gittah picka in the world. You at yo house. Dont cull im down. You'll run into a bad misstake. You an him gonna fall out."

Old Lightnin was sangin, "A Short-Haired Woman." An Brownie was goosin him up wit his gittah.

An finely I look over there: old Sonny asleep. He didn care nothin about no music; he done heard music all his life.

Brownie tuck his gittah off the back a his neck. Say, "Mance?"

I say, "What?"

He say, "You aint doin yo duties."

I say, "What is that?"

"You told Sonny you was gonna watch his woman. An here she over here talkin to anothuh man."

I say, "Durn it, she show is!" An so, I wadn gonna bother

that woman, cause she a stranger ta me. She wadn doin nothin ta Sonny, but I was sposed ta watch her. She kep alookin round, an talkin.

Finely I said, "Miss, reckon you hadn better move yo seat over here by me? I sposed ta watch ya."

She said, "Aw, shuh! Mista Lipscomb."

Sonny woke up. An she was laughin. An the house was full. An when she quit laughin, she lookt right at Sonny.

He said, "Mance!"

I said, "What?"

Said, "Where my woman at?"

I said, "Doggone, Sonny! That woman got away from me, an I dont know whichaway she went." Yonda she settin close ta me as my wife is now.

He said, "Goddurn! I told you ta watch my woman!"

I said, "Sonny, I done miscased how she look. Its a whole lot a women here. I dont know yo woman from nobody else's. Now, I got ta go an ask ya how she look."

Said, "Well I tell ya how she look. She's a heavysot mama. An she got big legs." BOY! That house jest hoop!

I say, "You reckon I kin locate her by them legs?"

"Durn right! Aint nobody here got legs like my woman." He's blind as a bat.

I said, "Sonny, I tell ya what I'm gonna do."

He said, "What?"

I said, "Now if you dont let me git hurt, an dont let nobody bother me, I'm gonna go round here, an feel these women's legs til I find the right woman."

Boy, we had that thang goin on fur two, three hours. I knowed how ta git a way wit Brownie an Sonny. Everthang I said to em is in a hooraw way. Oh, nothin but fun. But I jived them two fellas there til I got ready ta leave they house.

If you wanta know what kinda gittah I play, I stayed with that Harmony aminy a year. If you want me ta play a gittah, give me my old Harmony what Chris finely give me. I got all my songs nearly on that gittah. Got my initials on it.

But now I done moved over ta this Gibson. Because this gittah was give ta me. What I'm gonna do wit it if you give me sumpm, an dont use it? They didn give it ta me jest ta tote around or sell it ta you. They knowed what I was a man who was widely known in foedy-eight states. Some a them states, maybe this gittah be sold by you alikin me.

Say, "What kind a gittah is that you got?"

Mance in his bedroom with Gibson guitar, 1971. The photo on the wall is of Mance and Mississippi Fred McDowell (photographer unknown). *Photo by Bill Records.*

Well I tell em, "Its a Gibson." Or they know its a Gibson. Then they say, "Well I blieve I'm gonna git me one."

They thank they kin do with this Gibson what I'm doin. You know there's people that says, "Its the gittah." No. Its the man who *play* the gittah.

Well, I tell ya what I was doin: they had everbody lookin at me from here ta that highway. An around me an on each side. Not on the stage, out in the prairie land. An thats where Gibson give me that gittah what I been playin mostly these last three years: Ann Awba, Michigan. 1970. On the blues festival?

A blind boy got me ta leave there an go home ta his place, in Canady. Kids an grown-ups come up ta his school ta hear me, an he paid me fifty dollas. Fur one hour.

So, we got up that mownin: he's lyin in the back. He had all this quipments at his house he could put his hand on, an touch this an that. Know where everthang was. An I watcht im, see what he's doin. Said, "Mance, furgive me fur this house. I thank I do well, fur a blind man."

I say, "I thank you do too. I dont know how you git around wit all these thangs."

He says, "I'm gonna rang the bell an git us some breakfast, an have it brought here."

I said, "Well, I made about foe hunnud dollas at the blues festival. An I dont wanta intrude on you."

He said "Aw, no. I'll pay fur it." So he rung the bell, an here come the waitress. Brought me in some ham an eggs an, oh man, a fine breakfast.

Then I pulled my dentures out, an put em in a containa a water. An furgot em an got near about ta the airpoat befoe I misst em. There I was: toothless as a hen! Go meet all those people.

I was on my way ta Minyapples, Minnesota. Call it Twin City. I been there foe or five times. So thats where I got indentured fur those dentures: yeah, I give im my address an he mailed em ta me. But its two months befoe them thangs retch me. An he had done sent em three or foe times.

So I, you know, ta be outdone: I went back ta Docta Bawman. An he says, "What in the hell you doin wit yo teethiz?"

I say, "I swallad em."

Says, "Swallad em?"

I said, "Well, yeah. Why? I got hongry, an got ta eatin so fast I swallad em."

He say, "Well you'll hafta swalla some mow, then."

I say, "What you mean?"

"I'm gonna make you some mow," he said. "Hell, you caint do without no teethiz."

I said, "Okay."

He said, "But you hafta pay fur these, though. I caint make you a thousand dollas worth a teethiz an let you by as easy as you did befoe."

I said "Man, I dont care what they cost me. I want some. Make some a little better than you did the others."

Say, "I caint make em no better, but I kin put a little mow gold in em."

Course, I wouldn pay no thousand dollas fur em if I had ta buy em. But they do make me look mow like a—a human nature. I dont care how when you miss one teeth out yo mouth, people ever seed you once an know ya, they miss that teeth. An the people aint never seed ya, they dont know whats hapmd to ya befoe they seed ya. Thank thats nated to ya.

Well now, people lookin fur them gold teethiz everwhere I go. That young girl see me on the stage, you know? Sangin: open my mouth . . .

Said, "Well he show is sangin. I like that man. He show got a mouth full a gold."

I git off the stage an caint hawdly walk!

Oh, I tell you what: he's about the best tooth dentist in

iny state I been in. I done sent Doc Bawman patients from all over the country. Got ta have teeth like mine. I pulled em out an showed em all that works in there. An they carried it round there in their hands an showed em ever ten or fifteen people. Say, "Look here what this man got in his mouth? He *got* ta play his durn gittah, he got one in his *mouth.*" So I'm well equipted. I got a pitcher a them teethiz in a scrapbook. Layin in the bedroom in that box in yonda.

Old Dick Waterman got a good pitcher of me. He had me playin fur him, maybe ten or twelve times. He the same man bookt that girl—call her Bonnie Raitt, I blieve. Me an him would always git along together. I stayed wit im when I went out ta Boston, Massachusis. An he carried me from there ta New Yawk. At least he had me sent there in a caw. I played five places in New Yawk. One place was Syracuse. An left there an went ta Buffalo, where President Eisenhower built that college? Well, they had his name on ever check. I said, "These checks aint no good. This man's dead!"

Eisenhower checks. Lemme see. The other places I couldn rememba them places. Plenty a ice an snow was up there. Yeah, I know futures, but dont ask me about no names. A man done met a hunnud thousand people or maybe two hunnud thousand, he caint verify names.

Not once—mown one time. I played fur a hunnud thousand at Washington, D.C. Mississippi John Hurt? Yeah, we was there together. I been there twice: sixty-eight an seventy. What the name a that thang they carried on up there? Them devils: presidents was into that thang, man. An them there sinators. Snifazonian. Thats right. Thats where President Johnson first come ta hear me. They had mules an hawsses tied ta the trees, an cows an kids. All kinda thangs of a shape, fawm, an fashion runnin up an down, that the kids hadn seed in town.

An I was on the ninth stage. See, you move down ever ten foot, maybe from here ta that truck: I'm fillin the stage over there a while. Move there an play ta the next one. If you was qualified, you gonna go from numba one ta numba nine. What you call qualified, if you could play diffunt types a music on diffunt stages, why you went aaall the way. But if you would play but jest foe or five songs or two songs ta suit somebody, you got off on numba one stage. Then you go back an set down an here somebody behind ya: he may could do mow numbas than you did.

An they predicted, a hunnud thousand people was there. An lookt like five hunnud thousand could play: from here downtown. Back over this side, back here behind ya. Nothin but people. Show is sumpm frightenin. But I had done gotten ware a that then.

An they put me on top of a house, I call it a house: clam up there twenty steps high, an here's a man done got up there an promotin me. An I say, "Go ahead an talk, man. I'm give out." After while I clumb ta the top. An I reckon I had somewhere long about foedy thousand round that stage.

I had my mind made up when I got up there ta play a church song wit my knife slide. I played my pocket knife, see. An my promota pronounce who's gittin on the stage. Say, "Here's a man here, he comin from sich an sich a place. He's been knowin in so miny diffunt states, an he served so miny towns an . . ." Oh, he talk about ya so people could know who you was there.

I stood there an listened at im. But I was gittin my knife open so I could play slide. He say, "He gonna play this knife song."

An this lady down on the ground, she didn hear im. Lady said, "Lawd, have mercy. Why dont y'all tell that man—up there on the stage talkin bout this man—he's gittin his knife an gonna cut his throat?"

It tickled me! I didn say a word, lookt down on the lady.

Finely the man got through talkin. Said, "LETS GIVE HIM A BIG HAND! MAAANCE LIPSCOMB!"

Mance playing knife slide guitar on his front porch. *Photo by Bill Records.*

Then I crawl up on the stage. She whisper at em, say, "Y'all tell that man the man got a knife."

I sot down on the chair. Jest smilin at her. I blieve I played "Motherless Chillun Sees a Hawd Time When Their Mother's Dead."

That got about three verses, an she lookt up, said, "Wait a minute, mista!"

I say, "You talkin ta me up here?"

"Yeah! I'm talkin ta you. We thought you was gonna cut that man's throat, but you fixin ta cut our throat down here. I caint stand that knife playin."

Say, "You caint?"

"Thats too sad fur me," she say. "Kin you play sumpm a little easiern that? Man, that goes all through me."

Oh yeah. Lectric caint git that outa it. See, all you git

lectric outa is jest yo amp. The movements from yo hand: you kin quiver yo hand jest like I'm quiverin this matchbox here. Hear how that make a steady rattle? I kin shake this hand: that vibration dont need no lectricity. Lectric is a good loud tone. But its not no similar sad tone. But I git the sadness right here in my feelin with this knife.

Old Son House an all them boys, Muddy Waters saw me do that. Say, "What in the devil is you playin wit?" when he got off that stage.

I said, "I played a pocket knife."

An he said, "I dont blieve that."

Yeah, all the rest of em use a slide. An finally, Muddy Waters say, "Git off the stage an lemme see."

An I pulled my knife out.

He said "Man, I dont see how in the world you kin git that sound outa there with this knife."

An he played wit a slide: he got a piece a steel on his hand. He come out with that. He's tune his gittah where it'll be some good loud tone, an good sad tone wit his way a playin. He tunes it up in thribble E: he got a E first at the bottom, an got a E foeth, then there's a E sixth up top. Near about like one style Blind Willie Johnson would tune his gittah in. Man, you kin wham away on them three strangs, an if you kin sang: "I'm bawn ta die. Lawd have mercy on my wicked soul." Well you kin git by with that.

Yeah, Muddy Waters an Howlin Wolf, I seed them aminy casions. Last time I seed them together, they was at Ann Awba. Call it a blues festival.

You know how miny people there was predicted ta be there? Say it was a hunnud thousand people sposed ta be there. They had em on the ground. Didn have no room fur em in no town. Wadn no house in the world wouldn hold them people! Had em in a pen jest like this here: it was about twenty foot high. Two doze in there, two gates. One ta go in an pay, an one ta go out if you's tired. An man, you couldn see nothin but legs. You dont look at the people's faces, jest look down an see the legs jest this way away. Jest fur as you could see.

I blieve it was goin on three years ago. There was a foe-day schedule. J. B. Hutto played up there too. It was a whole strang of em played there. An you know, they stranded me fur the last man got on the stage.

A colored lady askt a man—bookin agent—say, "When y'all gonna put Lipscomb on?"

The man walkt off like he didn hear her.

She run, cot im. Say, "Why y'all dont put Mance Lipscomb on?"

He turned around an said, "Aw, you talkin ta me?"

An she say, "Hell yeah, I'm talkin ta you. I been here foe days ta hear him."

He say, "Miss, you dont understand what we doin."

"No, we show dont. Cause I'd a been back home if you'd a put him on first."

Say, "You know, all of em got a choice."

Say, "Well, a lot a people heard their choice, but I jest come ta hear Lipscomb."

Say, "Well." Lookt at his watch say, "Five-thirty, aint it?"

I never will furgit it, she say, "Yeah."

"Six o'clock, you see Mance Lipscomb on the stage."

Say, "Why you keep im out so late?"

Say, "You'd a been gone home if we put im on first, wouldn ya?"

She say, "You damn right!" Cuss!

Say, "Well, whole lot a others been gone. So, we got im here fur the last."

So I dont never root nobody out their position. Cause I done found out I'm not the only show. But they kin go along with me all night because I got so miny songs changed wit em, they gonna like some of em inyhow. I jest moved it around, tryin ta feel fur my audience. Cause I'm sangin ta my whooole gang a people. First thang you know, I plays a love song right there. An I sang joke songs, fiddle songs, blues an kids songs, story songs, I play all types a songs. Cause it strikes somebody's attainsion.

Inythang you ask me, I dont care how big the audience is, say, "Mance, play me Soanso." I never turn around an refuse ta do it. Because they paid ta come in there an see me an hear me. An thats where I git my money. Least I dont git it from one person, I git it from everbody. An they is as good ta me one as they is the whole bunch.

An so, I was always on the road, wadn nobody up here ta sorta see after my wife. You see that white house over cross the fence yonda? That where Little Mance at. Its been here three years now. I bought that from Mista Tom Mow. Got it out ta Allenfawm. An he had about fifteen or twenty houses like that ta be sold, cause they gonna rot down.

So I paid five hunnud dollas fur that house. An paid three or foe hunnud dollas ta move it here. An put a hunnud dollas worth a blocks in there. Cost a thousand dollas, all told. So, thats where that house was moved here, on account a it was my son, an protection fur my wife.

I wadn broke when I bought that house. I went out one week, an I brought seventeen hunnud dollas back, when I went ta Califownya. First stawted ta playin in Seattle, Washington. An moved from there an played at a place down below there—I blieve Poatland, Oregon. Thats two nights play. Then I left there an went on ta Berkeley. An played two or three plays over there. I makes purdy good money. But, I spent it. See, they thank I'm makin too much money, they been at me about payin income tax.

Well I got a govamint bond. An I put in three thousand dollars in two years, thats much as I allowed ta put in the savin loan, without iny income tax off a it. Well, I couldn hide that. But I went an got me a safe box. I kin hide that! Nobody knowed what I got in there but me an my wife without a book.

An then I turnt around an got me a lawya ta make my will out. So the bank couldn take over. See, a lot a people done put their money in a bank, dont let none a the kids know nothin about it. An it goes back ta the bank. After so miny years.

So I put so much money fur this girl, so much fur this boy. The next one I give him a will on down ta foeteen grandkids I raised. An three of em is adopted. Then I got one son, he got mama an papa's inheritance: he gits half of it.

So, they dont know what I got, cause if I tell em what I got, they'd worry me ta death about it: they got ta have this an got ta have that. So I knowed how ta keep em off me, until me an the old lady pass. Cause its my money, til I die. Then, some a that money is put up there fur a bier, where me an the old lady kin have a real good funeral. The kids aint gonna hafta give us nothin.

Because I made some money fur myself. An lot a money fur, you know, gigs. I played fur foedy an fifty thousand head a people at one time, jest me playin fur em. An you know that two dollas was low as you could git a ticket in there. Thats mounted up to a lot a money.

Man, you kin put on yo tuxeda suit, shined shoes an git out there. Say, "Aww, Soanso playin tonight!" Well, when you hear Soanso, you aint gittin what you thought you was gonna git.

Puttin me out there wit old brogan shoes on, I'm playin as hawd as I kin. They walk by, say, "Aww, what that old man doin? He aint nowhere." I aint got that tuxeda suit on! I aint got them shiny shoes on! An I aint got my bottle a beer up on top a my amplifier. I aint full a hell an I aint full a whatever that stuff you use: griefa.

An I aint got that big publicity, big name out there like B. B. King. I thought I was gonna hear sumpm when I saw him in Houston, about nineteen fifty-seven. I left my gittah in the caw. Went down ta play at a nightclub.

Say, "Lets go see B. B. King."

I say, "He here tonight?"

"Yeah!"

I say, "Well, now, y'all been talkin bout B. B. King: he dont have the same gittah I got. Do you blieve me?"

They say, "Aw he got a same gittah as you got."

I say, "No he aint. Here's a trebolo here an one there. One over here an one here. All those thangs is got knobs on em, controls? An alls he had ta do, jest hit one knob an turn it on an leave the others off. An he hit one strang an go down ta the lake an come back, an it still rangin. An hold his hand up in the air: clear! Aint got a fanger on them strangs. Lectricity! An you thank you listen at him, you lookin at that lectricity. I dont have no amp here. Jest clear pickin."

We done lost all our good pickas now. You goin with the wind now. Goin where the majority goin. An listen ta the majority.

But if they jest asettle it down an git right at the music: Blind Lemon, he's a musiciana, he played straight. All right, the next fella was this here Leadbelly. He was a fanger picka, like I am. Them two. The next man who is a clear fanger picka is Blind Blake. The next one is Blind Doc Watson. You gittin real music there.

See, I leave myself out cause I'm here. I jest proved mine up by playin it, but I kin prove out what they's doin: Blind Lemon, Leadbelly, Blind Blake, an Doc Watson, an Mississippi John Hurt, Elizabeth Cotton, an myself. Seven people could play actually, straight music.

But podna, I kin say this about me: I dont worry about givin you enough playin, cause I plays from sunup til sundown. An go eat suppa an play from sundown til tamarra mownin: still playin that gittah. I been doin that fifty-nine years. An follad it right on down, from my daddy befoe me. Only he fiddled fur the Suppas an I played gittah, when my time come. An man, I've had it hawd. We had shawt pay. Daywork: fifty cents an seventy-five cents a day. But we went through wit it, an we raised food an hogs an chickens an little thangs like that. We didn have much money. An we was happy an we was healthy too.

Dont you see whats happenin now? Everthang's a fast, fast time; everthang moves in a fast motion now. An if you be late, podna: you wake up in the mownin an everbody's gone. No, no. Its no good. It aint no strength to it. Its just a fullin. Cause you go ta the cafay: you dont know what you gittin. They're makin it in a fast way. All they wanta do is ta sell you sumpm an git rid a you an sell the next fella sumpm.

But, see, we take time with what we doin. Thats why we live long as we is now. I'm seventy-nine, an Elnora's seventy-six now.

I was right in Austin about two months ago. A boy was wantin me ta go over ta his house, play a little late music. An that come a rain.

I said, "I dont walk so well."

He said, "Well, we'll take care a ya. You dont hafta walk fur."

An so I got off the sidewalk an I slipt. An I fell foe I hit the ground he had me: pulled me up.

An you know the thanks I give im? I said, "Now fur you ta been an old man, you'd a fell down on top a me. Somebody had ta come git both of us up."

He jest died laughin, said, "Naw, I wouldnt!"

Now I'm gonna stick with these young folk. These young people is quick, man. Yeah, they got quick thoughts, an they got some power too. They got power in they head. They got power in they awms an strength too.

This young race a people done straightened out this world a whooole lot. Since this segregation [integration] goin on. Because a lot a cafays in Houston, about six or eight years ago, I couldn go in there an eat. But if I go ta yo town now, say, "Come on, lets have sumpm ta eat, Lips-comb." I go iny place I wanta now.

Right here in my town: fella carried me in from Los Angeles. He say, "Lets go downtown, git us some suppa. You know where a all-night cafay?"

I said, "Yeah, I know where two of em. But I'm not fitted in one."

"What you talkin bout, you aint fitted in one?"

I say, "I caint go in there."

Say, "What kinda cafay is that?" See, Los Angeles been wide open. Long time.

I said, "No, I tell ya whut. I'll go down there witcha, an you go in there an eat you sumpm, an I'll stay in the caw."

He said, "Aw, naw." Hapmd about nineteen seventy-two. M-hm.

So, that place wadn open: he was carryin on segregation. I knowed I wadn lowed in there. The other place I could go in there, but they was closed.

So he insisted me ta come on in.

An, they commenced ta lookin at me, you know. Lookin round. People askin what you want, or invite a menu: they was lookin at me so hawd they furgot everthang.

An the people from Los Angeles say, "What they lookin at you fur?"

I shuck my head.

"What you gonna eat?"

I says, "We aint gonna eat nothin! We aint got no menu."

They say, "Waitress?"

Waitress saw me settin ta the table facin them, she hear em an dont hear em all at the same time.

Say, "We want ta git sumpm ta eat!"

She wouldn turn em no answer.

He lookt around at me, say, "No wonder you dont wanta come in here."

I said, "No, I didn have no bizniss comin in here. I tell ya, I'll go out. An y'all git yo food."

He said, "Well, damn this place. If we caint git you no food in here, we dont wanta eat." An said it right befoe the whole house!

An they lookt around at im an lookt around at im. Two of em walkt up, he say, "Come on, lets go!"

Say, "You kin eat."

Say, "No, I caint eat. If Lipscomb caint eat in here, I aint gonna eat in here."

They lookt at us, say, "They must be some strange folks was goin out the doe."

So them peoples wit me commenced ta cussin at the doe when they went out: "Damn this place! You reckon you's a hitch on us?"

I said, "No reckon in it: I know it."

So, thangs done come to a hitchdown. Its been wide open now. You dont care nothin bout what race or color. An what I like about my kids an y'all's kids: they look at a person, whats inside of em. The hawt of a person. Not the color. You know, if you got a good hawt, you a good person. An if you got a bad hawt, they pass you up as a bad person. Leave you alone, see. So thats what this here segregation is.

The white folks an my own colored folks at home: they wont fit in wit me playin no gittah. An I wont have them. No, I dont play around here hawdly, no mow.

Well, I'm tellin ya, I aint studdin about them. See, a man known in foedy-eight states, an excusin his home—what he worryin about a home? Aint but *one* state there. An here I done been gittin out, playin in twenty-foe other states.

I played in Austin fifty-foe times. At the odditorium. Nightclubs. An some part in the university. Well I'm got tape over me in all these schools near about. Roger Abrahams, he's the first man I stayed all night wit. Stayed at his house an been wit his kids. I been knowin him, near about since I stawted ta goin out ta these places an playin. He brung me down ta the university; thats where he tot at.

Lemme see, I played at the Toad Hall. In Austin. An Robert Shaw come up ta the doe where you pay admission: they stopt im.

An he said, "I never paid iny money ta hear Mance in my life. I aint gonna pay it now."

An he meant what he was sayin, because see, me an him dwell together, we connected together, good friends. An if I go where he playin at, an cost me two dollas ta go in there—an he know it: why he tell em ta gimme my money back.

So, he was hoorawin the people, an maybe they couldn tell it. Cause they wadn used to it, see. It went on a lot a people's mind in a diffunt way, in their thoughts, that he was discruminatin me. But that might not a been in the ware a his meanins. Cause he was lettin em know he was a great fan a mine.

Mance and Robert Shaw at Armadillo World Headquarters, 1971. *Photo by Burton Wilson.*

An I couldn tell what was goin, in the go-along, cause I
was up there playin an couldn see it, couldn hear em. But I
do know if he'd a come an told me he had ta pay two dollas
ta come in there, well I'd a told the firm, "Give him his two
dollas back." Oh, I reckon they figgered it out right, cause
they let im come on in. An I didn see no money change
hands.

See, he love ta git wit me. He plays good barrelhouse
piana. An I'm a real good backup man. Sometime we plays
together, an I back him up. He dont hafta pay fur me ta be
playin under him.

Well now, I played in San Antone when this here place
was opened up here about six years ago. What ya call that?
That big place, they tow it down . . . Hemisfair. I was the
big shot there. I blieve they made a movie outa me there.
An they got my pitchers up there at that big old buildin
what they didn tear down. An called it a state institution
[Institute for Texan Cultures, now part of the University of
Texas at San Antonio].

Oh I got, lemme see, six records fur Ahhoolie. I got three
fur Warner Brothers, but they didn put but the one out.
Thats seven albums. Then I got some records combined wit
other people. Like you sang one song, I sang anothun, an
make a album outa it. I dont know how miny them split
records I aint got.

Frank Sinatra was tied up with them Brothers some
kinda way. He lives someplace out in Califownya, heard
me at one a my plays out there. I had jest stawted goin out
ta places an playin. So, he come up ta me an say, "Mista
Lipscomb, I got a little yacht settin out there in the ocean.
Wonder could you come stay wit me an my friends a couple
a days, an play a little music?"

I say, "Well, I dont swim too good. An I done been babtized. Naw, I blieve I'd be better off on solid ground."

Say, "You dont hafta git in no water, man. Jest walk

around on the decks an thangs an eat when you feel like it. Come on an go with us, Mista Lipscomb. Set out an enjoy the view."

So I got out there on that big waters. He had a little low girl wit im, she had shawt hair near about like a man. Called her Mia, I blieve. Purdy little old thang. An I sot out there an played fur them, two nights. She was holdin on ta him an he was holdin on ta her. Lookin at one anothuh. Say, "I show do like yo music, Mista Lipscomb."

I dont know what they didn have on that boat, man. I et inythang I wanta, they got it an brung it ta me. So, he told them Warner Brothers ta make a record outa me.

[From "Trouble in Mind":

Trouble in mind, an I'm blue, but I wont be blue all way,
Cause the sun gonna shine in my back doe someday.

Mance sang this to Frank Sinatra, who recorded his own rendition of the song.]

Then I got anothuh split record from Kirkville Festival. Seventy-two, thats when I met the boy puttin this book out on me [Glen Alyn]. Its twenty-five people in that album. Everbody who played there had one song. What that fella who played there, yodel like Jimmie Rodgers? He's a old fella got a whisky joint up there in Austin. Ken Threadgill [friend of Willie Nelson and Janis Joplin who received a platinum record for "Honeysuckle Rose"]. Man, he was so drunk: he had two quotes a whisky, one in each hand. An he was "E-yodelin-o lay-Deee, lay-Deee, lay-Deee." An he had his whisky goin, he'd turn it up an git anothuh drank an "lay-dee" again.

John Lomax an his wife, they askt me an him an Robert Shaw ta come over ta their motel room an see my movie. You know the one Les Blank an Skipper Gerson done? Call it *A Well-Spent Life*. Well, John Lomax, he put some money into that thang, so they give him his own copy.

So there we was all huddled up in there, settin on the flow an layin up in the bed an thangs. A buncha fans was in there wit us. Threadgill say, "Man, that show do brang back the memories." We in there talkin an laughin, hoorawin one anothuh.

Yeah, when I come onstage, they had three rows in front, didn have nothin but ribbons on em. An direckly here come President Johnson an his wife an daughter, sot down in the middle a all a them empty chairs. Buncha their friends sot down there wit em. Wouldn let nobody else close to em. Call him the president. A the United States. They say he come there jest ta hear me. He been a fan a mine since I went up ta Washington, D.C., an played at the Snifazonian. That was in sixty-eight.

Jawnus Joplin? She used ta sang at Threadgill's joint. An that lady I used ta stay wit in Austin, Shirley Dimmick? She give her some voice lessons. Now you take Jawnus: she sung behind me befoe she got on her first stage. An she knowed me fur an near til she died. That fella Tary Owens used ta run wit her.

I saw her somewhere long about three weeks befoe she died. In nineteen-seventy. I was gittin on the stage— Threadgill give that party out in the heights outa Austin. Called it a party barn. I thank it was somewhere long about ten thousand people out there.

So, she lookt at me an say, "Hello, Mance!"

I say, "What you doin here?"

She say, "Oh, I'm here lookin around like you. You want a drank?"

She loved ta drank. That what kilt her. An she had a fifth a whisky in her hand.

I say, "I'm gittin on the stage, save me a sniff when I git off." I didn want none, I dont know what it was, jest a big old red bottle.

An finely she say, "You know what you told me when I preach you puttin me on the stage first?"

I say, "Yeah."

Say, "You done furgot it."

I say, "No I aint. I told you if I had yo voice, an I had my fangers, I'd be all right."

An she say, "He show aint furgot it." An I aint never seed her no mow.

Now, anothuh little old girl come outa Austin, plays wit a band called Greezy Wheels. But she wadn playin wit nobody when I first knowed her. I trained her how ta keep time. She had all the notes an codes that she wanted. But she broke time. An from eight o'clock that Sunday, until about six o'clock that evenin I had ta go be on a program at the Awmadella—I say, "Mary," her name Mary Egan. We called her Fiddlin Mary. I said, "Now you reckon you got the time?"

She said, "Much as you done carried me over the motions, if I aint got it now, I never will have it. But I wanta git on the stage wit you tonight. Play fiddle wit you over there."

I say, "Now look. I'm gonna carry you over yo lesson one mow time. At six o'clock, I got ta go."

An me an her was up on the stage, she got ta playin fiddle, an I says, "Pat yo foot. Keep yo rhythm goin wit ya feet."

Now you watch her when you see her playin fiddle, she's doin that. Boy, what you talkin bout, that woman kin fiddle. She could fiddle then, but she didn have the time: But that feet, got her in that motion a havin that time. An she said, "I never did know that." I'll say I know them girls an boys.

An here come a new couple: I was down there at Monterey Festival, sixty-five, I blieve. Walkin around on the ground, eatin hambuggas, talkin ta people. I didn know nobody much, bout foe or five people. I done tried ta git ta know everbody, but everbody know me. An I dont turn nobody off from conversation.

Here come a young lady an young man, an this guy say, "They in love."

I said, "Well, I see that. She had holt a him an he had holt a her."

An I was facin em, an they commence ta lookin right in my face. I was goin towards them, they comin toward me: that made a conclusion.

When I got right by the lady, she say, "Would you sign this? Autograph this?"

I said, "What is this?"

She pulled my albums out from under her awm. She say, "You dont know me, but we flew from England over here ta hear you play."

I said, "Flew from England over here?"

She said, "Show did. This is quite a treat fur me an my husband; we newly married. I got yo album. Ta git autographt."

Oh man, yeah. They been tryin ta git me over there. You know whut they told me? I settin in the back a the caw. Kirk an Bruce up there, talkin an goin on. We was drivin back home from some gig I had in Austin. When they commenced ta talkin about how much I would git, man I woke up.

They say, "Mance, if you go over there, you worth somewhere long about sixty thousand dollas—cash money—ta go over there if you stay over there six days."

I say, "Well, they talkin one thang. Doin its anothuh."

They said, "Them people have been callin fur you. Comin over here in Texas. An they jest aint never run across ya, but they been askin about ya, they got yo records on juiceboxes over there. Got ya pitcher settin up there. You'll be kivered up wit people, in two states over there: New England an Great Britain."

But you know, I made mow money outa talkin than I made playin. Aint never made no mown a thousand dollas a night, playin. Them people estimated me: three thousand

dollas ta pay my indebtments off. At that benefit, at the
Awmadella? That was after I got outa them hospitals, in
seventy-foe.

Taj Mahal, he played at my benefit. He studied round me
bout foe years. He have his gittah backstage, an I be up
front on the stage. Then I'd git off an we would play together. One night I never will furgit it: I was out at his
place in Califownya, San Fernando, I blieve it was, someplace like that. That boy wouldn put that gittah down.

He built them thangs, what you call em? Dummy planes.
They go up in the air wit lectricity. They got a little box
he'd carry wit im, look sumpm like a little old hand radio,
ya know. An he'd turn a knob on, that thang'd fly up in the
air. Then he'd go an do sumpm else, an here that dummy
plane twist about, come an go—you know jest whatever
Taj want it ta do why, it'd go there.

An so, we was out in the country an he was flyin one a
them thangs about. An direckly, that thang jest droppt
right outa the air. Fell over in a conefield, an he went over

Mance, Bill Neely, and Taj Mahal at Armadillo World Headquarters (Austin) in 1971. *Photo by Burton Wilson.*

there ta look fur it. Wadn too long befoe he come back wit it; it was all busted up. Wing broke off it. An you know what he told me? Said, "This aint what I wanta do. Not wit you here. Lets go back home an play some music."

So show nuff, we hoppt back in his caw. Went on back ta his place. An we drug out them gittahs an went ta playin, podna. An stayed up all that night aplayin. An into the next day an that night! He say, "Mance, I know I'm wor- ryin ya, but I dont wanta go ta sleep. Jest wanta play music." Yeah, that boy got a *good* voice. He's a real good songster.

An then they give me three hunnud an foedy dolla, at that African program? What them folksong people put out. Jest ta set an talk to em. Over at the University a Texas. I had that in my mind, an their reaction the way they was lookin at me: jest everbody was settin, an cautionly lis- tenin. An takin it down. Some a them people tried ta rememorized it in their mind. Some of em had pencils, writ- in it. An then I seed some a that. An I knowed they was preciatin what I was sayin. Yeah, they showed my movie what Les an Skipper done. Shuh! Much as two or three hunnud of em settin out there—an I was facin em on the stage. I didn even play my gittah. Didn hafta do nothin but talk.

An I was tellin all them people bout goin ta church an thangs wont never do no good, if you dont place God in yo hawt, people. Cause when you be bawn a the spirit a God, you gonna feel it. Religion is a feelin. Its not a holla, an a hoopin an a shape, fawm, an the fashion: you've got ta feel it.

But the works: the pure works is in this hawt. Religion aint nothin but Love. Nothin but Love.

God made us here in this world, ta live peaceful an quiet an git along together. Everbody wanta be somebody. Wanta be the same person. Have the same feelin. Eat the same food, dance the same dance, sang the same songs. We git together. Have fun together. We share together. We lay down an eat an sleep together.

Because you kin live in heaven here on earth: peaceable an quiet, an nice ta people. The way you live, the way you die. If you live good, you die good: in a peaceable way. Well, I jest ta knows the day comin I'm gonna die, but I dont know how soon. An I dont know how long it'll be an how I'm goin a feel *when* I die, cause I never have died!

Now people, you jest rememba one thang: you caint git songs out yo mind that you kin git out yo hawt. See. Readins is good. In its place. But its not good in yo hawt wit songs.

So inyhow, we goin let y'all rest some. Gonna hit the road. Gonna play you a song, what you call the slide. I slide wit my pocket knife.

EPILOGUE:

Not Only
a Gittah Player,
a Teacha

Mance believed people could choose to go along through the world from a position of hatred or from one of love. He lived by the biblical moral "As ye sow, so shall ye reap." That translates into today's slang definition of karma: "What goes around comes around." Because Mance personified this natural law, his mastery of music carried a profound message to those who experienced it. He communicated his own choice through his actions, his music, and his very presence. He had a strong, clear sense of who he was in relation to himself, his hometown, and the larger world he experienced during the last sixteen years of his life. Mance opens up to these subjects in the epilogue.

He is remembered by many as a warmhearted philosopher and a man of great wisdom. Mance saw himself as a farmer, a guitar player and songster, a spinner of stories, a husband, the foundation of his family, and a teacher for a younger generation that offered him freedoms and recognition he had never dreamed of in his youth and middle age.

Even so, there were certain things Mance wanted to say that he preferred not to make public until after his death. Eight years of racial integration (1965–73) did not erase seventy years of subjugation. This was demonstrated by Mance's unwillingness to sing "Tom Moore's Farm" within earshot of Navasota and by his caution in revealing certain events of his past. The extent to which he *did* state what happened reflects his integrity and courage.

The songs "Tom Moore's Farm" and "You've Got ta Reap Jest What You Sow" are compilations, and the most complete versions available to me. The twenty-verse version of "Tom Moore's Farm" is a synthesis of several of Mance's recordings of it, including his "Anonymous" rendition previously alluded to. Such extensive deliveries are more like Mance's renditions at the Saturday Night Suppers, where if the dancers were responding well to his song, he'd keep making up or adding verses until they were sated with it. We can now appreciate the perspective of how much the plantation lay at the very heart of Mance's world and why he sang about it.

Mance closes this book with an Aunt Nancy tale. Three animals—Rabbit, Bear, and Man—square off on equal footing, and the story recounts what happens to one beast who is overly proud of his invincibility. Since Mance was part African and part American Indian, what better way to conclude than with a piece of traditional African/Native American wisdom and humor?

NOT ONLY A GITTAH PLAYER, A TEACHA

WELL, I'LL SANG this "Boss Man" over yo tape recorder.
Now where this song come about, why people invented this
song: its people like me an others who workt fur these boss
mens. An they rode over em wit pistols, shotguns. Jest like
they was a convict.

An people go along in the field an have thoughts ta come
to em, how they were treated. You rode over a boy or a man
or woman in the fields workin fur ya: he had ires inside a
him. But he couldn speak it out ta the boss man, because
he'd git shot down or whupt down.

But when he left an went to anothuh little group a people: this group over here git ta talkin about im. Say, "You
know I got a mean boss man." Somebody listenin at what
he say. An he go on, say, "He wont treat me right. He
works me hawd all day, an I caint sleep at night."

An then this stawted a song from that. An put verses to
it. Come out of planation. What you call a fawm. Of people
aworkin hawd. But they wadn sangin—didn even have no
music in the field—they jest talkin ta one anothuh. An
somebody heard em an they rememba what they said, an he
add anothuh verse in there, an first thang you know, that
was enough verses ta make a song. About that mean boss
man. An it goes thisaway:

[Mance plays his arrangement of "Big Boss Man":]

Told my wife this mownin, "Lets pack our thangs an go.
I aint gonna work fur that mean boss man no mow, cause they a
Big boss man, he wont treat me right.
Work me hawd all day. I caint sleep at night."

He standin on the turnrow, wit his pistol in his hand.
He done whuppt that woman, gonna kill that man. He's a
Big boss man. Dont you hear me call,
"You aint so big, Boss Man. You jest tall, thats all."

Next boss man I work fur, he gonna treat me right.
I kin work fur me all day, an let me sleep at night, cause is a

475

Mean boss man. Dont you hear me call,
"You aint so big. You jest tall, thats all."

I'm goin away, baby, ta wear you off my mind,
Keep me worried, bothered all the time, "Well, you
Big boss man, dont you hear me call,
Aint so big. You jest tall, thats all."

Early this mownin, chillun, an it wont be long,
My boss man gonna call me. Yes, an I'll be gone, cause he's a
Mean boss man, he wont treat me right.
Work me hawd all day, so I caint sleep at night.

Standin on the turnrow, hat on his head,
He git mad wit you caint understand what he said, cause is a
Big boss man, know he hear me call,
"You aint so big. You jest tall, thats all."

Next boss I git, gonna be right ta me.
When I go ta him, he gonna let me be, cause he's a
Mean boss man, jest wont treat me right.
Work me hawd all day long, people. I caint sleep at night.

Thats the boss man. Jest thank em up, an you kin add on all the verses you want. Now, that song dont end. I jest stoppt off. An we gittin back, wit our mouths. But we had ta say it, slow an low. Where he caint hear us. An the people made up these verses an the song about how they were treated an what he done to em, in the time I come up we call the time of De Pressure.

Put pressure on ya, you dont wanta do it but you hafta do it.

Boys I could tell y'all sumpm that make yo flesh crawl about the life I lived. An I'm still here, playin on this old gittah. But I jest . . . I lived it.

Like this here "Tom Mow Fawm." I dont claim I wrote it, because I'm stayin in Tom Mow's town. I called it A-nony-mous. Cause so miny thangs I could say about him: if it git

Oscar Coe, suspected Klansman, overseer, and livery stable owner, circa 1900–1910. *Photo courtesy the Marcus Mallard Collection.*

back to im he liable ta shoot me down yet. See? You got ta look out fur yoself. They say you kin kill a dog mow ways than hangin im. You kin shoot im down, you kin knock im down. Well see, I could be the dog that they's lookin fur.

Lets see . . . Oh well, he caint hear me. Lookt up an see how close the wall was to me, it aint goin out there:

[Mance plays his original arrangement of "Tom Moore's Farm":]

Aint but the one thang, people, I done wrong,
Aint but the one thang, see, what I done wrong:
Moved my famly down on Tom Mow's Fawm.

Go ta work in the mownin, dont stop til one o'clock,
Go ta work in the mownin, dont stop til one o'clock.
Hold back dinnatime, Mista Tom, you show caint hold
   back dawk.

Standin on the levee, spurs in his hawss's flank,
Standin on the levee wit his spurs in his hawss's flank,
Watchin his boys, man, from bank ta bank.

Tom Mow ask you, "How miny acres did you plow?"
Tom come an ask you, "How much acre you done plow?"
"Mista Tom, I done plowed so I jest caint tell nohow."

Git up in the mownin, you'll git ham an egg,
You wake up in the mownin, an git yo ham an egg.
Dinnatime come, you git you beans an bread.

Soon in the mownin, feed you ham an egg,
Soon in the mownin, you will git yo ham an egg.
Rang that bell, you better catch that gray mule's head.

Dinnatime come, you git yo bread an beans,
Dinnatime come, you gone, serve you bread an bean.
Rang that bell, you hafta catch that whirlin team.

Tom Mow whup you, dares you not ta tell,
Tom Mow whup you, he'll dare you not ta tell:
"You be at the lot in the mownin when my lot boy rang
   that bell."

Soon in the mownin, Captain, now so soon,
Soon in the mownin, baby, now so soon,
I dont be there. Tell Mista Tom, let someone have my
   room.

Wake up this mownin, I'll be seldom seen,
Git up this mownin, I'll be seldom seen.
Tell Tom Mow, let somebody else catch my team.

Tom Mow tell you, without a smile or grin,
Tom Mow'll tell you, without a smile or grin,

NOT ONLY A GITTAH PLAYER, A TEACHA

"Stay away from the cemetery, boys, I'll keep you from
   the pen."

Tom Mow folla you boys from end ta end.
Tom Mow will folla you boys from end ta end.
Ask fur five dollas, he'll haul off an give you ten.

Want some money, man, fur Christmas Eve,
Want some money, boys, man, fur Christmas Eve
Ask Tom or Harry, Clarence or Mista Steve.

One a these mownins, boys, an it wont be long,
One a these mownins, boys, an it wont be long,
Tom gonna call me, yes, an I'll be gone.

Standin on the turnrow wit his pistol in his hand,
He standin on the turnrow, pistol in his hand.
He done whupt the woman. Now he gonna shoot her man.

Little bitty woman, weigh about ninety pounds,
Little bitty woman, weigh about ninety pounds,
Walk so heavy til the little gal gouge the ground.

Who's that yonda, comin down the turnrow?
Who's that yonda, comin down the turnrow?
Aint Tom Devil, must a be Tom Mow.

Some people tell me, this song it never will end,
Some people sang this song, it aint no way ta end.
No, it wont end til when Tom Mow is yo true friend.

Reason why the boys like Mista Tom so well,
Reason why the boys like Mista Tom so well.
Sit down ta his table, look like the Rice Hotel.

Tom Mow got a way most iny man'll like,
Tom got a way most iny a you men will like.
Yo woman quit you, he'll have her brought right back.

Now you kin end that tamarra or next day or next week.
"He'll whup you, an dare you not ta tell. But you better be
at the lot in the mownin, when his lot boy rang the bell."
The bell is the system fur you ta git ready ta go ta the field.

"He'll folla the boys from end ta end." Up one row an down the other. Ridin on his hawss. An you ask im fur five dollas, he'd haul off an give you ten dollas. So he kin keep you in debt.

All them verses come right on his shoulder. Fits his shoulder like a rifle. But now I couldn sang that song an live there where I'm livin at. Oh yeah, Tom Mow's alive. He lives in Navasota in his home. I didn sang all the verses.

Is five brothers of em. Their daddy raised em up on a fawm in Washington County. Til they grow up an got some boys ta grow up under em, an *they* grown now they young boys is takin over.

All them five brothers bought land everwhere they *could* buy it. Jest like some people that couldn pay fur their land: Mow brothers come by that land by payin the debts out.

An got it all hovered up in between them five brothers. They got fifteen miles under the Mows. In a block! You's hafta drive fifteen miles befoe you got off the Mow Brothers Fawm. Right cross the river where they got a planation over in Brazos County.

An they done some a everythang, but Right. When they could do it. But now since this segregation come up, why they jest plain people now.

You talk ta these ooold fawmas round here—white fawmas. They say one thang an do anothuh. An they tell you one thang, an I tell anothun. Lot a diffunt, yeah. Let me tell ya, its lots a thangs I couldn open up the subject mongst a lot a people, cause you know what they'd do? You got sense enough ta know it would do me hawm, if I were ta explain ta you everthang that I know. Cause they right round here. An they know its so. When they git seventy an eighty years old, my age, let me tell you, young man, you still got some hatred here. You hear?

You watch some a these ooold guys: they look at you wit a keen an a disoddly look. You'll catch em. They come in there, an if you let a colored man come in front a them, they look at you wit a little instain. Thats what ya call that old ism in em yet. Thank ya oughta push me out the way an push them up there. But you aint studyin bout that. Cause you young.

You know what I do? I git out the way if I'm first. Then I ask the lady, "That old white fella, do he wanta git up ta the winda?" Yeah, I knowed my way around. Thats the reason I'm lived ta git where I am. An have the Principle an Pride as I got. If you dont know what you doin, you lost, podna.

Once you do Right, Right'll come back to ya. An you caint live Right unless you do Right. What I mean live Right among people, an git along wit people. An some of em you caint git along wit em if you *is* doin Right.

When I come up, you know what could hapm? There was one man in the precinct: we represent him ta be the bad-man, an all the rest a the peoples were scared a him. Cause he's done kilt somebody. Shot somebody or beat up some-body. An they'd bear around him as a badman. One man could rule fifty or a hunnud mens! Now it takes a hunnud polices to arrest one man. But when I come up, in my young stage of life, one man was the boss. Thats the reason we sang about this boss man. He was the boss. Aint no bosses now. Everbody's a boss now. Cause the people is fightin back.

Boy, this world done made a change. In the last, I'd say, goin on nine years—since I could witness to it about sixty-five. Where I was raised at an bawn an come up, people couldn even go in a white man's yawd. Unless he tip his hat. Colored man there'd pull his hat off. Hold it in his hand.

Come in their house? You wadn allowed in their house. An so I got this music away from em. Right here. See, they didn respect me as I was a man. I was what ya call a dog or sumpm. They dog would come in the house, an I couldn go in there. The dog could eat in the house, I couldn eat in there.

I look at some a those people that did me so much wrong, I caint git revenge only one way: git away from em. Walk away from em an git where you all at an other people who preciate what I'm doin. An I kin come ta they house an eat at they table.

Now them people in Navasota, they dont come ta my house an eat at my table. Y'all come ta my house, y'all set ta the table an eat wit me. You know why I do that? Because y'all treat me thataway when I'm away from home.

They say, "Mance is the Hippie Man. He got all them long-haired people comin round his house." They caint say nothin about it. If they pass there an see y'all huddled up around there, fifteen an twenty-five caws sometime jest stretcht right in front a my doe. Somebody from New Yawk. Some people from Califownya. An we set there an eat bahbecue, an they want some beer, whisky . . .

But all this music: they hate ta see it. An some of em likes it. You know who likes ta see me do that an want me respected? Is the young people yo age, an on back. You know, people git paid fur what they do. It might not speak in words, but it speak in feelins. Its inside a you, an that conscience'll folla you until you come admit ta me you done Wrong. If you live long enough. Dont, you'll die with that conscience in ya.

So them conscience is whuppin these people now back. Them old rascals what done caused my mama an papa ta be dead an rotten. An tuck from them. An I was raised on they fawm, an I raised some a my kids on it, at least I didn have but one. But I raised twenty-three grandkids out on these fawms. An they tuck our labor. An cusst us an buked us. An done wrong thangs, but it done come back to em. An now talkin bout Depression: de Pressure done turnt around. Done left the people who had the pressure. Gittin on the peoples who aint had no pressure.

Only people that is free a conscience—of what they did ta the colored man, what they did ta the Indian man—is you young race a people. Y'all dont have no hatred fur us. You gonna feel something, that you goin wrong. An you gonna turn around an do the right thang amongst all colors an all race an kind.

Thats why I'm happier, where I'm away from home. Sometime I'm three thousand miles away from home. Leave here, go on out ta New Yawk. Califownya. Cause people treat you right out there. An I feel free out there.

Ohh, it was some few white folks done good by me. You take Walter Mobley. An Old Man Bingham. His boy Lloyd was the one give me credit on that stawm fence there. He been dead bout foe years now. I kin mawk the time down, he jest a friend a mine died, an Lawd, I hated it.

So people, you dont see me on the streets in Navasota. Nobody dont bother me, cause I dont give em no chance. Go down an buy me some groceries an come on back. Because I'm lookin at that fella what done done me so bad, he's bent over, an some of em walkin wit a stick. There's some a the old devils right in every town in the world, man. They got that hatred in em yet. Y'all call it fogism. They try ta pull you back in them fifty-year-old back ruts. Dont thank it aint bad on nobody but the colored man.

I married Elnora in nineteen-thirteen. An I'm still got the same wife. Well we loved one anothuh when we stawted out. An I walkt up an down this road aminy night an talkt wit her, an found out that she had the ways that I wanted an she found out I had the ways that she wanted, an we connected then. She like me an I like her.

First thang you goin do is like a person. Then you dwell wit em, then you come ta love em. That like'll come ta be love. Then you kin share wit em. Its mow ta that than it is what you got an what she got. But, man, you aint got no foundation if it aint no love there. You jest well as ta go on down the road an hunt somebody else or let someone hunt you *one*. Cause its jest like that song, "If it aint no love, aint no gittin along. Always trouble, sumpm goin on wrong."

But if you love, you kin give over ta one anothuh. You kin sacrify fur one anothuh. Y'all kin eat a whole biscuit an divide it between y'all, when you happy. But if you didn love her, said, "Well hell, dont eat *all* the whole biscuit."

Well, if I didn love her, I wouldn take that. Love makes ya take thangs. An I kin go home an she look pale or bad, an she gruntin. But I feel sorry fur her if I love her. I wanta know whats a madda wit her. I say, "Do you need me ta go git you inythang?"

An she say, "Well no, I reckon I'll make it all right."

An first thang you know, I'll look at her an she feel a little better. But now I could walk off an leave her gruntin if I didn love her. Furgit about her, go hunt anothuh woman aint gruntin.

An so, look like everbody around me call me Daddy Mance. I aint everbody's daddy, but I treat em jest like I was their daddy. Thats what you call people creatin love amongst people: treat everbody the same. Didn make no diffunce how miny mothers they had split up, we cared fur all of em.

An you know, I call myself the hawt a the famly. Everthang they need, they hafta come direckly through me. I am the backbone a the famly. Been that way all my life. Ever since I been eight years old.

Do you know how ya stawt a fence? You put a hole down in the ground, dont ya? Then you take a beeline there, you wanta git it straight. Go round yonda an sight from this hole that ya put down in the ground wit a post in it, an go from one post ta the other. You know what you call them two postiz you put down first? A standby. A brace. Thats what you bead a fence by. Put a angle post between em, ta keep em straight. An the post'll stand up, an pull the wire, from end ta end.

Fence brace posts: "I am the brace a the famly." *Photo by Tad Hershorn.*

Thats the: I'm the brace a the famly. Its built from me. I am the brace, that stays. Everbody got ta be braced an come under my direction. Because I'm the standpoint. Its built off me, by me.

An here me a country boy. But I dont be nobody's fool. I kin talk wit you, wit foolishness, an say some funny thangs fur you ta laugh an alibi. But my head is full a bizniss. An my hawt is full a Right.

I dont hide my age, I'm seventy-eight. An I got mow advantage ta my reactions in my fangers than I had when I was fifteen years old. Cause I was workt ta death. But now I kin use my hand, perfect.

I teacht a boy in Califownya. He's been playin wit me five years, an he didn know how ta do nothin but strum on his gittah an hit there, there. I learnt im how ta carry bass an lead. You know a gittah: well, you've got ta learn that you kin transact yo fangers, ta do diffunt thangs wit yo fangers.

So I thank I left here fur a teacha. Not only a gittah player, a teacha.

I'll say, its a lot a fun. I dont care whats goin on, somebody got ta carry the fun on. An its one thang, I'm up in the age but they respect these fangers, ya hear? An they respect this knowin up here. See, I got foe ways at em: These fangers. These ears is two. An the eyesights is three. An remembrance up here is foe. They caint git by me, cause long as I kin hear an see, an rememba, an use these fangers, why they got to look at me an respect me.

But you know, nobody in the world kin master music. B. B. King. Mance Lipscomb. Lightnin Hopkins. Nary one of us is the best in the world. I'm jest playin my numba, doin my thang. An git my row hoed out. Now I leaves the other fella's row up ta him. Cause the best aint never got here yet. An you dont never say you doin sumpm bettern nobody. Jest say you doin sumpm nobody caint do, cause you doin it yoself. But dont figger you's the best in the world. Aint no best here!

I tell you, an improve this by one word. Its a little joke. But this joke come out ta be certainty fact:

Was a Bear an a Rabbit. Was travelin in a road. An the Bear was in the road, said he was the baddest thang on earth. The Rabbit was over on the side a the fence over in the pastor. He scared ta git in the road cause he knowed sumpm gonna hapm ta him. Somebody kill im or catch im.

An the Bear was goin up an down the road, say, "Ohhh, I'm the baddest man in the world!"

Rabbit say, "You keep on sayin that. Man, you goin ta meet somebody is a little baddern you."

The Bear went on up the road, an here he's hollerin an snortin an tellin the Rabbit, say, "There is some a the baddest man in the world!"

Direckly, he hear sumpm an look: "Brother Rabbit? I see sumpm comin down the road."

Rabbit peept out the bushes.

Bear say, "What ya call that?"

He say, "Well, thats a old man. But you gonna meet somebody is baddern you, an its gonna be a man. But that has *been* a man. That aint a Man what you meetin."

"Ahhhoh, he aint no man! I'm the baddest man in the world!"

The old man saw him comin, an he got out the road fur the Bear an hid.

Direckly, here come a *young* man. Wadn full grown, about maybe sixteen years of age. He carryin a hoe on his shoulder, he jest come out the field an on his way home.

Rabbit an the Bear is trotted along, together. Say, "Come here, Brother Rabbit! I see sumpm else comin! What ya call that?"

Rabbit peept out the woods, say, "Well, he goin *be* a man. He aint come up ta be a man *yet*. But you keep on down this road. You gonna meet a Man direckly."

Brother Bear say, "I'll show im who the *man* in this precinct!" He commence ta barin his teethiz an hollerin. An run at the boy, he drap that hoe an jump the fence, jest took a lope down that cone row.

Went on down the road. About two miles, an Old Bear spied sumpm else comin. Say, "Come on over here, Brother Rabbit, an take a peep an see what is this comin down the road?"

The Rabbit lookt up the road an said, "NOW! Thats what I call a *Man* you meetin now, Brother Bear!"

"Ohh, aint no man! Everthang you see, you say its a man."

Said, "No, this *is* a Man you meetin."

An the Man come on down the road. About twenty-five years of age. Had a durn shotgun on his shoulder. Jumpt off his wagon an met the Bear!

An Old Bear jest come up to im, bristled up ta the man.

Man lookt an saw im. Leveled down on im with that shotgun with some buckshot.

An shot the Bear, an he kreeled over.

An, the Rabbit look out, sees the Bear tumble over. Said, "Now, Mista Bear! Thats what I call a Man! That fella done tumbled you over? You done met a Man, Brother Bear!"

You know what that Bear say? "By God, I blieve you right!" Cause the Man done blowed his brains out.

So you blieve I'm right, you keep atravelin round here, you gonna meet a Man. Somebody above you an above me an the next fella, kin do sumpm that you dont know they kin do it. Oh yeah!

Jest take credit an thanks ta what you doin an be glad you do what you doin. An do the best way you kin do it. Cause you doin yo thang. But man, dont say you gonna do bettern everbody. See, its a great big world, an lot a thangs goin on in this world. We never would catch up wit this world. We jest here guessin our way through.

So, here's a song that I wrote, oh about, I reckon thirty-five or foedy years ago. These songs is made up by people's notions, an their mind, an thangs that hapmd to em. Cause I say me fur a parable, you catchin on ta what went on back yonda. All these songs is True Story Songs.

People say, "Thats all right, you gonna do sumpm ta me an thank you gonna git by, but you gonna reap what you sow." So they made a song outa that.

Well that was stawta ta the song. But the people made up that song as they went along, by verses. But when it ended up, ended up on a man an a woman. An he told her, say, "After all I done fur you woman, you told me you were through. Oh baby, you got ta reap what you sow."

She didn know what that meant. Until she got ta reapin what she sowed. So here's a song Richard Dean learnt me when I was a boy:

[Mance plays his version of "You Got ta Reap Jest What You Sow":]

After all I did fur you,
You say you hate me, an we were through.
You got ta reap, jest what you sow.

You got all my money, you left me cold in hand,
Taken my money, give it to yo other man.
You got ta reap jest what you sow.

Cried all last night, an the night befoe,
Changed my way a livin, not gonna cry no mow.
You got ta reap jest what you sow.

You dont love me, dont you dog me round,
Like you found me, put me down.
You got ta reap jest what you sow.

After all I did fur you,
You say you love me. Now we're through.
You got ta reap jest what you sow.

When you quit me, you didn even shake my hand.
Thats all right, you gonna understand,
You got ta reap jest what you sow.

Good-bye, I hate ta see you go.
I might not never see you no mow.
You got ta reap jest what you sow.

In the sprang, in the sprang, when the birds begin ta sang,
I would be wit you when yo comrade puts you down.

In the fall, in the fall, when the leaves begin ta crawl,
I would be wit you when yo good man puts you down.

If you wanta make a preacha laugh, change a dolla an give im
  half.
Yo last time, you ever gonna dog me round.

Oh, she laughed at im! But when it commenced bearin
down on her, she didn know she had it comin.

Its all right when you huggin the Bear. Got a tight grip
on him. But when that Bear git ta huggin you, you squeal
out!

APPENDIX:

Song Reference Index

All of Mance's songs featured his unique arrangements. He adapted them to the style he needed to accompany dancers at the Saturday Night Suppers. In the modern sense of songwriting, he "wrote" the music and lyrics to very few songs. His creativity was channeled instead into selecting timeless songs from a broad spectrum of musical styles. He composed blues couplets and collected many more from his people and passed them on, along with complete folk songs. He adapted his broad array of music into a single genre that would suit the varied needs of his audience: the dancers, gamblers, children, and women onlookers of the Saturday Night Suppers.

This book contains all or part of the lyrics of, or references to, fifty-two songs that Mance played, plus seven he did not play but was very familiar with. It includes complete lyrics to eighteen songs. Mance claimed a complete repertoire of 350 songs; well over a hundred were recorded. The songs in this book are a representative sampling of them. They are listed here alphabetically.

When possible, I have tried to attribute the song to its originator, or the person from whom Mance learned it, and to indicate whether the song's arrangement was close to the original or whether Mance had significantly altered its style.

The letters "ref" alongside the page number indicate a mere reference to the song. The letters "lyr" indicate extracts of lyrics juxtaposed with related text; "song" indicates the presentation of a complete or almost complete song.

"Alabama Bound"   Probably black minstrel song, learned from father in 1915.   192–93 (song)

"Angel Child"   Learned from field hand in 1918. Mance set it to music.   198 (lyr)

"Arkansas Traveler"   Black minstrel song, pre-1900, heard from father. Not in Mance's repertoire.   106 (ref) 127 (lyr)

"Baby Let Me Lay It on You"   Learned in 1926. Dylan recorded it as "Baby Let Me Me Follow You Down."   176, 436–37 (lyr)

"Baby Please Dont Go"   Written and recorded by Big Joe Williams in 1929 under the title "King Solomon Hill." Mance learned it off a jukebox in 1940 or 1942.   208–9 (ref)

"Big Boss Man"   A field song, which Mance set to music circa 1919–20.   139 (lyr) 475–76 (song)

"Buck Dance"   Instrumental, learned from Hamp Walker, played to accompany two male dancers trying to outdo each other.   195 (ref)

APPENDIX

"Hesitatin Blues"   Carnival or black minstrel song.   223 (ref)

"I Wanta Do Sumpm for You"   Recorded by Bessie Smith with Kansas City Joe, circa 1920s.   41 (ref)

"Jack a Diamonds (Is a Hawd Cawd to Play)"   By Mance, written in the early 1920s.   250–51 (ref) 251–52 (song)

"Johnny Take a One on Me"   Children's song, probably circa 1905. Mance arranged it as a dance piece.   92–93 (lyr)

"Keep on Truckin"   By Blind Blake. Mance said it was in a "ragtime style."   223 (ref)

"Key to the Highway"   By Big Bill Broonzy, circa early 1950s. Mance changed it slightly and added several of his own verses.   305, 368, 432–33 (lyr)

"Knockin down Windas, Tearin Down Doors"   Two-step song, learned circa 1920.   246 (ref)

"Lookin for My Jesus"   Gospel song, most likely pre-1900, sung in Navasota. Mance made a slide guitar arrangement of it, probably influenced by Blind Willie Johnson.   59–60 (ref)

"Masta Promised Me"   Probably pre–Civil War. Taught by father. Not in Mance's repertoire.   126–27 (lyr)

"Missouri Waltz" ("Til We Meet Again")   World War I fiddle tune, probably learned from father.   129 (ref)

"Mojo Hand"   By Lightnin' Hopkins.   183, 230–34 (ref) 229 (song)

"Mother Had a Sick Child"   Gospel tune, learned from Mama Janie's church. Mance made it a Blind Willie Johnson–influenced slide guitar arrangement.   58 (ref)

"Motherless Chillun Sees a Hard Time (When Their Mother Is Dead)"   Gospel song, learned from Blind Willie Johnson.   123, 211, 218–19, 420–21, 455 (ref)   219–20 (song)

"Nighttime Is the Right Time, Be with the One You Love"   Elnora recited two of its couplets. Bob Dylan varied some of its lyrics in his song entitled "It Takes a Lot to Laugh, It Takes a Train to Cry."   356 (ref)   356, 437 (lyr)

"Stagger Lee" ("Stag-o-Lee")   By Mississippi John Hurt. Not in Mance's repertoire.   210 (ref)

"Sugar Babe"   Learned from Robert Tim or Sam Collins in 1910. First song Mance ever learned.   42, 187, 194, 401 (ref) 188 (song)

"Take Me Back"   Pre-1900, learned from father.   195 (ref)

"Tom Moore's Farm"   Originally a field song sung when overseers were not present. Yank Thornton sang the melody to Mance in 1929, and several people contributed verses to it. 307–14 (ref and lyr)   474 (ref)   476–80 (song)

"Trouble in Mind"   Gospel song, probably pre-1920.   466 (lyr)

"When Yo Lamps Go Out"   Gospel song, probably pre-1900.   62–63 (song)

"Whoa Mule"   Probably a fiddle or banjo tune, pre-1900, taught by father.   125 (song)

"Willie Poe Boy"   Probably fiddle or banjo tune, pre-1900, taught by father.   126 (song)

"You Are My Sunshine"   Love song Mance played for whites at their Friday night dances.   243 (ref)

"You Gonna Quit Me Baby"   Carnival song learned in 1918.   195 (ref)

"You Got ta Reap Jest What You Sow"   Carnival or minstrel song, probably pre-1900, taught by Richard Dean.   102 (lyr)   355, 474 (ref)

"You Got ta See Yo Mama Every Night, or You Caint See Yo Mama at All"   Song Mance played for whites at their Friday night dances.   243 (ref), 488–89 (song)

Discography and Filmography

RECORDS

Mance Lipscomb: Texas Sharecropper and Songster. Arhoolie
F1001, 1960 Recorded in Navasota in 1960 by Chris Strachwitz and Mack McCormick. Fourteen songs.

Mance Lipscomb: Trouble in Mind. Reprise, Pop Series R-2012A
and B 10,046 and 10,047, 1961. Recorded in Los Angeles at
Warner Brothers Studies under Frank Sinatra's label; Mack
McCormick assisted in the studio. Twelve songs.

Mance Lipscomb: Texas Songster. Vol 2. Arhoolie F1023, 1964.
Recorded in Navasota in 1960 by Chris Strachwitz and Mack
McCormick. Thirteen songs.

Mance Lipscomb. Vol. 3, *Texas Songster in a Live Performance*.

Arhoolie F1026, November 1964. Fourteen songs.

Mance Lipscomb. Vol. 4, Arhoolie F1033. Ten songs.

Mance Lipscomb. Vol. 5, *Texas Blues and Three Other Songs.* Arhoolie 1049. Recorded December 5, 1968, and November 20 and 22, 1969, some at the University of California at Santa Barbara. Eleven songs.

Mance Lipscomb. Vol. 6. Arhoolie 1069, 1974. Ten songs.

Mance Lipscomb. Vol. 7, *You'll Never Find Another Man Like Mance.* Arhoolie 1077, 1978. Recorded in Berkeley, Calif., in 1964. Fourteen songs.

Blues and Trouble. Arhoolie F1006, 1960. One song by Mance.

Blues Roots. Poppy, early 1960s. One song by Mance.

The Great Bluesmen. Vanguard, 1960s. One song by Mance.

The Roots of America's Music. Arhoolie R2001-2, 1960 or 1961. One song by Mance.

The Second Annual Berkeley Blues Festival Concert and Dance. Arhoolie F1030. Held on April 15, 1966. Four songs by Mance.

Texas Blues. Arhoolie F1017, 1968. One song by Mance.

Texas Blues: The 1950s Blues Classics. Arhoolie RC16, 1960 or 1961. One song by Mance.

The Unexpurgated Folksongs of Men. Arhoolie Raglan 51, 1960 or 1961. Two songs by Mance.

Decca LK4664, early 1960s. Two songs by Mance.

There are numerous unreleased recordings of Mance Lipscomb, including those by Chris Strachwitz, Mack McCormick, Glen Alyn, Tary Owens, Mark Johnson, Billy Porterfield, Kurt Van Sickle, Bruce Willenzik, Bob Cochran, and dozens more. In addition, some captured Mance on film and video, many of which contain audio.

COMPACT DISCS, FILMS, AND VIDEOS

Mance Lipscomb: Texas Songster. Arhoolie CD 306, 1989. Twenty-two songs originally released on Arhoolie LPs 1001 and 1026.

Mance Lipscomb: At Home in Texas. Catfish CTF1004, 1993. Recorded in Navasota and Austin by Tary Owens in 1965 and 1966 (four songs unreleased prior to 1993). Eighteen songs, with additional monologues.

Ruff Stuff: The Roots of Texas Blues Guitar. Catfish CTF1003, 1993. Anthology featuring Texas blues guitarists. Two songs by Mance plus one song with Mance accompanying another artist.

Les Blank. *A Well-Spent Life.* Sound by Skip Gerson. 45 min. Flower Films, 1970. Filmed in Navasota.

Institute of Texan Cultures. Film of Mance Lipscomb at 1968 Hemisfair, in San Antonio.

Mance Lipscomb and Lightnin' Hopkins. Yazoo 502. 60 min. Video of films made in the 1960s.

Stefan Grossman Guitar Workshop offers several videos on which Mance is represented: *Fingerpicking Guitar Techniques; Bottleneck Blues Guitar;* and *Country Blues Guitar,* pt. 2.

Index

INDEX

Printed in the United States
94585LV00003B/5/A

9 780393 333275

Made in the USA
Coppell, TX
06 July 2020